What the experts have to say about
The Complete Single Mother

"*The* most comprehensive and accessible source of information for mothers parenting alone or preparing to, this book reads like a conversation with a warm and well-informed friend. Destined to become a parenting classic."

— Shoshana Alexander, author of *In Praise of Single Parents*
and a founding editor of the *Utne Reader*

"This is a virtual encyclopedia of knowledge that is indispensable for every single mother. You will love this book!"

— Jane Mattes, founder of Single Mothers By Choice

"My first reaction when I saw the scope of topics in the book was just, 'Wow!' New and experienced single moms, and even women contemplating single motherhood, will benefit from this unabridged guide to many complex issues. It's . . . honest, funny, touching, helpful, reassuring, and thorough."

— Janice Wright, senior editor, *American Baby* magazine

"Clear, concise, comprehensive—this book is packed with excellent advice. Run, don't walk, to buy it!"

— Jane Doller, M.D., clinical assistant professor of psychiatry
Cornell University Medical College

"Essential reading for single mothers!"

— Judsen Culbreth, editor-in-chief, *Working Mother* magazine

W9-CHX-434

"Constructive strategies for coping with major problems and everyday incidents that are special to single mothers . . . A great resource!"
— *Redbook*

"Substantial . . . chock full of resource information for single mothers."
— *Chicago Tribune*

"The advice is refreshingly positive!"
— *Detroit Free Press*

"[One of the] stars of the solo system!"
— *New York Daily News*

"Provocative, informative, and practical—a rare combination in today's publishing world."
— *Our Children* magazine

"Humor-filled, down to earth, offers tips on everything!"
— *New Age Magazine*

"Useful articles with a decidedly whine-free tone."
— *Philadelphia Inquirer*

"A wealth of resources for single moms."
— *Cleveland Plain Dealer*

COMPLETELY UPDATED SECOND EDITION

THE
COMPLETE
SINGLE MOTHER

COMPLETELY UPDATED SECOND EDITION

THE
COMPLETE
SINGLE MOTHER

Reassuring Answers to Your Most Challenging Concerns

Andrea Engber and
Leah Klungness, Ph.D.

Adams Media Corporation
AVON, MASSACHUSETTS

Published by Adams Media Corporation
57 Littlefield Street, Avon, MA 02322. U.S.A.
www.adamsmedia.com

ISBN: 1-58062-302-6

Printed in Canada.

J   I   H   G   F   E   D

Library of Congress Cataloging-in-Publication Data
Engber, Andrea.
The complete single mother / by Andrea Engber and Leah Klungness.—2nd ed.
p.   cm.
Includes bibliographical references and index.
ISBN 1-58062-302-6
1. Single mothers—Unites States. 2. Parenting—United States.
I. Klungness, Leah II. Title.
HQ759.45 .E54 2000
306.85'6—dc21
99-059671

This publication is designed to provide accurate and authoritative information with regard to the subject matter covered. It is sold with the understanding that the publisher is not engaged in rendering legal, accounting, or other professional advice. If legal advice or other expert assistance is required, the services of a competent professional person should be sought.
    — From a *Declaration of Principles* jointly adopted by a Committee of the American Bar Association and a Committee of Publishers and Associations

Interior illustrations by Lynn Jeffery, Stowe, Vermont
Cover illustration by Viki Woodworth

This book is available at quantity discounts for bulk purchases.
For information, call 1-800-872-5627

To our children, Spencer, Sarah, and Andrew, who taught us to live joyfully in the present. And to our sisters, the single mothers who have inspired us through their strength, hope, and the community they have brought to the new American family.

CONTENTS

--------- Part 1 ---------
BY CHOICE OR CIRCUMSTANCE:
How Did You Get Here?

Chapter 1: The Changing Face of the American Family 3

The Loss of the Tribe • The Divorced Parent as Victim • The Unmarried
Mother as Villain • Giving up the Victim Attitude • Choosing to Become the
Victor • The Heroic Goddess • Defining Family • Single Moms Are Number
One • Single Mothers Are Older and Wiser • Single Parenting Is Here to Stay
• A Shift Toward Matriarchy • The Strengths of Single Mothers • Stamping
out the Stereotypes • Single Parenting Is a Healthy Choice • The Future of
Mothers Outside of Marriage • The New Single Mother—Parent of the Future
• Meeting the Challenges Head On

Chapter 2: Becoming a Single Mother Through Divorce. . . 12

If This Was Your First Marriage • Not Again! • What You May Be Feeling •
Shedding the Victim Attitude • When You Can't Justify Divorce • Preparing
for Divorce • How to Select an Attorney • Consider Mediation •
Annulments and Gets • When He Threatens to Take the Kids • Sex with Your
Soon-to-be-Ex • What to Tell Everyone • What to Tell No One •
Recovering from Divorce and Growing Beyond It • How to Customize a Life
Plan • Wedding Rings and Other Leftovers

Chapter 3: Becoming a Mother Outside of Marriage 30

If You're Making a Decision • If Your Mate Doesn't Share Your Feelings • "My
Boyfriend Can't Make Up His Mind..." • "My Family Is Unsupportive..." •
"Mr. Right (or Mr. Adequate) Hasn't Shown Up..." • If Your Internal Clock Is
Ticking Fast • If Your Partner Left You • If Your Partner Has Problems • "I
Got Pregnant from a Brief Affair..." • If Your Birth Control Didn't Work •
Special Concern: Date Rape • If You Are in an Abusive Relationship • If
Abortion Is Not an Option • Familiar Themes • Handling Your Feelings
About Motherhood Outside of Marriage • Deciding on the Father's Role •
Establishing Paternity

———————————————— *Part 2* ————————————————

MEET YOUR NEW PARTNER—YOU!

Part 3

GETTING THE CONFIDENCE TO RAISE TERRIFIC KIDS

Chapter 16: Mothers and Daughters 259

Preparing Your Daughter for the Future • How Big a Loss Is It Not to Have a
Dad Around? • What Happens to Girls During Adolescence • Looking for
Role Models • Issues About Sex

Chapter 17: Raising Boys 268

The Oedipus Complex and Other Things You Shouldn't Obsess About • When
There's No Regular Male Role Model • Boys Don't Need Fathers But Do Need
Men • What a Good Male Role Model Does • Where to Find Role Models
• What To Do If Your Son Likes To Play Dress-up • Raising a Healthy Son

—————— *Part 4* ——————
RELATING JOYFULLY TO OTHERS

Chapter 18: Custody and Coparenting. 279

Joint Custody • Shared Physical Custody • Permanent Sole Custody •
Temporary Custody • When to Determine Custody • Terminating Parental
Rights • Why Fathers Seek Custody • Learn Your Rights Regarding Custody
• Child Custody Blackmail • Visitation • Drop-Off Centers • Exploring
Coparenting • The Transition from His House to Yours

Chapter 19: Child Support 299

How to Begin • If You Need Help • When Your Feelings Threaten to Overwhelm
You • Help in the Toughest Circumstances

Chapter 20: The Ex from Hell 310

˙If Your Ex Is Out of Your Life • Those Crazy, Hazy Post-Divorce Days • Don't
Shoot—Identify Him First! • The RAT (Really Always There) • Meet the
MAD (Minimal Access Dad) • The Strafe Bomber • The "Back-from-the-
Dead" Ex • The Cowboy • When His Family Becomes the Only Family • The
Under-DOG (Under Darling's Orders to Grovel) • RUN! (Really Ugly News)
• When Your Ex's Behavior with the Kids Is Upsetting • If Your Ex Poses a
Threat to Your Children

Chapter 21: Dealing with Your Ex-relations 325

Fighting Rejection • How to Deal with Former Family Members • When
Grandma Was Your Number-One Sitter • Facing Aunts, Uncles, Cousins, and
Others • Holidays and Celebrations • When Your Child's Father's Family
Remains a Mystery • Relating to Your Ex's New Significant Other • Sharing
Discipline with Stepparents • If Your Ex Is Remarrying • You're Still the Mom

ACKNOWLEDGMENTS

Sometimes those to whom we are most grateful cannot be thanked enough. And often those who offered their deepest support and encouragement are no longer around to receive the thanks.

I thank my late mother, Florence, who released me from her hold, but only after seeing to it that her constant refrain, "You can do anything you set out to do," had sunk in. To the spirit of Sherman Engber, the man who raised me, I owe deep gratitude for meeting the challenge by marrying my independent single mother and for loving me out of choice and not because he "had to." As real a daddy—if not more so—as any birth father could hope to be, he taught me that love has less to do with blood than unconditional acceptance. My parents also taught me their roles were genderless as my father, a tall, strong Bogart type, shopped and cleaned house while my mother, a former model, maintained the car and rewired our apartment.

I owe endless thanks to Sally McMillan, my agent, for preparing me for the rough process of writing such a book. With painstaking guidance, she returned the proposal four times before submitting it, yet because of her I have confidence and skills I never knew I possessed.

To Laura Morin, my first editor at Adams Publishing, I am deeply grateful for her trust in me, for being there at the eleventh hour, and for laughing at the right times. Cheryl Kimball and the staff at Adams Publishing deserves praise, too, for their efforts in standing behind this edition one hundred percent.

My thanks to *Working Mother* magazine; Universal Press Syndicate; Shòshana Alexander, author of *In Praise of Single Parents*; *American Baby* magazine; Jane Mattes, founder of Single Mothers By Choice; Gary Nielson and Carolyn Beyrau at the *Charlotte Observer* for giving me my first real break as a columnist; Moms Online and OxygenMedia for allowing me to become a "Web Journalist;" Mike Hooten, who claims my son, Spencer, as his spiritual son, my partner and best friend, Bob, who massaged my tired feet when he would much rather have been doing something else; and my extended family of friends particularly Tere Wood for reasons she knows all too well.

Probably my earliest thanks should go to Linda Dillon, who may have influenced me more than she knows. My first best friend did not realize it at the time, but she gave me much comfort when she matter-of-factly retorted, "So you'll raise the baby without him!" after I whined about being dumped by my son's father. And that's just what I did.

And finally, to my son, Spencer, the most beloved person in my life, for picking pretty flowers for me just when I lost sight of what is really important, and for forgiving me for being such a workaholic: It is for him and all the children of the new American family that this book is written.

— A. E.

Many people have given unselfishly of their time, experience, and wisdom to keep my professional life and my personal world on course. We all need a support system to sustain us. And I deeply appreciate mine, a nourishing blend of my loving children, loyal friends, and generous colleagues. I know that many of these people would be embarrassed to be singled out for recognition. So to you I make a promise: To continue to devote myself to helping others to grow, achieve, and go forward, with goals for a bright future and barely a backward glance at the shadows from a difficult past.

—L. K.

INTRODUCTION

I first met my co-author, Dr. Leah Klungness, in 1993, but we were unknowingly connected to each long before that.

Ten years before we met, Leah watched the moving van pull out of the driveway of her recently sold house in Syracuse, New York. Excitedly, she packed a few last-minute items to take with her to her new home. Her husband, already relocated in Charlotte, North Carolina, was waiting for the van and his family to follow. Leah, a schoolteacher, and her two children, Sarah, then three, and Andrew, eight, were saying their goodbyes to the house when the phone rang. Leah ran to pick up the phone, expecting her husband to fill her in on the final details of the move. Instead, he informed her that he didn't think they should be married anymore and that she and the kids should move in with her mother. Then he promptly hung up.

She was dazed. "I just couldn't believe it! There went most of my life—my bed, my furniture, every towel, plate, and cooking utensil, every toy and book my children had ever had—in that van heading toward our new home while he's telling me on the phone that he's found a new life! How could he just say he didn't think we should be married anymore? And what was wrong with me not to even notice any red flags?"

After stumbling around in shock for what seemed like ages, she gathered up the remains of her life—two flimsy suitcases, her children, $500, and whatever energy she could muster—and dragged herself off to her mother's, trying not to scrape her chin on the ground.

Like many other unprepared women whose husbands abruptly left them, Leah's entrance into single motherhood came with no warnings and no instruction manuals—only unanswered questions, paralysis, and fear.

She had already been accepted to the University of South Carolina's doctoral program, so she embarked on a plan of action to get her Ph.D. while raising her two young children alone. "I was planning to attend school while living in Charlotte anyway. Why change my plans just because I was no longer married?"

The following August, just a few months after her husband had left her and her children, Leah packed up from her mother's house, and she, Sarah, and Andrew moved into their new apartment in Columbia, South Carolina. "One of the driving forces I credit for motivating me to find us an apartment was that I wanted to get out of my mother's house, fast! True, we should welcome any options and choices we have when first faced with a disaster such as a husband bailing out. But living at my mother's with my two children was certainly not one of them."

When they arrived, Leah knew no one—she had no child care, no family, no support network. But she made a commitment to herself that come "hell or high water," she would complete her education. "I was determined to do what I always wanted to do—get my Ph.D. and become a successful psychologist with my own practice," she remembers. It was a major undertaking, trying to single-handedly raise two kids with no child support, get enough sleep, find time to cook, clean, earn money, study, and write her dissertation, but she met all the challenges head-on.

After extensive planning and artful prioritizing and compromising—which is much of the meat for this book—Leah's hard work and commitment started to pay off. Even though the family budget was painfully tight, and the only one without homework in the evenings was little Sarah, Leah began to feel that she was making some real progress. She earned her Ph.D. in the spring of 1986 and was on her way to working as a practicing psychologist. Leah and her children eventually moved back to New York, where she opened up a practice on Long Island, counseling families, children, and individuals, most notably single mothers.

Leah's life remains an example of perseverance and commitment. Her former husband has lost all contact with his children. By his own choosing, he became a faded memory. Leah's son, Andrew, is an attorney on the west coast and her daughter, Sarah, a college student who is considering a business career.

Just a few months earlier, and only a few miles away in Charlotte, North Carolina, I was going through my own dramatic entry into single motherhood. I was suffering from contractions, alone, in the parking lot of a local hospital because I refused to go in before midnight. The hospital's billing cycle started at 12 noon and it was only 11 A.M. and there was no way I was going to let them charge me their daily rate of $700 for just sixty minutes! Especially when I had no health insurance.

Needless to say, the grunting and groaning that accompanied the contractions caused quite a commotion because nearby members of the hospital's staff came rushing out to the parking lot, pushing a wheelchair and politely tried to shove me in. They raced me into the emergency entrance, where I had to go through more than the usual red tape of entering a hospital since I was uninsured, unmarried, and unprepared. ("Pack what bag? the baby wasn't due for two weeks and I was in the middle of a huge project at work!")

My live-in partner had decided on Labor Day, 1985, to leave town when I was four months pregnant at age thirty-six. Actually, he told me a day earlier that he was going on a job interview that Monday and would return the middle of the following week. At 4 A.M. the next morning, I awoke to the sounds of grinding gears and crunching gravel. I ran to the window and saw Jerry pull out of the driveway in a truck with his motorcycle on board, and a trailer pulling his boat behind him. Someone else was driving his car.

I waited one week, two weeks, a month for him to return, but no word. I couldn't ignore the sneaking suspicion that this was no ordinary job interview. During this time, I called at least fifty hospitals to see if they had anyone fitting his description, just to help prolong my denial. Four and a half months later, on January 3, 1986, when I had my son, Spencer, I got the hint that Jerry was not coming back. It wasn't until April 1 of that year that he briefly showed up to see if I still wanted him. Somehow, I couldn't forgive this guy who had left me on Labor Day and showed up on April Fool's Day claiming no pun intended.

Even though I was a new M.O.M. (Mother Outside of Marriage) like single mothers through divorce, I went through the usual course of dealing with loss, starting with denial and overstaying my welcome in the depressed and anger stages. I became obsessive. Being dumped was enough, especially if you've never been the dumpee. But to be pregnant with my thirty-sixth birthday only a week away was awful. On top of that, I had lost my partner to a woman who was twenty-five years his junior. My self-esteem was signaling "major meltdown."

Things got even worse. When Spencer was only nine months old, I was fired from my seven-year job as art director of an advertising agency. My boss was uncomfortable having an unmarried mother on staff and found an excuse to terminate me, giving me only one hour to pack up and go. All this occurred only days after I had major home improvements and repairs completed. How was I going to pay for all of it when I was still paying off the costs of Spencer's birth, let alone day care, food, and shelter costs?

Hitting bottom, it seemed that I had no choice but to accept the situation and stop feeling like a victim and get on with it. My mother's often-used refrain, "sink or swim" couldn't have spoken to me at a better time. I had actually made myself sick from the depression and anger and feelings of bad luck I had internalized. I decided to channel all that negativity into some productivity, thereby freeing up my creative energy. In fact, it actually occurred to me (although in retrospect) that the father of my child was someone with whom I did not want to spend the rest of my life. I also realized that had I not lost my job, I would still be working as an art director and copywriter in a mediocre job and not doing what I really wanted to be doing with my life. In a sense, both my boss and Jerry had done me a huge favor.

I ran a lucrative advertising and design service for a few years before the recession hit. By the time it caught up with me, most of my clients were already gone. But I was smart enough to sock away what I could when things were good, and by now my house was almost paid for.

Christmas of 1990 was the turning point when I became aware of the purpose of my life. While sitting in the pediatrician's office (for my son's umpteenth ear infection), I was thumbing through all the magazines boasting the same articles on "How to Avoid Stress and Supermom Burnout." You know the ones—they advise you to get your husband to help out more. "That's it," I said, leaping out of my chair. "Well, excuse me, but I forgot to bring the man who's supposed to bring out the trash."

With that, I started *SingleMOTHER*, a newsletter that prides itself as "a support group in your hands," and founded the National Organization of Single Mothers, Inc. (NOSM), because there wasn't anything out there for women like me. And I knew there must be more of us. I started selling subscriptions on the street, on airplanes, stores, anywhere I thought I could spy a distressed-looking single mom.

NOSM grew to become a network that was more than committed to helping single parents successfully meet the challenges of daily life. The organization and its publication, *SingleMOTHER*, became the voice of more than 11 million single mothers.

SingleMother has become the country's only national newsletter dealing with single-parenting issues in an upbeat, practical, and positive light. The organization has linked families through a network of empowerment.

One day, Leah was reading the *New York Daily News* when she saw an article about me and the *SingleMOTHER* newsletter. (Normally, she wouldn't be caught dead reading anything other than the *New York Times*, but thankfully her son insisted on getting the *News* for the sports section.) She was so impressed with what she read that she contacted me immediately and said she wanted to be part of this network that helped empower single mothers. Leah offered the perspective of one who experienced divorce and had attained her dream in spite of it. She shared her knowledge and success by contributing to *SingleMOTHER* even before we met in person in June 1993.

We realized that single mothers needed a book they could pick up anytime, anywhere, that would reassure them when sometimes the challenges of single parenting seemed impossible. We also were tired of seeing the self-esteem of "real" single mothers shot down by the debates over family values on television, radio, and in the news. This life style boasts popular celebrity status in Hollywood and Nashville (single motherhood is fairly popular among country singers). But the unfair stereotyping, poor publicity, and inaccurate analysis of studies that is the usual rhetoric began brewing a backlash against mothers raising their children without a husband at home. Economics was playing a major role,

too. It seemed okay to be a single mom if you were a rich celebrity, like Jodie Foster, Farrah Fawcett, Cher, Glenn Close, Madonna, Tanya Tucker, or a Spice Girl, but not okay if you were an average American woman.

Because Leah and I not only knew that the stereotyping of single mothering was false, but that single parenting actually could be a healthy and empowering experience in a woman's life, we needed to supply more information and more encouragement to prove that this was true. So we wrote this book.

The Complete Single Mother offers a fresh perspective to raising a family solo through its realistic, upbeat, and positive approach. Packed with valuable information, the book takes women through the first stages of accepting their single-parent life style, whether by choice or chance, to enabling them to unleash their creative potential to be a successful individual, parent, valuable friend, and worker. Here is a book that will answer all the questions you may have about single mothering but were either too busy or too afraid to ask because you felt that no one had the answers anyway.

The Complete Single Mother is for the new generation of mothers (and men, too, who are single parents) who will bring with them a new set of family values to the new millennium, values that are actually good and necessary for this country to survive. The single parent is bringing back community by seeking extended families, teaching that self-reliance is healthier than codependency, and proving that a family is not defined by who heads it, but rather by its ability to love and share and make its members feel safe. Whether by choice, chance, or other circumstance—adoption, divorce, death—if you are or will be a single mother, *The Complete Single Mother* offers reassuring answers for your most challenging concerns. For relatives, professionals, and others who work with and counsel single moms, this book will be a superb resource and reference guide, too.

The Complete Single Mother is for everyone who is affected by single mothering today. But, most of all, this book is for the woman who needs encouragement, confidence, and practical advice. It will help her organize her life around the realities and strengths of single parenting and not around others' expectations of who she is or should be.

— A.E.

Part 1

By Choice or Circumstance: How Did You Get Here?

1

The Changing Face of the American Family

MATRIARCHY MAKES A COMEBACK

Long before the age of Christianity, even before Judaism, Islam, and classical Greece, almost every culture and civilization on earth revered the "Goddess Mother."

Countless stories celebrate her as the source of all life—for giving birth and nurturing the earth. Almost always, they were mothers who were not attached to male partners. The single mother goddess Demeter went into the underworld to search for her daughter, Persephone. The legend tells us that Demeter spewed forth the seasons as she emerged from her winter darkness of mourning her daughter's loss and their reunion was celebrated as spring.

In some of these early societies, and in many aboriginal cultures being studied today in Africa and Australia, there was no fatherhood as we know it. In fact, renowned anthropologist Margaret Mead was among the first to call fatherhood a social invention. Women generally had multiple sexual partners, mainly for the purpose of expanding the tribe. They were the healers, the experts, and the moral decision makers, and the men were responsible for participating in the child-rearing process. Studies reveal that these early goddess-worshipping, matriarchal communities were happy and peaceful, and there is no evidence of strife or violence until late in the third millennium B.C., when they were destroyed and taken over by patriarchal nomads.

THE LOSS OF THE TRIBE

Of course, today's world is structured quite differently. Our present society does not place a high value on mothers, married or single, or even on children, for that matter. No longer are we concerned about the welfare of all our young people as the future of our country. Our culture has been criticized by many children's advocates for viewing our children's plight as someone else's problem. The African proverb "It takes a whole village to raise a child" is not widely accepted, and the community as a whole has come to regard the child-rearing process as strictly a parental one. Because of this, there has been tremendous pressure on the nuclear family—a family that is not only rapidly deteriorating but now represents a small percentage of all households.

THE DIVORCED PARENT AS VICTIM

Historically, the divorced single mother has been told that she is responsible for her "failed" marriage because it was her job to compromise and put her own needs last. Only when she acknowledged that she "got what she deserved" was she allowed to qualify as victim. If her husband left her, we ask, "What did you do to make him leave?" Many divorced women become caught in the vicious cycle of believing themselves to be victims because they allow others to treat them as such, and others continue to treat them as victims because they accept it.

THE UNMARRIED MOTHER AS VILLAIN

Conversely, when a single mother chooses her situation, as in the case of a woman who becomes pregnant outside of marriage because she felt ready for motherhood, she is eyed with suspicion. Even single mothers receiving public assistance, who decide to use that time to get their college degree, sink from victim status to that of villain because they are going after what they want. They have made a choice. Because victims evoke our sympathy and have no choices, most single mothers, regardless of their circumstances, would rather allow themselves to be labeled as such.

GIVING UP THE VICTIM ATTITUDE

It works this way. Suppose you told people that even though your partner left you four months pregnant in the middle of the night, you were actually grateful to him for not making you decide the fate of the relationship when you never really imagined spending the rest of your life with him. Or suppose you admitted that you became so sullen and withdrawn after finding out that you were pregnant, or so smothering, or angry, or possessive, that he found it easier to leave you first. Did you have any choices in this matter? Or was it easier to moan and whine about how selfish and loathsome he was and have others commiserate with you?

CHOOSING TO BECOME THE VICTOR

The truth is, most single mothers fall into the category of "Single Mother by Choice, Sort of." Choosing to be a victim is a very unproductive, senseless way to live. This is not to say we are not all victims of something larger than ourselves at one time or another. But everyone has a choice when it comes down to deciding how she wants to live her life. Whether you're divorced because your husband slept around, or whether you knew your baby's father for only a short period, if you want to succeed as a victor, not as a victim or a villain, you must first admit that you have made choices, even if you were not conscious of them at the time.

But it really comes down to this. If you absolutely must pick either victim or villain, go with villain. Why? The reason is that most people who judge others haven't been able to make their own choices, so they alternate between fearing (synonymous with hating) and admiring those who do. Those who most openly criticize the choice of single mothering are often people with their own unresolved family issues. For example, some people may not be able to separate from their own abusive relationships, or perhaps they secretly desire a child of their own. They may envy your freedom or feel threatened by the control you have taken over your own life. In other words, they may see you as a hero. And female heroes are not heroines but goddesses.

THE HEROIC GODDESS

Heroes are those who don't do the easy thing, but do the right thing. Heroes are courageous, stand up under fire, and often work for the good of others. They have had to face some form of injustice or inequity and are often lonely. As the "villainous" hero, it is up to you to protect yourself by setting boundaries, and it is up to you to help those who need it by setting an example of your own successful single parenting.

From this moment on, if you have ever felt like a victim, tell yourself that you will no longer be a victim in your eyes or in anyone else's. As a woman and a mother, you are powerful. You must resurrect the goddesses who lived before you by reclaiming the goddess inside you. Tell yourself, "I am a goddess. I am capable of doing heroic things. I am ready to take charge of my feelings, of my children, and of every other aspect of my life."

DEFINING FAMILY

There no longer is only one type of family. In fact, there never really was only one type of family, except that the nuclear family represented such an ideal that few people defined their environment as family if it didn't fit the model of a stay-at-home mom, breadwinning dad, and two or more kids. But today there are families consisting of children being raised by single women, men, grandparents, gay men, lesbians, stepparents, interracial couples, adoptive parents, and in communal arrangements.

Regardless of who heads the table, a family is where one can feel safe and familiar, and where children are accepted with unconditional love and a blessing for the future. Some say blood is thicker than water but, when you think about it, we are all of the same blood. With over 12 million single parents heading households today, the face of the American family is quickly changing.

SINGLE MOMS ARE NUMBER ONE

In 1994, 28 percent of all births were to single women. In fact, unmarried mom births topped one million, then a record high, and the steepest increase was among white, educated, and professional women. In the last decade, the percentage of college-educated white women who became mothers without marriage doubled; for women with professional or managerial jobs, it nearly tripled. In 1998, the Census Bureau reported that for the first time in its 60 years of compiling data on marriage and family, 53 percent of first births were to unmarried women. Sixty years ago, that number was only 18 percent.

Today there are 12 million single moms compared with 3.4 million reported in 1970.

SINGLE MOTHERS ARE OLDER AND WISER

The National Center for Health Statistics claims to be seeing a shift in the typical age of the unmarried mother. Increasingly, they're older than they used to be. Where once out-of-wedlock births were a teenage epidemic, the latest figures show teenager births to have declined, while the birth rate for unmarried women in their early twenties

through mid thirties has soared. Researchers predict that this trend will continue indefinitely.

Single motherhood crosses every demographic stratum. In fact, the rise of single-parent families is occurring throughout every industrialized democracy, with the exception of Japan although statistics show they are not far behind. There are already organized single mother support groups in Tokyo and other large cities.

Analysts give economic and cultural reasons for the rapid increase in the number of single mothers by choice. More women are in the work force today than ever before, and the gap between the earnings of men and women is narrowing. As a result, women don't feel as pressured to marry as they did decades ago. The women's movement has left many women with a new sense of independence. Many women no longer trust the institution of marriage, while the social taboos that have discouraged out-of-wedlock births have waned.

SINGLE PARENTING IS HERE TO STAY

Add the number of mothers outside of marriage to the millions of women getting divorced each year, and we can certainly say a final goodbye to the Cleavers and the Ricardos. Along with the outdated pearls that adorned the necks of the female leads of these television shows goes also their traditional status as the mainstay of the typical American family. In fact, today, only one in nine families is made up of a stay-at-home mom, a breadwinning dad, and two or more young children. Within the next few years, more than half of the work force will consist of single parents with children under the age of five.

A SHIFT TOWARD MATRIARCHY

You've heard the statistics: One in two marriages ends in divorce, second marriages dissolve at a rate of more than 60 percent, and more and more children will spend part of their childhood in a single-parent household. Many fathers are also becoming custodial parents.

This trend in our society toward matriarchal-structured households is felt not only by single mothers, but by our population as a whole. We're witnessing an increasing number of women entering the political arena and taking governmental posts. We see that more and more new businesses are being started by women, more than half of whom are said to be single mothers. Witness the panic that many conservative political and religious groups are spreading: They say the American family is breaking down, and with it our society. But what is really happening is that the family is undergoing a hierarchical change. The traditional structure is being democratized as the father-head-of-household steps down and women strengthen the family.

THE STRENGTHS OF SINGLE MOTHERS

Women in general are becoming more powerful, but the ones who have the best shot at gaining independence are those who have learned to depend on themselves. Raising a child solo and being forced to rely on one's own judgment and decisions, rather than depend on someone else, can be a very empowering thing in one's life.

Single mothers typically have many strengths and resources, but because society has placed such a low priority on their needs, self-esteem remains a problem. When asked if they felt good about themselves, most single mothers responded positively when in a support group situation, and negatively when isolated or alone. Indeed, in a 1990 Gallup Poll that asked single parents if they were doing a good job, most said yes, but wished they had more support and encouragement. Most single parents believe their life styles are acceptable, and many report being quite happy with their roles, but entertain doubts in the face of massive negative media coverage, started by the Dan Quayle flap ostracizing single moms.

STAMPING OUT THE STEREOTYPES

Contrary to the stereotype, most single parents are not welfare cases. Many are forced to receive assistance. Even with the increasing enforcement of child support, less than half of all mothers awarded child support receive the full amount. Some collect sporadically or receive inadequate payments, and many never see a dime. Yet the average stay on welfare has been four years or less, most commonly two years, during which time the majority either complete their college education or enter work-training programs.

According to the same Gallup Poll and a recent inquiry of members of the National Organization of Single Mothers, most single parents are nurturing, encouraging adults and spend nearly as much time with their children as do their married counterparts. Two-thirds reported feeling that they were doing as good a job as their own mothers. And many researchers have noted that single mothers give more attention to their children than married moms do, possibly because they don't have the frequent distraction of another adult. For instance, as early as 1987, a study presented at the Society for Research in Child Development in Baltimore rebutted evidence that mealtime in a father-absent family had negative effects. The paper actually showed that separated mothers emphasized the food preferences of their children, while married mothers catered to the other parent's needs. A Biola University study debunked myths about the poor development of sex role identity in boys of father-absent families. The study showed no relationship between father absence and masculine sex role orientation in boys.

But we don't hear enough of these results. We hear too much of the negative side of single parenting. *The Complete Single Mother* intends to bring to light the truth about single mothering by pointing out the extensive research, entailing over 500 studies, that has debunked most of the myths we've been hearing for too long.

SINGLE PARENTING IS A HEALTHY CHOICE

Ideally, a mother and father who share a strong marriage and each possess a healthy self-image and a positive commitment to child-rearing would be the most desirable choice. But many psychologists believe that the single-parent household, in many cases, is prefer-able to a two-parent situation, especially if there is constant arguing, substance abuse, physical or emotional battering, or even simply poor communication between the partners.

In fact the American Psychological Association's official journal, *American Psychologist*, reported that there is no support for the idea that marriage produces well-adjusted children. The study which appeared in the June, 1999 issue even claims that marriage can hurt women and children because males' unhealthy coping strategies place added stress on their families.

Male-female relationships are becoming increasingly difficult to maintain. A significant number of studies polling a cross-section of American wives have indicated that more than half are involved in unhappy and even oppressive relationships. *Ms.* magazine has published numerous articles describing the feelings of women before the feminist revolution got underway; almost all the subjects said they believed their own mothers never dealt with their own unhappiness. When researchers questioned the mothers of the baby-boomers, who were stay-at-home moms in the 1950s and 1960s, more than one-third said they were unhappy and relied on medication such as antidepressants and tranquilizers, and half eventually wound up divorced. According to Sheila Kessler's book *The American Way of Divorce* (Nelson Hall), divorce has always been a major part of American life, but the reason many women stayed married was that they feared the consequences and stigma of being a divorcee. Valium sales were sky high in the 1960s. It was no coincidence, according to Peter D. Kramer, author of *Listening to Prozac* (Viking),

RESEARCH ON CHILDREN OF SINGLE-PARENT FAMILIES

If you're concerned about the negative findings concerning the future of children from single-parent homes, take heart. Many thorough studies dispute what you may have read. Research is actually beginning to point to many benefits of being raised in a single-parent home. One carefully controlled study of more than three thousand participants has concluded that many of the warnings we have read in the past about single-parent families are myths perpetuated by those claiming to want to preserve the family but actually only wanting to preserve the hierarchical family with father as head. Here are some responses to the assumption of popular journalism that two-parent families are better for children, from researcher Shere Hite's new groundbreaking study, *The Hite Report on the Family: Growing up under Patriarchy* (Grove/Atlantic):

- Mothers from one-parent families are more likely to feel freer to confide in daughters because no "disloyalty" to the spouse is implied.

- Daughters from mother-headed families are more likely to confide in their mothers about personal problems involving sex and boys.

- Daughters in such families are less likely to see their mother as a "wimp" because she is an independent person.

- Boys who grow up in "mother-only" families experience less pressure to demonstrate contempt for things "feminine" and for nonaggressive parts of their personalities.

- Boys raised by single mothers don't experience the intensity of pain other boys describe feeling when they struggle to achieve a new identity based on patriarchal culture commanding them to "be tough," "stop hanging around with mom," or "don't be a sissy."

- Men raised by single mothers tend to have better relationships with women later in life.

- Children's overall respect for their mothers has increased significantly with the rise in single and working mothers.

- Since most two-parent homes still reflect gender stereotypes, children from these homes often feel pressured to "take sides" or "choose" one parent over the other. They may also feel compelled to help the weaker parent, causing cowardly or self-hating feelings that children from single-parent homes do not experience.

- It is more positive for children not to grow up in an atmosphere poisoned by gender inequality. Single-parent homes show male and female roles without gender stereotypes.

"that when American society wanted to keep women at home, the drug of choice was Valium." Today, American women have more options and are able to make more choices. They no longer have to fit an uncomfortable mold, the way many of their mothers did.

There are many two-parent households where the task of child-rearing is shared. But plenty of well-adjusted single-parent families abound as well. What's needed are resources and literature that affirm, educate, and support these families in their personal and parenting decisions.

THE FUTURE OF MOTHERS OUTSIDE OF MARRIAGE

According to the Population Reference Bureau, a private research group in Washington, an increase in the numbers of unmarried single mothers is predicted. U.S. census statistics show that the number of couples who wed after a premaritally conceived birth has declined over the years. In 1960, 52 percent of such couples got married; about thirty years later, that figure has dropped to below 27 percent—almost half. Carl Caub, a demographer with Population Reference Bureau has said "Since the pressure to marry isn't the same today as it used to be, there will probably continue to be a lot of women who raise children in a single state."

THE NEW SINGLE MOTHER—PARENT OF THE FUTURE

U.S. Census Bureau officials have acknowledged that "the tremendous increase in the number of single parents has been one of the most profound changes in family composition to have occurred during the past quarter century."

In fact, single mothers represent a growing $174 billion marketplace. Marketers are watching the rise in single mother household incomes and are now targeting this growing pool of women who make decisions on their own.

The message is becoming clear. No longer can single motherhood be explained away by phrases like urban dilemma, welfare dependency, and the demise of the family. Women are no longer marrying for opportunistic reasons—economic stability, a name in the community, a way to own a home and to have children. Today, women can achieve female adult status outside of marriage. The new single mother symbolizes the new reality, regardless of how she acquired her status. She is shattering all previously held myths and stereotypes.

The new single mother has heard the statistics. The divorce rate is staggering; four million women a year are beaten by spouses and partners; and Mr. Right—or even Mr. Adequate—may never come along. She knows that if she does get divorced, there's no guarantee she will collect full child support and that her standard of living will decrease while her ex's increases. It's no wonder that more and more women are opting for motherhood without marriage.

MEETING THE CHALLENGES HEAD ON

Let's face it: Times are changing. No longer are terms like "virgin bride" and "happily ever after" common. Scarlet letters and the label "illegitimate" have also faded. A happy family is not defined by who heads the household.

Instead of calling women who are single mothers by circumstance victims, and women who are single mothers by choice villains, our society should herald them all as victors. In spite of a culture that has failed to meet the needs of single mothers because of weak child support enforcement, inflexible employers, prohibitive day-care costs, and schools that are slow to recognize the single mother's schedule, most single mothers are doing a very good job. They are setting positive examples for their children and showing that self-reliance can be the key to responsibility.

If you are a single mother, you're not alone. Even if:

◆ Your child's father left you

◆ Your mate announced he doesn't want to be a father

◆ You're pregnant and he's got the bankbook

◆ Your fiancé died, leaving you pregnant and sort of widowed

◆ You left an abusive relationship

◆ Your ex-husband wants nothing to do with you or your child

◆ Your ex-partner wants too much to do with you or your child

◆ Your child was the result of donor insemination or adoption—

You can achieve whatever it is you want out of life. In fact, many women are convinced they would not have accomplished their desired goals had they not had to learn to rely on their own abilities and wit. Thousands of women have not only survived single motherhood but emerged powerful and dynamic people whose hidden talents and resources would not have been uncovered if they had not viewed the challenges of single parenting as an opportunity for personal growth. Some were single mothers raising children alone in the face of a life-threatening illness such as cancer. Other single mothers went from welfare recipient to corporate executive.

Don't confuse the challenges of single parenting with hard luck or unfortunate circumstances. With some creative thinking, a bit of planning, and *The Complete Single Mother* as a companion, you can not only raise happy, healthy, and productive children, but you will also be able to become the person you were meant to be—strong, decisive, independent, courageous and, above all—a joyful woman.

2

Becoming a Single Mother Through Divorce

HOW TO RECOVER AND REGAIN CONTROL

Recently, a number of popular magazines published results of studies that claimed that between 80 and 85 percent of women over the age of thirty-five were happier after divorce than while they were married. This may be hard to believe when you're in the throes of an agonizing separation, but according to numerous polls, it's true. For you now, however, the sense of loss for what was and for what might have been seems so overwhelming, it's hard to believe you can ever be happy again.

Loss can't be avoided. Everyone experiences loss, whether it is a loved one's death, a child leaving home, the loss of a job, or a divorce. Nobody marches down the aisle expecting to become another divorce statistic. Whether or not you dreamed of the white picket fence, station wagon, and 2.4 children, you are probably wonder-

ing what ever happened to your cherished hopes and fantasies.

IF THIS WAS YOUR FIRST MARRIAGE

For what it's worth, there most likely are some wonderful memories. There have been times you will never share with anyone else. You built a life together—friends, family, and neighborhood. You may go on to have other weddings or other children, but this was your first wedding and your first child. Because you have not kept your vows to cherish and protect one another, grow old together, and share in your children's growing up, you feel that your dreams for the future are now lost. When you grieve for your loss, also remember that it's okay to delight in the memories.

NOT AGAIN!

This may have been a second (or third) marriage filled with the promise that old mistakes would not be repeated. You did not expect perfection. You knew better this time that a marriage was hard work.

Like many, you probably thought that a second marriage should be the start of a new and different life. Particularly if you had children from the previous relationship, there most likely was great hope that this relationship would bring together a new, blended family. But things have fallen apart, and again it's necessary to grieve for the many hopes, plans, and dreams that are not to be. Equally important, however, is to cherish the times that were warm and wonderful, too.

WHAT YOU MAY BE FEELING

Feeling Stuck. There are so many ways to feel stuck. For some, being stuck means being forever labeled and defined as "divorced." For others, it can mean holding on to the painful feelings and dysfunctional behavior. Therapists often comment about how one can feel stuck regardless of economic or social status. Some of the most stuck women are in new marriages or relationships—or trying to be—with not a clue as to why they are unhappy.

In essence, being stuck means holding on to ways of thinking and feeling that no longer allow you or your children to move ahead. Rarely does it mean living a life in solitude. However, in order to avoid living in a self-imposed prison, you have to become "unstuck," because being stuck is not unlike being paralyzed or immobile. In order to move on, you have to let go.

Feeling Worthless. Even though it is important to remember that no feelings are wrong or unacceptable, don't fall prey to this one—the number one favorite of TV's popular soap operas. Emotions such as sadness, grief, guilt, fear, or anger can all be parts of the growing process, but your basic essence—who you are—should never be attacked by anyone, especially yourself. Feeling worthless is useless, and you need to stop right now! Your self-esteem needs to be enhanced and protected.

Make a list of the three things you like best about yourself. If you whip up the best tomato sauce in town, have a knack for growing flowers that are the envy of the neighborhood, or have terrific musical skills, write it down. Each morning review your list, and add something to it by the end of the week. For example, if your boss praised your reorganization ideas, make sure to add her remarks to your list. If you find getting started or adding accomplishments difficult, ask a trusted friend for help. As you review your growing list of admirable qualities, tell yourself, "I am worthwhile and accomplished." There may come a morning when you no longer require the daily reminder and wonder why you even have the list. But it's a good habit to indulge because when you value yourself, you wind up making good choices for yourself and for those you love.

Feeling Good!

Other women seem obviously devastated by the breakup of their marriages. Their pain is obvious. Frankly, I feel relieved. In fact, I'm thinking of having a divorce party with my girlfriends! What's wrong with me?

Nothing. It's normal to feel a sense of relief when you exit a marriage that went bad slowly over time. During this long, bad period, you were allowed to work through many of the initial emotions that newly separated or divorced women experience. Think back through the course of your marriage, and you will remember times of suffering through denial, rage, sadness, and fear. Good for you that these negative feelings are over and that your relief and renewed energy are letting you move ahead!

A divorce party can be a very creative idea, provided it is not a man-bashing festival, but rather a time for women to come together to renew their inherent power. If it helps, a little male-bashing can't hurt, but remember, this a time for you to go forward and not to stay stuck in negative feelings. Do what makes you feel good. One woman in a recent divorce found that having a "funeral" for her husband was a great cathartic. She sent her kids to

their grandmother's, invited all her girlfriends over, wore her sexiest black dress, and laughed, cried, ate, and grieved as many do at typical funerals. Even though this ritual allowed her to say goodbye to the dearly departed, she was careful not to involve her children in her method of grieving. Still, after years of misery, her life at last was taking a positive turn.

SHEDDING THE VICTIM ATTITUDE

America seems increasingly comfortable accepting the "victim mentality," which states, "I am not responsible for my actions." Just tune in to any talk show and you'll undoubtedly find the guest victim blaming his upbringing for the fact that he has lied and cheated on every woman unlucky enough to have crossed his path.

Those who are self-proclaimed victims follow a predictable pattern. When responsibility for personal behavior is jettisoned, there is always a price to be paid. You might notice that many "victims" never seem that happy or successful. They don't seem to have much energy left to point their lives in positive directions. So much energy is spent dwelling in the past.

This is not to say that you haven't been dumped on or suffered some terrible injustice. It's inaccurate to lump all victims into the talk-show mold when many women truly are victims of incest or domestic abuse. However, too many divorced women don't realize that they did have choices. And the first choice you should make is deciding whether or not you are a victim. Chances are, if you investigate a little further, you may find that you are simply allowing yourself to feel victimized.

WHEN YOU CAN'T JUSTIFY DIVORCE

My marriage has lacked passion for years. We have separate careers, interests, and friends. My husband does share some of the parenting of our two children but with a lack of enthusiasm and commitment. I have thought for a long time that I would be happier alone. I am having trouble sorting all this out and making a decision. Don't suggest marriage counseling. We've been there!

A large proportion of married women have contemplated ending their marriage at some point. However, only you can decide if the benefits of the marriage outweigh the limitations.

Think about how and why you and your husband created such separate lives. Away from the children, try talking honestly with one another. It is likely he also feels discontent. If counseling has not helped you resolve marital issues, you still need to explore and understand them for yourself, no matter what you decide to do.

Are you better off with him or without him? Make a list of the reasons you might want to stay married and the reasons you might want to divorce. Some women unconsciously postpone this decision despite much unhappiness or even abuse, waiting for another man to come along to rescue them. If this is how you feel, you need to take some time and sort out your feelings about yourself. Why do you think you need a man to survive? For some women whose marriages have lost that essential spark, making the decision to separate is laden with guilt. After all, they think, "What do I have to complain about? He doesn't gamble, drink, beat me." But don't you think you might deserve more?

If you are afraid to divorce because you don't know how to survive without a man, get out a sheet of paper and a pen and list all the reasons why you think you are nothing without a man. Then, list all the things you have done in your life of which you are proud. See how many of your accomplishments were not the direct result of your husband's input—things like being able to entertain lavishly on a shoestring budget or helping your company land that new account. Conversely, don't be surprised if a number of your husband's achievements were largely due to you. There is a reason for the saying "Behind every great man is a great woman"!

PREPARING FOR DIVORCE

Be careful about making major financial and career decisions, especially if you're not certain that you are getting divorced. And certainly don't make any joint decisions. For example, this is probably not the time to refinance your home to provide your husband with capital to start his own business. Use your period of indecision as a window of opportunity—a time to plan but not to act. This may be the right time to take a careful look at your own career. Are you moving in a direction that would allow you to be self-supporting?

THE DOS AND DON'TS OF DIVORCE

◆ Do treat your self-esteem like money in the bank. Value and protect it.

◆ Do choose life options that make you independent. Choose to control your own life.

◆ Don't make any long-term commitments right away.

◆ Don't expect a brand-new normal life overnight. Be patient and adopt the attitude of *Joy of Cooking* author Irma Rombauer. Savor the preparation as much as the meal. Remember, the real joy in living is to be found in the task at hand, and not in the end product.

◆ Don't allow yourself to feel like a failure just because your marriage didn't last forever. Partnership contracts can be dissolved when two people can no longer function effectively while connected, not unlike a business relationship. Try to look at this from a logical angle, not just an emotional one.

◆ Don't underestimate all you have to offer. You have talents, resources, and information to share. Reach out to others with positive energy, and positive energy will be returned to you.

◆ Don't confuse attorneys with friends, lovers, or therapists. Attorneys are paid guides through the legal jungle.

◆ Do tell yourself every day that you will succeed. Learn to say, "Yes, I can do it!" More importantly, believe it.

◆ Do remember that for children, it is the small things that count. Create happy memories now.

Does your present job offer the benefits you might need? Consider furthering your education or getting the training you may need soon so you can expand your options.

If you decide to go ahead with the divorce, you should discreetly document your finances and protect your assets before you begin legal proceedings. This is especially important if you fear that your husband will be particularly vindictive or angry. If you ultimately decide to stay together, knowing more about your shared finances will strengthen your marriage. Gathering this information will help you better plan and be in a stronger legal position if you do decide to divorce. Don't forget to follow these guidelines:

◆ Remove your name from any joint credit card accounts, and notify credit card companies in writing that you will no longer be responsible for charges made on them. Send the letters return receipt requested and then file all these documents in case you receive bills for your ex-husband's charges at a later time.

◆ You may also want to withdraw half of the money in your bank accounts or ask the bank to freeze the account. Notify your banker in writing, again with a return receipt requested, that you do not want any transactions to occur without both parties being notified.

◆ Close any equity lines of credit you and your husband may have. If you do not do this, you may end up losing your house.

◆ Make a list of everything in your home. Better yet, take photographs or make a videotape of your possessions. If you don't own a camcorder, you can rent one. Keep notes as to value and purchase date. Check your insurance files for these.

◆ Establish a separate mailing address by opening a post office box in your name. You do not have to live in a town to have a post office box there.

◆ Open a checking account in your own name. Apply for credit cards in your own name if you do not already have them.

◆ Do not cosign any loan with your husband. If you do and he later defaults, you will be obligated to pay back the loan in full.

◆ Consider what will happen to your health insurance if you divorce. Find out what your rights are in case of divorce.

Also be sure to make copies of the following necessary documents:

◆ Personal and business income tax returns for the past several years. If you used a tax preparer, this person is required by law to keep copies for three years. Otherwise, call the IRS (800-829-3676) and request Form 4506 (Request for Copy of Tax Form). This form need not be signed by your spouse, assuming the two of you filed a joint return. The IRS charges $4.25 for this service. Processing time is ten days to two months.

◆ Financial statements from banks and loan applications. Often things overlooked when filing taxes are remembered when trying to prove credit worthiness.

◆ Prenuptial agreements or any other agreements that show how income or assets are to be split.

◆ Business and home accounting records, including bank statements, ledgers, budget books, and check registers.

◆ Notes payable to you or by you, and outstanding credit card bills.

◆ Your husband's pay stub, pension agreement, and profit-sharing plan or other retirement program.

◆ Deeds or contracts.

◆ Personal or business insurance papers.

◆ Statements from brokerage firms, mutual funds, partnerships or other investments. This includes appraisals of any collectibles like antiques, jewelry, or sports collections.

HOW TO SELECT AN ATTORNEY

Those who find themselves dissatisfied with their attorney's services or fees probably don't realize that they did have a choice. Although shopping for a doctor or a lawyer should be done with the same patience and thoroughness you would give to purchasing furniture or a car, there is a marked difference: Most people don't know what they want when lawyer hunting. Why? Most likely it is because professionals such as doctors and lawyers are usually sought when a person is in a crisis situation, when the potential client is not thinking clearly yet is acting quickly. Moreover, attorneys and physicians often are placed on pedestals, making people feel that the professional is doing them a favor, rather than being in their employ. If you can see this, you shouldn't have too much trouble with the idea that picking an attorney is like shopping for a car. Both need to serve you well and be reliable, affordable, and comfortable.

Most people make do by simply asking a friend or looking up an attorney in the Yellow Pages. But to be an informed consumer when attorney shopping, here are some things to keep in mind:

- Call a lawyer referral service. Most communities list phone numbers in their local directories of sources that can refer you to someone who specializes in family law. If you can't locate one in your area, contact your local bar association. Most county bar associations will give out names of lawyers in the area. However, bar associations often fail to provide meaningful screening, which means that those who participate may not be the most experienced or competent.

- Another good source of referrals is a community center or public service agency. Your county's battered women's shelter, crisis centers, legal aid societies, women's resource cen-

ters or women's commissions, and children's legal services can be of help. Independent paralegals get regular feedback on lawyers' work and can make informed recommendations. If you know of someone who was recently divorced and was pleased with the services of her lawyer, call that lawyer first. If that lawyer cannot take your case, ask for recommendations. Group legal plans, available through some unions and consumer action groups, offer comprehensive legal assistance free or at low cost. Do your homework. Solicit recommendations from a variety of sources and compare the information you receive.

- Examine the attorney's areas of specialization or expertise. A common mistake made when asking friends for advice is that they often recommend an attorney whose specialty is in an unrelated field. For example, your brother may have found an attorney who is excellent for his business needs, but this adviser might know little or nothing about divorce or custody law. Avoid giant firms that primarily represent businesses. Such firms know little about matrimonial law and less about keeping costs reasonable.

- Keep in mind that just because you see an attorney on a consultation basis does not mean that you need to hire him or her. Most lawyers charge an initial consultation fee, but you should consider this a small price to pay for an opportunity to find the best fit for you and the best bargain. Use this initial appointment to assess whether or not this is the best attorney to represent you in your particular situation.

- Tell the attorney the exact nature of your legal problem as concisely as possible. Practice beforehand so you don't get caught up in an emotional discussion, which could wind up being costly. Remember, attorneys aren't psychologists. Don't waste your money venting your feelings. Do that through a support group, your clergyman or counselor, and special friends. Stick to the facts when interviewing a lawyer.

- Absolute honesty is essential. Remember, the attorney is bound by a code of professional ethics, and all conversations with the attorney are protected by the attorney/client privilege of confidentiality. But even though you can trust this person professionally, you need to feel trust in him or her as an individual. Get a feeling of whether or not you can communicate comfortably with this person. If you perceive this person as cold or arrogant, or if he or she is of a decidedly different personality type from you, the two of you may not work together well. Better to keep looking.

- Determine how much expertise the attorney has in family law. Ask how long he or she has been practicing and how many cases like yours he or she has handled. Ask how many were litigated successfully. A competent attorney will welcome your questions. The attorney should be eager to discuss his or her experience and knowledge in handling cases such as yours.

- See how realistic the attorney is about settling your case to your advantage. Avoid the attorney who promises you an unrealistically large sum of money. An experienced lawyer should be able to give you a reasonable assessment, but no guarantees. The judge has the final say. Also stay away from the expensive, flamboyant media celebrity lawyer. This kind of lawyer would probably pass your case on to a recent law school graduate in his office. Lawyers who make decisions without consulting you, who do not return your phone calls within a reasonable time period, and who generally will not tell you how your case is being handled are all to be avoided.

- Ask what your options are. For example, should you go to court, or would it be better to settle differently, perhaps through divorce mediation? If the attorney insists that his way is the only way, get up and leave. Trust your instincts. Any lawyer who offers to take you to dinner or bed or anyplace else should be avoided like the plague. Their conduct is unethical.

- Finally, at the end of the consultation, ask about fees. While most professionals can't promise an exact figure due to the potential complexity of the case, such as additional court costs or noncooperation from the other party, they should be able to give you a ballpark figure with a maximum range. And keep in mind that just because an attorney quotes a high fee, this doesn't mean that she or he is best.

A lawyer is your representative in perhaps the most important issues of your life—custody of your child, child support, your physical protection when domestic violence is an issue, and a fair settlement. Don't select this person without first knowing the facts. As a legal consumer, you have the right to shop around!

CONSIDER MEDIATION

Mediation occurs when, instead of each party hiring a separate attorney, both the husband and the wife agree to a single mediator. It is the mediator's job to reach an agreement regarding all aspects of the divorce, including custody and visitation. The agreement does not have to be fair or equal or right. It just has to be an agreement.

Mediation is not a good choice when your soon to be former husband wields all the power and you cannot negotiate with him on an equal footing. If you are intimidated or in any way fearful of your former husband, mediation is not for you. Mediation is also a particularly poor choice for women who have not worked outside the home or who do not have an accurate accounting of family financial assets. Women who give up too much during mediation for the sake of a quick settlement may have real regrets later when they come to realize exactly what they have given up.

Mediation can be a viable option for couples who need to preserve their working relationships after divorce—like the parents of young children. The compromise that is essential for successful mediation is good practice for the years of shared parenting ahead.

Communication skills are enhanced. Mediation deals with hard facts only, sidestepping murky emotional issues. Sometimes this approach helps divorcing couples defuse emotional issues and lessen the pain. Couples who have achieved a balance of power and knowledge and are accustomed to consensus building in the workplace can be ideal candidates for mediation. Not only are costs substantially lower, but also there is less animosity and emotional turmoil. Adherence to the agreement is typically greater.

Examine your own situation with care before making any decision about how best to handle the legal matters associated with your divorce.

ANNULMENTS AND *GETS*

Aside from legal considerations, you may have religious issues to deal with concerning your divorce.

For example, if you were married in the Roman Catholic Church, you must receive an annulment (the declaration of a marriage as null and void, as if it never existed) from the Church before it will recognize your civil (legal) divorce. A long and complicated procedure, an annulment is in no way guaranteed upon request; there must be extenuating circumstances, such as that one party was coerced into marriage. Without an annulment, you are still considered married in the eyes of the Church and consequently, remarriage is forbidden. This is because marriage in Catholicism is considered a sacrament rather than a contractual agreement, as it is in Judaism.

The laws of traditional Jewish divorce (*Get*) rank among those having the most serious inequities for women. If the divorcing husband and wife are both behaving amicably, receiving a *Get* can be a simple matter of signing a formal agreement. Because of the increase in divorce among all ethnic, religious, and social groups, there is an awareness among religious Jewish women that they are not equal to men under the laws governing Jewish divorce. A man is allowed to issue a divorce decree to his wife, but she cannot do the same. Moreover, because all power in Jewish divorce law rests with the man, she has to accept the decree regardless of her rights. If her husband wants to leave her and live with another woman and even have children with this other woman, that is permitted, but the wife cannot remarry, nor can she have children with another man without serious consequences to herself and her children. Worse, under the laws of Orthodox Judaism, if a husband was killed in war but there were no witnesses or his body was never found, his wife can never remarry, because he wasn't around to issue her the *Get*. She can be considered an adulterer should she have sex with another man, since she is still presumed married.

Since the acceptance of larger numbers of women into the rabbinate, these inequities are being addressed, and more changes to Jewish divorce law are being made as these women are interpreting the legal jargon with a more feminist perspective. Nonconservative Jews—those belonging to modern or Reformed temples— interpret the laws in ways that make divorce more tolerable for Jewish women.

WHEN HE THREATENS TO TAKE THE KIDS

Many husbands will demand custody as a tactic. These men and their attorneys know that losing custody of your child is your worst fear. By making this demand, they hope you will lessen your legitimate demands or accept less than equitable child support.

This is the kind of situation you are paying your attorney to handle. This is a bluff designed to frighten you. If these men wanted custody, they would have demanded it from the very beginning. Your worst nightmare is losing the children. Their worst nightmare is getting the children. Try to put this tactic into perspective and think before you let your maternal instincts dominate your good sense and judgment. However, if you find yourself embroiled in a custody battle, read Chapter 18.

SEX WITH YOUR SOON-TO-BE EX

I am in the middle of a divorce, but have had sex twice with my husband. This is confusing things terribly even though we both know it's over. What should I do?

One of the reasons some couples going through even bitter divorces continue to have sex is because it's convenient and certainly safer from a health perspective than sex with a new partner. Many just aren't ready to find another partner. Or maybe they are in denial emotionally about the divorce. Their heads are seeing attorneys and signing papers, but their hearts are somewhere else.

THE DOS AND DON'TS OF TELLING THE CHILDREN YOU'RE DIVORCING

♦ Do remember that children are not miniature adults. Just because your ten-year-old has the vocabulary and mannerisms of a young adult, don't assume that he or she is more emotionally capable than any other ten-year-old. Your child is trying to act bravely in the face of adversity. What your child is really feeling is frightened, and although the divorce may be the best thing for you, your child doesn't see it this way. Be sensitive to how your child views things.

♦ Don't stop parenting because you're going through major changes. Your child needs you to be a parent. He or she needs emotional support, consistent routines, and the assurance of love and care.

♦ Don't make your child your confidant, spy, or in-house therapist. This rule applies regardless of the age of your child. Teenage children are no better equipped, and sometimes less well equipped, to handle divorce than preschool children.

♦ Do keep divorce the business of adults. The ongoing negotiations and legal battles are adult things. Children take what they hear literally. When they hear the phrase "no money," they take that to mean "not a single penny." Lacking experience and maturity, they put two and two together from overheard conversations or inappropriate information offered by adults and almost never come up with four.

♦ Do share information that is relevant to them, however. If there are going to be major life-style changes like moving to a different house or a different part of the country, share these plans with your child when they are definite. Telling your child that you might have to do this or might have to move there burdens your child unnecessarily. Much of what you are worrying about now will probably not happen.

♦ Do watch what you say about their father. No matter what he has done, and particularly if he spent a significant amount of time with them before the divorce, keep

---

A woman may still love her husband and hope that sex will bring him back to her. Some people use sex as a weapon or bargaining tool—for instance, in the case of a man demanding sex in exchange for regular child support payments. This demand, in effect, puts the mother in a position not unlike that of a prostitute. If your ex-husband makes this demand, discuss the situation with your attorney right away.

Having sex with someone you are separating from extorts a great price. The emotional closeness sex brings can be confusing and can hinder your ability to detach from this person—a necessary step to surviving a divorce. See what needs you are trying to fulfill, and try to meet those needs without having sex with your ex. For example, if you need to be reassured that you are still attractive and desirable, try looking in the mirror and telling yourself just that.

(continuation)

in mind that he is still their father. Everything you say to your children about their father will be dealt with as part of themselves. Telling your children—even if it is the truth—that their father is a lazy, no-good bum may give you the momentary pleasure of knowing that they're siding with you, but what does acknowledging his shortcomings do for them? Remember, children think that half of them is made up of one parent. Positive comments work better, such as saying, "You draw very well. I'll bet you get some of that talent from your father." No matter what happened between Mom and Dad, your children will know that you are still their parents.

- Don't publicize your personal life, at least for the sake of the children. You may be ready to announce your availability, especially if you've been in an emotionally dead marriage for years. Or maybe your husband left you for someone else and you are desperate to show the world that you are attractive and desirable. You may have married very young and missed out on a lot or maybe you just miss sex. You have every right to make happen for you what you feel you need and want. But there is a big difference between what you need and want and what your children need and want. No matter what the circumstances were of your separation and divorce, your children are not yet emotionally ready to support your need for a life of your own. Give them time and keep your lives private. Later, you will find right ways to accommodate your needs into family life.

- Do try to live in the present. Today is as important to your children as yesterday or tomorrow. Although it's difficult to focus on your children when so many things in your life are up in the air, try to set aside a small part of each day when you handle "divorce stuff" such as keeping appointments with attorneys or real-estate appraisers. Allow another part of the day for even small things to do with your children. Freeze snow today for a snowball fight on the Fourth of July. Count happy memories instead of reading them the usual bedtime story. Bake purple cookies in weird shapes. Let them eat dessert first tonight.

Remember that sleeping with your ex, or any new love interest for that matter, is not a reliable gauge of your worth as a woman. Learn to love your body, your face, your talents.

WHAT TO TELL EVERYONE

This is definitely a situation where the less said, the better. The divorce may be taking up 110 percent of your time and energy, but to most other people the subject is boring. Obviously, some people thrive on other people's pain and love hearing the details. Unless you relish having your life dissected and analyzed by strangers, do not feed the gossip grapevine. Many women find a simple statement like "We reached a point where we no longer could be mutually supportive" or "I'd rather not bore you with these particular personal details" to be the best replies to probing questions. Share your feelings only with those you trust, and only if and when you feel like it. Eventually you will need to discuss some aspects of your divorce with pertinent family members—the children's paternal and maternal grandparents, aunts, uncles, close friends, and other relatives—but for now your priority should be to get your emotional house in order.

Your Parents. Your parents may be thrilled, or they may be devastated. They may think that your divorce is a giant blot on the family name. They may tell you that they told you so. It is hard to predict. Ask for their love and support. They may ask what they can do to help. Accept the help, but keep your requests reasonable. Your parents are probably not looking for a major change in their life style or child-care responsibilities. Perhaps your mother can pick up your daughter one day a week from school, or your father can fix a few things that need fixing. If they offer money and you need money, accept their offer but keep it a loan, with specified provisions for paying them back. You are not leaving a marriage to become your parents' child once again. Independence is a precious thing.

Your parents will not be better for knowing all the grim details. Your ex-husband will still be part of the children's lives, as will your parents. Telling them things that will make it difficult for them to look him in the eye or to act cordially toward him does no one any good.

His Parents. Having to deal with his family now only on a limited basis

might turn out to be one of the unintended perks of your divorce. You may be close to his parents, however, and want to keep up this relationship. Accept that things will be different. It is your former husband's responsibility to tell his parents of your divorce. You have no control over what else he chooses to tell them.

Do not expect your husband's parents to punish him if he neglects his children or fails to live up to his financial obligations. Do not punish them by withholding their grandchildren from them. Your children need their love and support. At the same time, you do not have to put up with any kind of nonsense. If his parents are mean and vindictive, stay away.

Your Boss, Coworkers, and Other Interested Parties. Your boss may like and respect you as a person, but he is not interested in the details of your marital breakup. He is concerned about whether you will be able to do your job as well as you have in the past. He does not want to hear you on the phone endlessly discussing the divorce with your girlfriends or speaking with your attorney. Your attorney works for you. Have him or her call you at home when you can talk without the office gossips on red alert. If you are feeling upset at work, go to the restroom and cry privately. Your coworkers will be sympathetic, but only to a point. Everyone has problems. The woman you may want to confide in and share your daily troubles with may have just found out that she has cancer or that her son is on drugs.

Do not allow your boss to find out about your divorce from someone else. Bosses typically like to be the first to know and hate to be surprised. Tell your boss in a matter-of-fact way and assure him or her that you will continue to produce as you have before. Practice your speech until you can do it in an unemotional way and, definitely, without crying.

Some women report that the best part of working is getting away from the financial and emotional problems that accompany every divorce and concentrating on getting a job done. More than ever, the income is important and you need to concentrate. Use work as a place to set aside your personal troubles and focus on what you need to do to build your new life.

WHAT TO TELL NO ONE

Accept the fact that most people have a very hard time keeping secrets. That is why attorneys and therapists are called professionals—they do keep secrets. It is absolutely guaranteed that whatever you tell one person, other people will hear about. You may not care. You may feel fine about having the whole town know that your ex-husband liked wearing pink nightgowns to bed. You may want to punish him by having people know that he was unfaithful or cheap or abusive.

But the bottom line is that this is not in the best interests of your children. Depending on how juicy the gossip is, they may be ridiculed by their classmates or may no longer be invited to other people's homes. People have short attention spans. After they are finished with the gossip you spread about him, these same people will turn on you. They will chitchat about why you put up with it or how you are rather cheap yourself. In short, your efforts to muddy his reputation may succeed, but some

mud will stick to you and your children. Find healthier ways to rid yourself of the anger you feel—by keeping a journal, talking with a trusted friend, or occasionally just punching a pillow.

RECOVERING FROM DIVORCE AND GROWING BEYOND IT

Most women exiting a relationship feel that their pain is like nothing anyone else could possibly have experienced and that they are the only person in such agony. Death seems appealing—except "What to do with the kids?" It's important to remember that other women have experienced the same feelings. No matter what your individual circumstances, there were feelings of love, commitment, attachment, and belonging. Great energy was focused on creating a life together. To expect to walk away emotionally unscathed is simply not realistic. To punish yourself by expecting instant healing or to deny the experience of loss will guarantee emotional numbness, which is as near to death as you can get while you are still breathing. Still, a few weeks of living in a semi-coma after the realization that you are divorced or divorcing is fairly common. It actually seems to serve as a resting period so you have the strength to complete the grieving process. Then you can begin the divorce recovery process.

Removing the Failure Label. When a woman's sense of personal identity is closely tied to a fantasy picture of marriage, the inevitable collapse of that fantasy can come as a crushing blow. Sadly, too many women define divorce as the ultimate personal failure. The fact that there were two people in the marriage seems forgotten. Yet accepting responsibility for others' behaviors or for making things go right is something women have been doing for a long time. Even the woman who came into the marriage with a record of success in school or in the work place can be vulnerable to a crippling sense of failure when her marriage ends in divorce.

Beginning in early childhood, we are expected to "play nicely" as little girls. Girls are brought up not to do things that make other people uncomfortable. As we were growing up, we might have overheard our mothers, grandmothers, or other female family members or friends talking about a particular woman who "just couldn't hold on to her man." Most of us were never quite sure then what that meant, but we knew it was almost the worst thing you could say about any woman. We began as adolescents to define ourselves according to the success or failure of our relationships—unlike boys, who were taught how to succeed in the board room. Even though the women's movement has brought astounding changes in the last twenty years, many women still allow a "failed marriage" to describe the outcome of their relationship rather than the "dissolution of a partnership."

Regaining Control. Negative, self-destructive feelings can leave you in a frazzle, causing you to feel out of control. Letting go of feelings of failure and helplessness can uncover the strength that you might not even have known that you possessed. This doesn't mean that your life will turn around overnight. Nor does it insulate you from experiencing some bumpy times ahead. But it does mean that control over your own life comes only with the understanding that it is not what happens to you that counts. It is how you decide to deal with what happens that ultimately matters. You may have had no control over events leading up to this moment. Define events as tragic, and your life may indeed be a tragedy. Define yourself as a helpless victim, and you will be just that. But you can take control now. Tell yourself, "I can move ahead. I will move ahead. I am never going to permit myself to be in circumstances like this again," and you will have learned from what has happened. You will become smarter, stronger, and better.

Knowing When to Give Up. When one spouse is prepared to face contempt, jail, and total destruction, there is very little the other spouse can do to get justice. When one spouse is prepared to do anything to hurt the other and to prevent a fair distribution of assets, sometimes the best thing to do is to give up. Lawyers seldom recommend giving up. It is their training and inclination to figure out how to fight back and get you what is due you. You must weigh the financial and emotional cost of continuing to fight back no matter what.

You shouldn't consider yourself a quitter should you choose to walk away from a spouse who has both the desire and the means to punish and abuse you through unending legal battles. Although in a divorce the first thing you are concerned with is protecting your financial rights, ultimately you have to ask two questions: Am I getting every penny I deserve? Is it worth living my life like this? Go with the answer to the second question.

Thriving After Divorce. Most of us know at least one woman who has survived the difficult and painful adjustment of divorce. She seems to have made the best of whatever her individual circumstances may have been. This woman has turned the divorce into an opportunity for personal growth. New successes, opportunities, personal happiness, and a genuine sense of fulfillment have come her way. She's doing great, and so are her children. This is a family that more than survives—they thrive.

Even if you've been divorced for years, you may still be living in a world that hasn't caught up with the realities of the day-to-day needs and challenges of the divorced woman's life. You need to identify your resources and put them to the best possible use.

Ask yourself how you can go about getting these needs met. What are your resources, and how can these resources be put to the best possible use? Make a list. Ask friends to help you brainstorm. You may find that you have more going for you than you first realized. For example, you may have gardening or desktop publishing talents that you could barter for the tutoring skills of a friend or neighbor. Remember that resources are not just money or possessions. Strong faith is a resource. Belief in yourself is the best resource of all.

HOW TO CUSTOMIZE A LIFE PLAN

Successful people all share two secrets: First they had a vision. Then they executed a plan.

Artists create with a vision of the image or emotion to be portrayed. Painters often rely on a preliminary drawing from which to complete their masterpiece. Writers develop an outline rather than keystroke randomly. Builders follow blueprints.

Like any good sailor, you need to chart a course so you don't just drift. But first you must see where you are going.

Women are typically less prepared than men to create their own vision different from the life that's depicted in fairy tales. Because helpless women are rarely rescued by princes in real life, and because there is no fairy godmother who with a wave of her wand will turn a pumpkin into dependable transportation to take you to a well-paying job with benefits, you need to decide how to make these things happen. Although careful planning and hard work won't guarantee that your life will be heaven, it's the most authentic, productive, and satisfying way to deal with what life offers.

Here are three steps for visualizing where you see yourself in the real world:

1. Make three wishes and write them down. Remember to give these some thought because even though you will be utilizing creativity, you don't want to suspend reality. For example, if you dropped out of college after one semester because you never wanted to hear the word "science" again, becoming a

world-famous neurosurgeon may not be a realistic wish. However, seeing yourself in the world of medicine may have little to do with longing for the prestige and respect given a doctor or scientist, but rather may be related to an interest in healing or prevention. Studying biofeedback techniques, volunteering at a hospice, or publishing an article on vitamin therapy might be realistic. Consider the potential earning power of your dream job. Think about becoming a hospital administrator or a counselor for adults with learning disabilities. Think about becoming a chiropractor or a homeopathic healer.

Likewise, if you are thirty-eight, have two left feet and never took a dance class in your life, becoming prima ballerina for the Joffrey Ballet doesn't look too promising. Yet if you visualize people, applause, and emotion, the stage may be very important in your vision. Try taking a music class, going to more concerts or ballets, or writing that play that's been in your head for years. Be prepared to be surprised by what you find out about yourself.

Taking Back Your Maiden Name

Resuming your maiden name after divorce can be accomplished at nominal cost even if you do not make this change as part of your divorce. This is how you do it. Take your birth certificate and divorce decree to the social security office and request a new card in your birth name. Use these documents to get a driver's license in your birth name. Notify credit card companies and magazines, and anyone else you choose, of your new name, and when necessary send them copies of your new license and social security card.

2. Review your wish list. You may wish for a better education or more knowledge of music and the arts. You may wish for companionship or romance. You may wish for greater happiness for your children. You may wish for more peace and serenity in your life. You may wish for more positive relationships with your extended family. You may wish for better health, more stamina, or more energy. Wishes that fall under a definite heading like financial security or improved health should give you a clear idea of where your visionary energies should be directed.

3. Now create a miracle. Look at your three wishes. Pretend a miracle has happened and your wishes came true. How would things be different? What would have changed? For example, if you wished for more companionship, would you see yourself sitting among a group of adults chatting and laughing on

weekends when "dad" takes the kids, instead of feeling lonesome in your apartment? Would you call some friends and invite them over for a potluck supper and an evening of good conversation? What is available at your local library, college or university, church or synagogue, or other organization? How about organizing a book club, support group, or film society, depending on your interests?

Don't worry, this process doesn't have to be overwhelming. Just take one positive step every day toward fulfilling your wish, and you will be accomplishing a lot.

WEDDING RINGS AND OTHER LEFTOVERS

My marriage has been over for five years. My former husband is happily involved in his new life. I think I'm adjusting okay except that I am still wearing my wedding rings. I can't seem to take them off.

Don't beat yourself up. Rings are powerful symbols of marriage in our society. Receiving your engagement ring brought you a moment of great joy. When the wedding ring was slipped on your finger at your wedding ceremony, it was symbolic of your life together. For you, taking the rings off will be the absolute final end of your marriage. You probably feel unready to date, so these symbols of marriage don't seem out of place. Maybe a small part of you has not completely accepted the divorce.

When you are emotionally ready, you will take them off. One day you will look at your hand and ask yourself why you are still wearing your rings. You will take them off and not think much about it. Remember to put them in a safe place, but not a place where you have to look at them every day. Your hand will feel strange and light for a few days. Soon, you will forget that you ever wore them.

My husband and I can't seem to decide what to do with our accumulated stuff. He says his new apartment is too small. I find much of it depressing, reminding me of less than great times. I find it interesting that even though we are long divorced, we can't seem to let go of this junk.

"Letting go" is the key phrase here. Whatever this junk is, it has come to represent the last vestige of your life as a couple. Neither of you wants to completely let go, or you would have disposed of this depressing stuff long ago.

When you are ready, try this. Say out loud that it is hard to let go of this stuff because it represents the last of your life together as a couple. Grieve and let go. Have a garage sale or rummage sale. Take the money and buy something that represents a beginning, not an end. Use the money to begin a stamp or coin collection for your children. Use it to try something new, like white-water rafting or canoeing. Give it to a charity whose work is life-affirming and constructive. Make an occasion out of whatever beginning you choose.

3

Becoming a Mother Outside of Marriage

THE NEW MOMS ON THE BLOCK

The majority of single mothers who give birth out of wedlock are called "single mother by choice" or "never-married mother," but this is often not the case. Although being stereotyped into either category is far better than such phrases as "knocked up" or "mother of illegitimate child," most of these women actually became mothers by chance.

In this book, we refer to these Mothers Outside of Marriage as MOMs. The similarity between a MOM and a single mother by choice is that both agree to "choose" to be receptive, to the idea of motherhood. But the MOM label could encompass those who arrived at motherhood by accident, those who prepared for motherhood "just in case," those who consciously chose to become pregnant, and adoptive mothers. At the risk of suggesting that on some

unconscious level most MOMs arrange the circumstances to allow for the possibility of motherhood, the truth is most have had the thought of mothering solo, however remote, cross their minds at one time or another. The woman who has told herself clearly that she does not now nor ever will want children and finds herself pregnant has experienced an accident. But again, it is still her choice whether to perceive this accident as tragic or as happy.

"Never-married" is also misleading because a huge number of MOMs have previously been in marriages or committed relationships. Certainly it would be wonderful just to call mothers mothers. But because our society does not treat all mothers and families equally, or offer policies that equally address all their concerns, this book distinguishes circumstances in order to be better able to meet the specific needs of those with unanswered questions.

IF YOU'RE MAKING A DECISION

Don't feel isolated. The numbers of Mothers Outside of Marriage have been multiplying. The rate of growth has increased more than 60 percent in the last decade; the highest rates were among white women over the age of 20. Statistics show that, contrary to stereotypes about unmarried moms, these "new MOMs on the block" are usually working women who have decided that having a child is more important than any disapproval they may face. They know that a nurturing mother and father might or might not be their preferred choice of family, but they are realistic about accepting the fact that the "dream family"—the house, dog, white picket fence, and Mr. Right—might not materialize. The new single mother has what it takes to raise a child; she just needs a little reassurance now and then. She is strong and independent enough not to feel overwhelmed by this responsibility, yet gentle and compassionate enough to give unselfishly to her child.

Technically, there is a difference between a Single Mother by Choice (SMBC) and a MOM. If you recall the brouhaha when television sitcom character Murphy Brown had her baby, she was referred to as an SMBC who was mocking fatherhood. Not true. She was a MOM. Unlike a true SMBC, who through adoption, donor insemination, or intercourse has marked on her calendar the events leading up to motherhood, Murphy Brown chose to make the best of her situation. When learning that her ex-husband, by whom she thought she was pregnant, wanted to go off and save a rain forest rather than stay with her, Murphy grappled with all her options, including remaining in a dead-end relationship or having an abortion. Finally she decided, as many of us do, "What the heck, I'm going to have this baby with or without him."

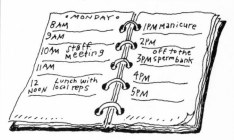

Most of us don't choose to become a mother at a precise time—say, attending a staff meeting at ten, scheduling a hair appointment after lunch, and at three going to the sperm bank to be impregnated. An SMBC usually has spent more time deliberately planning her upcoming motherhood, doing things like putting a certain amount of money away each month, moving to a district boasting good schools, and checking into the family leave programs at work. But regardless of whether they chose donor insemination or chose to raise their babies on their own after realizing that they were not in a partnership with someone who could be a father, all women who find themselves MOMs by choice—or sort of by choice—have many of the same experiences to share. There are so many reasons for becoming a MOM.

IF YOUR MATE DOESN'T SHARE YOUR FEELINGS

You're not alone if you find yourself in a relationship with a man who doesn't

ARE YOU READY FOR SINGLE MOTHERHOOD?

If you are considering single motherhood, it's very important to ask yourself some questions, since this style of parenting may not be for everyone. However, just because you can't answer every question the way you would like doesn't mean that you won't do a good job. If you haven't resolved the following issues, now would be a good time to work on them.

♦ Have you decided how you will explain your choice to be a single mother to your son or daughter? You should be able to present to your child a positive view of your family situation.

♦ Have you decided what the role of the father will be? Before your child's birth, you should consider the financial and emotional aspects of the father's involvement, if any, with the child. Does he want to play daddy, or does he not even want his name on the birth certifi-

cate? In some cases, it is best to get legal advice.

♦ Have you budgeted for all aspects of child-bearing and child care, including donor insemination if you are going that route? You should also make necessary legal provisions for your child should something happen to you.

♦ Have you thought about what you will tell family and friends, and are you prepared for any negative remarks? Knowing how to handle people's offhand comments is important, but be sure you are not simply trying to shock or hurt someone, or to prove that you can do something on your own.

♦ Have you resolved any issues about men and relationships, and are you sure that you are not angry at men or trying in some way to get even with a particu-

want children but never made this clear. Somehow, this doesn't seem to be a problem at first. You may have kept your desire for motherhood well hidden. And perhaps your mate has remarked in passing, "I may want kids, but not now, not for a long time," and you don't want to push him, so you wait for a more opportune moment to discuss marriage and fatherhood. But typically, it is only after you announce your pregnancy that any serious dialog begins.

Many MOMs say they knew subconsciously that their former partners were not father material. It often takes a few years to become aware that perhaps you stayed in such a relationship

to allow yourself at least the option of becoming a mother, whether or not the father was willing to participate. At first, it may appear that he is the only reason you are a single mother, but when you examine the matter further, you may find that you weren't really surprised by his decision not to be a father.

"MY BOYFRIEND CAN'T MAKE UP HIS MIND ..."

I've been in a relationship for five years with someone who has decided not to be a father. I've responded

(continuation)

lar man? It's important to place a high value on male and female relationships in order to give your child a realistic perspective of the world. No matter what the sex of your child, it is most important not to have negative feelings toward men. Also, you need to leave yourself open to the possibility that one day you might become involved in a committed relationship with a man.

- Are you having a baby because you are lonely and need something to fill the void? Hopefully, your life is already rich and satisfying, and you have the ability to mother yourself when needed.

- Do you think that having a baby will preserve the bond between you and a man you love even after the relationship is over? Think again. Having a child is not a guarantee that the relationship will continue.

- Have you learned what physical and emotional changes you will go through, before, during, and after childbirth? You should arrange to have a friend or family member be your labor coach and help you out the first few weeks after birth. Keep in mind that you won't always have a partner to share feelings with you or comfort you during the hormonal shifts and mood swings that go along with pregnancy.

- Do you have a strong support system? Just because you have lunch daily with your female coworkers doesn't mean they will be there for you in the middle of the night. Don't mistake work friends for real friends, and don't overlook those friends you normally would shy away from because professionally you have little in common. You need to create an extended family.

by announcing that I am considering having a child on my own. I don't want to spend my life waiting for my soon-to-be-ex to come around in order to have a child. I know definitely that I want to be a mother and to have a baby fairly soon, but I can't make him agree. I wouldn't want my baby's father to be someone who didn't want to be with us, anyway.

You're right—you can't make your boyfriend become a father. However, you can make the decision to become the best mother possible. If other options, like deciding to remain

childless or postponing the decision to start a family, are not right for you, then your decision to have a child is the best one for you and your child. You need to feel good about the appropriateness of the decision for you as the first step in successful single mothering.

"MY FAMILY IS UNSUPPORTIVE ..."

My family says I'm selfish to even consider having a child without a husband. They say I will deprive my baby of a father, but I want to be a mother.

Why not ask your family why they view your having a child as a deprivation to the child, rather than as a gift from a mother who really wants one? Is the cup half empty? You want to be positive and affirmative toward your own life and your child's. Remember that the child of a single woman who chose motherhood will one day be able to claim, "My mom really wanted me!" Isn't that healthier than the comments we hear from parents complaining that their children were "mistakes," or from a friend who claims his life problems revolve around his parents' revelation that his arrival was a burden?

"MR. RIGHT (OR MR. ADEQUATE) HASN'T SHOWN UP ..."

Many women are tired of waiting for Mr. Right, or even Mr. Adequate, to show up. He may appear after the age when you are safely able to bear children. In view of the high rate of divorce, many women are choosing to start families outside of marriage since they have no guarantees that a marriage will remain intact. Some go the sperm bank route and become pregnant through donor insemination, and others become pregnant by someone they have cared for and been involved with for a long time.

After carefully reviewing your options, you may join the millions of other single mothers who are now starting families and will be successfully raising them in the new millennium. A family is defined as a place where one feels loved, safe, and protected. It should not be defined by whether or not a man heads the household.

IF YOUR INTERNAL CLOCK IS TICKING FAST

Around the age of thirty, many women start becoming anxious about their biological clocks and their ability to be a mother. With all the advances in reproductive medicine, the risks of having a child at an older age have greatly diminished. In addition, many women report that because they waited until they had "lived a little" before having a child, they have more patience for child-rearing than do younger women who haven't achieved enough personal fulfillment.

IF YOUR PARTNER LEFT YOU

In a sense, the man who announces "I don't want a baby" has left you emotionally, especially if you discussed planning a family together. No matter what circumstances surround single motherhood, loss is a central theme.

Even women who consciously choose single motherhood by donor insemination are dealing with a type of loss—in this case, the loss of a dream family, complete with father, two kids, two cars, and a dog and cat.

If your boyfriend physically abandoned you, you need to ask yourself whether this is truly a tragedy or whether he may in a sense have done you a favor. If we take an honest look inside ourselves, we often find that even if we can't have the dream family, we still want the option of being a mother. It's just that it is very difficult in our present society to allow ourselves such conscious choices. Therefore many of us use abandonment as an excuse to be a "victim" of single motherhood.

If your pregnancy was planned but the father disappeared in the middle of the night, never to be seen again, you need to assess the situation carefully. You will find that most likely there always was some indication that becoming a father was not a commitment with which this person was comfortable.

Of course, there are no guarantees in life. Perhaps your pregnancy stirred up painful feelings in your partner, and the only way out was for him to flee. Being abandoned and being left in total shock is not unlike experiencing a sudden death in the family. In a sense, you feel widowed, but more unsettled, because widows often can accept their situation by recognizing that death is final and they have no power over it. When your partner leaves without explanation, you may wonder if there was anything you could have done to prevent it. Probably not, but there is something that can be prevented now, and that is blaming yourself. It is not your fault.

IF YOUR PARTNER HAS PROBLEMS

When I told my live-in partner of five years that I was pregnant, he simply said, "You decide," and went into the bedroom to watch TV. He's always been remote and a bit of a couch potato. Lately, he has been sullen and drinking pretty heavily, but only on weekends. Yet he always appears presentable and well groomed, has never become physically violent, and faithfully shows up for his job, which he claims to hate, every Monday morning. I want this baby, but feel unhappy and cheated. How can I decide whether or not to have this baby with him?

This is the most common question MOMs report asking themselves after learning that they are pregnant by a partner of many years. But first, it would be wise to look at the reasons you were drawn to this relationship to begin with. Perhaps sex with this person is more than satisfying. Maybe he's good-looking, has a good job and plenty of money, and drives a nice car. In spite of his weekend drinking, he might still be dependable enough. But feeling cheated is not surprising. After all, this person has put up many walls that allow him to resist communication and genuine intimacy. This might be his way of protecting himself and avoiding closeness to anyone, even you and your baby. If he is genuinely dispassionate and disconnected from others, it seems in character for him to be apathetic about your announcement. The fact that he shows up for a job he says he hates after a weekend binge means that he might have problems even he isn't ready to deal with. Having a baby might be a distraction from his own issues, and maybe this is why he doesn't have an opinion one way or the other. It also seems that he expects you to take most of the responsibility for this decision, which means he is unlikely to be an active participant in raising your child.

It's important to weigh the benefits of this relationship against the disadvantages. More importantly, keep in mind that communication is essential to the relationship. Without it, you are only making the motions of being in a partnership and are cheating yourself in the long run. Raising a child with a mate who has poor communication skills may not be wise, since people who tend to be disconnected with others have a way of sending out mixed signals—confusion that no one needs, especially children.

"I GOT PREGNANT FROM A BRIEF AFFAIR ..."

I'm a single mother by choice, sort of. At thirty-five I found myself pregnant after a brief affair with a younger coworker from my office. So far, I'm delighted that I have a healthy daughter, but I also feel a little embarrassed about how I got pregnant in the first place.

Unless your reasons for having a child are based on a need to get back at someone, to shock your family, to rope someone into a commitment, or to ease your loneliness, there is nothing to be embarrassed about. The delight and joy you feel about your daughter's arrival is the way it should be. Perhaps raising children in today's world is sometimes not so wonderful because of the many unhealthy social values that permeate our culture. But if new motherhood is met with a welcoming and positive attitude, then the steps it took to physically become a mother are not as important as how you mother on a day-to-day basis. If this brief affair filled needs for you in the present, chances are your delighted outlook on having a daughter may stem from the benefits you consciously sought out from that experience.

IF YOUR BIRTH CONTROL DIDN'T WORK

Imperfect birth control methods could easily have contributed to any of the above situations. Don't berate yourself for contraceptive failure. Even if you think it was because of a hidden wish to conceive that you were careless in the use of birth control, a combination of factors might be what makes this a blessing in disguise. If you've decided to go ahead and have your child, it is important not to blame the birth control but rather to welcome the happy surprise.

In most cases where contraception failed, and the thought of becoming a mother is something that you can't see in the cards, you may have considered terminating the pregnancy. Yet countless women report that once they became pregnant, all their earlier refrains of "I can't imagine myself ever wanting kids" disappeared. Still, pregnancy is only one step toward motherhood—it's a lifetime occupation that will change any woman. It is up to you to decide whether that change is for the better.

SPECIAL CONCERN: DATE RAPE

Statistics tell us that one in four women is the victim of some kind of sexual abuse at some time in her life. Date rape is a growing issue for many women, from the college student attending a campus party, to the account executive taking a client to dinner, to the woman introduced to a handsome new neighbor by a mutual friend. No matter how well you knew this person, or how intimate you had become before intercourse, if you said no to him and he continued, it constitutes rape.

If you decide to continue a pregnancy that is the result of rape, you should seek counseling from an expert in the field of victim recovery. Consultation with a criminal attorney would also be wise, since there are few legal protections prohibiting a convicted rapist from obtaining visitation, and in some cases suing for custody.

IF YOU ARE IN AN ABUSIVE RELATIONSHIP

Relationships can be abusive even if no physical injury occurs. It is emotionally healthy and empowering to end a relationship if you feel you can't be yourself. Remarks like "But he didn't hit you" or "At least he didn't cheat" are not reasons to stay with someone who belittles you or doesn't accept your value or worth as a person.

If you are in a physically abusive relationship, get out now. If you got out of one, reward yourself for your bravery and honesty. Our society too often credits those who stay in relationships "till death do us part," as it often does,

rather than those who have the courage to get out. You need to be your own best advocate. As many single mothers whose significant others were abusive say, "I left to save myself and my child. It was the right thing to do."

Still, rape or any form of abuse is a crime that warrants serious punishment for the perpetrator. If you got out of a harmful relationship, try to help those remaining in abusive situations by serving as an example. Also, helping other battered women is a key to your own recovery.

If you think you are in an abusive relationship but are confused right now, contact your local mental health center, which is often listed in the front of your phone book.

IF ABORTION IS NOT AN OPTION

You might be one of the many women who are basically pro choice but refuse to consider abortion for this pregnancy. Women who have had previous abortions often feel, by the time they reach a certain stage in life, that "This pregnancy is meant to be." Other reasons not to consider abortion may stem from religious beliefs. However, you should know that religions that forbid abortion under any circumstances often seem to have an underlying moral code stigmatizing single motherhood as well.

If abortion is not an option for you because of emotional, physical, religious, or moral reasons, you would fare best by accepting your single mothering status as a choice. Keep in mind, however, that if economics prevented you from receiving a decided-upon abortion, then economics will certainly be a serious issue in child-rearing. If you need more information on this, contact your local chapter of Planned Parenthood.

FAMILIAR THEMES

There are many other ways that women have discovered motherhood outside of marriage. Here are some scenarios shared by members of the National Organization of Single Mothers (NOSM). Do any of these sound familiar to you?

♦ Sandra, twenty-nine, was in a relationship with a man whose behavior when drinking she detested but tolerated. When she discovered she was pregnant, she urged him to stop drinking, even though deep down she knew she didn't want to marry him even if he remained sober. She wanted a baby but was afraid to have one on her own.

♦ Nancy, forty-one, lives on and off with a man who constantly belittles her. Even her eleven-year-old son (from a previous marriage) talks back and is disrespectful to her. Just when she's ready to let her partner know that it's over, his friends and family remind her, "He doesn't beat you or cheat on you. He's good with the kids. What's wrong?" She has resigned herself to her pattern of waiting to see if things will improve.

♦ Lisa thought her womanizing boyfriend would commit to a permanent relationship when he found out they were going to have a baby. He split,

saying the baby wasn't his, and she later learned that he had four other children he also denied fathering. Although she was initially in shock, after thinking about it she realized there had been red flags up all along.

♦ Susan, forty, wanted a baby, but everyone around her was unsupportive. She got pregnant through a long-time but distant friend after deciding not to go the donor insemination route for personal and financial reasons. Her family routinely asks her how she could be so selfish as to deprive her child of a father.

♦ Janine's partner of four years dropped her off at the hospital shortly before she was to give birth. He drove off and never returned. He left the United States.

♦ Claire is thirty-eight and getting very anxious about having a child. She's dating someone regularly, but doesn't think he would be a good husband or father. Yet she recently flushed her birth control pills down the toilet.

◆ Lili is nine weeks pregnant and is grappling with the decision whether or not to have an abortion. Her boyfriend shows no interest in the pregnancy, yet she feels dependent on him.

Maybe one of these themes rings a bell, or maybe your story is totally unique. Whether yours seems routine or sensational, there will be strong feelings that need to be worked through.

HANDLING YOUR FEELINGS ABOUT MOTHERHOOD OUTSIDE OF MARRIAGE

Before you can rid yourself of the guilt and other feelings you don't deserve to be burdened with, and before you "blame" the other person, you need to take an honest look at the circumstances surrounding your becoming a mother. Most likely, you told yourself a story that safely prevented you from outwardly admitting to wanting a child whether your mate stayed around or not. By saying we were surprised at his reaction to the news, we remove ourselves a bit from responsibility. And we receive more sympathy when we act as if we didn't have a choice. But if even on an unconscious level you sensed that tapping your full personal, emotional, spiritual, or even financial resources was not possible within the confines of the relationship you were in, then you have something in common with most MOMs. Because women tend to place more emphasis on the quality, communication, and dynamics of a relationship than men do, they are not as content with being

in a less-than-strong relationship, and therefore they feel responsible or guilty when that relationship quits working.

Getting Rid of Guilt, Shame, and Blame. Sometimes we think after a breakup: "It wasn't so bad. What am I doing now that's better? Why couldn't I have been happy the way it was?" We wonder if we secretly pushed the other person out of our lives. Other times, if we were abandoned or weren't deeply involved to begin with, we believe it was our fault because if we had been more lovable, we would be with somebody right now. And even if we removed ourselves from intolerable circumstances or left for reasons others can't explain as valid, we let guilt dominate us for having made any choice at all.

You're Not a Victim. Being a victim often seems to be the least disruptive way to go. But the truth is that few of us are really victims. We have choices.

The reality is that facing your feelings is necessary, just as it would be if your feelings were associated with any other major life-changing event. But because the events surrounding single motherhood—divorce, death, giving birth, buying or selling a home, moving, getting or losing a job—already rank high on the list of life's most stressful events, it can be particularly challenging, since our culture's fear of the unaccustomed adds excessive baggage we could do without.

Be Honest. The task is to be honest with how you feel so that you can separate the unnecessary baggage—the guilt, shame, and blame—from those feelings that are valid. Whether you sail smoothly or bumpily through what it takes to stand up to your feelings isn't important. The goal is to become more accepting of yourself and to get rid of the victim mentality that so many single mothers find themselves operating in.

Name It, Face It, and Erase It. Guilt must be given a name. Whatever you feel guilty about—dig it up, isolate it, expose it to the light of day. In order to name it, you have to be as specific as possible. We are not talking about blanket statements about inadequacy or failing, but about identifying as clearly as possible exactly what you feel guilty about. Guilt must be faced. It must be declared out loud and looked in the eye. Guilt makes us feel ashamed or it makes us blame others for our circumstances.

Because there is so much baggage each of us will discover along our way, we must identify the personal life dramas that have caused us to feel vulnerable in the past before we can reconcile our feelings about our guilt. Your feelings can't hurt you. In fact, by listening to them you can learn from them and uncover the joy of single mothering. What can hurt is allowing your feelings to fester and build up and overlap healthy emotions, causing you to act out of confusion and impeding your ability to make good decisions. The reward for facing your feelings about your entry into single motherhood is peaceful acceptance of the choices you have made. This acceptance is the first important step to living joyfully and fully in the present.

Hold Your Head High

I sometimes sense that my friends are uncomfortable around me since I became an unmarried mother.

Sometimes they're impressed, other times they seem fearful. Why is this?

People, particularly women caught up in unhappy relationships, alternate between admiring and fearing single moms because they see them as hero-victims. Most likely it's because real heroes—not the artificial ones the media create—emerge from painful experiences that could happen to any of us. So when we glimpse ourselves in these real-life heroes, we tend to get a little uncomfortable around them. On the other hand, witnessing your bravery and your independence may inspire your friends. Stop worrying so much about what others think of you. Take pride in yourself and your accomplishments.

DECIDING ON THE FATHER'S ROLE

If you are a MOM who has conceived with someone you know (and most have), there are potential legal and emotional issues that can complicate your life. These issues can also involve your child, so you need to be aware that in most states, the biological father's rights are the same whether or not you are married.

When a single mother finds that she and the child's father are not going to have a life together, she needs to define the father's role. It's best to find out what the father's motives are and get these in writing, if possible. That way, if the father claims he wants nothing to do with you or the child, but comes back later with threats about his rights as a father, you have some protection. Most likely, if he doesn't want to be involved, you will be left in charge.

However, we've all heard stories about the father from the past who declared that he wanted custody of his child, usually after becoming jealous of your new relationship, or finding that things hadn't worked out for him the way he had hoped.

If you are friendly with the father, you might be fortunate enough to have a good partnership. Your child would benefit from the two of you coparenting, as many divorced cou-ples are now doing, but without all the stress and emotional anguish of a divorce.

Regardless of how the father's role is defined, it would be wise to get a contract determining his involvement regarding visitation or financial assis-tance. Don't neglect this because you think his interests won't change. His involvement may be ongoing. For instance, he may want joint custody, or may try to prevent you from taking

---

THE DOS AND DON'TS OF BECOMING A MOTHER OUTSIDE OF MARRIAGE

♦ Do be aware of the implications for your child regarding your attitude toward the father. Your child will always be a link between you and this person. If you have unresolved issues about the father, seek counseling or emotional support before your child is born.

♦ Do seek legal counsel if you can't agree on what the father's role will be. Remember, even if this person is the last man on earth you'd like to see raise your child, he and all fathers have rights in every state, whether married or not. Learn about the laws in your state and protect your rights and those of your child.

♦ Don't try to rope someone into marriage, thinking that your accidental pregnancy will produce a change of heart in him. You may actually alienate him more and make him lose his trust in you.

♦ Do agree to a contract that clarifies your role and the father's if you were deeply involved with each other and he wants to remain somewhat connected, but uncommitted.

♦ Don't refuse to give your child's father access to your child just because he didn't want to get married. If he gen-uinely wants to be part of your child's life, don't "punish" him by refusing to let him in your life. Your child is more like-ly to be hurt than your ex.

♦ Do expect your feelings to fluctuate even if you are absolutely certain that it is best to have this child without the father. Because the traditional American dream of husband, home, and family is so emphasized in our culture, you will be going through a normal grieving period over the loss of this dream. Your outlook and the amount of emotional support you receive from others will determine how long you spend grieving for the loss of this fantasy.

a job that would require your moving to another state, or might even challenge your authority as a parent. If you can sit down and talk, prepare a list you can both live with and take it to an attorney. It's also a good idea to seek legal counsel during these negotiations to protect you and your child in the future.

ESTABLISHING PATERNITY

If you feel that you want the father to be involved, or if he reneged on his promises about being involved, you need to establish paternity before getting him to meet his obligations. For more information on how to establish paternity, see Chapter 19.

4

Choosing Motherhood Through Donor Insemination

You may be considering single motherhood—or may already have chosen it—for a number of reasons: a desire to reproduce the best part of yourself; a strong mothering instinct; the ability to get what you want out of life; and the awareness that your biological clock is ticking away. These reasons for wanting a baby would be the same whether you have a partner or not. In fact, the term "single mother by choice" can be misleading because it implies that the choice was to be single, not to be a mother. True, many women do want to have and raise children without a partner. However, most single mothers by choice prefer to emphasize the "mother" part of the phrase, because although it may not have been their choice to be single, it certainly

was their choice to become a mother. Many single mothers by choice eventually "partner," but generally they do not seek a relationship for the main purpose of finding a father figure for their children. Single mothers by choice have in common the fact that they spend a good deal of time planning their entry into motherhood, regardless of their former life style.

IF YOU'VE BEEN IN A RELATIONSHIP

You're divorced—maybe once, or maybe for the second or third time. You have finally decided that Mr. Right may not come along while you are still in your child-bearing years, and you feel it is unfair to deprive yourself of a child that you so very much want. Although single mothers by choice are often referred to as never-married, most have been either previously married or in a serious relationship and have decided that seeking out another partner is too risky and not worth the investment of time and emotional energy.

Or maybe you're like the majority of single women who prefer the "husband, two kids, two cars" approach to family life but find themselves in dead-end relationships. Like divorced women, rather than wait around for the right guy to show up, they have decided that no relationship is better than a bad one, and that having a baby solo with one caring parent is better than having two unhappy ones. Moreover, when a woman in a relationship expresses her desire to have a baby, this is usually when her partner's real definition of "relationship" surfaces.

If you currently are involved with a lover who seems ideal for now, once baby and family are mentioned he may let you know that this is not for him. Rather than discredit him for his feelings, it would be better to thank him for his honesty. According to a recent National Organization of Single Mothers (NOSM) poll, most of the MOMs queried said that they wanted a baby but their partner didn't. However, it was only *after* they'd announced their pregnancies that their partners stated that they did not want to be fathers, either verbally or simply by disappearing. About 95 percent of these women agreed that they wanted to be mothers and chose to continue their pregnancies, but admitted they would have preferred a different reaction from the father. They also felt they would have

been better prepared had the father warned them early on about his lack of interest in fatherhood. So if the person you are now with makes it clear he isn't interested in parenting, you can prepare yourself, emotionally and financially, if you choose to become impregnated by him.

To Exit or Stay?

I'm involved with a man who wants to spend his life with me but does not want to have children. I want kids, period. Should I leave or stay?

If you are involved in a relationship with someone who does not want children, but you seriously want to be a mother, you have some hard choices to make. It is difficult enough to exit a relationship. Trying to decide whether or not to become a single mother at the same time makes your choice much more agonizing. If you're sure you want to raise a child but this person wants no part of it, then do not involve him. Your partner should be involved only if he is to be the sperm donor, and even then you need to accept sole responsibility for your decision.

IF YOU'RE READY FOR MOTHERHOOD BUT NOT WIFEHOOD

A number of women are ready for motherhood, but the thought of marriage is not appealing. Where once the institution of marriage was the only road to female adulthood, for you who have reached that status successfully outside of marriage, having a baby completes a well-planned picture. Most single mothers by choice say that if they marry, it will be because they want to and not because they need to. Only a few decades ago, you needed to be married in order to own a home, have financial security, receive respect from the community, have sex, become a mother, and provide a name for yourself and your child. Whereas at one time the romantic ideal of marriage was for women to get their needs met by someone offering everything they could not possess on their own, now more and more women are choosing to remain single because marriage is no longer a benefit.

Although much has changed today, some women still feel they have failed if they can't find a suitable partner. It's important to keep in mind that getting married is one thing, but staying married is another. If you are choosing single motherhood because you think you would only end up getting divorced anyway, you may be right, but this should not be the sole basis for your decision. Conversely, it is not a wise idea to marry a person strictly because you want to conceive.

"MY BIOLOGICAL CLOCK IS READY TO EXPLODE ..."

You're in your mid-thirties, have achieved a number of your desired goals, and now your ovaries are screaming, "We want a baby!" You try to distract yourself with other things, but you still feel so pressured that you don't know what to do.

If you feel as though your time is running out, you're not alone. The NOSM study cited earlier reveals that

the average age for a single mother by choice is thirty-five. Most of these women agree that the real push toward motherhood came from the internal clock setting a time limit.

Your clock should serve only as a gauge to assist you in making your decision; it should not be the only reason to choose motherhood. Don't think you have to have a child before it's too late when you really may not want one. Motherhood simply isn't for everyone, whether married or single.

If you are in your mid-thirties, in reasonably good health, and fertile, there is no reason to rush into motherhood. Moreover, the risks of delaying motherhood have been reduced significantly thanks to the latest medical screenings that can alert you to problems early on, should they occur. Though we hear far too much about the risk factors associated with older women conceiving, most women in their thirties and early forties report no problems bearing children. In fact, according to some women, you may actually be glad you waited to experience motherhood because at this stage in life you are more mature and patient and can make better decisions.

THINKING IT OUT

Like so many women, you're ready for motherhood, and Mr. Ready for Fatherhood is nowhere in sight. Do you resign yourself to the fact that you may never get married and therefore may never have children? Or do you gather as much information as possible about single motherhood and see whether it is an option for you?

ARE YOU READY FOR SINGLE MOTHERHOOD?

Review the following checklist if you're considering single motherhood. If you can't answer "true" to all three statements, give yourself a little more time to think about this.

1. I am choosing single motherhood because I am ready to be a mother. For me, being married or not doesn't determine the quality of mothering.

2. I am aware of the importance of creating an extended family. Just because I have work friends or lunch acquaintances doesn't mean that I can call these people at 2 A.M. hysterical over a colicky baby. I know the difference between friends I can count on and those who were only meant to be part of my career or social life.

3. I am ready to discuss this issue with supportive friends, my doctor, a fertility clinic and/or an attorney, if necessary, to ensure that I get appropriate feedback and accurate information. If I choose DI with a partner, I will be sure that we have a legal contract stating our roles and expectations.

Like any life-changing decision, choosing single motherhood has advantages for some and disadvantages for others. If you have been thinking about this a lot lately, that's good. Thinking it out enables you to seek out good information. In fact, some women's groups offer talks and workshops for single women thinking of becoming mothers.

Considering single motherhood by choice is a lengthy process that involves identifying where you are currently in your life and visualizing where you see yourself heading. When a child is an indelible part of the picture you see, with or without a man in the home, you are ready to look at single motherhood as an option.

DEALING WITH DISCOURAGEMENT

I'm thirty-seven years old and want a child terribly. I just ended a five-year relationship with a man who clearly is not good father material. I'd like a child and have researched donor insemination, but my family is making me feel that I am selfish to deprive my child of a father. My parents have been married forty-three years and think I'm nuts to consider this.

You sound too smart to do anything nutty. After all, it's important that your decision be based on what you think and not on what others may consider crazy or selfish. First, you've made it clear that you want a child and that you don't want an inadequate father figure around. The first step toward being a good mother is wanting a child, and then wanting what is best for him or her. Second, you're smart if you have researched donor insemination because it means that you aren't going into single motherhood blindly. Your child will one day benefit from the painstaking care and thought you have given to this decision. The happiest children are the ones who believe unconditionally that their parents consider them a priceless gift.

Tell your folks that rather than depriving your child of a father, you are giving him or her a mother who made it clear, "I wanted you very much."

Stop feeling guilty and feel good that you are not adding to the world's problems by having children for the wrong reasons, but have chosen single motherhood for the right reasons.

REASONS FOR DONOR INSEMINATION (DI)

You may find yourself having to answer questions such as, "Why are you doing this when you can adopt?" or "There are so many children who need a home, why go through the expense and ordeal of donor insemination?" These questions may not come from others but from yourself, as part of the process of deciding to become a single mother by choice.

Many women choose DI because they are uncomfortable with the idea of engaging in sexual behavior for the sole purpose of becoming pregnant. Additionally, women at the height of their desire for motherhood may not know anyone with whom they would have intercourse. Still other women may have a certain person in mind to father their child, but that person may be reluctant to have sexual relations, although he might not object to supplying sperm.

Although DI is far more expensive than sexual intercourse, many women who choose this method feel it is safer, less worrisome, and more efficient than conceiving through sexual intercourse with a "live" one. The control over choosing the type of male they would like to have father their child, the reduced risk of catching a sexually transmitted disease, and the freedom from worry about hidden family secrets that a sex partner may harbor, such as inherited mental or physical handicaps, can make DI seem more appealing.

But don't take single motherhood by choice too lightly, whether you plan to conceive through intercourse with someone you know or through donor insemination using unknown donor sperm. If you are currently trying to become pregnant, it is imperative that you've carefully weighed all the benefits of single motherhood against the disadvantages. If you have come up with favorable results, then single motherhood most likely is right for you. Although there is no perfect situation or time or place to become a mother, you need to be sure that you have explored all your options and are making the best decision for yourself and your child.

Why Not Adopt Instead? When asked why they chose donor insemination instead of adoption, many women responded that they wanted to experience pregnancy and childbirth, a process they felt was one of life's most miraculous. Additionally, these women believed they would adopt a second child one day. Even women with fertility problems who are also considering adoption still would like to have the opportunity to reproduce what they feel is the best part of themselves.

Don't feel guilty because you would rather conceive than adopt. It's natural to feel this way. Perhaps, too, you know that you are not ready to undertake some of the concerns surrounding adoption, but you are willing to confront the issues associated with conceiving outside of marriage.

DECIDING ON A METHOD

DI by a Known Donor. The majority of women who become single mothers by choice through sexual intercourse usually do so with a friend or sexual partner, because to them it is more accessible, less expensive, less "clinical," and more natural than going through the donor insemination procedure.

I am seriously considering DI with the sperm of an acquaintance who has agreed to be the donor. He has donated sperm before and has furnished medical records and all sorts of background information. What else should I know?

Before conceiving with a known donor, the first thing to do is consult with an attorney specializing in family law, whether you have met this person only once or twice or you have been living together for years.

A known donor could one day renege on his promise to stay uninvolved after conception. For this reason, it is crucial to draw up legal contracts in the early stages of planning your pregnancy. There have been cases where men have sued for custody after having a change of heart about being a father, or because they are in a new relationship where their wife or partner is unable to conceive. As farfetched as this may seem, you need to be cautious in your decision to become inseminated with sperm from a known donor.

Ask yourself the following questions:

♦ Are you certain that this will never escalate into any type of relationship, romantic or not?

♦ Are you being straight with each other about what is expected from each of you, or are you kidding yourselves? Does either of you think the other will soften up and change his or her mind about the arrangement once conception takes place?

♦ If it is someone who has eagerly offered to be a donor, have you asked why he wants to do this? What would you do if he backed out when the time came, even though he has agreed for now?

♦ How do you know this person won't change his mind one day and want to become involved in your life? Have you thought out what would happen in the event that he might sue for visitation rights or even for custody?

♦ How can you assuage the man's fears that you will one day sue him for child support? Just because you now say you won't, what would happen if you lost your job, your finances took a downturn, or you or your child became sick?

♦ Have you made sure this person passes every possible health requirement in addition to having tested

CAUTION!

In all states, fathers have rights whether married or not. Never set someone up to unwittingly impregnate you. Deliberately sleeping with someone for the sole purpose of getting pregnant is deceitful, particularly if he questions you about whether you use birth control. Don't pretend that you are sterile or plan to conceive with someone else.

If a man suspects he is the father of your child, you could face a court order demanding that you establish paternity through a blood test known as HLA, which is highly accurate. If you truly want to become pregnant by a known donor, discuss this with him first and see if he will sign legal agreements that will waive his parental rights. Be aware, too, that you will not be entitled to child support.

negative at least twice—with a six-month interval between tests—for sexually transmitted diseases, particularly HIV? Have you looked thoroughly into his medical history regarding certain physical and mental disorders, including depression, personality disorder, alcoholism, drug abuse, or severe mood swings?

♦ Have you decided upon intercourse with this person, or do you want to be inseminated with his sperm without the physical entanglement? Intercourse has its advantages: less expensive, enjoyable, and easier to achieve success. But donor insemination is much less emotionally charged in general. Rarely does DI bring with it intense and unexpected feelings that can complicate your original plans, as can intercourse. Think this out carefully for yourself. Most men, if given a choice, will opt for the "live" donor method rather than ejaculate into a vessel.

♦ Have you discussed with this person what you will tell your child? It's best to agree on what you will say.

Anonymous Donor Insemination (ADI). If you are afraid or are imagining all sorts of unknown consequences as the result of having a child through ADI, you can relax. Many professionals believe that conception through anonymous donor insemination is one of the safest routes to go. Here are some reasons:

♦ Most sperm banks demand a thorough screening of each candidate.

♦ Donors are not accepted over the age of forty.

♦ Most facilities have pregnancy limits. As a safety precaution, a donor may not have his sperm used for more than ten pregnancies. The chance that your son or daughter will enter a relationship with a half-brother or half-sister is therefore extremely small.

♦ Donor shopping through a sperm bank catalog can ensure that you find someone who is "your type." Good health, intelligence, and physical appeal are just some of the traits you can request when choosing a donor. You may want someone whose looks are similar to your own or to those of the men in your family, or you may want someone with the same ethnic background. Whether your donor is an athlete, a social worker, or a college professor is a choice that is totally up to you.

◆ Did your mother always want you to marry a doctor? Well, the next best thing is to have one father your child!

Because selling sperm is an ideal way for a young student on a budget to supplement his income, many law students and medical students are attracted to this opportunity. Moreover, these young men often do not have an active social life while immersed in competitive studies, which means they do not ejaculate as frequently as sexually active men, a necessary factor in ensuring a higher sperm count.

What Exactly is DI?

I'm considering donor insemination because I want a baby before I am forty. However, I just can't seem to get past this image I have of me running to the doctor's office with a turkey baster filled with sperm. Can you update me on exactly what DI is? And is it the same as artificial insemination or in vitro fertilization?

The DI procedure is a more accepted way of referring to what was once called artificial insemination. There really is nothing artificial about it, since real human sperm is used! In vitro fertilization (IVF) is a procedure in which the sperm is actually placed in the egg in the laboratory, resulting in the formation of an embryo. Then the embryo is implanted in the uterus of the mother-to-be. This method, much

more expensive than DI, is usually used for women with fertility problems.

A popular form of DI actually does rely on a more refined, quite slim version of the turkey baster. Intracervical insemination (ICI) is the most widely used method, the easiest, and the least expensive. ICI requires depositing sperm on the cervix using a slender straw-type device with a plunger on top that pushes the semen through. Although this method appeals to many women because they can perform the procedure privately by self-insemination, most sperm banks recommend having a doctor perform the procedure just to be on the safe side. Certain symptoms such as infection, cramping, or fever could result and although the risk is minimal, you want to be sure nothing serious develops.

In intrauterine insemination (IUI), sperm is deposited directly into the uterus via a flexible catheter-type device. This method, which must be performed by a physician, cuts down on interference by antibodies on the cervix. Additionally, there's an increased chance of conception because the sperm travels a shorter distance. Some clinics report a marked increase in the conception rate, but most say it is only slightly higher than with ICI, because there are so many other variables that must be taken into account.

DI using frozen sperm has a 32 to 39 percent success rate when performed within the first three months of trying to conceive. However, sometimes it takes longer to become pregnant, just as it might for anyone conceiving in a more traditional manner. Women who have continued trying for three to six months report conceiving about 80 percent of the time. So patience and a positive attitude are particularly important, along with monitoring your ovulation cycles to ensure ideal conditions for conception. Your doctor or sperm bank can supply ovulation cycle kits that are relatively simple to use, although time-consuming.

The Cost Factor. The cost for DI varies based on the part of the country in which you are having this procedure done and whether you choose a private physician or a fertility clinic.

DI can cost from $250 for a one-day procedure through a private physician, and from $200 at the reproductive-endocrine department of your local hospital. However, because many doctors choose to inseminate for two consecutive days, the cost can almost double. You also need to consider the extra expense of purchasing sperm, which is not included in your doctor's office visit.

The cost of a vial of intrauterine sperm is about $200. The cost of intracervical sperm is about $175. Additionally, there are shipping charges for the tanks (the vials are protectively stored in tanks the size of old milk containers), ranging anywhere from $100–$150, depending on where you live. Keep in mind, too, that although some sperm banks will ship to your home, most accredited sperm banks ship only to a doctor.

Fresh sperm, although cheaper per vial, actually costs more, since there is an additional charge for a PCR-HIV test. However, the American Fertility Society and the FDA recommend against its use, since frozen sperm reduces the risk of disease. In fact, many fertility clinics and hospitals will not allow the use of fresh sperm even if purchased by the patient.

The cost of donor insemination is not limited to money. Emotional energy is expended, especially if you have trouble conceiving. Moreover, if you are using fertility drugs, they can exacerbate emotional stress. Be prepared to undergo certain additional steps, particularly if you are having difficulty locating clinics that treat single women as well as infertile couples. Some single women have to undergo psychological testing before a fertility clinic or physician will perform DI, whereas married couples don't require an evaluation.

How to Find a Fertility Center. The best way to locate a fertility clinic or a physician who is a fertility specialist is to call the American Fertility Society and ask for a recommendation in your area. Many sperm banks will also recommend physicians who have experience with DI. Keep in mind that just because a hospital has a reproductive-endocrine department doesn't mean that the staff members are board-certified reproductive endocrinologists. Although many doctors are well trained and qualify as fertility experts, only about 400 physicians in this country are board certified in this specialty. Do not seek a gynecologist or obstetrician who has little experience in this field.

Working with Your Physician. Be sure to choose a physician who has experience working with single mothers. Believe it or not, a number of doctors in the Southeast and Midwest won't perform DI on single women. If you feel uncomfortable with the doctor or the clinic you visit, keep looking. You also want to be sure to choose a doctor who is available twenty-four hours a day, every day of the week. You will be charting your ovulation cycle meticulously, and you want to make sure you are inseminated at the perfect time. You would hate to miss an entire month because your best time to try was at 2 A.M. on a Sunday. Remember, DI involves many variables, including timing, quality of sperm, doctor's expertise, body contour, and state of mind. Try to relax and focus on the process. It will happen if it is supposed to happen.

What Does AMA Mean? AMA means advanced medical age. Usually when a woman reaches anywhere between thirty-five and forty years of age, her ability to conceive decreases markedly. In women over the age of forty, there is a dramatic decline in fertility. Because we live in the age of advanced reproductive technology, you shouldn't overlook the possible complications and costly fertility problems that may accompany AMA. However, if you consult a good fertility specialist, you may find that you have a treatable condition.

If You're Having Trouble Conceiving. If you are thinking about taking fertility drugs, recently published studies report that these drugs often result in multiple births, which usually means low-birth-weight babies. Clomid and Pergonal are two drugs

responsible for causing multiple births, which may also result in these babies having physical and mental handicaps. Additionally, certain fertility drugs have been linked to an increased risk of ovarian cancer. Be sure you find out everything there is to know about fertility drugs from your physician before going that route.

Infertility can be an all-consuming process, what with counting and timing your cycles, taking a variety of drugs, and undergoing the financial and emotional drain of many unsuccessful attempts to conceive.

Women with infertility problems often become so obsessed with their bodies, it is a wonder they can do anything else. The more anxious they become, the harder it is to achieve ideal conditions for conception. And taking certain fertility drugs can exacerbate feelings of stress.

Make sure to talk to more than one doctor about your problem, and get an honest opinion of what is involved and what you are in for. It's true that many women conceive after years and years of trying, not to mention thousands of dollars spent in the process. Other women report that the emotional and financial drain was more than they could bear and that giving up released them from being totally self-absorbed. It's helpful to join a fertility group or support group where women with similar problems can offer suggestions, resources, and comfort. Only you can determine how much you want to give to this, and when it's time to give up and try another route, such as adoption.

Regardless of what happens, always know that you did your best, and try not to feel like a failure because you were unable to conceive. Sometimes

THE DOS AND DON'TS OF CHOOSING DONOR INSEMINATION

+ Do get your emotional house in order. Be clear about your reasons for wanting to conceive a child. Children are not consolation prizes for failed ambitions or disappointing relationships.

+ Do research all donor insemination (DI) options carefully. Both anonymous DI (ADI) and known DI have benefits and shortcomings, as does conceiving with a friend. Think ahead by viewing the big picture and choose the method that will work best for you and your child in the long run.

+ Don't buy into any guilt others may try to inflict upon you. These feelings are the result of their lack of knowledge and understanding and should not influence the informed choices you are making.

+ Don't discount the possibility of DI through a fertility clinic or medical facility because you think it's strange or unnatural. Some people still call it "artificial insemination" but there's nothing artificial about it. Additionally, many mothers who have used this method report having felt more control over their decision, less stress, and fewer emotional complications than those who have conceived with a partner.

+ Do have a solid support system in place. Single motherhood is a challenging life style. You need friends who can offer comfort and support. Even single mothers by choice can at times become overwhelmed.

this is nature's way of protecting us from what should not be. Remember, you can be a wonderful mother and become fulfilled by the process without having to "grow" the baby yourself.

WHAT TO TELL PEOPLE

Your reproductive organs are your own business. Just as people would think twice about asking you to describe your personal sex habits, they also should not assume that you are anxious to give them graphic details about DI or about what it was like to have intercourse with a donor.

However, some people are genuinely interested because it is a fascinating topic and also because they might want to investigate the procedure for themselves. Share only the information with which you are comfortable, and try to close all conversations with something like, "Well, I guess that proves having a child was a real priority for me!" The degree of comfort you exude will be felt by others. As this practice becomes more and more common, you will one day come to hail yourself as one of the early pioneers!

It is important to be very honest with your child about the circumstances surrounding his or her birth. Chapter 15 offers suggestions for explaining donor insemination to a young child.

MEETING THE DONOR

Do you think DI information should be available to children?

Yes. As in the adoption process, secrecy only causes children to wonder what their parents were like, why they didn't want them, and what is so horrible about them that their identities had to be concealed.

We're learning more and more today about how important it is for children to learn about their roots and about their identity. Moreover, it is important at least for doctors to have records on the donor in case some important medical information is required at a future time.

The reason donor information was routinely destroyed in the initial years of DI was to ensure married couples of confidentiality because of the stigma attached to being unable to conceive, usually for the man, and to avoid the possibility of the child having to deal with two fathers. In the case of single mother insemination, disposing of information helped protect the donors from being sued for child support and afforded the mother privacy and a guarantee that her custody rights were protected.

But today more and more sperm banks, realizing the importance of having information available to children, are giving the donors a choice to be contacted by offspring when the child turns eighteen. Some progressive facilities are even offering catalogs with donors' pictures, a wonderful way to feel an even more special connection with a special person.

IF YOU'RE IN A LESBIAN RELATIONSHIP

Women who plan to raise a family with another woman are good candidates for donor insemination. Most lesbian mothers already have a support system in place, usually within the gay and lesbian community. Additionally, if you or your partner are choosing motherhood, your child will benefit from having positive input from two maternal role models, as would a child from any loving, two-parent heterosexual home.

Because women planning to raise children with another woman are as "partnered" as any other couple, this book does not focus on their situation because it deals primarily with those raising children without another supporting parent in the home. However, you may want to consult the Resource Roundup at the end of this book for a list of organizations geared towards gay and lesbian parents.

5

Choosing Motherhood Through Adoption

A MEANINGFUL OPTION FOR MANY

If experiencing pregnancy and delivery or being your child's biological parent are not essential priorities, adoption offers the opportunity not only to love and nurture a child but also to make a significant contribution to our world. Many adopted children would otherwise have faced grim lives in underdeveloped or war-ravaged countries where basic necessities are in short supply and educational opportunities are nonexistent. Other adoptions, especially in cases where the natural parents have died unexpectedly, begin with a tragedy within the immediate or extended family rather than in a country thousands of miles from home.

Some single mothers who've chosen adoption may feel they don't want to add another human being to this already crowded planet, or they may be quite content to skip the infant stage altogether. Still others may have health problems, or may work in occupations that would make carrying a child risky, or harbor concerns about passing along a genetic predisposition to disease or mental illness to another generation. Whatever reasons contributed to your decision, an adopted child, no matter what her history or background, will come to know in a special way how dearly she was wanted and how treasured a part of your family she is. Remember, too, that adoption isn't always someone's first choice. But then most of us who enter parenthood, whether through planned or surprise pregnancies, have grappled with choices and realized that perfection just wasn't one of them. If you are an adoptive single parent, it's important to get past the events that led up to this decision in order to enjoy and raise a healthy, happy family. If you're thinking of adoption, you have many options and resources available, so do your homework first.

CHOOSING WHAT'S RIGHT FOR YOU

Maybe becoming pregnant isn't such an important issue for you, or perhaps you want to become a mother without the food cravings, the nausea, and the stretch marks. Likewise, you may know single mothers who have to deal with uncooperative exes or are embroiled in major custody battles, and you never want to find yourself in that situation. Or maybe you'd like to have a baby, but because of personal or religious beliefs, bearing a child without a husband is simply not right for you. You're focused and content with making the decision to adopt because you really want to be a parent and raise a family. Others may give you their opinions and advice, but the final decision is to do what is best for you, not for them.

FERTILITY FRUSTRATIONS

A number of single women who decide on adoption make the decision after failed attempts at donor insemination. Serious fertility problems can cause stress, sadness, feelings of loss, and frustration, and the tremendous costs of fertility treatments on top of the expense of DI add to the disappointment of being unable to bear children. You feel it is unfair to put forth so much

---

THE DOS AND DON'TS OF ADOPTION

- Do give yourself time to grieve the loss of your fertility if your decision to adopt is based on your inability to conceive.

- Do think carefully about all the different types of adoption and which one might be the best way for you to realize your dream of having a child. There is no single best method of adoption. Much depends on your individual circumstances and what particular qualities you might like your child to have.

- Don't expect the "perfect child" because no such child ever existed. Get rid of stereotyped notions, like thinking that children of certain ethnic groups are always successful and obedient students.

- Don't delay telling your child that she is adopted. Your child should be made aware that she is adopted from the very first day you bring her home, or as soon as she is capable of comprehending the idea.

- Do expect that your adopted child will have many questions and worries that will have to be addressed repeatedly as he gets older, and particularly during his years in elementary school.

- Do make sure that friends and family are prepared with the information you want them to have in order to help you make your child comfortable with his adopted status.

---

effort and receive nothing. It's normal to feel this, but if adoption is a consideration, there is much hope in knowing that you will realize motherhood eventually. Just don't rush into making a decision while you are still grieving the loss of your imagined pregnancy. Give yourself as much time as you need to accept this loss before you move ahead with possible adoption plans.

There is nothing wrong with choosing adoption as a second choice because you are unable to conceive. The fact is, the majority of parents who have faced the disappointment of being unable to conceive, whether single women or married couples, have chosen adoption because it gives them the opportunity to fulfill their dreams of being a parent. Infertility stands in the way of becoming a parent to a child that you biologically produce. Adoption removes that obstacle if parenting is your primary goal, and not experiencing pregnancy, giving birth, and nursing. However, if after exhausting all areas of infertility treatments, you find that raising a child who is your own flesh and blood remains critically important to you, then adoption may not be for you. After all, adoption won't change the fact that permanent infertility is plaguing you. But adoption can give you the opportunity to experience motherhood. One advantage, too, is that you can take your time to think it out, since your biological clock really doesn't influence this kind of decision. So relax, learn all you can about adoption, and then decide.

IF YOU WERE ADOPTED

If you were adopted, you have first-hand experience in what it was like to be raised by parents other than your birth parents. Regardless of your experiences growing up, there most likely were lessons learned that you could apply when raising your own child. Whether from a single-parent household, adoptive family, stepparent family, or traditional two-parent family, most of us say we want to do a better job than our parents did with us. If you were adopted, you have another special connection that can bond you to your adopted child.

HOW TO GET STARTED

- ◆ Contact adoptive parent support groups for suggestions on attorneys if you plan to adopt independently.

- ◆ Contact your state chapter of the American Bar Association or the American Academy of Adoption Attorneys for referrals to attorneys who are adoption specialists.

- ◆ Word of mouth can bring much success. Let people know that you are interested in adopting.

- ◆ Contact Adoptive Families of America (AFA) for a list of agencies if you plan to go that route. But because AFA and other support organizations cannot recommend or advocate any specific agency, you need to investigate and get a thorough history of any agency you deal with. Talk to people the agency has worked with, call your local Better Business Bureau, and contact your state adoption unit to see if written complaints have been lodged against the agency.

- ◆ Read the ads or place your own ad in a magazine that deals with adoption, such as *Adoptive Families*.

TYPES OF ADOPTION

You probably weren't prepared for all the different styles of adoption that are available. Most likely, your first concerns were the type of child you would like to adopt, the costs involved in adopting, and imagining what life would be like as a new mother.

Raising a child is a lifelong process, whether you bring your baby home from the hospital or home from an interim care facility. It is important to think ahead about the type of adoption that is most appropriate for you, because certain issues will affect your family for a lifetime. Would open adoption, in which your child has access to his or her birth family be best, or would he or she be best served leaving information about the birth family behind in a war-ravaged country? How will you help your Asian child cope with obvious differences if you live in a community where all the children come from the local region? Although there are numerous methods of adopting a child, following are descriptions of the three basic types of adoptions, whether domestic or international.

Confidential or Closed Adoption. In this type of adoption there is no information that could identify the birth parent, making contact almost impossible. The birth parents remain anonymous and are usually matched to the prospective adoptive parents through an agent or adoption specialist. Often, the adoptive mother and birth parents agree that there will be no contact, with the exception that when the child is eighteen, he or she may seek out the identities of the birth parents.

Partially Open or Semi-open Adoption. For many, this is the preferred choice, because you can meet the birth parents face to face with the agreement that they will not be involved in your life. You are assured of no disruptions in your home, yet the fear of the unknown has been eliminated because you will have been furnished with social and medical information on the parents and the child. Additionally, when the adopted child grows up and wishes to meet the birth parents, they can be available.

Open Adoption. This is the best bet according to many family experts. This form of adoption involves offering complete information that identifies both sets of parents. Not only do the adoptive parents and the birth parents receive complete information about each other, but there also can exist an agreement allowing ongoing contact, which serves to benefit the child. For many, this contact provides an extended family, a very necessary component of raising children today.

International Adoption. If you are connected to another part of the world because of family history, your work, or an affinity toward a certain region, you may be an excellent candidate for international adoption. Also, because homes for unwed mothers have all but vanished, the number of available babies in America has dwindled, making foreign adoption seem more attractive. Whatever your reasons for adopting a child from a distant land, you need to gather as much information as possible.

WHAT ABOUT THE BONDING PROCESS?

I have a biological daughter and have arranged to adopt an infant from Colombia. I wonder what the bonding process will be like.

Many mothers who have adopted infants after or while parenting a biological child report that bonding with adopted children when they are very young feels similar to bonding with biological children. Remember, bonding is a process, not an instant rush. Because international adoption often takes time, some moms have been unable to take their children home before two months of age. Although they may have missed having them as newborns, they report that everything else felt the same.

IS INTERNATIONAL ADOPTION SIMPLER THAN DOMESTIC ADOPTION?

Like domestic adoption, international adoption can be accomplished through the help of an agency, attorney, or adoption specialist, depending on the laws in the country from which your baby hails. Don't choose international adoption simply because you have heard that it is not as complex as domestic adoption. This couldn't be further from the truth. Although certain things are simpler—there may be less rigid criteria for the adoptive parents than in domestic adoption—there are some pitfalls to international adoption that you must consider. For example, because many international children have been abandoned, their personal, medical, and social documents are often unavailable.

You also need to consider how you will handle any obviously different physical characteristics the child may have, any prejudice that may be encountered through others' lack of acceptance of certain ethnic groups, and other issues of parenting an international child such as religious views, social values, and your child's feelings of cultural deprivation.

Like any aspect of adoption, or of raising a family for that matter, almost any obstacle can be overcome with love, commitment, and a knowledge of what one is dealing with. It helps to join an adoptive parent support group, particularly one that has members who have adopted children from foreign countries. Also, keep abreast of any changes in foreign governments that will affect the number and availability of children for international adoption.

Tips for Adopting a Child from Another Country

◆ Some parents who have adopted children from outside the United States recommend hiring an attorney who deals only in adoptions from the country you choose. For example, if you are planning to adopt a baby from an orphanage in Colombia, an experienced attorney can give you a realistic breakdown of costs, tell you the probable timetable to be expected, and advise you on exactly what you need to bring for the baby when you travel to the host country.

♦ The majority of intercountry adoptions are handled by private adoption agencies. Public agencies rarely participate in intercountry adoption. If you adopt privately, make sure the agency is aware of U.S. immigration laws. Employ an agency that has extensive experience in international adoptions. Most countries over-

seas that allow international adoption welcome single-parent applicants, with the exception of Korea. Most Latin American countries, India, and China also allow singles in some cases.

♦ Intercountry adoptions can cost from $7,000 to over $20,000, depending on whether you need to travel and reside in the country to complete legal formalities. If the initial figure offered by the attorney is about as much as you can afford, you might want to reconsider or wait until you have more money. Foreign adoption always costs more than

IF YOU'RE ADOPTING INTERNATIONALLY— TIPS FOR WHEN YOU'RE IN THE HOST COUNTRY

♦ Be prepared to wait. Courts move on their own schedule. Waiting longer than you thought you would does not necessarily mean that something is wrong. If you have ever traveled overseas and tried to bring back something as simple as an exotic food, you'll understand.

♦ Be prepared to be self-sufficient. Bring your own medications—prescription or over-the-counter—extra glasses, vitamins or supplements, and other preparations and toiletries that you normally rely on. Some people enjoy shopping or sightseeing while waiting. Bring that novel you've been dying to read. Because you do not know how long you will be waiting or what you will feel like doing, it's wise to supply yourself with some diversions.

♦ Follow local customs carefully. For example, in some South American

countries, taking pictures of the police is forbidden. Be sure to educate yourself about policies to avoid any unnecessary delays.

♦ Bring two hot pots (one to use and a spare) so that you can boil water in your hotel room for drinking and brushing your teeth. Make sure you have adapters. This is no time to test your resistance to Montezuma's Revenge or other ills of the international traveler. If your baby stays with you in the hotel prior to departure, you will certainly want safe water to make formula.

♦ Be prepared to donate to the orphanage in addition to any fees. The orphanage is grateful for donations of diapers, diaper rash ointment, sleepers, soft blankets, and other useful items.

anticipated because there are almost always unexpected expenses. Another tip: In addition to the agreed-upon amount of money to begin the process, some agencies or orphanages may request that you provide pictures of your close relatives so that they can match you up with a child who most resembles your family.

♦ Orphanages in foreign countries will usually be able to provide you with some medical and other pertinent information about the child and the birth mother but very little, if anything, about the father. Officials fear that if they press the birth mothers too much about the fathers' identity, they may, out of fear, fail to obtain proper prenatal care and might give birth to a child who will end up on the streets rather than in a loving adoptive parent's home.

The orphanage will send you pictures of your prospective adopted child. You don't have to accept the first child offered to you, although you may feel a little uncomfortable or strange about refusing a child. Try to remember that no one said you have to save the world. The fact that you are adopting any child who would benefit from being raised by you will make a small but very significant difference on the planet. You should feel proud of yourself for making such an important decision, but don't do anything you are not totally comfortable with. This would not be fair to you or the child, so be certain that you choose a child you really believe would work out best. Once you have chosen a child, the original birth certificate of the child is destroyed, and a new one is issued with your name.

♦ The amount of paperwork is unbelievable and can be overwhelming for you. An experienced attorney or intercountry adoption expert knows how to wade through it. For example, when you arrive in, say, Colombia for an independent adoption, the attorney will give you a sealed package of papers to present to the officials at the orphanage. Do not even think of breaking the seal. Follow your attorney's instructions to the letter.

♦ Make sure to select a pediatrician ahead of time before you leave the United States to pick up your baby. In case you have immediate questions or there is some emergency or crisis, you can call your own doctor. Be sure to advise your pediatrician of your plan so he or she can be prepared in case you call.

TRANSRACIAL AND TRANSCULTURAL ADOPTION

For many years, social workers and adoption experts frowned upon children of color being adopted by white parents. They felt that these children would lose their pride in their heritage and miss out on cultural teachings and traditions that would have been an inherent part of their lives had they been raised by parents with the same background. However, given that there are so many children of color waiting to be adopted, transracial adoption is now seen as a positive option.

If you are a woman of color who wishes to adopt a baby sharing your cultural heritage, this is greatly encouraged. The majority of potential adoptive mothers do choose a child with a connection to their own background. But if you choose to adopt nontraditionally, it would be a good idea to join a support group where members share similar concerns. Keep in mind that children of color have certain concerns that range from skin care and hair grooming to needing a connectedness to others who share their heritage. Moreover, many members of our society are prejudiced toward minorities, and you will need to handle this. Additionally, you do need to be aware that if you are considering adopting a Native American child, the Indian Child Welfare Act still has strict rules about adopting children of Native American ancestry. Do your homework.

ADOPTING CHILDREN WITH SPECIAL NEEDS

The largest group of children waiting to be adopted are children with special needs. Often called "waiting children," half are children of color, a majority have been physically, sexually, or emotionally abused, a huge number have Attention Deficit Hyperactivity Disorder or other types of learning disabilities, and many are older—eight years old and up.

Before you adopt a waiting child, you need to examine your motivations for doing so. Keep in mind, too, that part of the problems these children face is having a history of disappointment and loss due to multiple placements. Don't be scared away, because this can be a wonderful contribution toward making our planet a more beautiful, livable one, but it is important to be capable of giving this child what he or she needs. Insist upon receiving every bit of information on this child, which even means talking with previous foster parents. Most importantly, explore the availability of getting ongoing support for yourself and your family. Investigate subsidies and assistance you can receive, school services, medical services and coverage, and parent- and community-based support groups.

LEGAL ASPECTS OF PRIVATE ADOPTION

If you are adopting a child from the same state as your own, jurisdiction—or the authority with the power to interpret the law—is a minor issue. But should you choose interstate adoption, you need to be informed about the jurisdiction requirements, because every state has its own laws. Suppose you know a potential birth mother in a nearby state whose child you would like to adopt. Your agent or attorney will have to be sure that procedures comply not only with state regulations but also with the Interstate Compact on the Placement of Children.

PLANNING FOR THE COSTS

Adoption can cost from as little as $75 for attorney or court fees, to hundreds of thousands of dollars, depending on the state and all the bureaucracy and red tape that may be involved. Adoption experts can give you a ballpark figure, so make sure you ask about costs up front.

Adopting through public agencies usually requires minimal or no costs other than attorney fees for finalizing the adoption. Minimal costs are also incurred with foster-adoption because this usually involves little or no fees. In this situation, the child is placed in temporary care. Foster-adoption, however, is considered a legal-risk placement because the child may be returned to the birth parent's home or eventually placed with relatives. Adopting a child from a remarriage, or from a family member or other known person, can be relatively inexpensive. The most expensive adoptions are international or overseas adoptions, or where you have a pregnant birth mother whose medical bills you are also footing.

Never proceed with *any* kind of adoption without professional or legal help, even if it is your sister's child you are adopting!

ADOPTING MORE THAN ONE

Some women just want to double their pleasure. Maybe you came from a very large family and thrived on that, or you feel strongly that siblings should remain together. Or you may choose to adopt infant twins. Although the joys or troubles will not necessarily be doubled by adopting two or more children, the issues that you need to deal with will be multiplied. For example, just as in biological families, sibling rivalry will exist, and those tough parenting stages will be intensified by having to deal with more than one. Just as you shouldn't have another child just to

furnish your only child with a sister or a brother, you shouldn't adopt a second child for that reason. Your desire to love and nurture should be the factors in wanting more than one child.

EXPECTING THE PERFECT CHILD

I am thinking of adopting an Asian child because they are so smart—as practically perfect as you can get. They excel in school, particularly in the math areas, and I have always adored these children, who look like little porcelain dolls. Plus, money is not an object, and I've lived overseas and can speak a number of languages.

Stop right there. If you expect a perfect child, whether you give birth or adopt, you are setting yourself and the child up for disappointment. Moreover, you need to examine your motives for adopting a particular type of child, because you may have unresolved issues surrounding your own abilities. Your affinity for other cultures is your strongest reason to adopt, but should not be the major deciding factor. Although speaking your child's language is a boon because you can keep some of his or her culture alive, you still need to look at why you expect your child to fit into a custom-tailored niche. Also, it is unfair to stereotype a child and slot his or her attributes into categories, whether positive or negative. Children need unconditional love and to be accepted for who they are and not what they can do. Think this out a little longer and let the desire for an Asian child be the icing on the cake, and not the substance on which your decision to adopt is based.

MOTHERING A DECEASED RELATIVE'S CHILD

Most of us remember Diane Keaton as the single adoptive mom in *Baby Boom*. There she was, minding her own business at her high-powered marketing job when suddenly, following the death of a distant relative, she found herself the mother of an infant girl. Her life changed in many unexpected and funny ways, but the underlying message was hard to miss: Motherhood is a daunting challenge for the unprepared woman.

If you are thinking of adopting the child of a deceased friend or relative, you need to consider whether you are willing to change your life style and make the commitment necessary to mother this child. What was your relationship with the child prior to her loss? Adopting a child you barely know or have never met can be quite an undertaking, particularly for someone who never gave single motherhood

much serious consideration. It may be, however, that you are already a second mother to this child because of your close relationship. In that case, your decision and adjustment will be easier. If you had already agreed to be the child's legal guardian in case of the death of the parent, then you will be more emotionally prepared to face the challenges ahead.

MOTHERHOOD: THE SECOND TIME AROUND

Becoming a single mother through adoption is typically a decision that follows much careful consideration and planning. Adoption is sometimes not a free choice as much as a responsibility accepted in the wake of the last scene in a painful family drama or following an unexpected and sudden tragedy. Nearly 1.5 million children today are being raised by grandparents without presence of either parent. Most always, these grandparents are women who have become the custodial parents to their grandchildren because the child's parents are unable or unwilling to assume the responsibility of parenthood. Alcohol and/or substance abuse, mental illness, abandonment, child abuse or neglect, chronic unemployment, incarceration, or death may all be reasons why a grandmother becomes a mother—the second time around.

Assuming this incredible responsibility at a time when many of your peers need only worry about what beach to visit or what time in the day to play golf, can be at least at first, utterly overwhelming. Despite the obvious financial strains and genuine demands on your emotional and physical stamina, most (much older) single mothers report that providing care to their grandchildren, who are, of course, now their children, results in unexpected satisfactions and rewards. The chance to raise a child differently, perhaps correcting perceived mistakes or missteps, is a joy. Nurturing family relationships and continuing family history are sustaining. Children are a strong impetus to continue as a vital and active participant in your community, keeping you active and giving life a renewed purpose.

Your lifetime of experience is your best ally. Knowing that responsibilities cannot be fulfilled without authority, seek legal advice. You will want the power to make the important decisions regarding your child's health and well-being. Any financial arrangements with the birth parents need to be part of any legal agreement reached. Let go of what the neighbors or anyone else thinks. It does not matter and, in any event, at this stage in your life, you don't have the time to care. Expect your neighborhood school to be cooperative and unfazed by your family situation.

You will receive offers of help. Sort through these offers with care. Be selective. Decide what is genuine and what will be of value. Think about the choices, which will add to the comfort, security, stability, and emotional well-being of your newly reconfigured family. Graciously reach out and be thankful for what is truly meant and of lasting value.

Remember to take time for yourself. If you become so immersed in your new family responsibilities that you sacrifice who you are, you will become angry and resentful. All of us benefit from the opportunity to play. Join your children in the recreational activities that you also can enjoy, but don't forget your own needs for fun and relaxation.

Grandmothers assuming the custodial care of a grandchild may find they need financial assistance. The United States Congress passed the Personal Responsibility and Work Opportunity Act in 1996. It replaced the Aid to Families of Dependent Children (AFDC) with Temporary Assistance for Needy Families (TANF) programs. Medicaid eligibility is not tied to TANF eligibility. Supplemental social security, Medicaid, food stamps, and Head Start programs are all possible sources of help. Contact your local office for the latest information.

PREPARING YOURSELF AND OTHERS

There are adjustments that must be made before you can begin parenting. Most importantly, you need to prepare yourself and close friends and family members for the fact that your child has come into your life in a different way than most families experience. Because your child's background is different from your own, particularly if you have adopted transculturally or transracially, you should be aware that your child's heritage will be evident in day-to-day activities and will continue to evolve as he or she grows up. The differences should be neither ignored nor played up, but rather celebrated as an opportunity to learn and to grow.

Siblings, grandparents, and the adoptive mom herself must accept the new family member as one who will continue the family name even though there is no genetic connection.

GOOD NEWS ABOUT TEENS AND ADOPTION

Research has shown that for the most part adoptive families are strong and their teenagers are well adjusted. In a 1994 Search Institute study of 700 families with teenagers adopted as infants, half of adopted youth say that they are as happy as their peers, and 38 percent report being happier. More specifically, 73 percent say they feel good that they were adopted, and 84 percent say they are glad their parents adopted them.

Moreover, everyone needs to overcome any overly unrealistic expectations of the child. Although adoption brings with it unique challenges, the child should be treated with the same kind of love and commitment any child deserves.

IF SOMETHING GOES WRONG

No matter how carefully you plan, sometimes unexpected events occur and you are left with the cruel disappointment of not being able to take home a child you dearly wanted. In some tragic cases, adoptive parents have been forced to surrender a child to the natural parents or to an agency. All these life events are devastating. Do not listen to those who try to offer comfort by saying that you never really knew this child or that the child was not really yours. You suffered a loss as great as that of any biological mother. Allow yourself to grieve and mourn this great loss.

If your efforts to adopt came after unsuccessful treatment for infertility, this new blow can seem especially cruel and undeserved. Take the time to assess your situation and make plans to go forward with your life however you see fit. You are facing intensely personal decisions, and only you can decide what is right for you. Many mothers in your circumstances have taken advantage of counseling or have located a sympathetic support group. Consider these options if you are feeling unable to move ahead or are overwhelmed by your feelings of sadness and loss. Take care of yourself as the first step toward knowing what is the right path for you.

YOUR ADOPTED CHILD

Most likely, life with your adopted child will be normal, as long as your image of normal isn't that of a 1950s TV situation comedy. The time when most trouble occurs is when children reach elementary and junior high school, primarily because they spend more time with peers. They may be distressed at the differences they notice between their family and other families. Questions that may bother an adopted school-age child—may be: "Was I rejected because I was not smart or pretty enough?" "Were my real parents cruel or careless people who wanted nothing to do with raising a child?" "Was the adoption the tragic result of an accident, misunderstanding, or even a crime?" These questions can stir up feelings of abandonment, grief, loneliness, and guilt. Be there to listen and offer comfort when you can. Be happy to know that although the teenage years for many parents bring a host of problems, for the adoptive parent, things may actually improve because of the groundwork for family communication that already has been established.

TELLING YOUR CHILD ABOUT ADOPTION

The earlier a child is told that he or she is adopted, the better. You should refer to your child's adopted status as soon as the child comes into your life with remarks like, "I'm so glad I adopted you!" If you don't do this, the child will view the adoption as some kind of shameful secret and question why his life is shrouded in shame.

Some mothers try to wait until the child is of school age, but this is the most difficult time to tell a child. Preschoolers are untroubled by the knowledge that they are adopted. Between the ages of six and thirteen, however, children's feelings may change. Even children who have always known about their adopted status are much more inclined to be bothered by it than when they were little. Adopted children of this age are more likely to show signs of emotional difficulties as a group than biological children. Such signs include depression, withdrawal, aggression, and hyperactivity. By the time biological and adopted children reach adolescence, the groups are about equal in difficulty.

Even though the middle child years are the toughest, you can help temper this issue by discussing the adoption as soon as possible with your child. Always refer to the adoption in positive terms. For example, assure your child

(whether you actually know so or not) that his biological parents loved him and that their decision was based on a desire to do what was best for him. Describe your first meeting with your child in specific and loving detail—emphasize the pleasure that each of you felt and expressed at this first meeting. Make sure also to emphasize how the decision to adopt came from your heart and was based on how you felt about your child as a person. Point out your child's special qualities and how much you love those qualities.

Never deny or minimize the fact that being adopted is different from being a biological child. Adopted children may worry about their natural parents showing up and removing them from the mother they love. Invite your child to discuss these feelings of difference or fear openly, without concern that there is anything wrong with these feelings. Remember that your child is the first and foremost authority on how he or she feels about being adopted. Don't expect your child to resolve all of his or her feelings about being adopted. This process will unfold gradually and continue until adulthood.

Enlist the Aid of Others. Family and friends need to know how they can deal with your child's adoption in a healthy and constructive way. Be sure everyone knows that your child is aware of his or her adoption. Also, let them know how you would like them to respond if your child expresses concerns about being adopted. Do encourage special relationships. A close adult friend who is not a blood relative of yours can be an especially helpful confidant and role model for your adopted child. Like the child, this person is not biologically linked to you but nonetheless is an integral part of your chosen family. This gives your child a stronger sense of connection to the world around him.

WHEN YOUR CHILD STILL DOESN'T KNOW

I am the mother of a seven-year-old adopted daughter. I have never told her that she is adopted because I thought it would be better to wait until she was older. I can see now that waiting to tell her was not the best choice. Is it too late? How should I handle the situation?

If you have not told your child that she is adopted, then it is time to do so now as positively as you can. It is always recommended that you tell your child early on. For you, the right time is now—better now than later and, certainly, better late than never. Keep the dialog in a positive light, making sure that your child doesn't get the impression that you are alerting her to bad news, but rather to information that she was entitled to know earlier. Do not tell your child that you delayed because of her inability to understand or accept the news. Rather, make a special, private occasion out of the announcement and explain that you waited because you wanted to show your own parental love first when she was little.

Your heart was in the right place, so forgive yourself. You're working hard to remedy a common mistake, and now it's time to move on.

CHALLENGES TO EXPECT DURING YOUR CHILD'S SCHOOL-AGE YEARS

During the school-age years, troublesome feelings and behaviors may plague you and your child. For example, you may suddenly hear things from an angry child like, "You're not my real mother!" Other problems may include:

- Your child may suggest or allege that you kidnapped him.

- He or she may have problems getting along with siblings, especially if these are your biological children.

- Your child may develop fantasies about being reunited with his or her biological parents.

- There may be a reluctance or refusal to cooperate in family activities.

- He or she may demonstrate unusual shyness around relatives.

- Your child may have intense or inappropriate reactions to TV shows, movies, stories, or pictures featuring parent-child relationships.

How to Meet These Challenges. Feeling like a failure plagues most parents at some time whether they are single or married, have biological or adopted children. Your home situation plays a relatively small part. It is normal for adopted children to experience some of the toughest times during their school years, but the teen years are tough for any child! Try:

- Being receptive to what you hear without being defensive. Don't say, "That's a lie" or "You're wrong," but rather, "I'm sorry you believe or feel such untrue things."

- Communicating with your child often to soften some of the blows. Make it clear that you understand he or she is going through a tough time and that you are there to listen but not to be attacked.

- Do seek professional help if there are frequent and intense episodes of sibling rivalry and a consistent pattern of disruption at family gatherings. Trust your instincts if you have a profound and unshakable anxiety about your adopted child's emotional health.

6

The Widowed Mother

WHEN DEATH DIVIDES

Loss of a spouse ranks high on the list of life's most devastating events. There is simply no aspect of your life that is unaffected. The feelings of grief and loss are indescribable, and you wonder if you will ever again feel joy. In fact, at times, your own desire to continue living may not be all that strong. And much of what you are experiencing may not seem real, only a bad dream from which you will awaken.

But, as everybody most likely keeps telling you, you have your children and they need you. Your children give you a reason to continue your life with both purpose and happiness. It's hard to believe right now, but there will be joy again in your lives. There will be days ahead not clouded by grief, but filled with laughter and fun. By seeking out the joy and happiness in everyday events, you will see the light at the end of the tunnel. If you have hope, the light will grow brighter and stronger.

WHAT YOU MAY BE FEELING

Anger

My husband Tony, a firefighter, was killed while searching for possible victims after a fire in a nearby neighborhood. He was hailed as a hero. After the services were over, I watched his fellow firefighters and their wives return to their homes sad for the moment but with their own lives unchanged.

I'm so angry that Tony left me alone with two babies to raise. I also can't helping feeling anger and blame toward the fire department, toward his parents, who had encouraged his love of the job, and toward the residents of the neighborhood where the fire broke out. What's wrong with me?

Feeling angry is a natural part of grieving. There is nothing wrong with feeling angry. But remember that anger needs to be expressed appropriately without harm to others. Accusing Tony's parents because they had encouraged his passion for firefighting will not accomplish anything other than prolonging your rage. You could visit Tony's grave and tell him how angry you are at him for leaving. After all, if you didn't love him, you wouldn't feel this way. Allow yourself to feel angry at Tony from time to time, keeping in mind that you are trying to work through this. As the anger dissipates, you might want to tell a few close friends that you felt as if Tony had abandoned you. People will understand.

Inflicting pain on those who share your loss will not make your pain go away. When you realize there is no one to blame, your anger will no longer dominate your life.

My husband, Philip, died of cancer at the age of thirty-eight. There's no one to blame since Philip had lived a healthy life. He received the best of medical care from caring and compassionate physicians. Philip was able to die at home with dignity surrounded by the things and the people he loved. So why do I blame myself and let this anger consume me?

You might be angry at yourself for feeling angry. You may blame yourself for not yet being able to count the blessings of the many good years you and Philip shared or the dignity of his death. Moreover, like many widows, you may be punishing yourself for surviving Philip.

Your feelings are to be expected. Acknowledging the right to be angry at experiencing such a loss is the first step toward a new life. Maybe you are angry that Philip won't be here to help you raise your children, or to see the oldest teen leave for college. Tell him that you are upset he can't be here to help with the endless packing and transporting of belongings that are also college bound.

Continue to chat with Philip now and again. Many widows report taking great comfort from frank discussions about how they are feeling as if their husbands were still physically present. If you are feeling caught up in anger, try talking it out in this way.

Loneliness. Many widows lose not only a husband but also a best friend when their husband dies. This loss of companionship and intimacy is a difficult and painful adjustment. Remember, however, that some people are not capable of having the kind of deep, committed relationship you shared with your husband. You do have that capacity. You will have other relationships in your life that will fill the emptiness you feel now. Perhaps you will choose not to remarry, but your life will fill with rich and fulfilling relationships.

Try to seek out opportunities for companionship and conversation, even if it is just a brief chat with another mother at a Little League game. People may feel awkward and may not know what to say to you, so often you have to begin the conversation. What you say does not have to be brilliant or witty. You are simply looking for some social contact, so don't set your expectations too high. Small steps will lead to major progress at this difficult time. Give yourself the time to heal. You will always miss your husband, but that sharp edge of loneliness does go away.

Paralysis. Many widows report feeling nearly unable to move for a period of time after their husband's death. Managing daily routines is exhausting. Simple decisions, like what vegetable to give the children for dinner, seem overwhelming. Feelings of low energy, indecision, confusion, and, of course, sadness, are quite normal.

Simply put, the death of your husband was a major trauma. You need time to heal and let your emotional energies regroup. If you fight these feelings and force yourself to do more than you are able to do, you will feel worse and be able to accomplish less.

If you find yourself feeling exhausted, indecisive, or confused, lower your expectations for yourself for the time being. Do only what is essential. Whatever energy you can muster up right now should be invested in meeting your emotional and physical needs and those of your children. Let the dust gather, and let others be the stars at work for now. Healing is hard work and should be your main task now.

Worry. There is much to be realistically worried about when your husband dies. Your children are a tremendous source of concern, no matter what their ages. You have worries about finances and matters relating to the proper settling of your husband's estate. You may be worried about employment. You may have to get a job to make ends meet, or you might need to upgrade your job skills. You may be worried about where you are going to live. You may need to move and be concerned about the wheres and the hows.

With all that is on your plate, it would be strange if you were not worried. But endless worry can sap the joy out of life and exhaust you. You need to take control of your worries. Write them down. Rank them according to what is worrying you the most. Then, divide them into two categories: those you can do something about and those that are so far in the future there is nothing you can do about them anyway. Start crossing off the ones you can do nothing about. Prioritize the remainder. For example, which worries would be helped by talking them out with a friend or in a widows' support group? Which concerns don't seem that serious when examined in the light of day? Wondering who will escort you to your son's graduation ten years from now is a bit premature. Or maybe your health club membership expired with the death of your spouse. Can you find other ways to benefit from healthy activities and exercise? It is helpful, too, to set aside a certain amount of time each day—say, twenty minutes—devoted exclusively to fretting. Then, when you catch yourself worrying too frequently, you can say to yourself, "This is the wrong time for me to worry!"

Fear. Faced with unexpected challenges, many widows are afraid. They are afraid of being alone, of making the wrong decision, and of facing life and the responsibilities of parenthood. These fears are normal and natural and to be expected. It is important to acknowledge that fear is what you are feeling. Fear that is hidden or unexpressed will be devastating to you. Fear is such a strong emotion that if left unexpressed it will take on many hideous disguises. Fear can literally make you sick. It can look like anger and make you lash out at the very people most important to you. Fear can make you unable to move, like a deer at night with the headlights of an oncoming car bearing down on him.

Make friends with the power of fear. Say out loud, "I feel afraid." Sometimes simply acknowledging that you are afraid is enough for the moment. Fear can be a powerful motivator, or it can stop you dead in your tracks. Unlike other powerful emotions like loneliness, you are the only one who can know what you fear and make a plan for conquering the fear. For example, a very real fear you might have is the fear of the responsibility of raising your children alone. Don't let this fear turn you into a screaming mother from hell when you can allow it to mobilize you into the energetic, resourceful person you are capable of becoming.

Remember, we all have fears. It does not make you weak to be afraid. Often fear means that you are realistic about what you are facing. The real danger is letting our fears ruin our lives by preventing us from finding out where our strengths lie, or worse, making us nonproductive and too dependent on others. Try to live by the adage, "Feel the fear, and do it anyway!"

Unresolved Feelings. Talking it out or in some way expressing your feelings to your late husband is an important part of healing, especially if negative feelings are dominating your life. Perhaps you feel guilty about something you did and want his forgiveness. Perhaps you just want to say you are sorry about a decision or event for which you feel responsible. These feelings must be expressed and put in their proper place in order for you to move ahead.

Try writing your husband a letter and leaving it at his grave. If this is too public, then burn the letter and scatter the ashes. Maybe it is difficult for you to put your feelings on paper. Make a tape recording and play it at a place where you feel most comfortable. It is not important how you confront these feelings but rather that you do confront them. The only rule is that the feelings get expressed. Give yourself permission to create and enact any ceremony or ritual that will give you the forgiveness or peace you need.

WARDING OFF THE GRIEF POLICE

Among the more unpleasant immediate experiences widows face are the encounters with the "grief police." You know them—the well-meaning friends or people you hardly know who feel free to tell you the "rules" for grieving. These rules take the form of statements like, "He's been dead for six months. Why are you still wearing your wedding rings?" or "A year is long enough to grieve. Get on with your own life." Do not let anyone tell you that there are set timetables for grieving, implying that you are in some way behind schedule. Avoid others' distorted sense of priorities.

Most self-help books and tapes about managing loss are written by members of the grief police. These materials are based on the idea that grief can be managed. Grief, by its very nature, is unmanageable. There is no timetable or step-by-step guide to manage the experience of loss. One widow describes grief as like being behind the wheel of a car going sixty miles an hour with no control over the brakes or steering. You just told on tight.

Keep in mind that although you may never really get over a feeling of loss, you will get through this. When you do, the reminders of this loss in the future will be transformed from painful to poignant. Memories become more bittersweet until one day—as deep as the depths of your sadness and despair are—will come the ability to think of your spouse with warmth and fulfillment.

Remember, too, that there is no hierarchy of grief. Losing a husband of fifty years is not worse than losing a husband of five months or a son of thirty years. Others will be sharing your feelings of grief and loss—his mother, his father, your children. Respect others' unique way of mourning, but at the same time don't let them inflict their rules on you.

Finally, never forget that everyone experiences loss in some form or another. Of course, all grievers believe their pain at a given moment is unlike anyone else's—no one could ever understand the depth or strength of their feelings. But that is because loss is such a personal experience. Like everything else that occurs in life, you'll get through this. But only if you give yourself permission.

TIPS FOR RESPONDING TO NOSY QUESTIONS

Regardless of the circumstances of your husband's death, you will be astounded at the inappropriate comments and questions. Tragedy often brings out the worst in people. Remember to keep in mind:

- Contribute nothing to the gossip mill. People often assume that they have a "right to know." A few people in your life will ask out of genuine concern, but most people are simply curious or looking for gossip to spread. Choose your confidants with care.

- Respect your own privacy. Expect to be asked about the size of your husband's estate, how you are coping without sex, exactly how you plan to handle your money, and on and on. The best way to handle these "none of your business" questions is to say simply that it is a personal matter.

- Keep your sense of humor and use it, when at all possible. Try to keep a slightly amused, slightly surprised tone to your voice when confronted with nosy questions. Try laughing out loud if the question is particularly outrageous.

- When in doubt, say nothing.

FACING YOUR HUSBAND'S BELONGINGS

The most painful and heartbreaking task any widow faces is the disposal of her husband's belongings. Don't let others rush you into this task. Do things as you feel ready. Keep what you want to keep. Your children will want to have pictures and mementos of their father so that he can be remembered. Friends and other relatives might cherish something that belonged to your husband.

If you come across items of unknown value or your husband had a collection of some type, find out the value before giving it away or donating it to charity. Remember again that there is no timetable and that you are free to deal with this task at a pace comfortable to you.

PROTECTING YOUR CHILDREN FROM YOUR PRIVATE PAIN

Activities like writing your deceased husband a letter telling him how angry you are that he died are private matters reflecting adult needs and concerns. You may choose to discuss your feelings with close friends, a trusted clergyman, or a counselor. With few exceptions, however, the activities that accompany these feelings should not be shared with your children, no matter what their age. Your children are dealing with their own issues about their father and cannot shoulder your pain as well.

As you are dealing with your own feelings, you certainly want to help your children confront and express theirs. You might encourage older children to express their feelings in writing or on tape. Younger children can draw or paint. Make sure your children know that they can discuss

their feelings with you. If you cannot handle this—and many widows cannot—find a trusted adult in whom they can confide. Counseling can be very beneficial for families when a parent has died.

FINDING SUPPORT AND COUNSELING

Nearly all communities offer counseling and fund support groups for recent widows and their children. These may be available through your local hospital, mental health clinic, church or synagogue, or community center. It is a good idea to seek out these resources for yourself and for your children. Most often widows and their children report receiving great comfort from the opportunity to talk with others who are experiencing the same loss and many of the same kinds of feelings. A support system that enables you and your children to emerge intact from the emotional minefield of the grieving process is very important to your recovery.

If your children do not want to go, gently insist that they try it once or twice. Many children who have overcome the initial reluctance continue willingly. If your child does not want to continue, do not force him. Your child may not be ready for this group experience, or for the intensity of individual counseling. Later on, therapy or attending a support group might be just right. Remember, grief is not a timed event, and each of your children will grieve differently. Respect those differences and be ready to accommodate individual needs for private counseling or group therapy.

KNOWING WHEN TO RELEASE THE GHOST

Confronting feelings of anger or guilt and expressing them in some manner to your late husband may be healthy and appropriate. Expressing regret and asking your late husband for forgiveness or understanding can also be part of the normal, healthy grieving process. However, finding yourself conversing with your late husband about what to make for dinner or what movie to see is not healthy.

You will think about your late husband often. When you think of him, remember the love. You must let go of him to move on with your own life. Making his favorite dinner or seeing a movie he would have liked will not fill the void. No kind of meaningful life can be built with a ghost. Release the ghost of your husband. This is key to your survival.

THE YOUNG WIDOW

You may not have realized that widows come in all shapes, sizes, and ages. If you have been widowed while still relatively young and with children living at home, you most likely will receive more support and attention during the time immediately following your husband's death than do older widows. Your husband will have left many friends and survivors, and his parents might still be alive. Although you will want to reach out and accept the help available to you, it is important not to let this support dictate your feelings or shape significantly the plans you will make for the future. Older widows have had a style or pattern of living that they followed. But because of your age, you'll find others urging you to settle into a new life or expecting you to cope as they do. Their needs do not mean you have to stage a show or pretend on their behalf. Let them know that it is precisely because of your age that you don't want to do anything hasty with your life, or make too many decisions yet.

Above all else, be kind to yourself. The death of your husband was an enormous loss. Do not make it worse by burdening yourself with having to put on a brave front or feeling you have to create your new life overnight. Let the numb feelings protect you for a while. Let go of the numbness as you are ready. Your grieving will need to follow its own individual course.

My husband recently died in a car accident, leaving me widowed at thirty years of age. I just can't relate to elderly women mourning the death of spouses who didn't have much time left anyway. They don't appear to be in such a state of shock—a number of them tell me they actually feel relieved where I feel practically numb. Why?

Shock and numbness are often the first feelings young widows face. Often their husbands' deaths are the result of accidents, death in the line of duty, or illnesses only rarely found in men so young. The numb feelings are a natural protection, because with little or no time to prepare, there is simply too much to face all at once.

Particularly for young widows who lose their husbands unexpectedly, the feeling of being abandoned is overwhelming. You feel as though your husband has deserted you on purpose. No matter what the circumstances of his death, part of you feels that he had a choice whether to die or not and made a decision to abandon you. Women in their sixties and seventies also report feeling abandoned. But they sense it in a different way, particularly because they weren't left with minor children.

One woman was widowed at twenty-six when her husband died in an airline crash. She described being angry that she was left to face the "frontier" of raising their infant son alone. She knew her husband had nothing to do with the crash and certainly had no wish to die at thirty years of age, but she couldn't help blaming him for leaving her, as irrational and crazy as she thought this was.

NOT QUITE A WIDOW— LEGALLY

I'm in my early thirties and recently widowed, sort of. What I mean is that my fiancé died suddenly from leukemia while I was five months pregnant. I believe he had a little money put away for us, but contact with his family has stopped since my fiancé's death. I feel like I have no one to turn to since my family lives so far away.

Ask yourself if there is anything you can do to maintain relations with your fiancé's family—at least for mutual emotional support. Maybe they are aware of your fiancé's intentions and would like to offer you some assistance. Plus, they might want a relationship, however undefined or remote, with their grandchild, which

can be very beneficial for both you and your child. It is not clear why the lines of communication shut down, but maybe you could reopen them. You might also want to check with an attorney to see what legal rights you may have in a situation like this, especially if you know for certain that your fiancé had something to contribute financially to the future of your family. Chances are, he may have set up an account that is in your name, as well as his. Either way, investigate now.

MISSING HIS BODY AND TOUCH

This is the most personal aspect of your loss and probably the most difficult to discuss. Touch is a basic human need. Particularly if your husband's death was sudden or unexpected, loss of his touch makes you feel adrift and incomplete. You will miss his kisses, holding his hand, his mere physical presence. If your life together as a couple was especially rich and satisfying, you will long for the intimacy and pleasure you brought to one another. These needs will not be easily satisfied.

Some widows try to replace their husbands almost instantly, choosing almost literally the nearest warm body around. This will be a temptation because the pain you feel is so great and the loss so terrible. Looking for a substitute man in haste will almost surely compound your feelings of loss. There will be no shortage of men who will look to take advantage of your situation, particularly for the young widow. Some truly unscrupulous types will seek you out, especially if they think you are a wealthy widow. Their plan is to seduce you and steal your money. This is not to say that every man who might ask you out is a potential felon, but you need to be careful. You have been out of the social scene for a long while. You need to tread carefully and learn the rules and devise your own before you find yourself in a situation you in no way envisioned.

Many widows find that methods of self-satisfaction are the best substitute until they are ready to explore the social scene. Meeting your own needs can also take the form of small luxuries like manicures, pedicures, or massage. These may seem like small comforts in the face of what you have lost, but they may be the best and safest substitute for you now.

GETTING THE HELP YOU NEED

Many people will offer help, urging you to call upon them if you need assistance. Your instincts will tell you who is sincere and who is not. This is not the time to see how absolutely strong and self-reliant you can be. In short, accept the help.

Remember, other people cannot read your mind. You have to ask for what you need. Sometimes the simplest kinds of help are the most needed. If you have been too overwhelmed to cook, ask for a home-cooked meal. Feeling ready for a little entertainment? Ask someone to go to the movies or to the mall with you. Perhaps your children need a ride somewhere that you are having a hard time coordinating.

Asking for and accepting help, particularly during this difficult time, is not a sign of weakness and surely does not predict that you will be unable to forge a new life for yourself and your children. Asking for and accepting help is the first logical step in forging this new life. You have a lot on your plate now. Things will get better. Much of what you are coping with and having to handle, once done, will not have to be a concern again.

SUICIDAL THOUGHTS

It is normal to think about your own death when your husband dies. The desire for reunion, coupled with the feelings of sadness, makes most widows think at least briefly about ending their own lives. The needs of their children and their own healthy desire to live quickly take over. If you have had such thoughts, know that other women have had similar thoughts. Do not punish yourself by thinking that you are insane or a bad person or a terrible mother for letting such a thought even enter your mind.

If you find yourself thinking often about killing yourself and have thought about a plan or possible method, you need to tell someone you trust. You are in serious pain and need help to sort through what you are feeling. No one will think less of you. The loss of your husband is so overwhelming that you are finding it hard to think about continuing to live. Help and understanding are available to you. Ask.

WHEN WIDOW SPELLS R-E-L-I-E-F!

For some women, the death of their husbands brings only relief. Your husband may have physically or emotionally abused you. He may have had a serious drug or alcohol problem. He may have been continually unfaithful to you, causing you humiliation.

Cruel and abusive husbands are seldom mourned as are kind and decent men. If you worked hard at keeping his abusive or addictive behaviors a secret, you may be shocked to hear the comments of others, even at the funeral. Chances are, others were well aware of the kind of man he was and will not expect you to be all that grief-stricken. Your greatest loss at his death might be your pride. Your cherished fantasy that no one else knew may be destroyed.

If you feel only relief, then you have probably experienced much pain and grief during your husband's lifetime. You may have grieved for a loving marriage that never happened. If widowhood comes as a relief, then do nothing more than accept the blessing. You have endured enough. If you have feelings toward your husband that you could not express to him during his lifetime, do it now. Write him a long letter and, if you choose, burn the letter symbolically to express the end of your suffering and unwanted attachment. Enjoy the second chance life has given you. Free yourself from guilt. You have survived life circumstances that would have destroyed a woman of less strength.

The Merry Widow

My husband Jeffrey was a well-respected attorney. He was also a cruel man who ridiculed and demeaned me. As much as the members of our community deeply mourn, frankly I'm not grieving because I know Jeffrey was nothing like the public image he presented. In fact, I've forgiven him, as he begged me to, and am ready to live a little.

Cruel and abusive men often end their lives asking for forgiveness and understanding. You've experienced exhausting emotional pain during the time preceding your husband's death, so it's likely that you are "thanking" him for leaving, rather than forgiving him his abuses. However, these two feelings can go hand-in-hand, and either way are acceptable. But sometimes one can forgive a little too quickly, as in the case of a woman who was told her husband had only one week left to live. She immediately forgave him for his years of senseless emotional abuse. Feeling as though she had put her feelings in order by being unselfish enough to forgive, this woman went home and disposed of many of her husband's personal belongings, including socks and underwear. But to everyone's surprise, her husband staged a brief yet remarkable remission and was able to go home. Imagine her having to rush out and purchase new underwear and other personals for the husband she had already removed from both her home and her life!

SECRETS AND SURPRISES: THREE SCENARIOS

My husband, Alexander, was a high-school science teacher well respected for the personal interest and concern he took in his students. I knew exactly what kind of interest. Alexander was a pedophile. Protected by lax supervision on the part of school officials, my husband had his share of "interesting friends," as he liked to call his latest underage love interest. His sudden death by heart attack was an answer to my prayers, since I always feared exposure and a lengthy prosecution.

When I arrived at the funeral home shortly before calling hours were to begin, I found a strange woman kneeling at the casket sobbing. This strange woman was no stranger to my late husband. I found out she was George's girlfriend of several years! I'm totally speechless.

After going through all the financial records and legal papers that I had never seen until my husband's death, I was shocked to learn that my husband had been stealing from me for years. My retirement savings that I turned over to him for investment purposes had dwindled down to nothing. He even cashed in the life insurance.

There have been countless versions of these stories—the woman who discovered a stash of pornography when she cleaned out her husband's office, or the wife who found out that her late husband had not lost money in the stock market but rather had a serious gambling problem. Men you would never imagine as having an affair have been found to have kept mistresses in nice apartments or condos. Regardless of how you discovered your ex's misdeeds, or even if you already were aware of his "goings on," this proof can exert

some very basic changes in the way you feel about your late husband, someone you thought you knew so well.

Depending on his wicked deed, you may feel any or all of these emotions: shock, devastation, betrayal, humiliation. Remember that you are the victim. Do not berate yourself for not knowing about this part of your husband's life. He invested a great deal of time and energy in keeping this part of his life a secret from you.

Even though you may have been relieved by your husband's death because you knew he had some scary habits, you'll still need to purge some feelings. Keeping a diary or a journal might be especially helpful to you. As you get a better grasp on your emotions, you'll find more appropriate ways to express these feelings.

WHAT TO DO IF YOUR SPOUSE DIES SUDDENLY

Begin by contacting the Social Security Administration at their toll-free number, 1-800-772-1213, on any business day between the hours of 7 A.M. and 7 P.M. Some businesses advertise that they can provide name changes, social security cards, or earnings statements for a fee. Do not use such services. You can get all these services free from the Social Security Administration.

If you have no credit in your own name, this should be among your first priorities. Begin by obtaining a secured credit card. In this case, you deposit a certain amount of cash with the credit card issuer in return for a credit line of the same size. If you default on your credit card payments, the bank can seize enough money from your deposit to cover your debt. You can obtain a list of secured credit card issuers from the Bankcard Holders of America. Their telephone number is 703-481-1110.

Contact your husband's employer in writing regarding his employee benefits and inform them of your husband's death. Include the date of death, your husband's social security number, and a copy of the death certificate. Request information about the benefits you should expect to receive, such as 401(k), profit sharing, and partial tenure or retirement benefits, and the steps you must take to begin to receive payments.

Under federal law, as a provision of the Comprehensive Omnibus Budget Reconciliation Act (COBRA), you are eligible to continue health insurance coverage under your spouse's health insurance plan for three years at the same price the employer would have paid, plus a small administration fee. You will have to pay premiums, which you might not have had to pay when your spouse was alive. However, you will receive group insurance rates, which will be far lower than you could qualify for as an individual. Furthermore, your dependent children must continue to be covered under your late husband's health insurance policy, and the premiums must be paid under the same terms. Coverage under COBRA is not automatic. You must notify your late husband's employer within sixty days or you lose your right to coverage.

If enrollment under the provisions of COBRA is not available to you, consider enrolling in a Health Maintenance Organization (HMO) or Preferred Provider Organization (PPO). Doing without health insurance coverage is a

WHAT YOU NEED ON HAND

Although it is stressed over and over to "plan ahead," rarely is anyone actually "prepared" in the practical sense for the loss of a spouse. Here is what you should have on hand to guide you in the event of your spouse's death:

- A list of all the banks (and their phone numbers) where an account in either or both of your names was kept

- A list of all insurance policies and their numbers

- A list of all stocks, bonds, and mutual funds, with account numbers

- All real-estate holdings and copies of deeds

- A list of all other assets—for example, cars, coin collections, antiques

terrible financial gamble. Avoid this gamble if at all possible.

Determine Your Financial Needs. Your financial needs and goals will depend on many different factors. Much will depend on your age, the age of your children, your employment history and assets, and personal needs and desires. You will make costly mistakes if you do not have a plan. Your plan will depend on what your goals are and what assets are available to you. Following are four tips for protecting your worth:

- Hire a lawyer and an accountant you trust. Do not be afraid to ask people you like and respect for their recommendations. These hiring decisions are critical and unfortunately must be made at a time when you feel least able to cope. Invest the time and energy in interviewing people until you find the right fit. Ask about their experience in cases such as yours. Do not be shy about asking about fees and other costs.

♦ Beware of scams. You may be receiving a large lump sum of money from life insurance. Con artists are careful readers of the obituaries, so expect to be on the receiving end of a lot of sales pitches and possible con games. If something sounds too good to be true, it is! Anytime someone is trying to rush you into anything, that should be a clear signal to you to pull back and reconsider.

♦ Don't buy, sell, or invest in anything right away. You are coping with enough without having to deal with major decisions such as selling your home to buy a smaller house or condo, investing in hot stocks, or lending money.

♦ Keep your financial worth private. Many widows have regretted telling their children exactly how much money they had. Older children rarely have any idea how much money is needed to carry on with daily living and feel that the money their mother now has is sufficient to finance any particular whim. Younger children need to be reassured that their needs will be met.

Additionally, widows who have discussed their assets with relatives or friends were immediately besieged with requests for loans or urged to invest in a hot tip at the track. Your best advice? Be somewhat vague about your money with friends, children, and relatives.

Review All Your Insurance Needs. In addition to your health insurance coverage, you also need to review your car, life, homeowners, and disability coverage. Homeowners and car insurance may have been under your husband's name and may need to be changed. You should have life insurance coverage for yourself as part of your overall financial plan.

Revise Your Will. Among your first tasks will be to revise your will and to appoint a guardian for your children in case of your death. After you have settled these matters, tell your children of the plans you have made. Reassure them, particularly if they are young and their father's death was sudden and unexpected, that it is very unlikely that you will die also. This will be a difficult conversation with your children. Set aside a time so that it can occur without interruption and with ample time for all family members to say how they feel. Reactions such as crying are to be expected. However, your ability to answer your children's unexpressed fear about what would happen if you died will be an enormous comfort and an immeasurable aid in their healing.

What to Do About the Death Certificate. Death certificates are issued by the municipality or county in which your husband died. Where your husband died and where you live may be entirely separate locations. You will need a copy of your husband's death certificate to complete much of the business of settling the estate.

These copies need to be what are called "original copies," meaning that they are photostatted copies with the official seal of the issuing government office on them. Ask for ten copies so that you are not caught short.

Keep these copies in a safe place that is readily accessible to you but not where you have to look at them every five minutes. You do not need the constant reminder.

HELPING YOUR CHILDREN FACE THE LOSS OF THEIR FATHER

There will be little of greater concern to you than helping your children deal with the devastating loss of their father. No matter what the age of your children, their feelings and concerns will require much patient understanding and the healing power of time. Here are some thoughts to help you and your children face this painful loss together:

♦ *Let your children teach you about their experience of grief.* No one's love for

anyone else is exactly like someone else's. Your child loved his father in a unique and special way. Nobody knows how your child is feeling because nobody else is your child. Help your child find ways to express how he feels and then really listen.

♦ *Explain that death is natural.* Death is not a punishment, nor is it a horrible experience only for some. Know that not every child will understand death in the same way. Never tell a child that people die because they are bad or that death is like sleeping. You can imagine what young children would do with that information.

Don't force your kids to understand death. It is a mysterious stage in the life cycle, and although death is now a secret to us, we all eventually experience it. Some families rely on long-standing cultural traditions about how grief and death should be handled. In other families, death is a forbidden topic. It's best to be available to answer the sensitive questions that your child will pose. But it is important, too, to be able to say simply, "I just don't know."

♦ *Don't expect sudden understanding about God* when you explain your religious views about death. Teaching abstract spiritual and religious concepts is no easy task. As children mature, they are able to understand more and more. While we can teach only what we believe, be careful not to expect too much of yourself. It is a misuse of religious faith to tell a child that a loved one "is in a better place, so it is wrong to feel sad." At the same time, you need not feel guilty or inadequate if you are unable to give specific explanations of God and heaven or whatever your specific beliefs are. Openness to mystery is valuable not only in teaching about death, but in teaching anything about life.

- *Let time help.* Healing is a process, not an event. Children need to face the pain before they can heal, and this takes a long time. Telling children to be strong and get over it is cruel. You may want your children to give the appearance that all is well again so that you can hide from your own pain. But unexpressed grief results in unproductive and harmful behaviors, such as fighting with friends, failing at schoolwork, and demonstrating unsafe and poor behavior. Your children need time.

- *Tell the truth.* Children can almost always cope with what they know. Handling what they do not know is the problem. Children will fill in the empty spaces of what they are told with their imaginations. What children imagine is usually far worse than the truth. When children discover that they have been lied to, they feel humiliated and unloved. Lying gives children the message that it is okay to be dishonest at the very times when families should be pulling together.

- *Don't wait for one big "tell-all."* Encourage your children to ask questions as they need to ask them. Often children will repeat the same question over and over again. Some questions you will be unable to answer. This does not matter. What does matter is that you treat your children's questions with respect and

courtesy and try to answer them as honestly as possible.

- *Assure your children that they are not responsible.* Children often believe that their thoughts can cause something to happen. For example, a younger child may think that because she constantly left her skates out for her father to trip over, she caused her father's heart attack. An older child might feel responsible because he secretly wished his father would die for not letting him play video games until his homework was done. Children need to be reassured that nothing they did or thought caused their father to die.

- *Expect some physical distress.* Children's bodies will react to the experience of grief. Your child may complain of fatigue, stomach aches, sore throats, or trouble sleeping. You may be told that he is visiting the school nurse with greater frequency. Do not tell your child it is all in his head. He really does feel sick. These physical symptoms are the result of the stress this loss has placed upon your child. He needs support, understanding, and a little extra love and attention. If your child's physical problems persist, it is a good idea to talk the situation over with your pediatrician or family physician.

- *Babies need extra comfort, too.* Infants and toddlers are not too young to understand. If infants can give and receive love, then they can certainly grieve. Grieving in children of this age often takes the form of sleep disturbance, regressive behavior like thumb sucking or bed wetting, and strong emotional outbursts. It is important to support and nurture grieving young children, or their capacity to develop trust in the world around them will be greatly diminished. Hugging, holding, and playing with young children are the best ways to offer comfort and support.

◆ *Dispel the myth that loss means messed-up kids in later life.* The loss of a parent does not automatically lead to maladjustment in adult life. Although many people will take the attitude that your child will be forever emotionally crippled by his father's death, this is simply not true. What will determine your child's adjustment is how your child is helped to mourn this loss. If your child is allowed to express his feelings, ask the questions he needs to ask, and receive the guidance and love he needs, his chances for a meaningful and happy life are good. If your child is not allowed to grieve or is forced to keep to some grief timetable or told that crying or other expressions of feelings are signs of weakness, then no doubt there will be lasting emotional scars.

◆ *Maintain consistency at home.* Try to keep the household routines as stable as possible. Despite all that you must cope with, it is important that you maintain regular mealtimes and

bedtimes. Try to keep the demands on yourself as simple as possible. Gourmet meals are not needed, but your children will be reassured by the order and routine you maintain in their lives.

◆ *Be patient.* Do not work toward the goal of having your child "get over it." Children do not "get over" the loss of a father. They learn to live with it, reconcile themselves to it, and make peace with it. Your children will come to the realization that their world is different without their father. As they become more reconciled to his loss, they will look ahead with hope and begin to make plans for the future. They will not forget their father even as their lives go on without him. This process will require patience.

SURVIVING HOLIDAYS AND BIRTHDAYS

That first round of birthdays and holidays after your husband's death is very hard. It is impossible not to remember the special birthday cake your husband baked or the special surprise he arranged last Christmas. There is no reason to forget. Treasure the memory. At the same time, it is important to create new memories. This does not mean that you should completely change all your holiday routines and rituals. Nobody has the emotional energy for that. What you do want to do is to introduce one slightly different twist to the old routines—even something simple like an evening of cookie baking or making a few new ornaments for the tree.

Dad's birthday may bring much remembrance. The first few Father's

Days might be even rougher than his birthday. It is best to anticipate these days and make some kind of plan about how to spend the day. One husband and father is well remembered on his birthday by a secret good deed done by each of his children and their mother. Around the dinner table, plans are made and reports of the good deed are shared. Their father's generous spirit is carried on. Instead of sorrowful tears, dad's birthday is a time of sharing and doing good for others.

YOUR CHANGING SOCIAL LIFE

Immediately after your husband dies, you may find yourself receiving many invitations. After a short while, many of these invitations may stop. The sorry news is that you are probably not as welcome in your previous circle of married friends now that you are a widow. Some people really do consider an "extra woman" a social liability. In short, you will quickly discover who your true friends are. Your true friends will continue to include you in their plans. Those who are not your true friends will loudly proclaim their desire to get together when they happen to run into you at the supermarket, but somehow it will never happen. It is important that you reciprocate the invitations you do receive, even in a limited way. Nobody is expecting you to throw a grand party, but a simple coffee and dessert for a few friends will lift your spirits.

Probably before you have really thought about dating, someone will ask you out or one of your friends or coworkers will want to fix you up with someone. This will be a journey back into the awkwardness you thought you had left behind at fourteen. It feels funny to be having dinner or going to the movies with a stranger. Like that first plunge into the cold ocean, the first date will be the hardest. Take the risk. We are talking an evening here, not a lifetime commitment.

Remember, however, that your children's feelings and sensitivities need to be kept uppermost in your mind. Your children might be ready to have you date—so ready, in fact, that they ask your date if he would like to be their new daddy. Or they may be so unready to have you date that they embarrass both you and themselves by their rotten behavior when he comes to pick you up. Both these behaviors are clear signals that your children are not ready to participate in your social life even as simple bystanders.

DATING AND SEX

It is best to keep your dating life, particularly in its early casual stages, separate from your children. This means meeting him at the restaurant or having him pick you up at work. If you are dating a "grown-up," he will surely understand your need to protect your children. If he gives you a hard time, this is your first clue that he is probably not worth your time.

Having sex may the furthest thing from your mind as you take your first timid steps into the dating world. This does not mean that sex is the furthest thing from your date's mind. Be sure you are not sending mixed signals. For example, agreeing to return to his house or apartment after dinner may indicate to him that you are physically interested. If you are not, you need to let him know.

Your first sexual encounter will bring forth many confusing emotions. There is no reason to feel guilty that you want sexual gratification. After all, your husband may be dead, but you are not. Only you know when you are going to be ready, and no one can tell you what is right for you. The best advice is to think carefully before you have sex with someone new. Be clear in your mind about why you are choosing this person and why this feels like the right thing to do now. You need to take responsibility for birth control and practice safe sex. When you've taken responsibility for your sexual needs, you can allow yourself to enjoy the rest.

YOUR FIRST FAMILY VENTURE WITHOUT DAD

This will be my first summer traveling alone with my two children. My husband used to arrange our vacations, plan the travel routes and decide where we would all stay. He died two years ago and I just haven't had the motivation to venture out. I need some encouragement about getting out there and taking over his job.

Don't feel incompetent because your husband arranged your family trips as professionally as a travel agent. You may do a different job, yet chances are, if you really consider what you and your kids would like to do, and not what you think your husband

would have wanted, you'll be on the right road in no time. Remember, men and women have different outlooks when it comes to traveling. We've all met the guys who refuse to ask for directions and only rely on outdated maps, and moms who want to check their route by asking every gas station attendant for shortcuts.

Think of this as a new venture for you and your kids. Don't try to revisit all the same destinations you did when your husband was alive unless these are places that you truly want to see. For example, were beach trips something your husband loved but honestly, you could have done without the globs of sunblock and the sand sticking around for weeks in the car? Try something different that you and your children might enjoy such as checking out a dude ranch or spending a week in the mountains. If you're not that adventurous, then stick to something familiar, but remember, it doesn't have to be a play-by-play recreation of what your earlier vacations were like. You're bound to be disappointed if you have unrealistic expectations.

If you're traveling by car, you have a great opportunity to talk about dad. Ask the kids if they think dad would enjoy this trip. Or say something like,

"Your dad would laugh if he could see us trying to bait our own hooks," or, "I'll bet Dad wouldn't enjoy the mountains as much as we do because he preferred warmer weather." It's okay to reminisce about previous travels, but don't let the talk turn into negative comparisons. Remember, you're not trying to "please" dad. Rather you want to bring him along in your thoughts.

THE DOS AND DON'TS FOR WIDOWED MOTHERS

- Do remember that there is a life to be had without your husband. Building that new life does not diminish the love you shared.

- Do not be harsh with yourself if you feel only relief at your husband's death. If this is what you feel, you most likely have good reasons. Put the pain behind you and work toward a healthier, more satisfying life.

- Do not project too far into the future. Many things you are worried about today will never happen. Many things will happen over which you will have no control. Focus on today.

- Do make fun. Your children and you need the simple pleasures of family life. Cuddle up together on the couch and watch a movie. Make cookies. Take a walk to enjoy the sunshine.

- Don't sentence yourself to death by putting up too many walls. Yes, you are vulnerable to future pain, but that also means you are alive.

- Do treasure your memories of your husband and allow your children to do the same.

- Do make new happy memories together as a family. You cannot keep your home as a shrine to your late husband or celebrate every holiday in his memory.

- Don't try to find an instant replacement or substitute for your husband. A new man will not cure the pain or fill the void of your husband's death. He might be a distraction for you now, but you still need to work through the process of mourning.

- Don't let the world take advantage of you. Beware of scams and get-rich-quick schemes. Know that there are men out there who prey on lonely widows. They will try to win your heart to get your money.

- Do be open to new opportunities and adventures. The single life is filled with pleasures and excitement if you can open yourself up to the endless possibilities.

- Do reassure your child that no angry thought or deed can cause someone to die. People die because they were sick, or injured, or because they got old, but never because of an angry thought or heated words.

- Do let your children grieve. Avoid trying to distract them from their feelings. Grieving is a necessary part of life, since all living beings from time to time will experience loss.

PART 2

MEET YOUR NEW PARTNER—YOU!

7

For the Mother-to-Be

WHAT YOU SHOULD KNOW ABOUT PREGNANCY AND CHILDBIRTH

Remember the beginning of the movie *Close Encounters of the Third Kind,* where the sounds that were universally heard were recorded and then reproduced very loudly via a synthesizer? Well, imagine that there was some way to record the decibel level of all the women around the world who, upon learning that they were pregnant, collectively shouted, "I'm what?!" As sure as there are points on a Richter scale, this sound could no doubt blow up the planet!

But not every woman has the same reaction once the news has sunk in a bit. For some, particularly for teenagers, the shock is just too much. The emotional maturity as well as the financial and family support needed to handle this event responsibly just are not there. For these women, motherhood is unthinkable at this time in their lives, and they usually decide upon an early abortion or offer the child for adoption.

Others are not as definite about deciding whether pregnancy now is acceptable or impossible, and the choice of whether to continue or to terminate the pregnancy can be agonizing. Still other women may follow "I'm what?" with "It's about time!" particularly if they have been actively trying to get pregnant.

Whatever your initial reaction to the news, it's plausible to be "surprised" no matter how sure you thought you were. What is important, however, is that you don't let punitive and outdated social values dictate what is right or wrong for you, but rather let your heart and your conscience decide what is best. This decision is often most stressful for those who are fairly sure they want a child with or without Mr. Right but are getting negative feedback from family and friends. Find people with whom you can talk and from whom you will get positive feedback.

When you learn that pregnancy is first met with ambivalence by many women, whether they are married or not, you won't feel so alone. You are normal, and you will still be normal even if

91

you change your feelings about this news ten times in the course of a day.

HANDLING THE NEWS

If your test was positive, but his response was not . . . You've been a little nauseous lately, a little tired and irritable, or maybe your breasts feel slightly tender. Perhaps you just feel a wee bit different than you normally do when you are expecting your period. Even though you are due for it, and not particularly late, you get a strong sense (a sense that you're desperately trying to ignore, of course) that somehow, something is happening to your body. Something just makes you say no to that glass of wine with supper. You tell yourself that if you don't get your period in a few days, you will give yourself a pregnancy test, but you reassure yourself that you are probably not pregnant. But then, if you are, it's not such a bad idea. After all, you would like a child one day. It's just that your partner or whomever you've been spending time with may not welcome the news the same way you had hoped. Or maybe your partner isn't good news anyway.

You hold your breath as you wait for the little line or dot to show up in the applicator of your home pregnancy test. There it is, and even if you have previously entertained fleeting thoughts that you could be ever so slightly pregnant, you're now totally dumfounded. But of course you still run out and buy four more kits, and on the way to work the next morning, you perform the same ritual in the cup for your doctor. Okay, so now there is no question that you really are pregnant. Like most single mothers by choice, sort of, you didn't actively plan this baby. Much of how you are feeling depends on what degree of involvement the father wants and how you feel about this.

If You're Considering Abortion. If you've just learned that you're pregnant and you have no commitment from the father, you may be asking yourself whether or not to abort. You're not the only person who has asked herself this question. But you are the only one who can answer it.

Don't panic. Take a little time (and a few deep breaths) before making a decision too hastily. Be aware, too, that this is not the time to become saved, born again, or take every grain of your religious dogma to heart if you weren't that invested in it before. Try to keep guilt, family values rhetoric, militant attitudes, and old-fashioned scares out of your rational thought processes. There is no rush. You have a few weeks to make this decision with safety and security.

My pregnancy was really an accident. I used birth control pills up until six months before I became pregnant and relied on spermicides after that. I'm worried that because I became pregnant while using spermicides it may affect my baby. I want to have this baby but am concerned about spermicides or even the pill damaging the embryo.

Almost half a million women become pregnant each year while using spermicides, and many continue to use them even a few weeks into their unknown pregnancy. No one knows for sure, but it appears that if so many women conceive this way without risk to the baby, it is safe to conclude that there is not much to worry about. If you're really concerned, there are tests that can detect abnormalities early on. Discuss your concerns immediately with your doctor. By the way, you don't need to worry about the oral contraceptive usage because you stopped taking birth control pills way in advance of the recommended time to stop.

Bouncing Between Joy and Heartache. Although you may have been initially terrified at the news of your pregnancy, like most single mothers by chance, you decided to keep and raise your baby. Although their pregnancies were neither planned nor purely accidental, single mothers by chance usually report wanting a child. But because they have had to endure abandonment, rejection, or other negative and sometimes unexpected reactions by the father, these women's emotions bounce between joy and heartache.

If you have successfully conceived through donor insemination, you may still have mixed feelings about becoming a mother. First, trying to get pregnant through donor insemination can be an exhausting effort. Unlike trying to conceive with a partner, trying to conceive through donor insemination is not much fun. Additionally, this process certainly costs more money. But congratulations are in order here. Even when physiological changes are causing you to feel strange or uncertain about your decision, remember, all women go through confusing feelings during the early stages of pregnancy.

Don't underestimate those hormone fluctuations!

If You Thought Your Partner Needed a "Shove"

My boyfriend of six years and I can't seem to make the commitment. I thought that when he learned I was pregnant, this would be the push we both needed. But he's acting strange, and I'm not sure if he's even going to stay around.

While it is true that strong relationships often need a little nudge to push them toward making the big "C," don't expect your partner to make a commitment to parenthood if his commitment to you was not there to begin with. And even though shotgun weddings are becoming a thing of the past, we'll never know whether high-profile celebrity couples are just putting on a public display of delight when responding to the news of their impending parenthood. The best method for dealing with no reaction, a confused response, or a totally negative or angry reaction from the father is to arm yourself with some strategies for coping that include focusing more on your life, not his.

"My Partner Can't Decide How He Feels About My Pregnancy ..."

My live-in partner of two years is undecided about my pregnancy. He says he loves me but doesn't know what to do. I feel like my life is on hold while waiting for him to make up his mind. I had an abortion with him last year and don't want another one.

It's difficult enough to decide whether and when to become a mother, let alone worrying about whether your partner is receptive to the idea. Again, the level of devotion this person has demonstrated to you during your relationship should be an indicator of how much you should let his reactions affect your decision. For example, wonderful as he is, if this man has a history of unfulfilled promises, then you may be relying too much on his input. Conversely, if this is a man who gives serious thought to every aspect of his life, then be sensitive to the fact that news like this may unbalance him. Surprise pregnancies can often frighten men because they feel that they have no control over the issue. With time, however, he can get used to the news, and you can both sit down and work out a plan. Still, there is a risk that he may not respond to the news of your pregnancy the way you had hoped. It is for this reason that women are encouraged to look toward motherhood with a can-do attitude, regardless of whether a man is in the picture.

Do keep in mind, however, that some men are delighted with the news of impending fatherhood, although they may not show it. It is certainly the mature man who recognizes that his life is irrevocably and forever changed. That insight alone will give any man pause for thought. So don't expect any literal jumping for joy, but don't necessarily expect a rejecting, condemning, or hostile reaction.

When the Test is Positive, but His Response Is Negative. As much as

you think you know a person, when you tell the father of your baby-to-be the news of your pregnancy, be prepared for anything. Some women who expect their mates to gush over the news are astonished to hear such hostile remarks as, "You must be nuts to think that I would marry you" or "How could you do this to me? I'll never give you a dime" or "Get an abortion, or get out!"

It's natural for you to feel ashamed or embarrassed initially that you could have gotten so close to someone and know so very little about him. After all, they say that the way a couple handles a crisis is what determines whether the relationship will strengthen or deteriorate. Even for engaged women, when a surprise pregnancy is announced to the fiancé, the reaction can be so strong that these women often wonder why they didn't see any red flags before. It's also very common for a man with whom you've had a brief sexual encounter, or even a long-term sexual relationship, to respond angrily with accusations that you were setting him up. You may hear comments like "It's not my baby," which can add to your twinges of humiliation.

What you need now is emotional support, not hurtful comments. Try to get support from friends, family, your clergy, a support group, your doctor, or friendly neighbors. Don't set yourself up for more pressure or stress by continuing nowhere conversations with the person by whom you became pregnant. But at the same time, be open to the possibility that he may grow to accept the news. It's not uncommon to hear men admit that at first they were negative when learning about their mate's pregnancy, but later committed to the undertakings of fatherhood.

On the other hand, if your partner insists upon your having an abortion, do not succumb to pressure or react hastily. Remember, this should be solely your decision.

Have You Ruined His Life?

My partner has accused me of trying to ruin his life by becoming pregnant. I feel so upset about this because it isn't true.

Don't let negative responses from your baby's father set you up for a guilt attack. You are not ruining anyone's life, and you are not responsible for all the damage that you may be accused of. This is simply one way that your baby's father can assuage his own guilt and feelings of not coming to terms with his responsibility in this pregnancy. This is not to say that he has to burst into a chorus of "Thank Heaven for Little Girls." He need not tell you he's overjoyed when it isn't true. But the man who, quite uncertain whether fatherhood is or is not for him, is willing to talk rationally with you about his feelings is exhibiting more responsible and mature behavior.

Should You Stay with the Baby's Father? No matter how rocky your relationship is, you may simply be staying with the baby's father because, although he was horrified at the news, he didn't rush out and catch the first flight to the coast. Counseling can help you decide whether to work it out or move on. But this can be one of the most difficult decisions to make because most women still buy into the two-parent ideal and feel they are being unfair to their children by not providing a father. At the same time, however, there is the knowledge that you deserve better, that this is no longer a valid reason to stay involved in a relationship that requires struggling and possibly an unfair amount of compromise on your part. And even if the relationship is terminated, this does not mean that there will be no involvement with the child's father. It just means that the traditional form of parenting most likely won't happen.

If Your Partner Leaves. The majority of single mothers by chance— those who became pregnant with a man they knew—have to deal with making decisions based on a future that does not include the father. Most men who exit a relationship after learning of their partner's pregnancy do so because they simply can't or don't want to deal with the responsibility. He may tell you that:

◆ He feels tricked.

◆ He wants you to choose between having an abortion or losing him.

◆ He is ambivalent and thinks you should do what you want.

◆ He feels he is not ready to be a father.

Unfortunately, these reactions are also the toughest to accept at first. But try not to become unglued at these comments. Believe it or not, in most cases, the father may have reasons for being unable to stay in this changing relationship that have absolutely nothing to do with you or your child. Don't berate yourself because, as hard as it is to make sense out of this, it's really not a personal attack on you.

THE EMOTIONAL ROLLER COASTER

Accepting Your Pregnancy. Even though you know that you are pregnant, you may periodically forget. Like many single women who claimed they wanted a child someday, you didn't expect it to be like this. Accepting the

news from your doctor doesn't necessarily mean that you have accepted the reality of being pregnant.

In a diary she kept during pregnancy, one mother reported how it felt when she first realized she was pregnant. No, it wasn't after the blue line appeared on the pregnancy test, or right after her doctor told her she didn't have food poisoning. It was one morning, months later, when she woke up and realized she was very, very pregnant. Wherever she went, it seemed that her blossoming belly arrived there first. It entered the elevator before she

---

IF YOU'RE PINING OVER YOUR CHILD'S ABSENT FATHER

Keep your thoughts positive! Try focusing on:

- Increasing your confidence, self-reliance, and peace. This time alone can be one of growth. A healthier set of emotions can emerge just as your child is growing strong and healthy inside you.

- Empowering yourself. Take this time to read up on your legal rights. Visit a law library and educate yourself. (Who knows, maybe some of this will filter through to your baby, the future lawyer!)

- Reminding yourself that you are part of a fast-growing group of women. If this is so unusual or weird, then how come almost 30 percent of all births last year were to single women? Don't let yourself forget that you aren't alone.

- Learning what can be changed, what must be accepted, and how you can grow wiser by recognizing one from the other. You may want to keep the lines of

communication open with the father, but if your expectations exceed what he is able to give, be careful. Don't focus on his life—work on yours.

- Taking a positive action or two. Channel your anger or grief into constructive areas like working out in an expectant moms' class, preparing your child's room, reading about childbirth, or taking daily walks.

- Knowing that there are just no guarantees in life. But the ability to rely on yourself is as close as you can get.

- Accepting your pregnancy. Visualize yourself and your child together. Do not think only about snuggling with an infant whose helplessness and total dependency might be overwhelming to you now. Think about having conversations with your child, teaching your child the skills you have mastered, and sharing in activities you enjoy. Imagine you and your child playing together at the beach.

did, complained loudly at any uncomfortable moves, and was the first to snuggle down at night. "That's when I knew I had company that was going to stay for a while."

Of course you already "know" that you're pregnant. After all, you've been told by more than one person, you've been shopping for maternity clothes, it's been all your mother thinks about, and you probably have satisfied some strange food cravings or eaten things you would never have let sit on your plate before. But one day the part of your brain that dictates how you respond or react to things figures out that you're pregnant, too, and all of a sudden you realize that you really are going to have a baby. The months before, you had been going through the motions of being pregnant because only your rational self knew that you were. The good news about the rest of you catching up with this information is that now you can accept your pregnancy and be comfortable with it and start enjoying it.

You don't learn to accept your pregnancy the way you might learn to ski by taking an intensive training course. Acceptance of this momentous life event is a gradual process requiring what you know in your head and what you have come to believe in your heart to come together. Every mother experiences this acceptance in a gradual way, no matter what her circumstances. You can help this process to take shape by talking about your pregnancy with close friends or family.

Try to Enjoy Your Pregnancy! There is an old saying that you can spot a pregnant woman even if you only see her from the shoulders up. She has a glow and a look of happiness. Well, the glow part might be true due to increased levels of pregnancy hormones causing a reddish tinge to the skin. But the look of happiness can vary from woman to woman.

Even women who have desperately tried to become pregnant don't always walk around with a beatific smile on their faces, especially if their pregnancy brings with it nausea, physical discomfort, and swelling and fluid buildup. And let's face it: Along with the dreamy thoughts of a sweet-smelling, cuddly baby to look forward to are sobering moments filled with such petty annoyances as constant urinating, miscalculating door openings, and those little hemorrhoids.

But at those times when you do experience that lovely fullness, the deep and soothing satisfaction that was never achieved through eating or smoking or even through sex will now seem to transcend all problems of life on earth. If you allow yourself to bask in the feeling, you, too, can be one of those women who accosts everyone who crosses her path and rattles on interminably about how her pregnancy is a period of intense joy and bliss. If you have any reservations about turning into a bliss ninny, don't let that stop you from enjoying what can be a very special period of your life. In fact, most women report that their pregnancy months allowed them to get away with varying degrees of aggressiveness they never would have dared before. For example, now you can demand a seat on the bus and still be looked upon as a lady. You can avoid waiting at restaurants, airports, crowded theaters, and even on line at grocery stores if you practice some subtle yet feminine grunting. Everyone loves a pregnant woman—

but only if she promises to deliver across town.

Telling People You're Pregnant. Tell the people capable of sharing your joy first. This might mean telling the warm-natured elderly woman who rides the elevator with you every morning, the chatty mailroom clerk with whom you've shared heartfelt stories, or the man behind the deli counter, even before telling your mother or sister. Why? The response of genuine joy from friendly acquaintances will fortify you against the negative reactions you may experience from others. And don't feel that only unmarried mothers receive negative reactions. Comments ranging from "How can you bring another human being into this sick world?" to "Aren't you concerned about overpopulation?" are pretty routine for married women, too. Of course, if your family would be overjoyed, tell them first.

I'm worried about telling my boss about my pregnancy. What do I need to know?

Know your rights and options before telling your employer. Choose an appropriate time, and share your plans with him or her in a calm and logical fashion. Your boss may not be overjoyed initially, but don't take this to heart. It may mean that he is concerned about your absence from the work force, as he would be with any productive employee.

If your boss cuts your hours, demotes you, or terminates you, and you believe it is because you are unmarried and pregnant, or simply because you are pregnant, you have

rights. The Equal Employment Opportunity Commission states that discrimination on the basis of pregnancy, childbirth, or related medical conditions constitutes unlawful sex discrimination. Women affected by pregnancy or related conditions must be treated in the same manner as other applicants or employees with similar abilities or limitations. This means that your boss cannot treat a married pregnant employee differently from the way he treats you. Contact your local Equal Employment Opportunity Commission office for more information on hiring, pregnancy and maternity leave, child care, health insurance, fringe benefits, and filing charges of discrimination.

Dealing with Questions About the Father. As you begin to "show," people will start asking you many questions. Strangers on the street will come up to you and pat you on the belly. Nothing in the world attracts more attention than a pregnant woman, except maybe a new baby.

You might be walking down the street one day, and an old acquaintance runs into you and says, "Congratulations! I didn't even know you were married!" Because many women find that the second trimester of pregnancy is the most stable, hopefully you will be relaxed enough to respond appropriately. You can either ignore the comment and smile graciously, or if you're feeling whimsical at the moment, you might remark, "Well, I had no idea that I was married either!" Depending on the attitude of the person commenting on your marital status, it would be best not to be sarcastic or defensive, but

COMEBACKS TO REMEMBER—JUST IN CASE

Some people make inappropriate remarks or ask rude questions of unmarried expectant mothers without realizing it. Here are some snappy comebacks to offhand comments about your situation:

"I just heard you were pregnant. I didn't even know you were married!"
"I'm not married. I hope I'm still pregnant!"

"Oh, you poor thing, carrying this baby all by yourself. How do you do it?"
"I think all women carry babies by themselves, don't they?"

"Are you sure you know who the baby's father is?"
"No less sure than you are!"

"How are you going to have a baby all by yourself?"
"Oh I'm not. I'm having it in a hospital with a doctor and pain medication … just in case!"

"You need to find the father of that child right now!"
"Well, if you really need him, here's his address."

"How? Check the lost and found?"
"But it took forever to get rid of him!"

"You need to find a father for that child right now!"
"Okay, but I didn't know I lost one."
"Great. Got any tips (and a flattering dress I could borrow)?"

"Don't you think it's cruel to bring a baby into the world without a father?"
"Actually, I think it's far worse to be brought into the world with the kind of men some children must endure as fathers."

"Isn't it selfish depriving your child of a father?"
"In this case I think I'm being generous!"
"No, he's getting a mother who really wants him!"

"You're not married! How'd you manage to get pregnant?"
(Don't answer this one unless asked by your child. In that case, tell him grown women can have babies and you will explain how when he reaches the appropriate age.)

rather to be straightforward, with an air of confidence. It is important to let people know that you would like their good will rather than their preaching, but at the same time, you need to accept that their beliefs may differ from yours.

Family Pressures and Other Realities

My mother and sister keep urging me to marry the father of my child, which is totally out of the question. For that matter, they would have me marry any man with a pulse, just to give my child a "name."

Sometimes parents and siblings are so unable to accept that you will be having a baby on your own they don't realize they are putting pressure on you. Resist their pushy yet well-meaning efforts by explaining that the baby's father and you are not able to have the kind of relationship a sound marriage requires. Share with your family your plans for taking care of this child on your own. Don't disclose everything, only what you are comfortable with. For example, if the father is to be involved in some way, you may wish to explain that he will visit once a week, or help with child support or medical bills.

Your decision to have a baby on your own is a new way of thinking to some families, making it difficult for them to accept the idea. In fact, you will need to practice being calm and rational because your news may be met with irrational behavior on their part. Don't try to change them, just seek their acceptance if not their tolerance. Be sure to let them know that you wish they would respect your decision, but if they don't, avoid threatening them with such retorts as, "If you don't accept my decision, then you'll never see the baby" or "I won't be part of this family anymore."

Requesting Assistance from Your Family. It's a good idea, early in your pregnancy, to determine the amount of help, if any, you can expect from your family. The important thing is not to make assumptions about what family members are willing to do to help. For example, just because your sister is great with her three little ones and really seems to enjoy staying home with them, this does not mean automatically that she will be happy to watch your baby so that you can return to work. She may be counting the months till she can go back to work herself, at least part-time, or she may be on "kid overload" and not want the responsibility of another baby to care for even during the day. Your mother may share your joy at the impending arrival of the baby, but that does not mean she wants to be on twenty-four-hour-a-day babysitting call.

Not surprisingly, many single mothers find themselves strapped for cash and consider borrowing money from their families. This is not necessarily the most promising start to an independent life, but it is not unusual. Many married couples rely on family members for financial support during the first few years, particularly if there are unexpected events like pregnancy or job layoffs. If your parents or other family members need convincing that your decision to become a single mother is the best one, you might want to investigate other loan sources before asking your family. If you must borrow money from your family, make a businesslike arrangement with them. Agree upon the amount, a method of payment, a payment schedule, and late charges, if any. This arrangement allows you your independence and keeps you in control of your own life.

If You're Resentful of Couples. A number of women who were in relationships that came to an abrupt halt because of the news of their pregnancy find that they often look at couples and wonder why their own partners couldn't be the kind to handle this. Combined with the rush of pregnancy hormones early on, the lack of grieving time for the loss could contribute to feeling angry or resentful of other relationships that appear intact. Since we hold so dear this image of the overjoyed new mother blissfully residing with her adoring husband, it's difficult to think realistically about the quality of the relationship the couples we spend so much time envying really enjoy.

The truth is, many couples are not as happy as they seem. In fact, a great number of women may actually resent the freedom you are enjoying in addition to the blessing you have brought into your own life with the expected arrival of your new baby. Rather than waste energy resenting couples whose happiness and contentment you envy, make the study of these couples a project. Decide what it is in their relationship that you envy or at least find desirable. Are these the very qualities and features that were missing in your previous relationships? Very likely. Decide, then, that you too deserve what you are witnessing and resolve to seek out these qualities in future relationships.

Letting Go of the Daddy Fantasies

I can't believe my baby's father isn't around during my pregnancy. He decided he couldn't handle it and left when I was barely in my second month. I get so depressed watching those baby food and diaper commercials and think of all that he is missing out on—the pregnancy, being part of the birth, holding the baby. How do I begin to deal with these feelings in a positive and productive way?

You need to be concentrating on yourself and not on how much fun the father is missing. He may be so much on your mind because the end of your relationship was so abrupt. It is natural that you still have feelings for

him and that you haven't shut them off like a faucet.

Maybe what you should do is get together with some girlfriends and give a good, old-fashioned wake to signal the final goodbye to your ex. Wakes are designed for tears and laughter, so you'll want to cry while remembering the good times and the bad times and laugh at some of the silly times. Some types of wakes are notorious for great food. Eat and drink (but no alcohol for you) and give away possessions of his you may still have that you no longer

---

THE DOS AND DON'TS OF HANDLING YOUR FEELINGS ABOUT AN UNINVOLVED FATHER

- Don't dwell on the idea that you are inadequate or that his rejection is due to a flaw in your character.

- Do think more about yourself right now and about your soon-to-be-born child. Your responsibility is to yourself and not to the emotional issues your child's father is contending with.

- Do ask yourself: Is it single mothering I am afraid of or am I really upset over the father's reaction and possible departure?

- Don't try to counsel the father, help him cope, or apologize to him.

- Do accept responsibility for the decisions you are making now.

- Do acknowledge your feelings of regret or disappointment. Until you accept the reality of this loss, you are flirting with depression.

need. But don't forget to keep some special mementos for you and your baby to share. The purpose here is to express your sadness at his departure, say what is in your heart, and then say goodbye. You need this ritual to allow you to go forward. A wonderful and exciting new part of your life awaits.

Your Changing Life Style. Naturally you are going to have concerns and worries about how the baby will affect your day-to-day life. This means you've thought realistically about how being a mother will profoundly affect every aspect of your life. If you are thinking of motherhood on your own, you need to be prepared and eager to embrace major life-style changes. Does this mean only coffee with the girls and never again any all-night parties? Will your conversations with your girlfriends change from talking about men to the best way to burp a baby? Will flannel nightgowns worn in celibacy replace romantic weekends in lingerie? No! What motherhood will mean is that in order to have what you want, you must prioritize and form a plan. Obviously your baby is a priority and so is your work or career. But day-to-day priorities can shift, sometimes as often as hourly. Like other single moms, you can learn to be superorganized—a talented manager who is fast on her feet. Don't worry about not doing everything—the myth of the superwoman was mercifully killed off by the excesses of the 1980s. Handle each day that comes along the best way you know how.

Worrying About Being a Good Mother. Almost all women worry about this. If you had a super relationship with your mother and believe she did a terrific job raising you, then you may worry that your abilities won't meet the standard she set. If your own mother was neglectful or uninvolved, you may worry that without a role model you will flounder. Or you may dread the "like mother, like daughter" scenario where you feel doomed to repeat her mistakes, or worse, magnify them.

True, there is no better teacher than good example, but keep in mind that your mother or whoever raised you lacked many of the resources we take for granted today.

If your mother or primary parent was neglectful or abusive, you've no doubt thought about how her behavior has influenced your life and your perceptions of self. Having this baby may partially be your attempt to right the childhood wrongs done to you by providing your child with the guidance and nurturing you never had. It's a worthy goal to incorporate these hard-won lessons into your parenting skills, but be sure to seek guidance, too, if you believe that you can create the happy family you never had and thereby magically erase the pain you experienced growing up.

I'm due in a few months and desperately pray that I can be a better mother to my baby than my alcoholic mother was to me.

Make every effort now to put your aspirations and hopes for this new life in perspective. If you haven't yet come to terms with the effects of your mother's drinking on your life, then it is time to join Al-Anon or seek out a therapist experienced with situations like yours. It's never too late to begin healing. In fact, you may benefit more from this recovery than you would have when you were younger, when you may not have been as motivated. If you feel you were basically neglected by an indifferent parent, find a support group for pregnant women run by your local mental health agency. By receiving comfort, support, and guidance now, you can sort out the past to ensure a good, strong start for your child.

Handling Last-Minute Anxiety About Your Decision

I'm about to become a single mother in a few weeks. As my due date approaches, I'm becoming more and more anxious. I don't know whether I made the right decision, or why I couldn't work things out with the baby's father. I alternate between feeling depressed and elated and am now worrying about the kind of mother I will be. I knew I did not want an abortion at thirty-six, knowing it might be my only chance to have a child, but now I'm confused. What's wrong with me?

Nothing is wrong with you. It's surprising that your obstetrician didn't alert you to all the emotional ups and downs that accompany the final months of a first pregnancy. New mom jitters are normal and are part of every healthy woman's first experience of motherhood, whether she is married or not. Any major life-changing event challenges us to question whether or not we are capable adults. You would have reason to worry more if you didn't experience these feelings and didn't place much weight on the importance of becoming a mother. Just remember that your hor-

mones leveled out for a while, and now that you are preparing for childbirth, they are getting ready for act three. So relax, it's not all in your head!

You also need to lighten up on yourself for not working things out with the father. There is no way that you can control the feelings and behaviors of another.

THE PRACTICAL ASPECTS OF YOUR PREGNANCY

Choosing a Practitioner. You have many choices when choosing a practitioner to accompany you during your journey through pregnancy and childbirth. But not all choices are good for all women. Choose what works for you financially, emotionally, and practically.

Family Doctor. Many women opt to continue under the care of their general practitioner or family practice physician. These physicians can be good choices for keeping you healthy through pregnancy and delivery because they know your health and family history, and you may already have established a rapport, so important in achieving physician-patient trust. The family practice physician has had more training in obstetrics than the general practitioner, but if you envision a fairly risk-free pregnancy, either one may be the way to go.

Obstetrician. Some soon-to-be-mothers feel they receive more qualified care from a board certified obstetrician. An obstetrician is considerably more trained in pregnancy and child-bearing than a general practitioner. You certainly want to consider an obstetrician if you have a high-risk pregnancy. The only drawback is that this will be a new relationship and you may or may not feel as comfortable with this doctor as you do with your familiar physician. You may have to shop around. Some obstetrical practices rotate who you see. You might see the same doctor throughout your pregnancy but then be delivered by whoever is on call. If this set-up bothers you, you might want to look for an obstetrician in solo practice, although there is no guarantee that any doctor will be available to you at the precise moment of your delivery. Your gynecologist might also be an obstetrician, but don't assume that this doctor delivers babies just because he or she has provided your gynecological care.

Certified Nurse-Midwife. Increasingly, many women are choosing a nurse-midwife for their prenatal care and delivery. In fact, hospital births under the care of midwives increased nationwide from 0.6 percent in 1975 to 4.4 percent in 1992. This choice has several benefits, not the least of which is lower cost. The personal touch is appreciated by many mothers, since the midwife's' only role is to work with mothers delivering babies. Most women using midwives feel they have the added support of someone who can answer all their questions. The potential drawback of using a nurse-midwife comes in the case where a routine delivery takes a turn for the unexpected and complications arise. You want to make sure that a resident physician is available for consultation with the nurse-midwife along the way and is available instantly should you suddenly need care the nurse-midwife cannot provide.

Telling Your Doctor about Previous Abortions

I had two abortions in the past five years, but I have not told my doctor. I already feel uncomfortable being a single mother and worry that he will misjudge me as promiscuous or irresponsible. Should I tell him in case this could affect my pregnancy?

Most likely, having had two abortions, if they were performed properly and early in the first trimester, will have little or no effect on your pregnancy. However, it is best to tell your doctor so he will have a clear picture of your medical history. Additionally, now is the time to learn whether this doctor has the compassion, patience, and understanding necessary to be what you require in a physician. If you feel he is judgmental of your life style, or disapproves of decisions you have made, then you should find another doctor, one with whom you feel comfortable and are able to be honest. Trust your feelings. You will be sharing one of the most precious periods in your life with this person. For the next few months he will become very important to you and it is essential that you have a rapport with him.

IF YOU'RE AN OLDER SINGLE MOM

Welcome to one of the fastest growing groups of single mothers, woman over forty. A woman who postpones childbearing has often achieved goals like advanced degrees or enviable careers. Such accomplishments often give the older single mothers a financial cushion and greater degree of job flexibility. These assets, combined with well-honed organizational skills, give the typical older single mother great advantages.

Many such older single mothers report that the decision to choose single motherhood often means that career, hobbies, and travel have simply taken a back seat to a desire for the fulfillment and satisfaction of a child. The husband hunt may no longer interest or excite the accomplished single mother to be.

Despite the many advantages to postponing motherhood, there are certainly trade-offs. Fertility starts to drop after thirty-five, so getting pregnant may be more difficult than for a younger woman. Genetic screening, such as amniocentesis, is the standard recommendation for woman over thirty-four. The older the mother the greater the likelihood of complications in pregnancy and delivery. Once, however, an older mother becomes pregnant and genetic problems have been ruled out, older mothers without pre-existing health conditions usually do not require special prenatal care and have healthy babies as often as younger woman. In fact, recent studies have shown that the age of the mother alone is not as big a risk factor as had previously been assumed.

Woman considering a later-than-usual-in-life pregnancy should do some advance planning. See your physician for a thorough check-up to identify and treat any medical conditions that could interfere with a healthy pregnancy and delivery. Make every effort to get yourself in peak physical condition. Of course, stop smoking. Some physicians recommend taking prenatal vitamins and folic acid supplements while trying to conceive. Discuss this option with your physician as part of your pregnancy planning.

Prenatal Diagnosis. There are a variety of specialized tests your doctor may order if he or she has reason to be concerned about possible genetic defects. You may also request tests that you feel are warranted given your personal circumstances and private concerns. Make sure that you give your doctor a thorough health history so you two can determine together the right course of action for you.

Maternal Serum Alpha-fetoprotein (AFP) Screening. A simple blood test that is often done before recommending amniocentesis, this screening detects elevated levels of AFP in the mother's blood, indicating a possible neural tube defect (spina bifida) or brain deformities. Extremely low levels can suggest a risk of Down's syndrome. However, because this is a screening only, further tests are usually administered.

Amniocentesis. This is usually performed on mothers over thirty-five, primarily to determine if the fetus has Down's syndrome. Amniocentesis can also identify neural tube defects, metabolic disorders, and genetic and inherited disorders including hemophilia, Tay-Sachs disease (found mainly in Ashkenazi Jewish couples whose ancestors can be traced originally from Eastern Europe), and sickle cell anemia. But because Tay-Sachs, cystic fibrosis, and sickle cell anemia traits call for matching gene pairs—that is, one gene from the mother and one from the father—they are rarely passed on, so few babies are born with these disorders. Testing for these diseases is recommended only if either or both parents have a good chance of testing positively, or if you've already had a child with genetic defects or have close family members with hereditary disorders.

This is how amniocentesis is performed. A long, slender, hollow needle is inserted through the abdominal wall directly into the uterus, where a small amount of amniotic fluid is withdrawn. To avoid poking the baby, the doctor is guided by viewing the image generated on a TV-like screen through ultrasound.

Your physician may perform amniocentesis as early as fourteen weeks into your pregnancy and as late as the nineteenth or twentieth week. Earlier testing is currently being analyzed and refined because the cells from the test require about four weeks of cultivation. If defects are found and the mother wants to terminate her pregnancy, this allows her to terminate the pregnancy at an early stage.

Ultrasound. This test uses sound waves bouncing off the uterus and fetus, allowing visualization that is far safer than X-rays. Used widely on women of all ages, ultrasound can verify a due date by pinpointing the age of the fetus, in addition to seeing if you are going to have twins, diagnosing fetal size and movement, and determining the general condition, health, and sometimes even sex of the child.

Ultrasound is performed by lightly massaging a clear gel onto the abdomen, after which the doctor moves a metal device around the area until an image of the baby is seen on a nearby monitor. This is a totally painless procedure, aside from the complaint some women have of how cold the smooth metal is on their bellies.

Chorionic Villus Sampling (CVS). This test is usually performed between the eighth and twelfth week of pregnancy. It is becoming more popular than amniocentesis because it allows for an earlier, and therefore less potentially traumatic, termination of pregnancy when abortion is called for. CVS can detect thousands of disorders caused by defective genes or chromosomes. Hopefully, it will be performed more and more in doctors' offices, but presently it is performed in medical facilities such as hospital outpatient centers.

Depending on when you have the procedure, it can be done transvaginally (through the vagina) or transabdominally. In the transabdominal method, a guide needle is inserted through the abdomen and uterine wall to the placenta, where another smaller needle passes through the guide needle, withdrawing a sampling of fifteen to twenty cells to be examined. A local anesthetic is used, and, as in amniocentesis, ultrasound imaging is used to determine the exact location of the fetus. Although not risk-free, if performed at a good testing center the test is almost as safe as amniocentesis. The transvaginal procedure is done the same way, except that the cells are taken via the cervix rather than through the abdominal wall.

Other Tests. New tests are being developed constantly. Your doctor will advise you of the best route to take.

Fibroids and Age

I have always had fibroid tumors but was told since my early twenties not to worry because they usually only affect older women who are trying to get pregnant. But now I am thirty-six and pregnant with my first child. This is adding to my fears that maybe I am too old to have a baby.

You are not too old to have a child and most likely will have no problems. Most pregnant women with fibroids carry to term successfully. Fibroids occur most often in women over thirty-five, and because so many older women are now opting to have children, fibroids during pregnancy are reportedly becoming more common—almost two in every hundred pregnancies. Occasionally, certain developments can occur, so it is best to discuss this with your physician and alert him or her to any treatment you may have previously had for fibroids. Generally, the worst thing most women can expect to endure is discomfort or pain from the pressure of the fibroids around the abdominal area. This usually is not a reason to worry, but you should still report every symptom to your doctor, particularly if you notice any irregularities such as spotting.

When There's No Man to Dump the Litterbox

This sounds silly, but one thing I worry about since my partner left is who will clean the cat litterbox while I am pregnant. I heard that cats and cat litter cause a disease that can harm the fetus. My partner gave me the cats and now that he is gone, I don't want to have to give them up, too, since they're part of my family. How would I know if I have the disease?

You don't have to give up your cats, but you do need to exercise caution even though your chances of contracting toxoplasmosis, the name of the disease in question, are low. First of all, if you have lived with your pets awhile, you have probably already contracted the disease (more than half the population of the United States has been infected) and most likely have built up an immunity. Also, fewer than one woman in a thousand gets the disease while pregnant. However, toxoplasmosis can cause serious fetal damage, so prevention is the best cure.

- Try to delegate the cat-care chores to a family friend, relative, or neighbor. If you must remove the cat litter yourself, wear rubber gloves and be sure to wash thoroughly afterwards.

- Change the litter daily, and be sure that if the cats go outside, you don't allow them to defecate in sandboxes or garden areas.

- Better yet, don't let the cats out, because other animals can cause your cats to contract the disease.

- If you'd feel better, have the cats tested to see if they have a current infection. If the results are positive, board the pets or have a friend keep them for the duration of your pregnancy.

- If your cats tested positive and you feel you need to be tested, call your

EIGHT TIPS FOR A HEALTHY PREGNANCY

1. *Seek quality medical care.* If you are over thirty-five, or have special medical problems such as diabetes or high blood pressure, be sure to choose an obstetrician who has experience with your particular condition. Even if you are the perfect picture of health, be sure to start spoiling your child now by getting the best prenatal care possible.

2. *Eat right.* Whether or not you suffer from nausea or are starving every second, it is important to maintain a diet high in complex carbohydrates, green and yellow vegetables, fruits, calcium-rich foods, and a moderate amount of protein and iron-rich foods. Although you need more calories when you are pregnant, your general eating patterns should be the same as your basic healthy eating plan. It is not difficult to add an additional 300 to 400 calories daily, but be sure these are not empty calories. Seek the advice of your prenatal practitioner. Especially if you are overweight, underweight, or very young and still not fully developed yourself, be sure to follow your practitioner's instructions for the right amount of daily caloric intake for you. And always be sure to drink at least 64 ounces (2 quarts) of fluids daily, preferably water, to flush out toxins and waste, help reduce the chance of urinary infections, and minimize bouts of constipation.

3. *Lose the image of the perfect pregnancy.* Don't buy into myths that all pregnant women are happy, fulfilled, or have a certain glow. Be open to having good days and bad days, such as you or anyone else who is human would experience. The less anxious about your pregnancy you are, the less risk you will endure.

4. *Don't worry, be happy.* There comes a time in life when you simply won't be able to get everything done. It's called "motherhood," and pregnancy is a practice run. Stop trying to accomplish everything you think must get done and start focusing on yourself and your new baby. This means giving up the idea of being superachiever-career-mom and relaxing a little into the role of normal pregnant woman!

physician right away. But remember, your chances of having toxoplasmosis during your pregnancy are slim.

- Remember that toxoplasmosis is also transmitted through uncooked meat and unpasteurized milk. Avoid these, and be particularly sure when eating out that meat is well-done or the very least medium-well done. Save the steak tartare for a future dinner date!

Is It Safe for Me to Use an Electric Blanket?

I told a friend recently that now that my partner and I have separated, I'd have to buy an electric blanket to keep my toes warm this winter. I was sort of joking, but she was pretty serious about my not using an electric blanket while pregnant. Why?

(continuation)

5. *Keep in shape.* Avoid gaining weight too fast, and consult your prenatal practitioner about beginning an exercise program. If you've never exercised before, now is a good time to get started. Walking, cycling, and swimming are good picks for a novice, and be sure to pick up a good exercise video or book for expectant mothers. Unless you are proficient at some rigid workout routines, never start an exercise program during pregnancy that includes rigorous training such as jogging or weightlifting.

6. *Beware of your responses to feeling abandoned by the absentee father.* Worrying excessively about him can make you emotionally susceptible to a difficult pregnancy. You're having this baby without him, and you will do just fine!

7. Avoid drugs, tobacco, and alcohol. Most bad habits can be eliminated through a program that helps you replace the bad ones with good ones. Quitting abruptly works fine for some, whereas a gradual withdrawal works better for others. For example, if you are a smoker and find out that you are pregnant, it is certainly best to quit, but don't feel that you must accomplish this cold turkey. Because we now know that tobacco companies have been adding addictive chemicals to the nicotine in cigarettes, making it that much harder to quit, stopping suddenly may cause more stress and anxiety than you need.

8. *If you are addicted, get help, now!* If you suffer from a serious addiction, seek help through a twelve-step program such as Alcoholics Anonymous or Narcotics Anonymous, or see a counselor. Attend meetings that are smoke-free. Never use a nicotine patch to quit smoking while you are pregnant. Never replace any drug with another substance unless it is approved by your doctor.

   If your drug use or drinking is chronic and/or if you refuse help from qualified experts, twelve-step programs, or certified alcohol or drug treatment centers, then you would be wise to consider postponing childbearing until you have this disease under control.

There are three reasons not to use electric blankets. First, they have been linked to potential fetal damage or miscarriage that scientists believe is caused by the electromagnetic field they create. Second, electric blankets and even heating pads can increase your body's temperature, a factor that is associated with fetal damage. Finally, who needs the cords and extra energy usage? Why not get yourself a plump down comforter instead? You can also try warming the bed with the electric blanket first, but be sure to turn it off before getting in.

Sexual Desire During Pregnancy

I'm seven months pregnant and all of a sudden am feeling particularly frisky, but not in the athletic sense. Why do I feel such strong sexual desires when there is currently no one in my life, and the last person in the world I would want to reconnect with is my baby's father, who disappeared the minute he learned I was going to have a baby. I'm looking forward to having my child, but I'm concerned that I'm having these feelings because I haven't had a love interest for so long and may be missing male attention. Also, would masturbating cause any damage to the baby or me?

Masturbation will not cause any harm other than rocking the baby, since orgasm causes the uterus to contract. But don't worry, it won't be enough to induce labor. Still, if you are concerned, talk to your doctor. There is no question he or she has not answered many times before. Do not worry that your doctor will be shocked or think less of you.

Your feelings about missing male companionship might be why you are feeling amorous, but most likely it is physiological. During pregnancy, the hormonal changes that occur cause increased blood flow to your pelvic region. This results in engorged genitals, which can be responsible for the heightened sexual desire you are experiencing. Conversely, women who have had sex during these stages of pregnancy sometimes report a feeling of incompleteness due to a bloatedness that persists after orgasm, leaving them feeling they didn't quite have one. The pressure on the bladder caused by the baby's position is another reason for that sensual feeling you and many other women report.

Special Concern: If You Miscarry. If you start to miscarry or suspect that you

are about to, you should of course call your doctor immediately. At this vulnerable time in your life, it is also crucial to have someone with you. Most doctors will give your body a chance to complete an early (first-trimester) miscarriage on its own before intervening. However, you can lose a dangerous amount of blood during even an early miscarriage, and may end up needing emergency medical attention. If you can't have someone with you, your best bet is to go to the hospital.

PREPARING FOR CHILDBIRTH

For Women Only

I'm due to have my first baby in a few months and am really nervous. The father with whom I had a long-term relationship decided parenthood wasn't for him, and he left. Although this is probably for the best in the long run, I get so depressed when every half hour I see a commercial for our local hospital's birthing unit. They always show an impassioned father devotedly coaching his tearful yet happy wife through labor. Why do I think this is the only right way to have a baby?

You are watching too much TV if you've seen your local hospital's spot more than once. Not only is it unnecessary to be coached by your mate, but according to French obstetrician Dr. Frederick Leboyer, fathers have no place in the delivery room. He believes that this experience should be limited to women only. In *Birth Without Violence* (Random House), Dr. Leboyer writes, "Pregnancy and birth are incomprehensible experiences for a man. For the mother, they are like a mystic voyage, a pilgrimage which men cannot join."

Listen to this advice from a man who knows that his place in the delivery room was that of physician only. You probably have more women than you realize available to you on this momentous day. Think about having your sister, your mother, or your best friend accompany you. By all means, you should select a birthing coach so you are well prepared to participate fully in this most miraculous "women's only" experience. But even if your birthing coach is a man, this will still be your voyage.

Feeling Less Alone on the Big Day

Although I realize that motherhood is a lifelong process, right now I'm concerned with making the big day, meaning the birth, as stress-free and pleasant as possible. Is there any way for a single mom who has a lot of family support but still feels alone to feel less alone?

This may sound as though it is coming out of both sides of the mouth, but in a sense you are not alone and yet you are. Even though childbirth is experienced by billions of women, binding them to one another in an enormous spiritual sisterhood, other emotions that accompany this process are yours alone to feel. Aside from the level of pain (and don't let anyone kid you—if pushing out a baby were painless, childbirth would be an activity that could be accomplished while napping!), the flood of feelings that can gush out along with the baby can be as individual as is each new life's fingerprint.

The one issue that may make you and other birthing single mothers feel

---

IF YOU'RE FEELING ALONE

Consider taking along photos of famous single mothers to the hospital or birthing facility when you are ready to deliver your baby. One new mom who tacked up pictures of famous unmarried women who had given birth said that looking into their faces served as a distraction from the pain and was reassurance that she wasn't alone in this. Author Maya Angelou; entertainers Tanya Tucker, Gypsy Rose Lee, and Isadora Duncan; actresses Farrah Fawcett, Glenn Close, Jessica Lange, Ingrid Bergman, Catherine Oxenberg, and Catherine Deneuve; and Cleopatra and Sir Isaac Newton's mom, Hanna Ayscough, are just some of the women who were single when they gave birth!

---

alienated, particularly if you are giving birth in a hospital or medical facility, is not being the better half of the happy, cigar-offering new dad in the waiting room. And with the introduction of men in delivery rooms more than twenty years ago, this image of the happy father seems more apparent. But there must be many women giving birth without men in the delivery room. Last year, 53 percent of all first births were to single women, and if you combine the number of military wives and those who separated early in pregnancy, millions of women in this country give birth without the assistance of a husband or mate. In fact, millions of American women have given up on having the obligatory male who is ready with suitcase in hand and a ride to the hospital. Many modern-day women take a taxi or have a friend or family member drive them and send someone to their place later to collect all the necessities.

Childbirth Classes. Lamaze childbirth classes are a must, whether you want to experience this process with or without pain medication. Above all else, they teach you what to expect and how to comfort yourself. Don't worry that the class will be crowded with cooing couples named Biff and Muffy. Hospitals and childbirth educators report single mothers attending classes in record numbers.

You can attend Lamaze classes with your mother, sister, other family member, or friend, or ask your doctor or childbirth instructor to pair you up with another pregnant single mom. Your instructor might also be willing to demonstrate techniques with you as her partner. Most would love to have a free mother with whom to work to present the lessons in a more practical, hands-on manner. Don't overlook male friends or relatives, too. Some communities have "childbirth companions," usually volunteers who work through hospitals or clinics. Your local women's commission, nurses association, or new mother support group can recommend someone. Your childbirth educator can also recommend a nurse/midwife to help deliver your baby. You should also consider hiring domestic help, a godsend to any new parent, but especially the new single mom. Having someone come to your home and perform tasks such as light cooking and cleaning and perhaps even help you care for yourself and your new baby is worth it if you can fit it into your budget.

Don't overlook the opportunity to record the big occasion. If you are so inclined, find a friend who would like to come along and videotape or take pictures. It is best if this person is not your birthing coach or companion.

Your coach will be busy enough attending to your needs without the added responsibility of being resident photographer.

MANAGING YOUR LABOR AND DELIVERY

If You Go into Labor in the Middle of the Night

I'm terrified that I will have contractions in the middle of the night with no one around to help me and I'll end up having the baby alone or, worse, dying alone during childbirth. I chose single motherhood, but I sure envy those who have a man around to pack the bag and get them to the hospital on time!

Relax. Even if you begin having mild yet inconsistent contractions in the middle of the night, you have a long way to go before you approach active labor, when the contractions are strong, occur three to four minutes apart, and last for up to a minute.

Besides, if you have been to childbirth classes, you will know that the first stages of labor, called early or latent labor, can last a few hours or even a couple of days. Rather than panicking and calling everyone you know, follow these simple steps:

◆ Try to go back to sleep because, most likely, this will be the most rest you will get for a while, and you need it. If you can't fall asleep, but feel comfortable and can get some rest, do so. Watch TV in bed or listen to music. Think pleasant, dreamy thoughts about your new baby.

◆ Do something relaxing or positive. If your bed feels like it's made of live wires, rather than lie there wide awake timing your contractions and watching the clock, get up and make a cup of tea and review your pregnancy and childbirth literature. Or if that makes you too anxious, try reading, putting last-minute touches on the baby's room, or organizing your post-pregnancy wardrobe.

◆ Put your coach on alert. When a reasonable hour approaches, and you know your childbirth coach most likely will be awake, call to give her a status report, but don't make her drop everything and come running. Plan how and when you will stay in contact over the next few hours, and be sure you both have clear signals on how to reach each other.

◆ Know when to begin to time your contractions. If your contractions begin coming a little closer than ten minutes apart within a half-hour time span, you should begin timing them.

How to Know When to Go to the Hospital. If you experience mild to strong contractions that range from five to twenty minutes or more apart and last up to half a minute, you are probably entering the second stage of labor, or active labor. The second stage of labor is when you should contact your doctor or nurse-midwife and let him or her know how far apart your contractions are, how strong, and the duration of each contraction. If you are with your labor coach, have her help you gather up your last-minute belongings and head to the hospital or birthing facility if the doctor says it is time. Even if your contractions are sporadic and not that strong, if your membranes rupture, it is time to go to the hospital.

You should be in the hospital by the time your contractions are about three to four minutes apart and last up to one minute. Have your labor coach begin assisting you in your breathing exercises. Try to remain calm and patient, because even though the rest time between these contractions grows less and less, this stage can last up to an average of three hours, and in many cases a lot longer.

What to Do When You Get to the Hospital. If you are not preregistered, you will need to do this now. You will be asked to fill out forms, sign routine consent releases, and answer a number of questions about when you last ate and how far apart your contractions are. This is the time to tell the staff that you are a single mother and introduce your coach or friend or relative who is accompanying you. If you have no one with you, be sure to ask if you can talk to a nurse who can remain with you during your labor and delivery. In fact, talk with the nurses at the nurses' station and see with whom you feel most comfortable and who is available to assist your doctor.

The Transitional Labor Stage. This is the most exhausting phase of labor, with contractions that can be so overwhelming, it's not unusual to beg for death, as Murphy Brown did in her memorably hilarious delivery before 4 million viewers. You should already have had medication (if requested) before this stage, but nevertheless it's not unusual to feel that you are becoming unglued, frustrated, literally maddened, or insane. Hang in there, listen to your coach, maintain your breathing pattern, and if at all possible, try to visualize relaxing images and think about how lucky and close to finally having your baby you are!

Here Comes Baby! A flood of feelings accompanies the actual birth of a baby, feelings that may be so new and strange you may be overwhelmed by them. You may look at your newborn and experience sensations beyond comprehension. The intensity of the emotions surrounding what went on with your former mate—love, hate, loss, grief or relief; the intimate connection to a man you've never met if you were donor inseminated; the unexpected passion you may feel for your doctor—these are normal, common feelings expressed by nearly all single women at the moment their child enters the world. It's okay to feel overwhelmed, and you have permission to react by crying, laughing, remaining motionless, or doing whatever else you feel compelled to do. It's okay, too, not to feel anything or to experience conflicting feelings. Don't

be disappointed if you don't feel an overwhelming surge of love for your new baby such as you may have seen in the movies. Many women don't experience this, so don't worry.

Congratulations, Mom. You've done it, and you've done it well!

Will Cesarean Birth Lead to Less Bonding?

I feel like such a loser. First, my baby's father left because he "wasn't ready for this." Then, after months of trying to prepare myself for motherhood, there I was in the delivery room with coach, video camera, and support only to find that I had to have an emergency C-section. It's not so much that I didn't experience "natural" childbirth. I worry that my child and I won't bond as completely as we would have done with a vaginal delivery.

A baby does not have to travel through the birth canal in order to bond with its mother. Mothers who were under sedation while giving birth, those who have adopted infants, and women who have undergone C-sections have been able to bond successfully with their babies.

Try to remember that bonding is a process that develops over time, not something that is accomplished in minutes. In fact, many experts believe that real bonding doesn't occur until late in the baby's first year. It takes time for you to accept and feel warm toward this little stranger who made his grand entrance in such an attention-getting manner. Keep in mind, too, that the concept of bonding was introduced to mainstream culture sometime during the 1970s. Does this mean that people who had children before the 1970s never bonded? Surely mothers and children have bonded successfully for millennia before this word became popular and regardless of the events surrounding the birth.

Your dreams of the perfect child you were carrying for nine months would normally culminate in the perfect birth, but you need to stop thinking that it didn't go right. Look at the positive side of C-section. For one thing, babies born via C-section don't emerge with squishy, funny-shaped heads as many do who travel through the birth canal. So start thinking that the perfect birth is

---

THE DOS AND DON'TS OF PREGNANCY AND CHILDBIRTH

♦ Don't engage in emotional psychodramas with your baby's father. You need peace of mind and even some levity if possible. Try lightening up a bit.

♦ Do try to get as much rest as possible. You'll need your energy later for childbirth, for the first few weeks at home with baby, and, in most cases, for the next eighteen years!

♦ Do prepare now for whatever you need so that you can devote about six weeks to yourself and to your brand-new baby. Whether it is working out arrangements with your boss, stashing away some extra cash, painting, papering, or whatever else you need to do to get your house in order, don't procrastinate thinking you'll be home with baby anyway. Do it now, especially if you have bouts of nervous energy that accompany the latter stages of pregnancy.

♦ Do make arrangements to take care of things—crib set-up, diapers, food, nursing utensils, outside help—so you can come home with your little newcomer and, without too much distraction, begin the incredible bonding process.

♦ Don't assume that bonding is like all those nursing ads you see in popular magazines. Bonding is a process, not a conclusion or completion of an event.

♦ Do expect some startling emotions to play on you. Remember, your hormones are having a wild party, particularly right after birth, so it is normal to laugh one moment and wail the next.

♦ Don't think that because the father is out of the picture, you are alone. Link up with a pregnancy or new mom support group. Just having the phone numbers of women you can call can ease some of your anxiety and anticipation.

♦ Do talk to your baby before it is born. Rub your hands over your tummy (even if you are not showing yet) and tell your child how you feel. Saying, "I'm scared to meet you but excited, too," or "I hope I do the right things" brings immediate comfort.

♦ Do keep a pregnancy journal or diary. In fact, this can be the starting point for journaling as a lifetime activity. Keeping a diary does not have to command the attention a full-time career does but it should be as habitual as brushing your teeth, eating properly, and having basic health checkups. Because the fluctuations of emotions are so pronounced during pregnancy and shortly after giving birth, chronicling your feelings in a journal not only keeps you in good mental health, but gives you an opportunity to begin a "friendship" with your child.

one where mother and child survive to come home to a new life together.

If You Give Birth to a Baby with Physical or Developmental Challenges. The birth of a baby with serious medical problems suddenly thrusts you into an unfamiliar, intimidating world. In fact, a number of women have reported that they became single mothers right after their baby was born because the father was unable to deal with the challenges that lay ahead. The best way to rise above the confusion and crisis is to arm yourself with knowledge. Learning all you can about your child's condition is also a way to cope emotionally with the feelings attached to having a baby born with medical problems, whether or not you were prepared.

♦ Familiarize yourself with the Patients' Bill of Rights and become an advocate for yourself and your child.

♦ Don't be shy about asking questions of medical, educational, and other professionals. While it is difficult to get second opinions in a life-threatening situation, research the best care for your child regarding long-term conditions.

♦ Work through the hospital social workers when you need extra support in dealing with medical staff or in locating resources.

♦ Research facts and medical data thoroughly. Demystifying your child's condition will also help you rise above the fear.

♦ Take care of your own physical, emotional, or spiritual needs. It is the only way to stay strong for yourself and your child.

♦ Do whatever you have to do in your own heart and mind to love and accept your child for what she or he is. Your attitude will imprint your child's self-image for the rest of her life.

♦ Do not let a medical, therapeutic, or educational opinion lock you and your child into a life sentence. Be open to new possibilities. In the world of medicine and special needs children, things are always changing.

FILLING OUT THE BIRTH CERTIFICATE

Most hospitals will ask you to sign the birth certificate only hours after you have given birth. As if you didn't have enough to worry about, now you're wondering how to fill in the space asking for father's name. For most women giving birth, this can be an extremely emotional time, particularly if the father has fled.

If the father filled out legal documents acknowledging paternity before the child's birth, you can put his name on the birth certificate even if he is not at the hospital. Many hospitals, following laws in their states, forbid you to place the father's name on the document without his being present or without your furnishing a legal, notarized document stating that this man is indeed the father.

Just because you cannot legally, in most states, put the father's name on the birth certificate without his agreement is no reason to go to pieces if the space is left blank or the word "unknown" is printed there instead. You know who he is, and it really doesn't matter what it says on the birth certificate. Your child is a legitimate little person having the same rights as anyone else. Don't ever let anyone tell you any different.

ESTABLISHING PATERNITY

Even if your child's father has offered little or no support and probably will remain uninvolved in your child's life, you would be wise to get him to acknowledge paternity if you plan to seek child support. You should not try to establish paternity if you are sure you do not want the father involved in your lives, emotionally and financially.

The least traumatic way to deal with establishing paternity is to have a talk with the father of your baby months before you are actually faced with signing documents. Hopefully, he will acknowledge that he is the baby's father and feel comfortable with this information. Ask him if he plans to take some responsibility for this child and to what extent. If he's hesitant to respond, say that you will give him some time, and suggest that you talk again. Assure him that you realize this is a big load to drop on him at this time and you can understand that he needs time to get used to it. For more information on establishing paternity, see Chapter 19.

8

It's Me and You, Kid

STARTING OUT

Regardless of how your journey into motherhood began, the first few weeks and months are destined to be filled with many unexpected challenges. No matter how much reading you've done, there isn't much short of plain and simple experience that can quite prepare you for the demands of this job.

Care of your infant may be your first real experience with sleep deprivation. You soon find out that the "all-nighters" you pulled in high school or college were child's play compared to the relentless demands of a crying infant at 2 A.M. It is a strange and humbling experience to be awake and functioning at an hour when the rest of the world is asleep.

And then there is the advice. Naturally, you heard your share during the pregnancy. Now you find that everyone has an opinion about something. Perfect strangers feel free to tell you that you are doing something not quite right or, more likely, disastrously wrong. Some of this unsolicited advice can be quite helpful, of course, but other little tidbits can make you wonder if you're up to the challenge of motherhood.

Although you've most likely prepared for the first few months after childbirth, you may have overlooked some things that need attending now. Potentially tough decisions like establishing custody need to be considered now, as do other simpler yet equally important parenting decisions such as how you will feed your newborn and if you want your baby to use a pacifier. Whatever you need to do to make your initial period with your new bundle more enjoyable, do it now.

NAME THAT BABY!

While many new mothers are thinking of cool names for their babies, unmarried moms are wondering what last name they should use—their own or the baby's father's.

Legally, you can name your child anything you want, even if it's Marilyn Monroe or Elvis Presley (just remember you can't put the father's last name on the birth certificate without his consent). Even though many women give their babies their father's last name, here are some reasons for using yours.

- Men normally have their greatest contributions named after them. Bridges, cities, airports, highways, buildings, and schools are often named after the man or men who had the most input in the project. You contributed the most work in bringing your child into the world—carrying and caring for him or her for nine months, going through labor and childbirth, and in almost all respects, undertaking the majority of the parenting tasks. It only makes sense that your greatest accomplishment should be named after you.

- Historically, children (and wives, for that matter) were considered the legal property of the husband. With the strides made in women's liberation and the increase in women as breadwinners, this is a totally outdated assumption. Not that you should ever adopt an attitude of *owning* your child, but since you are the responsible parent, your child is yours.

- Consider what happens if you get married sometime in the future. Stepfamilies become awfully confusing when a woman remarries and has another child with her new partner. There are stepfamilies today in which one mother has three children living with her, all with different last names.

- Certain cultures operate under a matriarchal lineage, meaning that all children are assigned the mother's maiden name. Among these cultures are Native American groups such as the Navajo. These cultures experi-

ence fewer struggles in which children are used as bargaining pawns, experience less trauma, and have an overall minimal amount of paperwork when a marriage dissolves. In these families, such as those in many Spanish-speaking countries, it is assumed that children remain with the mother if the marriage is terminated.

- Keeping track of a family tree would seem simpler, too. Most maternal relations tend to remain in a child's life, such as grandparents and siblings on the mother's side, but the majority of divorces estrange not only the father, but often his family, too. If all children were named after mom, we could connect to our roots more easily, not to mention with more accuracy. We usually know who a child's mother is, but we don't always know who the father is!

- A nice gesture would be to use the father's name as the child's middle name, giving a biological or even a spiritual connection to the birth father, but avoiding all legal implications. Remember, whether or not a child has the last name of his father has nothing to do with the father's rights, his obligation to pay support, or his responsibility toward the child.

CHECKLIST OF MUST-HAVES FOR BABY'S FIRST YEAR

Be sure you have everything you need on hand before you return home with your new bundle. You'll want to make the transition from single-with-cat status to single-with-child as smoothly as possible. Scrambling around for last-minute necessities is something you don't need to be doing. Here are items that you should have on hand:

◆ *Car Seat:* Many hospitals will not discharge the baby to you if you don't have one, because child protective car seats are mandated by law in many states. You can buy a used one, preferably one that converts from infant to toddler use, or call your local health department about loaners or rentals. Many communities offer programs making car seats and other items available for temporary use for a nominal fee.

◆ *Umbrella Stroller:* These are cheaper and easier to maneuver than the larger, fancier types. Remember, your child's most immediate goal is to get those little legs moving fast, so he can run away from mommy! Don't invest a fortune in something that is necessary but has limited usage.

◆ *Snugglesack or Papoose Carrier:* A must-have—you're a single mother who will not have another pair of arms available to her as often as your partnered counterparts. Slings and cloth carriers that strap the baby to your body are not only comforting, but will free up your hands to conduct business as usual.

◆ *Bassinet:* If you can't find an affordable crib right away, a bassinet is perfect, particularly if the baby will be rooming with you for a while. But shop around or seek a loaner—some bassinets are so fancy that you might end up spending more than you would for a standard crib. Babies outgrow bassinets quickly!

◆ *Crib:* Make sure that the crib you use meets all safety standards, particularly if it is a hand-me-down or a garage sale find. If you are buying a new crib, investigate the kind that later converts into a child's bed. Visit juvenile furniture stores or look through catalogs to get ideas.

◆ *Playpen:* Find one that is as portable as possible. If you introduce your baby to a playpen early for brief periods, it can provide a welcome respite for both of you.

◆ *Diapers, Creams, Changing Supplies:* Consult your pediatrician or health-care provider about the products and procedures he or she recommends. Ask for samples, if available. Keep a stash on hand, but try not to use too many unnecessary preparations.

◆ *Layette Items Like Blankets, Undershirts, Sleep Sacks, and Simple Shirts:* You will probably receive many of these newborn items as gifts because people enjoy buying them. Newborns are changed frequently, so you will want a supply on hand. Friends will also offer hand-me-downs since babies grow out of these items quickly. Accept what is offered to you. You can always return or pass on what you did not use.

◆ *Pain Reliever/Fever Reducer:* Open a bag and tell your baby's doctor to load you up with samples of recommended products. This doesn't mean you will use them all, but they're nice to have in an emergency.

◆ *Thermometer:* A rectal thermometer is a must. Every phone call you make to the pediatrician will begin with the question "What is your baby's temperature?"

◆ *Bottles, Breast Pump:* If your baby is relying on your breast 100 percent of the time, you will still need a breast pump to keep some frozen milk on hand, just in case. You'll also need bottles for you or a sitter to feed baby the milk you pump.

IF YOU HAVE A CESAREAN

The number of births by Cesarean section has been rising steadily in the United States for the past several years. Sometimes the decision to have a Cesarean is made on the spot, with no opportunity for you to prepare. For this reason, it is helpful to know what to expect if your doctor tells you ahead of time that you will be delivering in this way or your labor becomes unexpectedly complicated and a Cesarean is needed.

If you have a Cesarean, you will be in the hospital for a couple of extra days, need more medication, feel more tired, and generally be more uncomfortable than you expected. You will need to take extra care of yourself, so it is important to enlist the help of a friend or relative.

You will probably not be rooming with the baby at least for a day or so after the birth. Cesarean-born infants are often placed away from their mothers for at least several hours after birth for observation. This is because these infants have a higher probability of respiratory difficulties after birth. Your little one may also be groggy from the anesthetic. You will not be feeling all that terrific yourself after a Cesarean, so neither of you really will be up to the long-anticipated moment of being introduced in person. Do not worry that this delay will in some way prevent a loving attachment between you and your child. Very shortly, you two will be madly in love!

Here are some tips for getting through the first several weeks:

◆ Find some way to get help with household chores, like shopping or cooking. These may be too difficult while you are recovering from this kind of birth.

◆ Try to walk around your living room, however, even on your first day home. Mild exercise like this will speed your recovery.

- Breastfeeding is an especially good choice for you. Keep the baby right beside you and enjoy the convenience of not having to prepare or heat formula. Save your energy for important activities like cuddling.

- You may feel especially alone and sad following a Cesarean, particularly if your partner left you. Try to seek out other mothers who have had this experience. Ask your doctor or contact your childbirth instructor about support groups that might be right for you.

THE BENEFITS OF BREASTFEEDING

The benefits of breastfeeding for the baby are well known, but did you know that:

- Breastfeeding will help you lose those pregnancy pounds. About ten pounds of the weight a pregnant woman gains is to support milk production after the baby is born. Breastfeeding uses up those fat stores.

- Breastfeeding flattens your tummy. The hormones involved in breastfeeding stimulate uterine contractions so that your abdomen regains its pre-pregnancy flatness more quickly—good not only for your self-confidence but terrific for helping you fit back into your "pre-baby" wardrobe.

- Breastfeeding is convenient and cheap. There are no bottles to sterilize, no formula to fix, and no rushing home because you forgot to bring a bottle.

- Breastfeeding will benefit you and your baby even if you are only able to do so for a month or six weeks.

WORRYING ABOUT DOING THE RIGHT THING

I am getting a lot of advice from neighbors and friends about caring for my newborn son. Even though I've read every book on infant care, they act as if I can't hack it because I couldn't stay married. So now I'm worrying that I will make a mistake and won't be doing the right thing.

Don't worry about making mistakes. Accept the fact that you will make mistakes. An important part of being a good parent is the ability to learn from both your mistakes and your successes. It doesn't matter whether you are married or not—people love to give new mothers advice, so don't take it to heart.

Your most important source of information is your baby himself. He will be your best and most trusted teacher. When you are on the right track, he will be relaxed and his face will be calm and content. If you are on the wrong track, he will thrash around. His cry will be breathless and piercing. He may turn red, and his limbs may stiffen. All these signs will give you a message, and in a short time you will know exactly what the message is. The "right" answers come not from a doctor or a book but rather from your baby.

BABYPROOF YOUR HOUSE NOW!

Many single mothers like to make their home safe for baby as part of their preparations during pregnancy or may already have taken some safety steps, especially if their house is a welcome destination for the children of friends and relatives. Begin immediately if you have not already made your home safe for baby. Start by sitting on the floor of each room so that you can see your home just as your baby does. This will open your eyes to many potential hazards. Remember to use common sense. There is no substitute for supervision and, if something seems dangerous, it probably is.

Be sure to:

◆ Install safety latches on all low cabinets and drawers.

◆ Put plastic wrap and plastic bags where your baby cannot find them. Plastic bags can cause your child to suffocate. Get into the habit right now of tying your plastic bags from the dry cleaner into knots before disposing of them.

◆ Get rid of the water and the buckets. Babies are fascinated by water, so never leave a filled or even partially filled bucket unattended. A baby can drown in one inch of water.

◆ Give your house plants a review. Many household plants are poisonous. Keep all plants on high shelves or hanging so that they are out of your baby's reach. Know the names of the plants you have so that if your baby ever eats part of one, you will be able to provide the information that poison control centers need to help you. Better yet, dispose of all poisonous plants.

◆ Small items are a big worry. Babies put everything in their mouths—this is how they explore the world. To prevent choking, keep small knick-knacks, bowls of candy or nuts, and anything else with small parts away where baby cannot reach them.

◆ Look over your curtains and blinds. Keep window-blind and curtain cords and even long telephone cords out of the reach of your baby. These can cause your baby to strangle. Tie these cords securely out of your baby's reach.

◆ Cigarette lighters should be banned from your home. Babies and young children are fascinated by these devices. They are colorful—a wheel turns and makes sparks, and fire comes out. What's more, these fit easily into little hands. Ask your guests to leave their lighters at home. Smoking around young children poses a health risk, so your best bet is to decide from the start that your home will be a "No Smoking" area.

BE PREPARED FOR EMERGENCIES

Whether you are starting back to work or just venturing out for a little free time, you need to prepare in case of emergency. Find out from your pediatrician which hospital you should take your baby to if there is an emergency. Make sure you know how to get there because, most likely, you will need to rely on yourself to drive.

If you do not have 911 service in your area, post in a "can't be missed" location in big easy-to-read print the numbers of ambulance services equipped to handle emergencies involving children. Post also the number of your local poison control center and your pediatrician's number.

Baby-sitters need to be able to reach you at all times. A beeper is ideal for single mothers, as are cellular phones, particularly as they become less costly. You might hint for these items as baby gifts.

Leave written authorization with baby-sitters that allows your baby to be treated by medical personnel if you cannot be reached. Some state laws do not permit a child to be treated without parental authorization. Given that you are the only parent, this is especially important.

Record on paper and leave with all baby-sitters any allergies your baby might have, the immunizations he has received, and any medication he might be taking. Carry this record with you also at all times.

HELPING YOUR BABY LEARN TO SLEEP THROUGH THE NIGHT

By about four months of age, most babies do not need a late-night feeding. You can probably enjoy a six-hour break, more or less, when your child begins to skip her nightly feedings. As important as not needing a late-night feeding to sleep through the night is, your little one must also be able to cycle between deep and light sleep several times. This development will be especially welcome if you are back at work or are just anxious to have things in your life settle down a bit.

Sleep experts have found that all of us cycle between deep and light sleep, coming up to a state of light sleep called REM (rapid eye movement) every ninety minutes or so. Every three to four hours we come into a more active state, closer to waking.

A REM cycle is characterized by very individualized patterns of activity. As a baby comes into light sleep, she is likely to cry out and to thrash around. Sometimes, if she is on her stomach, the resistance of the bed calms her and subdues all this activity. If the baby is on her back, she is more likely to be startled, move her legs and arms around, and become upset and cry.

If the baby has developed a pattern of self-comforting, such as finding her thumb or blanket, or if she finds a cozy, comfortable position, she'll settle down. Some babies like to maneuver themselves into a corner, where the pressure on their head reminds them of what they experienced in the womb. Active babies obviously have a harder time settling themselves down and often manage to get themselves to a fully awake state. If this happens, the baby will want to be held and comforted, and you will want to respond to this need.

Most babies can settle themselves during the ninety-minute stage of REM. It is at the three- to four-hour cycles that the baby has a harder time getting her behavior under control.

Some babies cry out as if in fear or pain. They aren't awake, but sometimes their own activities awaken them. If you become part of the process by which your baby comforts herself back to sleep, it will be more difficult for your child to develop these skills independently. If you rush in and pick her up every time she whimpers during the night, it is unlikely she will sleep through the night any time soon.

When There's No Mate to Help on Sleepless Nights. One of the biggest complaints single mothers have about going it alone with an infant is not having someone else to get up when the baby awakens all through the night. But if you keep in mind that it is mostly mothers, married or not, who arise with the sleepless baby, particularly if they are nursing, you'll realize that lack of sleep is a common symptom plaguing all new mothers.

Should Baby Cry It Out?

My brother, who will most likely be my baby's only male role model, recently said that the reason I feel compelled to tend to my four-month-old every time he fusses is because we were neglected as kids. He told me that because I didn't want to repeat this pattern, I was allowing my own needs to interfere with my baby's development. How do I know the right thing to do? Honestly, I could use a full night's sleep, but I refuse to let my baby cry it out like some people suggest I do.

The fact that you are able to listen to your brother and consider his words indicates that you have come a long way from what must have been a difficult and painful childhood. And it's true that childhood experiences might have an impact on choices you make as a mother.

But you are right not to let your baby cry it out. No baby should ever be allowed to do that. Crying it out does not teach your baby anything except fearing that his mother will desert him at the very moment he needs her the most. It is important to understand that there is a difference between letting a baby cry until he falls asleep from exhaustion and allowing a baby to learn to settle down and be comforted on his own. Helping your baby become independent at night will make him feel good about himself. For that reason. getting your child to sleep through the night is an important goal.

If Your Baby Cries Round-the-Clock

Sometimes when my fussy baby is crying nonstop and nothing I do is helping, I have fleeting thoughts of abandoning the baby or wish I had never had her. Of course I would never actually leave my baby for an instant and I am so thankful to have her, but I'm so burned out from the hours of crying that I can't help thinking such bad thoughts. Is something wrong with me?

Nothing that a long period of rest and relaxation wouldn't cure. Howling babies can make even the most patient mother have feelings of intense frustration. Only a dishonest mother would never admit to having thoughts of getting rid of the baby.

Single mothers particularly, because they don't have the availability of another set of arms to help comfort the child, find constant crying hard to tolerate. Don't feel guilty that you have had such thoughts because it is your very honesty in facing these feelings that is working for you. Researchers have proven that excessive crying by an infant affects everyone around him by causing many common symptoms of stress like quickening pulse, a rise in blood pressure, faster heartbeat, and breath holding.

To survive what may at times seem like round-the-clock crying with the least amount of stress, you need to understand why babies cry and find methods of comforting not only the baby but yourself, too.

Why Babies Cry. Crying is the first form of baby talk. This is the only way babies can communicate their needs. Sometimes babies have crying spells for absolutely no reason at all. In time, you will learn to interpret when your baby's cry means he is hungry, needs changing, or is simply tired or colicky. Most newborns will cry for up to one and a half hours daily! So don't take it to heart if your baby seems to be crying a lot. It's probably nothing to become overly concerned with. But if crying is constant, where no source of relief is in sight or baby appears to be in pain, call your pediatrician.

Ways to Manage the Crying

Answer the call. Remember, your baby is talking to you. See what she wants, even if it is just to be cuddled.

Determine the cause. Is baby wet or uncomfortable being swaddled in too many blankets? Or is she simply hungry? Maybe your newborn needs burping or gentle rocking to relieve him of a colicky tummy.

Assess yourself. Are you tense or upset? Babies can pick up on the emotions of the parent, so take a moment to regroup and relax yourself. Chances are this is exactly what you both need.

Be consistent. Feedings and changing times should be at the same time every day, if possible. Sometimes a break in routine can cause excessive crying.

Rock together. Rocking can be soothing to you both. The motion of rocking back and forth in your favorite chair is very sedating for both mom and newborn.

Go for a drive. The drone of the engine while you take a brisk cruise in the car often will lull baby to sleep.

Seek a change. This means for you and the baby. Hand the baby over to another person, grandma or grandpa, a friend, neighbor, other relative, or baby-sitter. Get a little fresh air for yourself and take a walk.

Protecting Against SIDS. Sudden Infant Death Syndrome, otherwise known as SIDS, causes seemingly healthy infants to cease breathing, almost always during sleep, resulting in death. Mounting evidence has linked SIDS to a stomach-down sleeping position. Let your baby sleep on his back or snuggle him between soft, wedge-like sleep positioners. Sleep cushions designed for this purpose support the baby's back yet allow free movement of arms and legs. If your baby suffers from severe reflux (spitting up), sleeping on his tummy is still recommended. Your pediatrician is your best source of information if you have specific questions or concerns. Never, ever put soft pillows in a baby's crib!

DEALING WITH POSTPARTUM DEPRESSION

Nearly two-thirds of all new mothers experience the blues, or postpartum depression (PPD), after childbirth. Sometimes the depression starts within days; other times it doesn't kick in until a few weeks later. Often the postpartum blues can last up to a couple of months. In the most severe cases, 2 in 1,000, the depression becomes incapacitating enough to require intensive professional help.

Prevention and knowledge are always the best medicine. Being prepared for the emotions you might experience right after childbirth can help you understand that the symptoms of PPD are experienced by many women and the effects are not lasting. For example, it is perfectly normal not to feel bonded to your baby from the first instant or even not to feel immediate love for your newborn. It is also perfectly normal to feel a little disappointed that the baby looks somewhat lopsided or is a shade of red you have never observed before. You might have secretly wished for a girl and feel sharply disappointed about not having a daughter.

The guilt and anxiety over these feelings are sometimes enough to trigger a period of mild depression for some postpartum women. These debilitating symptoms can include uncontrollable crying, feelings of self-doubt, guilt, anxiety, insomnia, persistent nervousness, and lack of concentration. Knowing what to expect can often prepare you enough so that you can ride out a brief postpartum storm.

If you experience any of these symptoms of PPD, talk out your feelings with a trusted friend or family member. When you are depressed, it is difficult to muster the energy you need to seek out help. Family members and friends can help by giving the support and direction needed.

If your symptoms are unbearable, get help promptly. Don't be ashamed to ask for help—you are not the only woman who has felt this way. Don't worry about mild symptoms of depression that last less than two weeks. However, if months pass and you feel there is no hope of ever returning to the old you, you need to see a mental health professional, such as a psychologist or certified social worker. Treatment may include progesterone therapy, psychotherapy, antidepressant medication, and/or attending a support group.

If you feel like hurting your baby but have not become violent, call a parents' hotline in your community. There will be counselors to talk to you and reassure you that you are not alone in your feelings. If you feel violent, call a child-abuse hotline or go to the nearest neighbor for help. Get professional counseling immediately at your local mental health center. Don't be ashamed of your feelings; this is not the time to worry about what others think but about the potential for inflicting damage. Those who seek help fast avoid the possibility of compromising the relationship with their baby and regain new confidence as a good mother.

WHEN THE WORKING MOM HAS A PROBLEM WITH SEPARATION

I have returned to my full-time job after being home with my six-month-old son. He seemed to handle the separation well. I am a wreck. I find it difficult to separate from him and am reluctant to put him down for the night. Any suggestions?

Having been away from the baby all day, it is natural that you find it hard to separate from him at night. It is okay that you need your baby at night. It means you love him and are attached to him as mothers should be. Many working mothers find that warm, intimate rituals at night, such as rocking in a favorite chair and singing a cherished lullaby, and setting aside special time in the morning for snuggling and cuddling, helps. You feel like an emotional wreck because you are dealing with so many different feelings now. Concentrate on savoring every delicious moment with your precious baby boy.

COPING WITH THE NIGHTTIME BLUES

There are many theories for getting baby to sleep. Two somewhat oppos-

ALERT!

Depression reduces your capacity for nurturing, which may have lasting effects on the baby. If your doctor dismisses your concerns about postpartum depression, know that recent studies show that primary-care physicians miss the diagnosis of depression more than half the time. Seek the help of a qualified mental health specialist if your symptoms are overwhelming or persist for longer than two weeks.

Be particularly prepared for symptoms of postpartum depression if:

- You have a personal or family history of depression.

- You have pronounced symptoms of premenstrual syndrome (PMS), which include irritability and depression.

- You experienced a complicated pregnancy or a difficult labor and delivery.

- You experienced childhood sexual abuse.

- You are already under stress. Woman who were abandoned by a mate or are dealing with unresolved issues about the baby's father may be more susceptible to depression.

ing and much-studied approaches are 1) to work toward developing consistent routines and regular schedules, which allow babies to settle into good sleep-wake patterns. Sometimes this means letting the baby cry for gradually increasing periods of time. This approach is based on the work of

Richard Ferber, M.D., Director of the Center for Pediatric Sleep Disorders at Boston's Childrens Hospital. Dr. Ferber believes that sleeping alone is a crucial step in learning to separate without anxiety, and 2) "shared sleep," a term coined by William Sears, M.D., referring to what has also become known as "the family bed" where you let the baby sleep with you. While these approaches seem to take opposing tactics, their ideas are disseminated with the well-being of both baby and mother utmost in mind.

Both approaches have strong proponents and have also come under sharp criticism. Proponents claim "Ferberizing" helps create an independent child and ultimately is easier on the mom, especially if a new relationship or marriage comes onto the scene. Opponents of the "Ferberizing" method of approaching baby's sleep say that the idea of letting the baby cry goes against a mother's basic instincts and extracts too high of a toll on her. Proponents of the Sears method point to strong bonding and quite simply the best possible night's sleep for Mom, leaving her more refreshed and able to face the challenges of motherhood. Opponents of the Sears method have philosophical problems with the baby sharing the bed, and they have been joined by recent medical studies that show dangers of injury and even suffocation when a small baby sleeps in bed with one or more adults.

Only you can ultimately come up with the best solution for you and your baby. But from birth to six months, do what you need to do to get through the night! Expect to be exhausted and frazzled for these are truly zombie months. Do what you feel is right for you. Discuss sleeping arrangements with your pediatrician or health care provider. Make informed choices together to keep your baby's safety and well-being paramount.

Many mothers have found it comforting to set up a cradle, crib, or bassinet within arm's reach of your bed. You can comfort your baby if he or she needs it, you don't need to go far if your child needs a middle-of-the-night feeding, and you can sleep easily knowing you are right there if your child needs anything.

These are important considerations and you need to check out your options and make the decisions based on your personal beliefs, preferences, and life style.

THUMB SUCKING AND BRACES

My six-month-old daughter sucks her thumb when she is tired or frightened or upset. Her baby-sitter tells me that I had better start saving money for braces because she will definitely need them. I get no child support and I can't start worrying about braces when paying for child care is expensive enough. Should I be taking her thumb out of her mouth? What about a pacifier?

Don't worry about not having money for braces right now. First of all, there is little difference in the need for braces between children who suck their thumbs and those who do not. Most children who need braces require them because of what happens when the tongue is thrust against the upper teeth or because of heredity.

THE DOS AND DON'TS OF STARTING OUT WITH YOUR NEW BABY

- Do carefully consider your options regarding paternity and custody and act accordingly. Delay may subject you and your child to danger, hassle, or interference. Know that in many cases the decisions you make will be final.

- Do accept the help that is offered to you. Just because you are a single mother does not mean you have to be isolated. In fact, your first lesson in successful single motherhood will be well learned if you find yourself increasingly comfortable asking for the help you need.

- Do plan ahead of time and purchase or obtain the baby items you will need. You have no idea now how complicated a trip to the store becomes when you need to take the baby with you.

- Do make your pediatrician your trusted guide to issues related to your baby's health and development.

- Don't take all the advice and criticism too seriously. Listen to what is said, take what you can use, and disregard the rest. Remember, however, that the most valuable parenting skills and advice are often gotten informally from sources you might least expect.

When Thumb Sucking Is a Problem

Thumb sucking is a symptom of emotional problems:

- When a child appears to be withdrawn

- If a child sucks intensely a great percentage of the time

- When a child is over the age of five or six

Discuss this situation with your pediatrician and consider counseling to determine why your child's thumb sucking is persisting.

WHEN BABY SAYS "DA DA"

I am a single mother by choice in the sense that I knew that the baby's father was not going to remain in the picture. He did visit a few times after my son was born but has not been around since. Now my baby is gurgling his first words, and I can't understand why he is saying "Da Da." Does this mean that my baby is looking for Daddy? I'm confused and wonder if all babies know that they should have a father.

Don't worry. This is one of the first stages in normal speech development. The babbling sounds you are hearing are your baby's attempts at communication and have no meaningful association to your baby. They are just easy sounds for him to make because they involve simple movements of the tongue. So relax, and enjoy conversing with your chatty baby.

9

Taking a Closer Look at You

YOUR PHYSICAL AND EMOTIONAL HEALTH

One of the big messages contained in this book is that the real expert on living successfully as a single parent is you. The day-to-day challenges of ordinary living supply the substance of real life, no matter what your circumstances. Every day you are parenting, growing, and working at your career brings experiences that you learn from. There aren't too many mistakes, only lessons. Yet as single parents, we get so caught up in the mundane details of our own lives that often one activity, responsibility, or chore seems to blend into another, leaving us to wonder if there is any time for us. This section deals with creating a framework or a foundation from which to make more selective choices about how we choose to spend our time and about evaluating how effective these choices have been.

IT ALL BEGINS WITH POSITIVE SELF-ESTEEM

It's no big news that many of the problems we experience, the poor choices we make, or the less-than-ideal situations we find ourselves in result from negative feelings within ourselves, or what is now popularly referred to as lack of self-esteem. Self-esteem is a word we hear all the time. The trouble is that there are as many definitions of self-esteem as there are talk show hosts talking about it.

Here is one of the best definitions of self-esteem, developed by the California Task Force to Promote Self-Esteem and Personal and Social Responsibility: "Self-esteem means appreciating my own worth and importance and having the character to be accountable to myself and to act responsibly toward others."

There is much substance in the words "appreciating my own worth and importance." Our present society does little to honor or support the task of nurturing our children. Single parents often lose sight of the fact that society's devaluation of parenting holds true for all families, whether headed by one parent or two. However, coupled with the unpleasant associations people often unfairly make about the task of single parenting, it is easy to see how feelings of self-worth and importance can be diminished.

You must continue to remind yourself, however, that these feelings come only from you and not from anyone else. Think about it: People see themselves through the eyes of others and behave in the way that is expected of them. When a person is told repeatedly that he is horrible, chances are he'll begin to believe it and to behave that way. Likewise, a person who is continually praised and reinforced positively will display a "can do" attitude.

The only expectations that you should strive to meet are the ones that you create for yourself. If you rely upon others to make you feel worthy and important, you relinquish your vital sense of who you are. Specifically, when you allow other people's views to alter your opinion of yourself, you risk losing the ability to care for yourself. And it's only when you can care for yourself that you can effectively care for your children.

CULTIVATE FEELINGS OF SELF-WORTH

How do you acquire feelings of self-worth and importance within your-self? Think of the word "cultivate" and about all that is involved when a garden is cultivated. Gardens, whether spectacular or modest, need time, nurturing, and attention to flourish. Individuals who treat themselves with patience, love, and encouragement are called self-nurturers. If you neglect yourself or fail to take into account your own needs and desires, it is a lot like a garden with inadequate water or sunshine. There certainly won't be much yield from that type of garden, just as an individual may be lacking the necessary energy with which to be productive at work or to nurture children.

That is why so many successful, emotionally healthy people typically give themselves little rewards or treats to acknowledge their accomplishments. Try it yourself: Even simple things like patting yourself on the back or scheduling some extra private time to read a magazine or go for a walk can increase your self-respect and admiration for your achievements. Or tape affirmations to your mirror, refrigerator, headboard, or desk. Look at them often and say them out loud upon waking in the morning, retiring at night, or whenever you need a boost.

Another self-esteem enhancer is to reach out to others. The more self-assured you become, the more you will be able to become an integral and visible part of your community. Volunteer in a local organization like the PTA or volunteer emergency squad, or reach out to other single parents by initiating a support group. Helping others creates a win-win situation: Your self-esteem gets fed, enabling you to give more, and so the cycle continues.

YOUR PHYSICAL AND EMOTIONAL HEALTH

Your health is your most important asset. Although heredity plays a part in determining whether or not you are predisposed to a certain illness, basically this is an area of your life that you can largely control through proper diet, adequate exercise, routine medical checkups, and stress management. Given all the media attention focused on health issues, research studies with conflicting results that confuse us, or the latest exercise craze or fad diet, it is natural to feel uncertain and over-whelmed. Don't let every new finding or fad influence you or cause you to abandon healthy habits that have worked well for you.

Diet. Is there a library big enough to store all the information that has been written even in the last couple of years about diet, nutrition, weight control, and energy? In addition to all that has been written about nutrition, the com-plicated relationship that many people, particularly women, have with food is becoming increasingly recognized. It's the same set of choices as with drugs or alcohol. If food or other weight-related issues are controlling issues in your life, get help fast!

But even if we don't fall into the "need-help-with-food" category, many of us, given the hectic schedules and multiple demands we face, still need to be reminded of a basic fact: Food fuels our bodies. And eating nonnutritious, empty calories is not going to get us very far. There are people who aren't particularly emotionally involved with their automobiles but still are very careful about the quality of fuel they put in their car. Yet how many of us know of similar types who wouldn't think twice about wolfing down candy bars and pastries during the middle of a time or energy crunch?

There are many healthful and bene-ficial food choices out there that are actually cheaper than unhealthy, processed, or ready-to-eat foods. Simply stated, juice is better than soda. Fruit is better than chips. Legumes, beans, and grains are far better and cheaper than fatty meats and dairy products.

Taking control and balancing your eating habits is especially important to single mothers. We need to be a shade more attentive than other parents, par-ticularly those in a two-income house-hold, because our financial and time constraints can lead us to make poor food choices. The fast food outlets can seem a welcome haven to the weary single mother. Processed and prepared foods can seem a blessing when, in truth, they offer us very little of the nutrition we need.

Does this mean Pop-Tarts kill? Does eating leftover pizza for breakfast put you in psychological reverse? Of course not. Just be sure to maintain a balance in your overall eating patterns.

Exercise. Only twenty to thirty minutes a day of steady aerobic activity three days a week is enough to supply us with all the benefits we need for our physical and emotional well-being, according to most physical fitness experts. Many single mothers have found that it's not too difficult to slot a half hour in the morning for aerobic exercise, like low-impact or aerobic dancing while watching a video or listening to music. Vigorous walking and old-fashioned calisthenics like the ones your high school gym teacher used to make you do are also effective. Running is terrific for some, but may put stress on your joints. Whether you run or walk, an added benefit if you miss adult companionship is exercising with a buddy with whom you can chat. Ask other moms in the neighborhood about joining you for early morning or evening walks. Just be cautious about where and when you do this. Stick to public places that are well lit and safe.

Work Out with Your Kids! Physical fitness is not only a prescription for enhancing your physical and emotional well-being, but it can also be a great opportunity for parent and child to share quality time. Some single mothers take their children along to the local track or park. While mom runs or power walks, the children can play and she can still keep her eyes on what they are doing. Other single parents rent videos and work out with their kids in front of the television, or take a brisk evening walk before supper. The point is, you can find some activity to share with your child while benefiting from exercise if you decide that it is a priority.

The Secret to Jump-Starting Your Day. Wake up before the sun and do whatever it is that feeds your soul. Sound impossible? Or just plain crazy? Well, it works and here's why: When we try to carve time out of our day to fit in personal prescriptive routines like working out, meditative exercise or prayer, bathing and primping (and we don't mean a quick shower!), or studying or creating art, the knowledge that this activity needs to be performed lingers long and hard in our brains. Emptying our brains of tasks to be done by recording them on paper has always been a terrific stress-management tool. But imagine how accomplished you can feel not having to check a calendar or appointment schedule to see when private time can be slotted in because this has already been done and your day is now ahead of you.

There is no question that those folks who walk five miles in the dark morning, meditate while the moon is still out, or write the great American novel (or self-help book) while the kids are still asleep are the ones who get their goals met. Feeding your soul at 5 or 6 A.M. or even earlier, if necessary, makes you feel that the day hasn't gotten ahead of you. When the sun comes up and you've already coddled yourself with those extra, but oh so necessary, perks, you'll be ready to meet the challenges of your daily life head on, with a concentrated, intense dedication that is found in the attitudes of those who live fully in the present.

So go to bed early tonight, and wake up one step ahead of the rest of the earth!

Stress Management. This section won't elaborate on popular stress-reduction techniques (biofeedback, yoga, reflexology, deep breathing, and visualization) because we are bombarded with this information in every magazine and self-help book that deals with living in the modern world. Also, this information is not any different for single mothers than for those who are married or divorced, male or female, gay or straight.

What is unique to single mothers is that their stress seems so built in, so inherent to their life style, that the thought of taking time to learn how to reduce stress can cause more stressful worry. Tell a group of single mothers that you have discovered the latest stress-management technique and they will collectively refrain, "But where will I find the time?" So first, before we deal with stress, we have to understand our stress. And because we think of our stress as coming at us from every direction—job stress, money stress, parenting stress, family stress, and relationship stress—the sources seem endless. The more the sources of stress, the less possible it seems that we can begin to grapple with this fundamental life issue. Managing stress, however, is really a matter of "knowing your enemy." When you realize that stress results from having too many demands on too few resources—in other words, everyday life—you'll realize that all stress, no matter what the source, is essentially the same.

Following are common symptoms of stress, along with some simple cures:

Constant Fatigue. Make sure you get enough sleep. Some people require only six hours of sleep a night coupled with a twenty-minute catnap during the day, while others require a full eight hours or more at night. Figure out what sleep pattern works best for you, but remember that the quality of sleep is more important than the amount of hours actually slept. Most people find that sticking to a sleep schedule, going to bed about the same time and rising about the same time each morning, is of great benefit. If you have bouts of insomnia, ask a health-care professional for some tips on how to improve the quality of your rest. Many single mothers have addressed this problem successfully using homeopathic or herbal remedies.

Just as your children need time to relax and make the transition to bedtime, so do you. Find out what works for you. Some mothers enjoy a relaxing cup of tea or the opportunity to read uninterrupted. Even five minutes of slow, steady, deep breathing while sitting up or lying down is beneficial, since it slows your pulse rate and adds to your general feeling of well-being. Organize for the next day before bedtime, but never, ever take your problems to bed. The one thing everyone deserves to have is deep, dark, delicious sleep.

Frequent Illness. Be sure to eat nutritious foods and stay away from energy zappers like sweets and highly processed foods. Limit consumption of heavy or rich foods and alcoholic beverages. Don't smoke, or at least cut down, and avoid other smokers, since exposure to second-hand smoke contributes to frequent sore throats and upper respiratory infections.

Discuss with your physician taking a daily multivitamin that has at least 500 milligrams of vitamin C and, if needed, supplement your diet with a good B-complex vitamin that is especially potent in vitamins B6 and B12. Keep in mind that antioxidants are very important in your diet since they have been proven to combat the risk of getting many diseases, especially cancer. Eat lots of foods rich in beta-carotene (dark-green leafy vegetables such as collard greens, kale, spinach, turnip greens, mustard greens, and Swiss chard, and yellow-orange fruits and vegetables such as carrots, pumpkins, sweet potatoes, cantaloupes, peaches, mangoes, and papayas); and rich in vitamins C (asparagus, broccoli, cabbage, brussels sprouts, cauliflower, green peppers, melons, oranges, tangerines, and strawberries) and E (almonds, hazelnuts, peanut butter, vegetable oil, sunflower seeds, and wheat germ). The best part is that most of these foods are inexpensive!

Depression. Working out for thirty minutes three times a week will not only give you more energy, but can ward off depression, since the brain releases endorphins when the heart rate is elevated for that length of time. In addition, exercise can help prevent you from coming down with common ailments such as colds and helps keep your immune system functioning optimally.

If depression persists, despite eating properly, taking vitamins, and exercising regularly, seek out a support group or talk with a counselor, friend, or family member. If your depression seems overwhelming or you alternate between depression and extreme hostility and anger, see a psychologist or psychiatrist. Some types of depression are a medical condition and require treatment by a qualified physician. In addition, most cities and counties have resources and services for women through hospitals and community agencies. Check the listings in the local phone directory.

Anxiety About Time Constraints. Deal with conflicting or competing demands in a realistic manner by prioritizing and compromising. Never rely on your memory to remember chores or tasks that must be completed—write everything down for daily or weekly scheduling. Learn how to say no! Establish a routine that is highly organized, even if it borders on rigidity. You'll avoid retracing your steps and other time-wasters like searching for your child's lunchbox or looking for your shoes or stamps. The occasions when you break the routine to indulge in something frivolous will seem like an exquisite pleasure. Teach your children how to manage and organize their time.

Understanding Chronic Stress. The stress of living with children can be all-consuming when you are not getting emotional support from friends, family, and community. In fact, a 1994 study conducted by researchers at Duke University Medical Center found that women who work outside the home and who have children living with them produce high levels of chronic stress hormones, day and night.

By measuring the neurohormones epinephrine and norepinephrine (more commonly known as adrenaline and noradrenaline) that are responsible for the "fight or flight" response in our bodies, the researchers found that women with chronic stress have higher levels of a hormone called cortisol. Here is how this works: Normally epi-nephrine and norepinephrine dissipate as rapidly as they initially kick in. For example, when you quickly swerve to avoid a car accident, you feel the adrenaline rush for a few seconds. The excess is excreted in urine, but if very high levels are produced, cortisol is released to prolong the effects of the other two hormones in the body, there-by causing chronic stress—up to 36 percent more when compared with childless women.

few resources, we must recognize it as a fact of everyday life. Coping effectively with stress involves not so much isolat-ing its sources but, more importantly, looking at stress in a global way and try-ing to increase the resources available to cope with its inevitability.

Don't take this as a message that it is unhealthy to have children, when the message of this book is that children can be the greatest joys of your life. But it does mean that single mothers in par-ticular need to learn how to manage their stress by first understanding that they may be at a greater risk for higher levels of chronic stress. Secondly, it is especially important for single mothers to learn techniques that will work for them to help control the chronic levels of stress most of us will experience.

Guilt is a far more insidious enemy than stress. Guilt is private; guilt is not easily talked about; guilt can even be viewed as deserved because we made poor life choices in the past.

You may already have learned how to sort out your feelings surrounding your reasons for becoming a single par-ent and discovered that much of your guilt was unearned. As each day pre-sents you with new challenges, you must remember to remain aware of the two types of guilt—earned guilt and unearned guilt.

Insidiously, stress and guilt go hand in hand. They feed off one another, gaining strength from each other in a self-defeating, debilitating cycle. Knowing what to do to stop this guilt-stress cycle seems simple enough. It's actually doing it that seems impossible. There is so much about which single parents feel guilty. Moreover, single parents genuinely feel that this guilt is deserved. We often feel powerless in the face of circumstances surrounding what we believe to be our own unique "guil-ties." To tackle stress, which is nothing more than too many demands on too

Simply put, unearned guilt is the unnecessary one—we feel guilty because we don't make much money, we don't have a designer home, we didn't become the person our mother thought we should be. Earned guilt is conscience. In other words, it's okay to feel a little guilty if you helped yourself to your friend's best lipstick and then lied about losing it. It's even okay to feel a little guilty because you con-sciously changed plans at the last minute and caused someone special disappointment. But it's also okay not to feel guilty if you take some private time by reading instead of watching your child show you for the fifth time that day how she does ten cartwheels in a row. Saying, "Mommy needs to do something for herself right now and doesn't want to watch you" is no reason to succumb to the "I'm-a-neglectful-mother" guilties.

If you're divorced or widowed and still plagued with guilt about the kind of wife you were, or are a single mother outside of marriage and doubt your ability to handle the choice you made because you worry you are not good parent material or you got what you deserved, go back and reread the chapters dedicated to you and your particular life circumstances.

Time Management

If I read one more "how to organize" article in popular women's magazines—you know, the ones that advise "take a bath and get your husband to take out the trash"—I'll hit the roof! Any advice on time management for those of us who forgot the husband?

Assess your time investment. Figure that there are 168 hours in a week and see where your time goes. Keep a log for one week and jot down everything you do. Then see what time-bandits you can get rid of. Don't forget the staring, daydreaming, distracted-by-TV time. Everyone gets the same amount of time, whether you are rich or poor, married or single. Decide what your priorities are and spend your time accordingly.

The Busy Mom's Favorite Tool: The Egg Timer. Here's a simple but effective tip:

Invest in an inexpensive kitchen or egg timer. The uses are endless, particularly when used as a handy helper for managing kids. Here's how:

♦ When you need private time, set the timer for fifteen or twenty minutes, and concentrate on attacking or completing one special project or at least a segment of a job until the timer goes off.

♦ Use the timer when putting your preschool child in timeout. Experts advise one minute for each year of age. Avoid going over ten minutes.

♦ Set the timer to give your child undivided attention. Set the timer for about thirty minutes and let him know that this is his time and that when the timer goes off, you are going to do something else. Turn on the phone answering machine or simply let the phone ring. Allow no distractions.

♦ Set the timer for approximately twenty minutes daily to give yourself some private time. Relax, exercise, laugh, or write in a journal. Obviously, this is not possible when your children are infants or toddlers. Let your older children know, however, that this is your time and you are not to be interrupted.

YOU ARE LIKE A WAREHOUSE—STOCK UP NOW!

Suppose you are part of a group of single-parent employees at a major financial corporation sales incentive meeting. The speaker asks the audience of approximately sixty adults, "How

---

THE DOS AND DON'TS OF TAKING CHARGE OF YOUR TIME

♦ Don't wait for the opportunity to find the time to do what you need or want. Life can change in the blink of an eye. Time is never found, altered, hastened, or slowed down. You can only take charge of it.

♦ Don't jam your head with repeated thoughts of how much you have to do and how you will never get it done. This trap often happens when you are in a place where you have no choice but to wait.

♦ Do write down things you must do or remember. Never keep anything that needs doing locked up in your brain. Think about saving up the many short errands and jobs for a once-a-month marathon. Or devote half a week to accomplishing as much as you can.

♦ Do ask yourself, "Will something terrible happen to me or my children if I don't do this right now?" Although it is usually best not to put off what can be done immediately, chances are if you answered no, you are too tired or stressed out and should save this task for another time.

---

many of you think that being a good parent means putting your child first?" Hands shoot up so fast that there is no time for anyone to think that the second part of this query might be a trick question. Would you be one of the handraisers? But wait. The speaker follows immediately with, "And how many of you believe that you, the parent, are number one?" Would you glance around to see if the others would recoil in horror, noting perhaps two women and one man hesitantly raising their hands? Where would your hand be if the speaker shot back, "Right you are!" to the minority who got it correct?

Look at it this way. You're like a warehouse. If you're not well stocked with inventory, how can you possibly give to anyone else? By making yourself number one, you will have on reserve a supply of "nurturing" that you can readily lavish on your children. Thinking about this for a minute, don't you agree that it is a pretty logical concept?

COMMIT TO YOURSELF

Believe it or not, the essence of being a good parent is putting your own needs first. Instead of endless self-sacrifice and denial of your needs, you should focus on making yourself the best person you are capable of becoming. It is this determined focus on yourself as a complete human being that creates the life energies vital to parenting, which is simply the process of supervision and guidance that allows children to emerge as independent beings. It is from your growth and development that your child grows and develops. After all, who arrived here first, you or your child? Just as the earth revolves around the sun for life-sustaining energy, your child thrives on the nurturing, caring, and warmth that you provide. You are the nucleus of your family, just as one day your child may become the nucleus of his or her family.

This commitment to self does not mean, however, that your children are left to their own devices while you pursue Zen meditation in some distant location. This commitment to self also does not mean giving yourself permission to accept a job in which 100-hour

PARTNERSHIP (WITH SELF) CONTRACT

My name is _____. I am a single mother who is committed to self-discovery and to furthering my joy and growth as a remarkable woman with my new best partner—me.

I agree to the following ideals:

I don't have to be mom and dad to my child(ren). I just need to be a loving, guiding parent.

Allowing myself time for my feelings to emerge has been a wonderful cathartic for me. I promise to allow a few minutes every day to express my feelings, no matter how great or rotten I feel that day.

If and when I remarry, I promise to continue to nurture myself above anyone else and not to stop growing because I am in a relationship. If I find that I can't grow because of the confines of a restrictive relationship, I will change that.

I will listen to and learn from my child(ren) as well as teach.

When people tell me how scary it must be to be a single mom, I will show them my bravery.

When people misjudge single mothers in my presence, I will educate them to the truths.

When people question the legitimacy of children whose birth certificates don't bear a man's signature, I will correct them gently but pointedly.

As a single mother, I have discovered how creative and resourceful I am. Within the next three months I will have chosen _____ as an outlet with which to explore myself more fully. _____ and _____ are two other interests I hope to pursue that I might not have considered had I not been a single mother.

I have chosen a friend, support group member, relative, or spiritual teacher named _____ to contact once a week if for nothing else but a reality check.

In the course of raising myself and my children, I have learned that this is not a transitional time until another husband or father for my child(ren) comes along, but rather a time that encourages me to deal with the here and now. The task is not so much to get through each day, but rather to appreciate the joy that is in the process. To that end, I agree to the above commitments, which have no specific time goals, but I agree to begin this new journey with myself on the following date: _____.

_____
(Signature)

work weeks are not uncommon. Simply stated, commitment to self does not give you permission or license to abandon, minimize, ignore, or in any other way compromise your responsibilities and duties as a parent. What this commitment to self does mean is that you also have the responsibility to develop your own unique talents and skills to their fullest and not use your children as an excuse for not moving ahead with your own life. This idea of commitment to self shouldn't just pop into your mind every so often when you read magazine articles recommending occasionally pampering yourself in a hot bath. Commitment to self must be a priority and must be evident in all you do every day for both yourself and your children.

Demonstrate your commitment to yourself by completing the Partnership (with Self) Contract. As with any other important document, review its provisions carefully and know that you are making a promise to yourself when you sign it. Review the provisions of this contract often. Make it your guide to more joyful living in the present for both you and your children!

THE ART OF PRIORITIZING AND COMPROMISING

Coping with stress is usually a daily activity and often can be an ongoing battle. Successfully fought battles have two components: strategy and planning. The strategy is to decrease the demands and increase the resources. Planning is simply putting the strategy into action.

How in the world do we go about decreasing demands when everything around us seems so pressing and urgent? If there is, indeed, any one trick to reducing stress, here it is: Priorities must be set and compromises must be made. Which priorities will be set and what compromises will be made are yours to decide and are unique to you. Is it really necessary to have a floor you can eat off of, or a spotless kitchen? Or is it critical that you get to the dentist? Trade off and put off chores that are not urgent. Move to the top of the list an evening exercise class or an afternoon of roller skating with the family. Plus, make sure you enlist the help of your children in performing chores they are capable of doing. For instance, five- and six-year-olds can help set the table, or put away laundry and feed pets.

But keep this basic premise in mind: Whatever today's priorities are can be just for today. Very little is cast in stone. Flexibility is important. Remember, too, that it's the little things that tend to wear us down and cause us to experience debilitating stress. Knowing what little things drain us is critical not only to coping with stress, but to our overall sense of well-being.

Deciding What's Important

I'm a recent single mother of two teenage boys. How do I go about setting some priorities? It seems everything I need to do is so different from all the other families in my neighborhood. I mean, I work, my kids are involved in numerous activities, I'm taking a nursing course at night, and my house is one giant dustball.

You set priorities based on what is important to you and your family, and not on what others are doing. And it sounds as if you are doing a very good job of that, so don't let guilt stress you out over a job well done.

For some single moms, clean clothes come first because they are hard to fake. Their children's appearance is a priority for them. For others, the little things that get to them are a dirty bathroom and clutter like overflowing garbage pails, dead flowers, two-day-old newspapers, and junk mail. If you would expend your last breath taking out the garbage rather than look at it, then most likely your kids and you know this and will typically respect the need for, if not a clutter-free house, at least a clutter-managed one.

But if older children's rooms are another matter, where overlooking the destruction is a very big compromise for you, then closing the doors and walking away might help, although not always. Messy bedrooms might frustrate all other parents as well, but you need to recognize that as a single parent you have a finite amount of emotional energy and time. Remind yourself that there are bigger parenting issues during the teenage years than dirty clothes on the floor.

Hoping that your children remember what you taught them about honesty and integrity rather than your monologues about bathtub ring or the value of organized dresser drawers is a healthy compromise. Your time together as a family will become increasingly precious as your children grow older and more independent.

"Does Compromising Mean I Have to Be a Martyr?"

I'm a never-married mom of twin boys and have found that compromising has definitely been a plus in reducing stress. But sometimes I hear from my family and friends, particularly the childless ones, how I shouldn't have to compromise, that I don't have to be a martyr. So now what?

Nonsense. Compromising is such a sophisticated negotiating tool that those who are successful at it may seem like martyrs to unsuspecting fledglings who don't know the difference between compromise and selling out.

If you are able to overlook dust as well as waxy yellow buildup in exchange for seeing that you get your nursing degree or that your kids are in the kayaking club, then clearly you are on the right track. However, if your children are allergic to dust, then again, only you can decide what stays and what goes.

INCREASE YOUR RESOURCES

At first, increasing our resources seems like an almost impossible task. Most of us are struggling with the double burden of too little time and too little money. It often seems that the more we are linked by technology like television, which can take us anywhere and show us anything, the more isolated we become from the families around us and from the resources in our own communities. It's a mistake to assume that because you are a single-parent family, you shouldn't network and seek support from other types of people and families. Whether it's the single woman down the block, the married couple next door, the retired couple across the street, or school-age individuals such as a friend's teenage son, you

NEED SUPPORT? GET ON LINE!

One of the best support group ideas for single mothers who are strapped for time, have limited access to baby-sitting or transportation, or simply need a friendly shoulder at the strangest times is the on-line forums offered on telecommunication services such as Woman's Wire, CompuServe, America Online, and Prodigy. You can travel the Internet and discuss the joys and concerns of single parenting with regular members and visitors without leaving your chair. You'll need a computer, modem, communication software, and a few hours of "driving practice," but it's worth the investment. For an additional few dollars a month, often less than a long-distance phone bill, you can contact other single parents at the Parents' Place (http://www.parentsplace.com/) or E-mail the National Organization of Single Mothers by typing INTERNET:SOLO-MOTHER@AOL.com or INTERNET: 74601.1373@Compuserve.com

can expect to discover resources, allies, and support if you search carefully enough.

This search for resources begins with your willingness both to give and to receive help. Look around you with keener eyes. Do you live near a college or university? A student may need cheap housing. Maybe you have a spare bedroom in exchange for low rent and child care at night so you can attend a class yourself. Do you have a skill such as bookkeeping, word processing, or haircutting that you can barter in exchange for plumbing, cleaning, or home repair?

Is there a community bulletin board at your child's school, day-care center, pediatrician's office, local hospital, or athletic club? Why not post your name

and a note stating that you would like to get to know other parents who would be willing to exchange rides to or from school or other activities? Naturally, you would first need to be entirely comfortable that your child will be transported safely by a responsible, dependable adult. But once you have this assurance, think of the advantages. For instance, another mother may need to work late one or two nights a week. If you offer to pick up her child on those late nights, she may be happy to take your child to a scheduled activity such as Brownies or swimming. Don't be afraid to reach out and include anyone in your community, married or not. The worst possible answer might be an occasional no. But isn't it exciting to consider the possibilities that could come from yes?

Decide what is important and what you and your children need to gain some control over in what is for everyone a hectic, unpredictable world. Priorities and compromises do not take away from what we need. Rather, they give us less stress, less guilt, and more of what we all deserve—increased happiness and peace of mind.

Start a Baby-Sitting Co-op. Feel as though you cannot afford a social life because of the high cost of baby-sitting? Think about organizing a baby-sitting co-op, which is nothing more than each parent banking hours of baby-sitting toward receiving equal hours of baby-sitting. Begin with parents you know and trust. It does not matter whether you recruit single parents or married moms. In today's unpredictable economy, almost everyone would welcome such a venture. This is also a terrific way to network with people in your community.

If your group grows large, you will

want to appoint a secretary to keep tabs on sitting schedules and hours. Make your arrangements directly with a member, but you will need to make sure to notify the secretary as soon as possible.

LIVE IN THE HERE AND NOW

Any activity can be fun if you allow yourself and your children to enjoy it. Don't know how to do this? Take this advice from Alcoholics Anonymous: Start acting as if you're happy. Better yet, start acting as if you're successful, as if you're fulfilled, and as if you're sitting on top of the world. These attitudes soon become your beliefs, and sooner than you realize, this is exactly how you will feel for real.

Copy this idea and hang it on the refrigerator, bathroom mirror, or any place where you can refer to it. Do another single mother a favor and make her a copy, too.

THE DOS AND DON'TS OF TAKING CARE OF YOU

- Don't waste time regretting failures and feeling guilty about things you don't do or have. Give up all rescue fantasies.

- Do pat yourself on the back every now and then.

- Don't attribute every crisis or problem your family faces to single parenthood. Every family has its own set of difficulties and has a rough time now and then.

- Do relish your independence. Let people know how nice it is to make your own decisions, to eat what you want, not have to shave your legs, and so on. Remind yourself that there are many advantages to being a single parent.

- Do keep a determined focus on making yourself the best person you can be. From your life energies will come the energy to enable your children to grow and thrive as independent human beings.

- Do keep your personal warehouse stocked. Make a daily determined effort to nurture your physical, emotional, and spiritual needs.

- Don't let stress rule your life. Learn how to compromise and prioritize and be flexible enough to know that goals and priorities will often change from day to day.

- Don't limit your support network to single-parent families only. Seek and give support to all kinds of people and families.

- Don't give in to your child's every whim. Single parents who are guilty of giving that extra toy or candy bar to replace the missing parent spoil their kids in the process. Spoiling children leads to more and more time-consuming battles over control. You are the parent, and your word is final.

10
Money Matters

MAKING YOUR FINANCES COUNT

There is no denying that the strongest force in our society is the power of money. Men have known this far longer than women, who are still faced with emotional obstacles that can sabotage asset-building efforts. Historically, men had role models to lead them into the world of banks and boardrooms, while women were taught that their self-worth was measured by how long they kept their families together and happy. Attorney Ann Owings Wilson and financial counselor Linda Bessette, authors of *From Paycheck to Power: The Working Woman's Guide to Reducing Debts, Building Assets, and Getting What You Want Out of Life* (August House), have discovered while counseling their clients that the best-laid money management plans will be undermined if the client harbors self-defeating myths, assumptions, and emotional obstacles. Addiction is one form of emotional obstacle, whether it be a dependency on a relationship, food, chemicals, or shopping. Myths with messages like "girls will be taken care of" and "nice girls don't discuss money"

are also serious emotional obstacles for many women.

CHANGE THE WAY YOU LOOK AT MONEY

If you have let some of these obstacles get in the way of managing your money, you need to change the way you think about money before you can become financially responsible. Whether you are currently getting a divorce, entering a new relationship, or pregnant and want minimal involvement with the child's father, you need to avoid situations where you will not be in control of your financial future. The first step in managing your finances is to take charge of your economic situation, no matter how bleak it looks.

Falling prey to all too common financial pitfalls can sabotage your efforts to become financially fit. All these traps that many women have found themselves in could be avoided by learning the difference between money matters and money myths. Just because you may be an investment banker from nine to five during the week doesn't mean that you are viewing money realistically when it comes to going in together on a condominium with your boyfriend or keeping joint checking accounts with your husband.

It's also important to have a clear understanding of the meaning of money as control when it exists as a dominant part of the male-female relationship. For example, your partner may feel he works harder than you because he earns more money and therefore leaves you solely responsible for cooking and cleaning. Many of these issues can be resolved by clearly distinguishing emotional issues from practical ones, and negotiating "house" rules early in the relationship.

This is not to say that you shouldn't ever get involved romantically with a man unless every financial aspect of his life is up front. However, you should recognize that in general men and women have fundamentally different views of money. It is also important to understand the role money can play in empowering a man's life and how your financial independence frees you to make decisions that are in your best interest, too.

THE TRUTH ABOUT THE THREE MAJOR MONEY MYTHS

MYTH #1: *Money is synonymous with love and commitment.* Money is a medium of exchange. When we have certain needs and wants, they are satisfied through money. Money is how we measure our achievements in the workplace. However, many women report having trouble equating money with business. When control of money instead is connected to feelings of negative self-worth, nagging and persistent doubts can follow. Women who feel that they can't offer much in a relationship other than money often wonder, "Does he love me for me or for the money?" Feelings of self-worth never improve if women create situations where money substitutes for personal qualities they feel they are lacking.

MYTH #2: *He doesn't control me, only my credit.* Wrong. Too many women think that because their former partner or husband handled all the family finances, he should continue to do so even after a divorce. Wives who were not a major part of the financial decisions during a marriage often relinquish too much power to their spouse during a divorce.

Financial entanglements are often also a sign of not being able to let go. Severing money connections is an important step toward disengaging yourself from a dead-end relationship. Remember—the one who pays is the one who makes the choices.

If you are getting divorced, be sure that what appears to be your seemingly fair split of the debts includes not only totaling up the dollar amounts but also looking at what debts are outstanding and in whose name. Make sure that money coming to you comes directly to you. Do not accept terms in a separation or divorce agreement whereby the former spouse agrees to make mortgage or credit card payments or any other type of loan payment.

MYTH #3: *It cost me nothing!* You've heard the expression: There is no such thing as a free lunch. Because money is a symbol of power and control, be cautious before agreeing to an arrangement in which someone else pays your bills, such as maintaining your auto insurance or paying for your child's swim club membership or child care. There will be a price to pay in some form, whether in blood, sweat, or tears. It is up to you to determine what that will be and if you are willing to pay. Weigh the advantages against the disadvantages of any economic agreement. Ask yourself, "What do I have to gain not only financially, but in time, convenience, and peace of mind?" More importantly, ask yourself, "What do I have to lose in terms of time, convenience, and peace of mind?"

COMBINING ASSETS DOESN'T NECESSARILY MEAN COMBINING HEARTS

My significant other and I had wanted to escape the rat race of New York and open a New England bed and breakfast.

I guess I saw this venture as the end of our "dating years" and the beginning of real commitment, including marriage and kids. I saw the combining of our assets as proof positive of commitment and did not insist on drawing up legal, binding

documents. The bed and breakfast succeeded, but the relationship failed. Had I kept my finances and heart separate from the beginning, with the financial obligations spelled out, I would have at least been in a financial position to move on from this failed relationship. But doesn't a business attitude seem to diminish the romance?

Money is not love and needs to be kept separate. In other words, don't allow unmet emotional needs to color your money management decisions. Money is not commitment, nor can it buy self-esteem, in spite of its ability to purchase many material things. It is so important to remember that money is business.

In fact, the quicker you get the business side of dealing with money out of the way of new relationships, the more intense the romance can become because you never have to worry that you owe or are owed anything.

YOU NEED TO BE THE DECISION MAKER

In a situation that is fairly common, a couple had long been divorced—kind of. The wife was deeply hurt and confused by her husband's announcement that he wanted out of the marriage. They had two young children, and she felt overwhelmed by the responsibilities that lay before her as a single mother. Fortunately, or at least so she thought at the time, her ex, following the divorce, showed no signs of abandoning his responsibilities, financial or otherwise, to the kids. She and the kids were allowed to live in the house, which had been a wedding gift from her mother-in-law, until both children were out of college. Having owned a home for a while, the newly single mom was no stranger to the many expenses that come with homeowning, over and above the mortgage and taxes. She insisted in the divorce agreement that her ex take some responsibility for expenses like home repair.

That can work out just fine, depending on what type of agreement you may have. But if you have an elaborate agreement by which your ex has to pay a proportional share of home repairs and anticipated expenses—only if he agrees that the repairs are necessary—you're in for a run for your money. Your ex-spouse may get to choose the painter, contractor, or whomever, and has to agree to the cost of the repair. Initially, you may be satisfied with this type of arrangement because you're glad that you are not going to be paying all the home repair costs. But in cases like this, especially if your ex is something of a control freak, he is going to have a lot more than just some say-so in the situation.

"My Ex-husband Wants to Pay My Mortgage Directly to the Bank"

I'm getting divorced after many unhappy years of marriage. I had little say or control over the family finances during our marriage, so I did not raise any objections to the suggestion by my ex that there be a provision in my divorce settlement that he would make the mortgage payments directly to the bank. After all, I'll have enough on my hands with two teenage boys to look after. Why should I have to go to the trouble of depositing his check and then turning around and writing a check to the bank as a house payment every month?

It's not that much trouble, and if you don't do it that way, you may find yourself in worse trouble. Consider what happened to one single mother who agreed to a similar arrangement. She changed her way of thinking after she received a notice from the bank that she was three months in arrears on the mortgage. The bank was demanding immediate payment or foreclosure proceedings would begin.

Like her, you would find yourself stunned. You would need to spend more money on attorney fees once you discovered that your ex may have simply grown tired of writing that check every month. Most men who originally agree to such an arrangement later on admit, "Why should I be paying for a house I'm not living in? The divorce was your idea and your fault. You are the one who wanted out. You want to take care of yourself. Go ahead."

True, it is not written in stone that your ex will renege on his promises. But if, like many before him, he does, it can take a lot of scrambling, borrowing, and overtime for you to hold on to your house when you find yourself in this predicament. Other women have not been so lucky. Judges tell women every day, as they are about to foreclose on their homes, that the court can do nothing to enforce family court orders requiring former spouses to make mortgage or other types of payments. Work out the settlement differently, so the money is in your control, not your ex's.

"My Ex-husband Is My Handyman …"

My ex has agreed to help me from time to time by paying for certain repair and maintenance bills, as long as he selects the handyperson or contracting help and determines what really needs to be done and when he can do it. I don't think this is so bad. It's not like he's intrusive or anything. Besides, there is no one else in my life right now to help me, right?

Think again. Some women in your situation have found that they were still a little angry and confused and wanted their ex around assuming "husband" responsibilities. Sometimes, the presence of that person in your home can enable you to remain in denial that your marriage is over. Do you ever think about reconciling your marriage? Maybe deep down, you feel that as long as he is around the house for any reason, he will see what he had thrown away and reconciliation is possible. Or maybe there are other things going on, but you still find yourself emotionally entangled. Your ex may be more than willing to agree to the home repair conditions, because his needs for control are satisfied that way and he, too, is emotionally entangled.

If he is the one who initiated the breakup, he may be the kind of man who had few or no regrets about leaving his partner but feels rotten about leaving his kids and the home he considered to be his. Or he may just need something to do to occupy his unwisely utilized time. There is always something to do around a house, and home repair responsibilities might give him the perfect excuse to come and go in the house as he sees fit. Consider whether you would like to have unannounced inspection tours, or risk having him march through the house like a commanding general issuing orders about everything from the CDs left scattered on your daughter's bed to the kitchen floor that he feels needs mopping.

At first you may welcome these visits. But if you have any desire to build a life for yourself and your family, it won't take long for you to see his unannounced visits for what they are—intrusive, controlling, and unnecessary. You may be able to let go, but he is not.

"Just One Last Repair Before I Change the Locks ..."

My ex has remarried and divorced, all in the course of eighteen months. His newest ex resented his coming here to help me around the house sometimes. Now he is living alone, but he has a girlfriend who can't stand that he still comes by my home just to check on things. The truth is, I'm sick of his coming by, but I haven't told him because it was easier to let his girlfriends and ex-wife do that. I'm thinking of changing the locks, but not until he fixes a leak that I just discovered in the roof. Is this a bad idea?

It would be more appropriate to have a talk with this man and ask him to please call first, before just walking in. Of course, if he doesn't comply, changing the locks is a good idea. However, don't proceed too hastily. It's not going to be hard to guess what might happen next if you try to get him to repair your roof while distancing yourself from him. Knowing that you are serious about changing his "entry requirements," he may stall or look for excuses to postpone working on your roof. He may offer to come by, but only at a time when it would seriously inconvenience you or when you would have to take off from work.

Rather than continuing this emotional entanglement or putting up with a leaky roof, it might be best to come to some sort of negotiation where he pays you so a roofer of your choice handles the repair. If that still presents problems, find a reputable company to temporarily patch the roof, and repair it when you are able to pay for it without involving your ex.

Time Is Money

I had a long relationship with a married man much older than myself. For a long while, his other life did not bother me all that much. I had a promising career and good friends and did not wait by the phone. As my thirtieth birthday approached, I began to feel that inexplicable longing for a child. Later, I found myself pregnant and was delighted. When the baby's father realized that his life would go on uninterrupted, he, too, seemed pleased that I was going to have a baby. I thought it best to plan for the baby as the single mother I was, without reliance on the father, although his offer to pay the baby's educational expenses was irresistible. He kept his promise to pay my daughter's educational expenses, but he chose a private school to his liking. This school was close to

his office, because he does occasionally like to go to school plays and science fairs and that kind of stuff. It's a fine school, but it is located very far from my home and office. I wish I had never agreed to this because I am paying every day in time and inconvenience.

People most often will do what is good for them. Your daughter's father is doing exactly that. He wants his daughter to have a good education and wants to participate in the most convenient way possible for him.

You have a couple of options. You can tell him that you no longer wish him to pay for your daughter's schooling, thereby giving you the right to enroll her where you please. Denied the opportunity to manage your daughter's education, he may decide to seek greater control and even sue for partial custody. Of course, he may do nothing and simply retreat further from your daughter's life. So instead of seeing her father at least at school events, her contact with her father may diminish. This change may be good for you, but it would not be in the best interests of your daughter.

There is always the future to consider. The cost of a college education is enormous. His ability to provide a free college education for your daughter would be no small advantage in life. There is no denying that, for now, his control over where your child attends school is an inconvenience, using up both your time and energy.

What would you be doing with this time if your daughter was enrolled somewhere closer to home? One thing you might be doing is working extra hours, perhaps in part to help save for her education. Why not consider the time you are spending back and forth to her school as just that—a part-time job the earnings from which you will use to finance your daughter's education? Your daughter's father's offer to finance her education should be in writing. There should also be provisions as part of his estate planning to enact this agreement should he die before your daughter's education is completed. This is just good, sound business sense.

GETTING YOUR FINANCIAL HOUSE IN ORDER

The first step to getting your financial house in order is to put your financial goals in writing. Be as specific as possible. Saying "I want a lot of money" is not clear enough to be a specific goal, but stating "I want to provide my child with one half of his college costs" or "I want to buy a house" or "I want to own my own business" is a specific goal. It may seem confusing to write down goals when you aren't really aware of what condition your financial house is in. But deciding first on your goals leads you to the second step—finding out where you stand—and ultimately to a plan of action.

Some people give up before even attempting the first step, believing that meeting their goals is impossible, especially after they learn what it costs to buy a house, send a kid to college, or retire. During this step, no one is asking you to pay for anything. Just write down your goals. Don't wait to find time to write down your goals; make time now. List as many realistic goals as you can. "Realistic" means leaving out the magical thinking such as "After I win the lottery, I will buy a racehorse!" Whether you have three major goals or

twenty, you must be specific, write them down, and keep them in a file labeled "Finances." Put the file away for a few days, if you are overwhelmed, and pull it out when you are ready to proceed to the next important step.

Establish an Operating Budget. It's critical to find out how much money you owe and how much you are spending in order to establish an operating budget. This critical step is often ignored because it is painful to take a hard look at how limited your resources might be and how much debt you really might be carrying.

Ginger Applegarth, author and financial planner based in Boston, says that for many people, the toughest part of the second step—finding out where you are—is getting a grip on ATM, or cash machine, spending. At least it was for her. A single mother who spent five years totally disabled without disability insurance, Applegarth advises jotting down on the back of the receipt from the cash machine exactly how that money will be used. Often we find that we really didn't need to spend some of that cash.

Although fewer than 60 percent of all Americans use a budget, it is important that single mothers keep a record of income and outflow on a monthly basis since getting control of spending is crucial to managing money. Another reason is that if you are seeking or collecting child support, your finances need to be well documented.

If you find you need to take this hard look but feel you lack the skills or just can't face it alone, this is a good time to ask for the assistance of another single mom who might possess some savvy money skills. Most mothers going it alone understand financial problems and there is no reason to feel embarrassment at your predicament. The calculating eye of another person who has taken hold of her finances might be just the incentive and role model you need.

Get Yourself out of Debt. Don't let this hard-headed look at your financial status discourage you. Start saving whatever you can, even if it means just squirreling away a couple of dollars each week. Getting yourself out of debt can seem to be a slow, painstaking process, but you must be patient. Otherwise you'll get frustrated and put yourself back where you started with a wild shopping spree.

Step 1. The first step is to get a credit card with the lowest rate possible that will allow you to transfer your other outstanding balances to that card. Many

Taking Aim at Credit Card Debt

Here is how to get out from under excessive credit card debt. Contact the Bankcard Holders of America and request a Debt Zapper Kit. The cost is $15.00 from BHA Debt Zapper, 524 Branch Drive, Salem, Virginia 24153. You supply the number of credit cards and the total amount of money owed. Debt Zapper will help you lay out a repayment plan based on paying off the card with the highest rate first.

credit cards are still charging 18 to 22 percent a year. If you have a credit card debt of $5,000, you can save over $400 a year by moving from a 20 percent card to a 12 percent or lower card. Consolidate all your bills into one low-interest monthly payment, if possible.

If you have no credit in your own name, establishing credit should be a first priority. Begin by obtaining a secured credit card. In this case, you deposit a certain amount of cash with the credit card issuer in return for a credit line of the same size. If you default on your credit card payment, the bank can seize enough money from your deposit to cover your debt. You can obtain a list of secured credit card issuers from Bankcard Holders of America at 703-481-1110.

Step 2. Cut up all your other cards, saving one for dire emergencies only. Notify all the credit card companies (except the one card you saved) to close your account. This is a smart idea because even if you have no outstanding balance, the credit line existing for these cards might be so large that it prevents you from getting other types of credit like a mortgage refinance or car loan. Having too many credit cards can seduce you into spending money that you don't have.

Step 3. You need to start an investment program. Again it is important to write down specific goals. These goals will be influenced by your age and the kinds of responsibilities, assets, and resources you already have. What is it that you really want? Are you interested in saving money for retirement, or do you have more immediate goals like starting a business? How much risk can you handle?

Save, Save, Save! Some women begin by investing in mutual funds. Investment programs like this can often begin with as little as $50. Remember that no one investment plan is right for everyone. How you invest your money is ultimately your decision because it is you who will reap the reward or suffer the loss. Enlist the help of a financial planner, take a course or attend a seminar in financial planning, or even subscribe to investment magazines. Learn what's out there and what investment vehicles might be right for you.

Investigate the opportunities for savings that may be available through your employee benefit package. Are you taking full advantage of the flexible benefits plan? Does your company offer a 401(k) or 403(b) plan? These plans allow you to set aside part of your salary into savings or investments whose earnings are tax-free until withdrawal, which is usually at retirement. Many companies are willing to match the funds the employee sets aside in these plans. Find out what kind of pension, if any, your company offers for which you are eligible. Use that information to plan your career moves and possible job changes more wisely.

Tax Planning Is Essential. Understand what your deductions are and plan carefully to minimize your tax liability. Know the tax consequences before you make major decisions like purchasing a home or selling off investment assets. Keep receipts and other supporting documents in a safe, accessible location. Ask your tax adviser how long you should keep records and copies of your returns. Even if you don't make a lot of money, don't avoid careful filing of tax returns. You may be eligible for Earned Income Credit (EIC), which can give you an additional $2,400 a year!

INCREASING YOUR ASSETS

Some Tips for Earning Extra Income. Entrepreneurial women are starting half to two-thirds of all the nation's new businesses. You can become self-employed if you market a special skill or talent. Here are some best bets for starting your own business, either full-time or part-time:

Start a Word-Processing or Web Business. The investment for a home word-processing business is around $2,000, including the computer, modem, and word-processing software. When advertising your services, be sure to emphasize a specialty such as evening and weekend work for small businesses, or another selling point such as free twenty-four-hour delivery.

For another $500, you can start a Web design or development business. Although there's a lot of competition, the world is running its business on the "Net" so this could be lucrative.

Be a Professional Organizer. Got a thing about being organized? Professional organizers plan sales and auctions for individuals, whether they are managing an estate or simply want to bring garage and attic sales to a professional level. The National Association of Professional Organizers can advise you on the legal steps you need to take to get started and provide information about bonding and licenses that are necessary to protect yourself.

Be an Event Planner. Almost every organization sponsors major events for fundraising, issue awareness, and membership drives. Activities such as dinners, musical entertainment, trips, tournaments, and contests need to be thoroughly planned. Event planners are not on staff but are usually hired on a free-lance or contractual basis. A knowledge of promotions, publicity, and public relations is a plus when dealing with newspapers and local television and radio stations.

Provide Courier and Personal Services. Today's working parents have busy lives. They often need someone to do the most basic yet time-consuming errands. Some courier services are franchised, but to zero in on a more personal target for your services, a small personal service business might be just for you.

Be a Music, Art, or Exercise Instructor. If you have a particular talent or skill in a specialized field that does not have too many regulations, offering tutoring, piano lessons, personal training, or kids' jewelry-making classes can be a great way to supplement your income. If you can find enough business, full-time classes can become your sole method of making money.

Try Lawn Care or Landscaping. If you have always enjoyed working outdoors and are able to buy the basic equipment, this could be a terrific way to earn extra money. Some single mothers with a creative flair and a green thumb have created thriving businesses caring for lawns, gardens, window boxes, or flower beds.

Start a Child-Care Business. If you are interested in operating a home-based child-care business, get a copy of Patricia Gallagher's *Start Your Own At-Home Child Care Business* or *So You Want to Open a Profitable Day Care Center* ($19.95 each) by sending payment to Child Care, P.O. Box 555, Worcester, PA 19490, or call 215-364-1945 to find out how to get started.

Be a Medical Transcriptionist. A medical transcriptionist takes the notes doctors dictate after performing operations or examinations and transcribes them to the written word. Typically, training takes about six months part-time. After completing the program, a medical transcriptionist is able either to set up shop at home with her own computer and printer or to work in a physician's office or hospital. The hours can be flexible, and the pay is quite decent to start. Medical transcription is needed everywhere and jobs are plentiful.

Try Decorative Painting. House painting or interior painting is a familiar job. There has been a great revival recently in decorative painting with techniques such as stenciling, trompe l'oeil, rag painting, sponge painting, and a variety of other styles. Most people apprentice themselves to established painters and learn the techniques on the job. Your own home or that of a friend could be your best advertisement.

Provide Cleaning Services. As long as there are people living, breathing, and making a mess, there will be always be jobs for people willing to clean up. This is where a resourceful single mother can create a profitable part-time or full-time business. Offices, large and small, as well as homes are all possible job sites. Be prepared with references and know that cleaning is hard, demanding work.

Scale Down! Not only is scaling down necessary, but it is becoming chic to live simply by reusing and recycling. Here are some rich ideas for cheaper living to help you start spending less while living better. The money left over should go into your savings or investment plan.

- You can eat six healthy home-cooked meals for the price of one fast-food dinner. Packing your child's lunches saves an additional $100 to $200 a year. Moreover, many public schools encourage parent participation, so why not join your child for lunch, if he or she likes the idea? Brown bag it at work and rack up another $60 a month, or $600 to $800 or more a year. Make brown bagging fun by letting your child fix the midday meal that you will take to the office while you are making his or her school lunch. Allow meal planning to be your child's choice occasionally.

- Never go grocery shopping when hungry. Use coupons, but only for those items you normally buy. You can let your kids cut out the coupons while helping you with your shopping list. Plan menus and don't be swayed by packaging or TV advertising.

- Become semi-vegetarians. Buy rice, beans, potatoes, pasta, and legumes in bulk and save even more. Remember that these foods are located at the perimeter of the store and never at eye level, which is all the more reason to bring the children along to retrieve those items on the bottom shelves! Store in airtight containers. Avoid expensive meats and prepared foods. Simple vegetables, soups, and stews are cheaper and far healthier than processed food. Be on the lookout for healthy recipes and create opportunities for exchange with other single mothers. Boredom often leads to unhealthy and expensive food choices.

- Consider shopping at a salvage company that offers substantial discounts on dented cans, broken cartons, and institutional size containers of food, paper, and dry goods. Depending upon where you live, some salvage companies also have freezers full of meat and prepared foods that were deemed undeliverable to grocers and restaurants because of expiring freshness dates. Usually, these items are safe to buy but can't be accepted by restaurants, stores, and hotels. For example, if a skid of flour (which may contain a number of cases) has even one broken bag, the entire case becomes unusable. The salvage company sells the individual bags at a cost to consumers that may be up to 60 percent less than supermarket prices. Some savvy "salvage shoppers" report stocking up their shelves and freezers with items they normally couldn't afford because they cost two or three times as much elsewhere. But be wary of overstocking with limited space and appetites: better to go in with a friend or family member or you may wind up throwing out your savings.

- Have a cooking marathon one day every weekend and store extra portions in meal-sized serving containers in the freezer. Use powdered milk in recipes instead of fresh. Collect recipes, learn to use leftovers creatively, and grow your own herbs. Join with other single mothers who cook in quantity and trade a pot of stew for a pot of chili. Your children will learn to try new things and be offered more variety, and you'll have less hassle and save time in the long run.

- Find the day-old-bread store in your community and stock up. Promptly freeze your purchases to ensure a longer shelf life. These shops also have pizza shells cheaper than at the supermarket. Make your own pizzas and let your child help put on the toppings.

- Time-crunched single parents tend to frequent fast-food restaurants more than they should. Next time you go out to dinner, find a family restaurant with discounts for kids. Often these places let kids under six eat free and those under twelve eat for half price. And be sure to choose small restaurants with simple menus. These places often need fewer people to make and serve the dishes and therefore often have lower prices.

The typically less frenzied atmosphere is also a welcome change.

- Worried that your child will miss his or her kids' prize meal from the local burger joint? Order one of these for yourself on days when you only get a half-hour break from the office and save the toy for junior. In fact, these are great to stock up on and use as rewards when your child does something particularly useful. Remember, one or two of these cheap meals a week won't hurt if you remember to round it off with a salad or fruit brought along from home. Be sure the toy is safe for your child's age. Many fast-food places offer toys for children under three.

- When visiting your doctor, ask for free samples of everything. Say that you are a single parent and on a strict budget. Stock up on over-the-counter remedies such as ointments, pain relievers, diaper creams, and decongestants, and don't forget those latex gloves. Besides cleaning, they're great for those of us who color our hair! Additionally, latex gloves should be worn when administering first aid to visiting children or anytime you come in contact with blood or fecal matter. Staying healthy saves money and lives!

- Don't buy too many cosmetics or perfumes. Request these items as gifts when reminding indecisive friends about your birthday or Christmas. Better yet, window shop at a large department store, and request free samples of everything the cosmetics department has to offer. Indulge yourself, and use the extras for little gifts or stocking stuffers.

♦ Offer yourself and your children as hair models for beauty school students. You can get a nice haircut, styling, and sometimes coloring (just for you, of course, and stay away from anything that requires too much upkeep) for practically nothing. Just be sure to keep your style simple— something that is versatile and keeps its shape with minimal care.

♦ Learn to sew, or swap skills with a single mother who does. Many children's clothes, like shorts and simple tops for toddlers and preschoolers, are ridiculously easy to make, even for the amateur. Your child will enjoy picking out the fabric. Even teenage girls who are notoriously picky about clothes will enjoy a cozy flannel nightshirt handmade by mom.

♦ Think swap and not shop. Organize and find other single mothers with skills to barter. Some women are fabulous cooks and terrible housekeepers, other women just the reverse. Could a swap of services benefit both? Absolutely. Be clear about the rules and keep careful records. Not only can this be a big money saver, but it also can lead to wonderful new experiences and opportunities. Many successful small businesses have begun by women swapping or bartering their skills and discovering just how valuable other people found these talents to be.

♦ Give up or at least cut down on some of your bad habits. Giving up just six cigarettes a day will save you over $250 a year. Cutting back just four canned soft drinks a week saves you another $100 annually. Give up smoking altogether and replace sugary drinks with water (much healthier than soda), and you'll have quite a nest egg to show for it, not to mention the added years to enjoy it.

♦ Don't shop till you drop ... unless it is at garage sales, flea markets, and consignment or thrift shops. Never buy expensive toddler outfits for your young ones, because after five minutes of wear they are as used as anything you can pick up second-hand. And at the rate that kids grow, you wouldn't be able to keep up. Also, believe it or not, toddlers and infants simply don't care about making fashion statements.

♦ Find the discount movie house in your neighborhood and sneak in your own popcorn. Or for a day of fun, rather than spend a bundle at a theme park, take the pack to a park, zoo, or historical site. In fact, some peanut butter sandwiches, a dog, and a kite can make for an invigorating day for under a couple of bucks.

♦ Don't overlook the library as a source of family entertainment. Take advantage of their free activities, including films and video series, storytelling and puppet shows, poetry readings, and guest speakers. In fact, you probably wouldn't have enough time to take advantage of all their classes, workshops, and special programs if you did nothing else.

Fashion Tips for the Money Conscious

◆ Stick to one color family for your work clothes. For example, buy work clothes that can be accessorized with black—shoes, handbags, belts. Maybe brown is your color. The point is that sticking to one color family allows you to afford better-quality and longer-lasting items because you have to buy fewer things.

◆ Buy classic styles that do not easily become dated. Blazers, basic shirts, the little black dress, and tailored skirts and slacks can be combined to create dozens of looks from just a few basic pieces. For fun and to look fashionable, rely on well-chosen accessories like scarves or costume jewelry. Quality matters; buy the best you can afford.

◆ Respect the unwritten corporate rules when choosing clothes for the office. Take special note of how your boss dresses. If she never wears pants to the office, then perhaps dresses and skirts are your best get-ahead bet. If you work in a more trendy, casual place, then the corporate suit with matching pumps will look out of place. Men have known for years the importance of the corporate uniform. Smart women who get ahead also know the importance of image. You will not get promoted if you do not look as though you already have the job.

◆ Indulge yourself in color and style for your casual clothes. Casual wear costs less, and during your time away from work, you really are free to dress as you like.

◆ Keep yourself and your clothing meticulously clean. Hang up your work clothes and let them air out when you get home. The more quickly you air out your things, the fewer times expensive things will have to be dry-cleaned or laundered. Fewer dry-cleaning bills and longer clothes life will save money. Repair loose buttons and make other small repairs promptly. There is nothing like a missing button on the front of a blouse at precisely the wrong moment to ruin a day.

◆ Avoid purchasing too many items that require dry-cleaning. Stick to fabrics that are easily laundered and do not easily wrinkle.

◆ Take advantage of discounts on items like pantyhose and buy in quantity. Order with girlfriends and increase your savings.

◆ Be wary of outlets and avoid the temptation to buy simply because you are there. If you would not have paid full price for it, it is probably not a bargain no matter what the tag reads now.

◆ Catalogs may save you money in the long run if shopping around for bargains takes you away from your job and the potential for earning money, not to mention the costs you incur for gas and parking. Time is as valuable as money, so if catalog shopping works for you, go that route. Get on the mailing list of discount clothing catalogs and take advantage of their special sales for regular customers. Just be sure not to overspend simply because you have a credit card in one hand and a phone in the other.

- Your appearance will affect how others judge you on the job. Unless you have unlimited resources, careful planning is essential. Make no major purchases on impulse without giving thought to how this item will fit into your wardrobe-building plan. The purple and fuschia jacket may have instant appeal in the store, but it will never give the service that the well-tailored basic black jacket will.

- Many large department stores have personal shoppers who will help you select clothing for no additional cost. You are under no obligation to buy, and often these shoppers can show you many ways to mix and match so you can get maximum mileage out of your minimal clothing dollar. This service can be a real blessing for the time-crunched single mother who hates to shop.

- Organize a single mothers' clothes swap. That teal and magenta jacket that one woman is sick of, the scarf that goes with nothing, the dangling earrings that annoy you, or the wool coat that causes one mom to have an allergy attack might be just what someone else is looking for. Everyone gets something new and the chance to socialize. Every item is considered an even exchange. What doesn't get exchanged gets donated to charity.

- In bigger cities and towns, there are exchanges run by women's groups that help women trying to get back into the work place. Many of them offer gently used business clothes for little or no cost. Investigate these by calling your local women's commission or the library or just ask around.

- Seek out secondhand clothing stores or consignment shops, particularly for items to fill out your wardrobe or for special occasion items you will wear only once. Make friends with the owner or manager and she may contact you when something terrific in your size comes in. Keep in mind, too, that if you have a special event to attend that requires formal dressing, you don't have to purchase an item that you will never wear again. Consider renting a formal from a store specializing in this. In fact, many of these places also rent jewelry and accessories.

BANKRUPTCY

Single women are the single largest group of people who file for bankruptcy, making up 39 per cent of the nation's annual 1.4 million filings. There is strong bipartisan support for bankruptcy reform. Special attention is being paid to the effects of proposed legislation on child support collection.

If you are considering filing for bankruptcy, remember that creditors are often willing to negotiate with you. This possibility should be explored first. Legal advice is essential. Bankruptcy law is complicated and varies from state to state; you need an attorney who concentrates on this area of the law. Be sure you know where you will stand financially after you file for bankruptcy and what effect this filing will have on your credit history and for how long. Generally, filing for bankruptcy will greatly limit your ability to obtain a mortgage or car loan, often for many years. Bankruptcy is a last choice option.

IF YOU NEED PUBLIC ASSISTANCE

Regardless of your circumstances or reasons for becoming a single mother, if you find yourself unable to take care of yourself and your children adequately because of a severe lack of funds, you should apply for financial assistance.

As the result of the major overhauling of our previous welfare system, aid to families is now the responsibility of individual states rather than the federal government. Rules and procedures differ from county to county and from state to state and even program names may vary. For example, Massachusetts calls their welfare program (as referred to in this book) TAFDC (Temporary Aid to Families with Dependent Children); welfare benefits in North Carolina are paid under the state's WorkFirst Family Assistance program (WFFA); and Wisconsin has named its program Temporary Aid to Needy Families (TANF). Depending upon which state you reside in, different time limits and guidelines may also be set. For example, some states offer a maximum cash payout for up to five years, others limit their benefits to two years, while still others may limit assistance to, say, two years but allow clients to reapply within a five-year period. Your best bet for seeking financial aid is through your Department of Social Services (DSS). Look under government listings either located in a special section or in the beginning of your phone book for the phone number and address of your local DSS.

Ten Steps for Requesting Assistance with Dignity. Familiarize yourself with this ten-step plan first to increase your chances of successfully obtaining benefits.

1. Keep in mind that you will encounter caseworkers who will try to dismiss you because that is their job, regardless of what you are told. The more requests they can deny, the better it is for the Department of Social Services. Remember, too, that every state will have a different set of standards, so do your homework first!

2. When you go to DSS to fill out the many applications required to apply for aid, be sure to bring every document you can think of, including everyone's birth certificates, death certificate (if spouse died), divorce or separation papers, monthly expense and income statements (including gas and electric bills and canceled rent checks or receipts), and anything else that shows you have substantial need. Because there is the risk that states will be required to deny benefits to children where that state has failed to establish paternity, be sure to bring proof of paternity, or request that an action be started to establish paternity.

3. Don't be intimidated, but do expect some unwelcome behavior on the part of the caseworker. These people are inundated with caseloads and can barely muster up the energy to keep their mouths horizontal, let alone avoid frowning. Be sure to take a pen or pencil and paper with you so you can take notes. Nothing gets a caseworker's attention more than a potential recipient who writes down everything the caseworker says. Above all, be sure to note his or her name and ask for the correct spelling. For some reason, the intimidation process seems to reverse itself when

you are poised with pen in hand and a look that says, "I'm ready when you are!" Never forget that knowledge is power.

Note: If you encounter abusive behavior on the caseworker's part, don't let him or her see you cry. Maintain your composure and explain that you have a legal right to this information and would prefer that it be given to you in a straightforward, noninsulting manner. (This is not to give the impression that all caseworkers are abusive monsters, but the majority of women who have been through this procedure have met with unpleasantness.)

4. You mustn't give up. Moms seeking TAFDC benefits often fall prey to discouragement, humiliation, and intimidation. Keep these three common feelings in mind and don't let them force you to give up. In some cases, it might take four or more visits to DSS and even more telephone attempts to finally collect what you are entitled to.

5. Don't avoid applying for food stamps (a separate program) because you are not receiving cash assistance. Food stamps are based on your income compared with your shelter costs, which include rent and utilities. If your shelter costs come to more than half of your total income, you are usually awarded close to the maximum amount of food stamps. Remember that the amount is determined by the state. People receiving social security or disability benefits, the elderly, and even employed persons are eligible to receive food stamps based on the comparison of income to expenses.

6. Don't assume you are not eligible for AFDC because you own a house or a car. You can own a house as long as you live in it. Your car's value, may not exceed the amount set by your state. Also, if you have a savings account, find out what the maximum dollar amount is allowed. Unfortunately, because some women have a little nest egg in case of emergency, this may cause a denial of benefits. Be informed of the maximum assets you can claim.

7. If the case worker suggests that you are not eligible, make certain that you ask for the denial in writing. One woman requesting aid mentioned that she owned her own home, but couldn't keep up the payments after her husband left. The caseworker was astounded at the value of the home and gave the woman the impression that she was not eligible to receive a grant, causing the woman to give up seeking help. Later she learned that as long as she resided in the home, she was eligible for benefits. Another caseworker attempted the same manipulation to suggest that no homeowner could receive state welfare, but the woman requested the so-called denial in writing, whereupon the caseworker immediately changed her tune.

8. Always ask for the address of the hearing office, so you know where to request a hearing whether or not you are immediately denied benefits. If the person responds by telling you that the address is on the forms, ask again, saying that you don't see it and you would like to make note of it immediately.

9. If you request a hearing, do so in writing at the state level. Your local DSS office will give you the address and telephone number of the state's social services department. Be sure to keep your request brief. You are not arguing your case, simply requesting a hearing. Saying, "I was denied TAFDC benefits because …" is enough. Note the date, name of caseworker, and address of office where you were denied. Chances are, you won't need a hearing because most caseworkers will do their work once they learn that you are asking for a hearing. If you do require a hearing, keep in mind that if the state receives your request for a hearing before the date of termination of TAFDC, reduction of payments, or whatever you are being threatened with, you must continue to receive your benefits at the current level until your problem is resolved. Don't accept anything else, and if necessary, go to a Legal Aid office for help.

10. If you are still getting a hard time from your caseworker, insist upon the names of all supervisors in the department. Go to the higher-ups, the office heads, even the director of the agency, making sure that copies of every document are sent to them and that your caseworker knows that you have sent these copies. Additionally, send copies to the media, politicians, and your representatives at all three levels—state, county, and federal—and also send copies to local and national women's organizations. You can call your local election commission to get the names of your representatives in the state

and federal government. If you run into problems such as lateness with checks or reduced amounts or are just told that you will have to wait, be persistent. Keep calling, and repeat, "I did not receive my benefits." You may sound like a broken record, but that's a great way to get someone to intervene. Never forget that the squeaky wheel gets the grease.

Ways to Earn Money Legally and Not Lose Your Benefits. A family of four on welfare often receives benefits not amounting to much more than $300 a month give or take some, depending upon where you live. Obviously, this is not adequate to meet all the needs of raising a family. There are ways to supplement your income, but you must be sure that these ways are legal in your state because anything else constitutes welfare fraud, which carries with it a very serious punishment. This could include a stiff fine, jail time, or even losing your children. Here are ways some states allow you to earn more money while receiving assistance:

Attend School. Grants, loans, work study, and paid tuition are exempt from TAFDC punishments. (A punishment means taking away benefits, usually the mother's, but could result in the whole family suffering.) Additionally, getting your education means that you are learning skills that will allow you to one day earn a living that pays more than minimum wage. Don't be bullied into thinking you have to sign up for a "Welfare to Work" program when you are getting an undergraduate degree. True, you can't receive full benefits if you are getting a master's degree, but the requirement may be waived for those who are earning their GED or completing college.

Do Reimbursable Volunteer Work. If you volunteer for an organization and get reimbursed for "expenses" at an agreed-upon rate, you may not lose benefits. For example, you may volunteer at a public agency and receive lunch in the employee's cafeteria at no charge and be reimbursed for transportation and child-care costs. Although the amount of money you receive will be slight, the training and contacts the volunteer work provides might well lead to paid employment and an end to your need for public assistance.

Provide Foster Care. Some single mothers have found that taking in a foster child not only is emotionally fulfilling, but the money allotted you for this program is often exempt from TAFDC punishments. Don't forget that the major portion of the allotment is intended for the care of the child, but a portion also reimburses you for the time and effort you expend caring for this youngster.

Self-Employment. Your state may allow the same deductions as the IRS when you work for yourself. Additionally, you are eligible for EIC (Earned Income Credit), which can give you over $2,000 when you report your income on your taxes.

Become a VISTA Volunteer. Volunteers in Service to America (VISTA) stipends are exempt from penalties. Of course you don't earn much for work-ing a full schedule, but if you receive, say, $550 a month for being a VISTA volunteer, you still get to keep all of your TAFDC benefits. VISTA volunteers work only for nonprofit agencies. You can reap the rewards of helping others and gain valuable job experience! Some VISTA volunteers work part-time. Check out all options that might interest you.

Own Your Own Rental Dwelling. If you own a duplex, you may be able to rent out half and declare your rental income without losing benefits if you write off your expenses the same way you would if you were self-employed. Again, TAFDC allows exemptions similar to those of the IRS, but remember that if you make a profit, you lose benefits. Also, you must reside in one part of the duplex or rental property.

Take in a Boarder. This person cannot be biologically related to your child. In other words, you cannot have your baby's father live with you and report his payment of room and board as income. You would lose benefits. Remember, welfare fraud—meaning you earn a living under the table and get caught—can result in severe penalties, including incarceration.

Gifts. Basically, the rule of TAFDC punishment is that if you get cash, you lose benefits. However, there is nothing saying that you can't receive what are called in-kind gifts. If your mother wants to buy the children's winter wardrobe, or your boyfriend wants to give you a pair of shoes or a microwave oven, it's perfectly okay.

SEEKING OTHER SOURCES OF HELP

Keep in mind that there are several programs that are made available through government agencies and non-profit organizations that can assist you in making ends meet while you are gaining marketable job skills.

Medical Insurance Programs

The Department of Social Services has a federal Medicaid program that provides health insurance for low-income families. If you do not qualify for this particular health coverage, ask a DSS caseworker to give you a referral to other agencies or the local health department for other types of health insurance for low-income individuals.

Food Programs

DSS also has a food program. Food Stamps are food coupons that are allocated on a monthly basis for low-income persons to use at the grocery store. However, these coupons are limited to the purchase of certain foods. Alcohol, tobacco, and other non-food items are excluded. The WIC program (Women, Infants, and Children) provides food coupons for specific food items from your local supermarket to benefit pregnant women, infants, and children up to two years of age.

Local non-profit organizations also have food supplement programs (and sometimes cash aid programs as well). The following national organizations (listen in your local phone directory) can refer you to help in your area:

United Way, Salvation Army, Catholic Charities, Food Bank

Area churches, Jewish community centers, and homeless shelters can put you in touch with programs providing food and other assistance.

PROVIDING FOR YOUR CHILDREN IF YOU SHOULD DIE

Because the future rests with those who will experience it, the responsibility of all adults is to see that their children, and then their children's children, and so on, will have a safe planet, where they are protected from unnecessary suffering and where they all start out with an even chance at success. Unfortunately, with our country's social policies regarding children, the task has been placed solely on the shoulders of the individual parents. It would be nice if all children had access to funding for college, creative endeavors, health care, experimentation, and simply pleasurable things, but for now, it's up to you to take care of these things.

Here's a story to which many single moms can relate, particularly if they have very young children.

A woman was waiting for her doctor to examine her for what she complained was serious cramping, backaches, and fatigue. She was frantically struggling to wrap herself up as gracefully as possible in the sterile white hospital gown, but wasn't having much luck. The perky little nurse, whom the depressed woman decided had no idea what a stretch mark looked like and had never experienced an unwanted body hair, popped her head in the examining room and reminded the woman that the gown snapped in the back. Whatever dignity remained was now waning.

When the elderly doctor entered the examining room, the woman, who was in her late thirties and obviously quite distressed, tried to appear composed but was unsuccessful at mustering up even a hint of decorum. Ignoring her feeble attempts to calm herself, the doctor was busily scribbling on a chart when he asked, "So why are we here today?"

"We have ovarian cancer," blurted the woman.

This got his attention. "And what makes you think you have ovarian cancer?" he said, looking up slightly disturbed.

"Gene Wilder. Gene Wilder said I had all the symptoms." She was now sweating and becoming more agitated.

"Gene Wilder the actor, or Gene Wilder the gynecologist?" snapped the smallish man.

"The actor, of course. Remember all those ads he did for the American Cancer Society about the symptoms of, you know, it? Bloating and swelling, constant lower backache, and sudden fatigue. His own wife, Gilda Radner, died from it, at only forty-two."

"That's because she probably had it," said the doctor, who was getting noticeably annoyed. He started thumbing through the charts. "Hey, weren't you here just six months ago claiming you had a brain tumor?"

"Look," the woman said. "I never had a migraine before and didn't know what it felt like, okay? So sue me!"

"Wait a minute." He was furiously flipping pages. "Nine months before that you insisted you had lupus or Lyme disease and then back in 1991 ..." the doctor continued.

The woman started sobbing. "Look, I'm sorry. It's just that I'm a single mother and I worry every time something is wrong with me that it's terminal and I'll die. I can't help it. I worry about who will take care of my child if something happens to me."

The doctor softened a bit. "Listen, you don't have any indication of ovarian can-

cer. And all your tests from your last visit look pretty normal. In fact, everything is fine with you, except maybe you could use some peace of mind. You want my advice? I suggest you get some kind of will, make plans for your child's future—just in case—and then please go live a nice life."

Don't Worry, Just Be Prepared. Worrying about who will take care of your child in the event that something happens to you is a common thread that binds single mothers, following a close third after guilt. (Never having sex again has been running neck and neck against guilt in a tight race for second place, and lack of money is still number one.)

Chances are, you will live a long and healthy life if you don't make yourself crazy with worry or drive into the back of a truck while reviewing your daily schedule on the freeway. But it is definitely a good idea to get certain things out of the way—for example, planning for who will raise your kids if something should happen to you.

Having a plan gives your children a double gift—first, your peace of mind, which will allow for less stressful parenting, and second, a safety net in the event that something happens to you. Peace of mind allows for a healthier outlook both physically and mentally, and what better start to longevity than that?

First Things First: Get Life Insurance. Almost all tax and estate attorneys recommend that single mothers purchase life insurance even if they have other assets. Basically, there are two types of life insurance: whole life insurance and term life insurance.

Whole life or cash value insurance does have its appeal because it is like an investment that has a cash value.

Because it provides tax benefits and funding that is available to you as the cash surrender value (the amount you receive if you cancel the policy) or as a loan at a very low interest rate, financially solvent single moms might want to go this route. Another plus is that the premium doesn't increase with each birthday, but your policy's cash value as it accumulates interest does increase.

Term insurance, however, is usually recommended for single moms, particularly for those with limited funds. First, whole life insurance as an investment is not one of the fastest money accumulators. Your money could be invested in more aggressive ways. Term insurance offers the same protection as more costly whole life insurance, but its only purpose is to pay a benefit in the event of your premature death. The policy's term can be one year or five years, and you can pay the rates monthly, just as you would your other bills.

Speak to a general insurance agent who represents many companies and find the best type of policy for your needs. Some types of insurance policies are decent investment vehicles as part of an overall financial portfolio. As part of the decision about how much life insurance to buy, it is important to know if your children will be eligible for social security benefits or other death benefits should you die before they are adults. These benefits may be more than you realize. Make a rational decision about how much life insurance you need and can afford. Be careful not to be influenced by irrational fears that your children will be penniless.

Money-Saving Tip: For information on finding the best rates for life insurance, write:

LIFE INSURANCE TIP

Avoid paying premiums directly to a person unless you know he or she is a reputable agent. Be sure to pay life insurance premiums directly to the insurance company, if possible. However, if you are paying life insurance premiums to a local agent, make certain to keep receipts, payment book stubs, and canceled checks as proof of payment. Contact the home office periodically to be sure that your policy is in force. Many scams have been reported by people paying independent agents who moved from one insurance company to another, defrauding their customers with false policies.

Insurance Quote
3200 N. Dobson Road
Building C
Chandler, AZ 85224

Or call toll-free, 1-800-972-1104. They will screen out insurers whose prices fail to make the grade and will point you in the right direction.

Estate Planning. Estate planning is also an integral part of your investment program. You know the importance of having a will simply for your peace of mind. But it is critically important to have a will to provide for your children. If you die without a will, state laws will largely determine what happens to your assets and who becomes your children's guardian. You also want to be sure that an ex you don't want to see get your money is legally prohibited from doing so. Unless you know something about estate planning and wills, avoid a will kit. It's best to go to an attorney for even a simple will because if it is prepared inaccurately, certain provisions can become invalid.

I wasn't married to my child's father, and he's seen my four-year-old daughter only once. How could he possibly get my daughter's inheritance if something happens to me?

PLANNING FOR YOUR DEATH: BENEFITS OF A LIVING TRUST

• Living trusts avoid probate, whereas a conventional will requires it. The probate process lasts up to two years and can cost up to 8 percent of your estate.

• Living trusts are private, whereas a will or a trust under a will is a matter of public record.

• A living trust is rarely contested. Because it's difficult to challenge, disappointed relatives, such as your child's father, are unlikely to be able to get their hands on the money.

• Living trusts cost more than wills but are worth it in the long run. Costs in creating this kind of trust are tax-deductible, and there are no annual court accountings and the legal fees that go with them.

• A living trust allows the trustee to collect life insurance immediately without court delays.

• A living trust gives you control and is created, activated, and managed while you are alive and well. Moreover, it is portable, meaning you don't have to revise it as you would other types of trusts if you move to a different state.

It is possible that an estranged father could get custody of the child and therefore have access to her estate. In practically every state, a biological father has rights, whether or not he was married to his child's mother. Because most courts will appoint the biological parent as guardian if no one else is named, it is essential that you choose a guardian to be named in your will in the event of your premature death. Be certain, too, that you don't leave your daughter as beneficiary of your life insurance. There have been cases where an estranged parent showed up at the time of the custodial parent's death and, knowing that minors cannot be awarded the insurance money, gained access to the inheritance, depleted it, and even put the child up for adoption later. Don't let this scare you, because it is unlikely to happen. But to be safe, put your estate as beneficiary, or better yet, have your attorney execute a living trust, particularly if you have a net worth that includes a home, insurance, or other money.

How to Choose a Guardian. First, talk privately with the person you would like to appoint as your child's legal guardian. Ask this person if he or she is willing to assume this important responsibility. If the person says no, accept this and understand that he or she has good and valid reasons for the refusal. Never try to talk anyone into accepting this responsibility. It is not important whether the person you choose is male or female, single or married, or childless. It is only important that your child's prospective guardian would be able to care for your child in a loving and caring manner. Don't disregard asking a lifelong friend with whom

THE DOS AND DON'TS OF MONEY MANAGEMENT

- Do remember the golden rule: He who has the gold rules. The person with resources is always the person with choices.

- Don't allow or expect others to make financial decisions for you. You can enlist the aid of an adviser, but only you can decide what and how much you want to invest in something. Remember, too, if something sounds too good to be true, it most likely is.

- Don't invest in anything you don't understand, and never make financial decisions in haste.

- Don't let emotional obstacles get in the way of managing money. Feeling guilty because your relationship fell apart is not a reason to refuse what is financially yours, such as part of the proceeds from the sale of a house, car, or boat, or even accepting spousal support if your job was taking care of your family.

- Do remember that money is not commitment, love, or attachment. Money is just business.

- Don't be afraid of money or sabotage any money-making efforts because you think you are acting masculinely, or it's not important enough to you. Money is genderless.

- Do remember that control of your credit is control of your life.

- Don't overlook the total costs of what is offered you. In other words, nothing is free—time and energy are also costs.

- Do start today to make a financial plan. Think about your goals and how to achieve them. Above all, write them down.

- Do investigate your employee benefits package. Understand all the benefits available to you and make the best possible use of them.

---

you feel close, even if that person has not spent a lot of time with your child.

Have a Lawyer or Financial Planner Create a Trust. Generally, a popular method of planning for your child is to create a trust, which is property or money that is to be left to your daughter or son upon your death. For many single moms, this usually means the life insurance benefits. Never leave your child as beneficiary, because naming your child can pose the risk of the child's father controlling the assets, thereby gaining access to the child's inheritance. Remember, insurance

companies won't release monies to a minor, which is why estranged parents have been known to show up and gain access to the money.

Now You Need a Guardian of the Trust. Be sure to appoint a guardian of the trust. If you fail to name a guardian in your will, the court may assign guardianship to the natural father, regardless of his involvement with your child. The trustee should be someone with financial knowledge and in whom you have the utmost trust and confidence. Don't choose the same person who will be guardian of your child. This can create too much temptation. Besides, you want to ensure that the guardian and trustee keep a check on each other. You could name your mother, your sister, or a long-time family friend or attorney as the trustee. Never name a bank. Banks charge high fees and often pay the lowest rate of return. Better to pay a financial adviser as trustee if you can't find anyone.

Shop Around for a Qualified Attorney or Estate Planning Expert. There are will kits, but each state is different and you want to be sure that the father cannot get his hands on the money. You should be able to find an attorney to draw up this kind of will for about $300, a fair price for protecting your children's future. When you speak with the attorney who will draw up your will, speak candidly with her or him about the situation with your former husband or partner and about any unusual family situations that might exist. Do not be embarrassed to be as open and honest as possible. If you have other legal matters now unresolved, make sure you inform this attorney. This is not the time to hide anything. Remember that everything shared is protected under attorney–client privilege. Unless this attorney graduated from law school yesterday, there is probably nothing you could say that would be new or surprising.

If you have a net worth over $100,000, execute a living trust—a document in which you state how you want your property managed if you become disabled or terminally ill.

Talking to Your Child About Your Death. You can obtain real peace of mind by allaying fears your children may harbor of losing their only parent. Remember—this is about allaying their fears, not creating fears where none existed before. It is probably necessary to have this kind of discussion with a young child only if there is a real absence of extended family, either because you have no close relative or because your family lives at such a distance that your child rarely sees them. If you have lots of family close by or your child's father is an integral part of her life, then it might not be necessary to bring up this subject until the child asks, which is typically not until they are school-age.

If you feel you need to discuss this subject with your child, or your child asks, say that you plan to be her mommy for a long, long while but if the time comes when you can't be, Aunt Jane or Cousin Donna would love to take care of her. Keep these conversations age appropriate. Reassure children that having this kind of "backup mommy plan" is something that all good parents do and that you are not planning to go anywhere.

Another way to feel as though you have your house in order is to talk into a tape recorder or write a letter for your child to open in the event that something happens to you in the future. In fact, it is a great idea, whether you live to be thirty-five or ninety-five, to have personal messages prepared for your child to open at different stages of her life—for instance, one when she turns twelve and another when she is fifteen. The act of leaving a loving part of you is a wonderful gift of reassurance for your children and rewards you with a great amount of comfort as well.

11

"Home Economics"

COMFORTABLE AND AFFORDABLE LIVING ARRANGEMENTS

Regardless of your financial status, your shelter costs will account for a substantial portion of your income—from one-third to three-quarters of your income for many families and even up to 90 percent for extremely poor families. Finding adequate housing when you are on a shoestring budget is often a difficult task.

Perhaps you've already planned for this and you and baby are in a cozy apartment, or you and your brood of three teens have moved into a smaller but still comfortable house. Aside from the financial considerations, there are others factors that must be considered in order to decide what kind of housing arrangements will work best for you and your children, particularly if you are recently divorced and can't maintain your previous residence, or if you were single in a studio apartment and need a room for the new baby. If you became a single mother by losing a loved one to death, these decisions can sometimes appear even more difficult, because emotional issues can cloud the realities that must be faced.

Fortunately, for today's single mother, there are many exciting possibilities, such as sharing a residence with another single-parent family, or moving from a house to an apartment (which means no more mowing the grass, or rebuilding your own place from start to finish!). Flexibility, careful planning, and weighing all your options are essential. Don't be surprised if you wind up liking your new living arrangements more than you did your old ones.

CHANGING YOUR LIFE STYLE

Like many other suddenly single mothers trying desperately to cling to a past life style, you may find that maintaining your past living habits is not working out very well either emotionally or financially. For example, if you live in a busy city and the cost of keeping your car garaged is almost as much as the rent on your apartment, can you forgo car ownership even though you were awarded the car in the settlement? Why not take public transportation and bank the extra money you'll suddenly have?

One single mother recalls her change of life style as something like "going from the country club to the welfare line." As it turned out, she did not require welfare but had been so entrenched in her previous life style that she did temporarily imagine that she would be destitute. Cutting back does not necessarily mean you are not doing well. It can be a time when you learn to simplify your life to your advantage.

Your emotional outlook has a lot to do with how smoothly the transition from one life style to another is made. You don't have to become a totally different person, but it's healthier to accept the fact that single people have different (and often more enjoyable) living habits than married people. By accepting that you are no longer married, you may find it easier to redefine your living style to suit a more independent you.

FACING THE FEAR OF HOMELESSNESS

Homelessness is a fear that haunts nearly every single mother. Even those who chose motherhood after doing some serious financial planning worry that they could lose their jobs or their health and end up homeless. If you visit a homeless shelter, chances are you will find someone who claims they never imagined being there or hear a story about a person who had all the trappings of a successful life until one day, everything went wrong and they lost it all.

For most single mothers, the fear of homelessness is exactly that—an irrational fear. True, your life may change significantly and you may have to scale down your standard of living somewhat, but moving to a smaller place, eating in more often, and clothing your kids from the local thrift shop hardly mean you are headed on a path towards homelessness.

On the other hand, if you do suddenly find yourself homeless due to a sudden change in circumstances, you are not alone, and you are not a failure. It is very difficult but critically important not to let yourself fall into the role of the victim—"I'm poor, therefore I'm worthless." Let your children know too, that although they may not have four familiar walls at this time to call home, home can represent your dreams and values that will one day be realized. For now, however, you need to find temporary housing, either in a shelter or through a crisis assistance center, if you can't find living arrangements through a friend or a relative.

STAYING OR MOVING?

One of the biggest issues newly divorced or widowed single parents face is whether or not to remain in the same house that they lived in when married. The decision of whether to keep or sell your house, condominium, or cooperative apartment certainly should not be rushed, but neither should you avoid a decision for too long.

Make a realistic assessment of your new expenses and income. Determine if keeping your current home is even affordable. A basic rule for determining whether you should reside in any living space is to calculate what percentage of your monthly income your house payment represents. If you're paying out one-quarter to one-third, then you're okay. But if your mortgage eats up well over 30 percent of your total income,

your best bet would be to look for something more affordable.

Don't kid yourself into thinking that you can't manage now but will magically be able to manage at some unspecified future time. Be realistic. Do not rely on child support payments to pay the mortgage. You never know when the payments will stop, and even though you may take legal action to continue the child support payments, any delays could cause your lender to foreclose on your property. But if you can afford to stay where you are, you are then ready to ask yourself whether you want to.

Even if you can afford to keep the house, if you really think you want to start fresh somewhere else, do so. Don't let yourself feel guilty about staying put for the sake of your children. Unless the change would be an immediate and serious educational disruption or cause them to miss out on important milestone events, remember that children are adaptable and resilient and may find the change a welcome, positive event.

Getting Answers to Your Mortgage Questions

I'm getting divorced and want to keep the house but my partner and the co-owner of the property won't *explain the details of the loan or answer my questions about it. My husband has always handled these details, with the result that I now have no idea what is going on. However, he says that if I want to buy him out, it's okay with him. Where do I start?*

If you find yourself in the middle of a divorce or separation from a significant other with whom you jointly own a home, and have no idea of what you own or owe, contact the current mortgage holder and ask questions. You have a right to any information concerning the loan's terms, payments, and equity, and to learn what your options are. Don't be afraid to keep asking questions until you understand. Find a lending officer with whom you have a rapport. Single mothers tend to be more comfortable with other women, but some men, particular single fathers who are mortgage lenders, can also be helpful.

Banks seem to work hard at maintaining an aura that often intimidates us or makes us feel as though we are somehow intruding, with our silly little questions and our piddling amount of money. Nonsense! Banking is still a service industry.

Bank personnel like to act as if they are doing you a favor, when actually it is they who should be grateful for your business. You may feel intimidated when seeking information about your mortgage, but try not to accept these feelings. Be pleasant, but be clear that you understand you are entitled to the information regarding the services the bank provides, and to more specific information regarding your particular loan or account. Even though loan officers may need to be a bit more creative in the financing options offered to single mothers, they still should welcome your business. Remember, also, that most loan officers are not used to being bargained with, and if you make a reasonable offer, it will usually be accepted.

Consider Refinancing

My child's father, who was my housemate, wants to move out of state. He says we should sell the house we bought together and share the proceeds, but I don't want to move. I love this house and it is perfect for raising a child. The payments are just too high for me. Do I have any options?

You might consider refinancing and using your share to buy out your former partner's share. By extending your terms—in other words, refinancing for fifteen or thirty years, depending on what's left on your mortgage—you can make smaller monthly payments. Or, you can pay off your former partner and maintain the same payments you have now by getting a housemate to absorb some of the costs.

How to Cut the Interest on Your Mortgage Payments. Most people don't realize that although they can deduct the interest on their mortgage to reduce their taxes, the amount of interest paid out over the years can be enormous. For example, let's say you have a 30-year loan at 11 percent interest. During the first five years of paying off your mortgage, you will pay $19 toward interest for every $1 you paid toward principal. In short, a lot of money goes toward interest. Of course, by the time you get to the end of your mortgage-paying years, you will be paying less interest and more principal. So

how do you shorten the life of your mortgage? Usually, just refinancing your home at a 15-year term would make your monthly payments too high.

Here's what to do to easily cut the interest on any mortgage. Simply make an extra payment once a year along with your regular mortgage payment and designate it to go strictly to principal. In other words, if your monthly mortgage payment (interest and principal) is $450, simply pay an additional $450, or a total of $900, but be sure that the extra $450 goes toward principal only. By "tricking your mortgage" (perfectly legal, but rarely suggested by lending officers, since mortgage holders love getting that interest!) you can cut the time on a 30-year mortgage almost in half, and avoid paying thousands of dollars of interest in the process.

REASONABLE RENTALS

If you're already in an apartment that isn't quite as large as you'd like to have to accommodate a new baby, but you have a dining area or sleeping alcove that could serve as a nursery, by all means do this if it means avoiding a rental increase. However, if your current rent is too high, and your building has other rental apartments available for less than what you are now paying, check with the landlord about getting something a little cheaper or see if he will reduce the rent in exchange for your painting the apartment or performing certain maintenance tasks.

If you definitely need to look for a place, you should be aware that finding a reasonable rental for you and your family is a little trickier than it used to be. In some larger cities, the tactic among those in the race to find the

HAVE A HOUSEWARMING

Throw a party to celebrate moving into your new place. One newly divorced single mother tells of what she did when her husband selectively took many items, both valuable and incidental, out of their home without her knowledge when they first separated. When she first discovered the theft, all she could focus on was how she did not now even own a hammer. She asked each guest to bring a hammer as a housewarming gift to her new place. She mounted these hammers as a unique and very creative wall display, which also served as a daily reminder that she had survived. She could even laugh publicly at what had once been a frightening time in her life.

most desirable apartments is not to look in the paper's classified section, but rather to read the obituaries and see where a recent "vacancy" has occurred.

Less drastic techniques include calling a rental agent daily at a place where you really would like to live. One of the best ways to find out about available rental units in an apartment complex is to talk with the residents already living there. Searching the classifieds, being on the lookout for yard signs announcing a vacancy, checking listings and notes posted on community bulletin boards at your local college or university, post office, or health and human resource agencies are other ways to apartment hunt. Don't overlook placing an ad yourself in your local newspaper, apartment guide, or school newsletter. Enlisting the aid of real estate agents is another good idea, because often these people sell homes to people exiting from apartments.

Some of these agents will also charge you a fee, so be sure to ask about possible costs up front.

Retirement homes can be another source of information on affordable apartments, because many of the residents may be giving up their apartments in order to live in a place with health-care professionals on staff. Ask the director of the home if you can post notices in the recreation room announcing your need for an apartment. Often residents may know of others moving into the retirement home who may give you a lead on an available apartment.

SUBSIDIZED HOUSING

Your Department of Social Services can refer you to subsidized housing programs that are provided by local housing authority departments. These programs can assist you in finding a place to live and even provide some financial relief with your rent. Keep in mind that most housing assistance programs require you to pay a portion of your monthly income. If you're required to contribute, say, one-third of your income toward rent, they will pick up the remaining balance of your rent.

You can also contact your local housing authority for a list of subsidized and HUD (Housing and Urban Development) housing in your county. These housing developments base their rentals on a sliding scale but you may also find low-rent apartments in higher-rent areas. Since there is usually a huge waiting list for these apartments, you might want to move into a non-subsidized unit. By doing so, you can get to know the landlord or building manager, prove what an exemplary tenant you are, and often move up the waiting list faster for a subsidized rental when it becomes available.

HOMESHARING

Homesharing—two or more single-parent families maintaining one residence—is gaining increased popularity. Basically, homesharing usually consists of two mothers sharing an apartment with their children or purchasing or renting a house together. Networks are currently being developed to help single parents find others who may be looking to share an apartment or rent out part of a house.

One single mother, who was a day-care provider, feared that she wouldn't be able to afford the house that she had previously shared with her spouse. A friend of hers introduced her to another single mother with one daughter who had to give up her apartment because the building was going co-op and the woman could not afford to purchase her apartment and pay the monthly maintenance fees. The day-care provider rented out a portion of her house to her new friend and her daughter. Both greatly benefited from this arrangement, because the woman who lost her apartment had always wanted to live in a house in the suburbs without being saddled with a mortgage, and the homeowner did not have to lose her house since she was now getting help meeting her mortgage payments.

Buying a House with Another Family

A few months ago I met a young woman at my son's karate class and we've become fairly good friends. *She's a single mom like me and has always wanted to buy a house but couldn't afford it. We've discussed going in on some real estate together, not only as an investment, but so we can have more living space and our children can attend an excellent school. Even though I'm fed up with my tiny apartment, I'm a little worried. It seems to work great on those TV sitcoms, but what happens if we don't get along, or if one of us loses a job, or gets transferred? What happens if one of us decides to get married and move out? What do we need to know about buying a home together?*

Certainly, a *Kate and Allie* situation can work well in real life if you consider all the pros and cons of homesharing or joint home ownership before venturing into such a commitment. Many single-parent families are successfully sharing living space, and based on your forethought and your intelligent, thoughtful, and realistic questions, it's clear that you are doing your homework first. It's critical that you weigh the advantages against the pitfalls of joint home ownership.

Deciding if Joint Home Ownership Is Right for You. Buying a home can be a lot easier today than it has been in the past. Interest rates have been fairly stable, and through certain programs offered by some lenders, down payment requirements have dropped to as low as 5 percent in many cases. Years ago, not having a husband's signature on the mortgage document was very uncommon. Today, more than one-fourth of all home buyers are unmarried, and more and more of these individuals are pooling their resources and purchasing properties together.

Joint home ownership can be complicated, since all the factors that need to be considered when you individually purchase a home are now twofold (unless your prospective partner is your clone). You may prefer an area with a fabulous elementary school, but a problematic high school. If your co-owner or partner has older children, this may present a problem. Additionally, the location of your jobs, family, and friends may appear to be at opposite ends of the earth when you are considering these factors in your decision-making process.

Joint home ownership is first and foremost a partnership, not unlike being married. As in marriage, you should be informed of all the possible things that can go wrong. Be aware of the responsibilities of home ownership, and know all the details of the financing. Having information means that you are headed in the right direction.

The best thing to do initially is to sit down with your prospective partner and work out a scenario with possible problems and workable solutions. Because any kind of joint ownership—whether involving a married couple, or two single mothers who have pooled their resources—invites certain problems, severe financial disruption can be avoided if a realistic plan is devised.

Next, it is wise to seek the advice of an attorney before even seeing a lending officer. An attorney can best advise you whether or not the scenario you have agreed upon is workable and can alert you to any possible complicating factors or unforeseen situations you might not have considered. Tax planning will also be important here. You will need to decide, for example, how deductions will be apportioned. Your attorney will also outline costs, such as additional legal fees or special types of insurance coverage, which you will need to factor into your decision making. Carefully review all the information provided so that you can make the best-informed decision about whether or not this housing arrangement is right for you.

If you decide to proceed, your attorney will draw up an agreement, not unlike a prenuptial agreement, in order that both of you will have your rights protected in the event of a dissolution of the partnership. At this stage you may wish to be represented by separate attorneys so that each of you is equally protected. As in any partnership, your individual interests may conflict, and such conflicts need to be ironed out early. Although the benefits of joint ownership are many—the ability to afford a larger down payment, lower monthly mortgage and maintenance expenses, and the joys of gaining an extended family—knowing what to do in the event that one person opts out of the partnership is most important.

When One Family Does Too Much

I and my teenage daughter live with another single mother and her young daughter, who has slight learning disabilities. This woman schedules everything, right up to how we spend our weekends, but sometimes I want private time with just my daughter. My housemate's three other young children will begin summer vacation soon. My housemate thinks that my daughter will be in charge of caring for them. But I don't think it is fair for her or a good practice to be tied up taking care of all the young kids in this household (who are not even family related), and miss out on being with her friends. What do you think?

When you say, "not even family related," you are shortchanging yourself on the definition of family. Family is defined as a place where love is shared and a place that feels safe. One of the reasons you probably entered a homesharing situation was not only to save on bills and expenses, but also to create a sense of extended family. However, you are right that a teenager should not be expected to be the caretaker of all the youngsters in a household. A certain amount of responsibility is necessary and important for all teenagers to help them make the transition from childhood to adulthood, but resentment can occur if they are expected to do too much.

BE CREATIVE WHEN DECORATING

Fixing up your house or apartment can give you many opportunities to show off your talent, ingenuity, and creativity. First, you don't have to ask permission from anyone else if it's your own place. Keep in mind, too, that lack of money or the small size of your dwelling does not have to prevent you from making your place homey and inviting. One single mother who moved out of a huge apartment into an itty-bitty bungalow was so determined to provide a warm, attractive home that her simple but clever decorating schemes had her visitors referring to her new place as the "cozy country cottage." She even planted "no-maintenance" wildflowers, which reminded some of entering an English garden. Other moms haunt the secondhand stores and flea markets after becoming inspired by decorating magazines. Here are some more ideas:

♦ Barter with others for help with painting and other big home fix-up tasks. Fix meals in exchange for having your peeling paint sanded. Invite everyone for a fix-up party.

♦ Get travel or movie posters, usually free from travel agencies or video stores, to decorate your kids' room.

♦ Be a little flamboyant: Paint a shelf jade green or your trim turquoise. Finish the cabinets in fuschia or hot pink, or make your bedroom look like a cabaret dressing room or an island getaway with remnants from a fabric store.

♦ Don't overlook the value of cleanliness and order, which cost almost nothing and go a long way toward making a house a home. Think about the woman who turned that teeny bungalow into a cozy cottage!

How to Make a Home-Sharing Arrangement Work. Hold regularly scheduled family conferences, including the children (if they are old enough to sit still for a while), to review any changes and allocations of responsibility. Children feel good about themselves when they are allowed to participate in the decision-making process. Ask each of them what household tasks they like to do best, such as hanging the towels back up before leaving the bathroom. Allow your teenagers to voice concerns about baby-sitting or any other problems they might have.

All your children will learn valuable negotiating skills and will get firsthand practice in how to compromise for the common good.

You and your housemate will also need designated times to meet away from the children to discuss finances, pay bills, or discuss any home repairs or other joint decisions that must be made. Just as in any type of partnership, communication skills are critically important. Not only do you live with this person, but she is also your partner. Use your business manners and avoid namecalling or losing your temper. Make every effort to discuss your shared interests reasonably and with respect for each other's feelings. Insist on similar treatment in return.

Remember that all collaborative efforts are shaky in the beginning and need an extraordinary amount of cooperation for success. Things will be tough at the start, but the outcome will make all your efforts worthwhile.

Define responsibilities clearly by putting up a chore chart on a wall in the kitchen. You and your partner should assign everyone tasks, leaving to yourselves the major ones like paying bills, deciding on major purchases, and lawn maintenance. Older children and teens can be responsible for preparing meals, cleaning, and shopping. Even younger children can pitch in by setting the table, putting laundry away, keeping their toys picked up, and helping to cut coupons (using safety scissors, of course) for grocery shopping. If one of you has more members in her clan, she should have to absorb a larger share of the cleaning duties, especially if her kids are messy.

Make sure to reward extra effort and cooperation. For extra baby-sitting time teenagers might give, suggest that these favors be returned by driving teenagers to meet their friends, taking them to sports practices or games, or to school activities. One thing that younger teenagers really value is having someone taxi them around until they get their driver's license. Even when they are legally allowed to drive, many of them are unable to afford a car, so borrowing the family car can also be a welcome reward.

What if the home-sharing arrangement is not working out? Incompatible business partners terminate their relationship. If this is your home, after giving a reasonable notice to your housemate, you can start posting notices at work, local schools, churches, universities or colleges, real estate and rental agents, women's shelters, community centers, and day-care centers stating that you are seeking another single-parent household to share living space and expenses. If the house belongs to your housemate, then you must begin the search for a new place to live. The same search techniques will also work for you. You should also investigate other types of housing options in order to ensure that you make the best choice for yourself.

COHOUSING

Cohousing is a concept that began in Denmark in 1972. It consists of private apartments or houses that form a small-scale community around shared common facilities such as playrooms, kitchens, dining rooms, and laundry areas.

Cohousing is different from some other group living arrangements, in that everyone owns or rents their own living unit. What makes cohousing particularly appealing to single parents is that the other adults in the community provide companionship. It is economically advantageous because the lending, sharing, or shared ownership of seldom-used items such as sewing machines, video cameras, or camping equipment is encouraged so you can borrow and use such items without going to the expense of purchasing them. Additionally, members of the cohousing community pitch in on child care and food preparation.

MOVING IN WITH YOUR PARENTS

In the late 1980s, newspapers and magazines ran story after story about the back-home movement, featuring interviews with many of the unmarried, professional single working men and women, single-parent families, and young married couples who sought relief from the troubled economy by moving back home to live with their parents. Because living with your parents is in all likelihood not the living

arrangement you would choose first, it is easy to lose sight of the fact that this represents a major adjustment for your parents also.

Changes Your Parents May Undergo. Your image of one or both of your parents as caretakers and providers may not have changed, but it is likely that since you grew up and left home, they *have* changed. For starters, they probably enjoyed the changes that came with an empty nest. They were able to set their own schedules and priorities. They may have enjoyed having company more often and taking spur-of-the-moment vacations. If one of your parents is deceased or single, it is likely that this parent has made a fine adjustment to the post–single-parent life. He or she probably enjoys many activities and friendships and is doing his or her best to live joyfully in the moment.

Your arrival with the children will probably cause your parents to have some mixed feelings. On one hand, they are probably glad to be able to help you and sad that things have been tough for you. In addition, it is a blessing to be a real part of their grandchildren's lives and to be able to share with them important events and exciting changes. On the other hand, their life styles will most certainly be disrupted. There will be noise, sticky fingerprints on everything, toys with a million pieces, and requests for a snack at all hours. There might now be a line at the bathroom, where before your parents had the luxury of privacy. There will be added expenses like bigger water and utility bills, and generally more wear and tear on the house and its contents.

Establish Some House Rules. Before you and your parents come to an understanding about the details of daily living, you must recognize that your parents are sacrificing and compromising on your behalf. They may be more than happy to do so, but if you are going to retain your grown-up status, the adjustments your parents have made must be gratefully acknowledged by you. It is also critically important that you work out businesslike financial arrangements. In all likelihood your financial resources are quite limited—otherwise, living with your parents would not have been your first choice. Try to pay them something no matter how small an amount. As your financial situation improves, increase your contribution to the household proportionately.

Decide who is responsible for food or shopping and how the cleaning chores will be divided, and discuss curfews, loud music, allowing guests in the home, and baby-sitting arrangements. Even though you are dealing with Mom and Dad, agreeing to a formal arrangement may define your roles even more effectively.

When Living with Your Parents Is Difficult. Knowing that your parents have compromised still may not be enough to enable you to deal effectively with how you may be feeling. A little communication might go a long way toward solving any problems you might be experiencing. You may want to write your parents a letter. After you write it, review it and either throw it away if it contains too much anger, or edit out the accusatory parts, and rewrite it and give it to your parents. Ask if all of you could sit down quietly away from the children and discuss what is expected of you, and what all of you see as appropriate roles in the day-to-day care of the children. Ask what might be making them uncomfortable with their current situation.

Because of financial strains resulting from a very nasty divorce, I had to move back into my parents' home, and let me tell you, my mother is driving me crazy. Don't get me wrong—she's a wonderful lady— baby-sits, feeds them if I'm late getting home from work, cares for them when they are home sick. I know that she loves us. But, if I so much as attempt to discipline my kids (without spanking), she says I'm being ineffective. Or before I go out on a date, she gives me the third degree. She often waits up until I get home. I'm thirty-four years old, not fifteen. Why does she treat me like a failure just because my marriage didn't last as long as hers? If I wanted to have someone constantly control me, I would have stayed married to my tyrannical ex.

Although moving back home is an economic necessity for many new single moms, one of the major issues cited by women who have moved back with their parents is that of being treated like a child again by one or both of them.

Some mothers, particularly mothers of the baby-boom generation or earlier, were themselves raised to believe that a woman's success was measured by how long she could hold a family together, and not so much by how she felt about herself or her ability to create her own life. So these moms often feel responsible for what they see as their daughter's failed marriage. If you try and see things more from your mother's perspective, and understand where it comes from, you will cope more effectively with your current living arrangements.

Acting like a grown-up will also go a long way toward helping your parents treat you as one. You might simply say

---

TIPS FOR LIVING PEACEABLY WITH YOUR PARENTS

- Don't expect your parents to give up or alter lifetime habits just because you and the children are now living with them. Insisting that they do so will diminish their own feelings of security and self-esteem and maybe cause disruption in everyones' lives. You have the capacity for greater flexibility and you may need to demonstrate this skill more consistently than will your parents.

- Remember that your parents' energy levels are not as high as yours. A trip to the grocery store to buy a carload of supplies may be routine for you, but might be exhausting for your mother. From simply a fairness perspective, heavy chores should be your responsibility.

- Help your parents to locate resources that might make their adjustment to this situation easier. You may want to get them books or videos that describe parenting ideas for grandparents or materials that have influenced your parenting choices. But don't present these materials in such a way as to suggest they are less than wonderful grandparents. Say something like, "I know how hard it has been, and how wonderfully you've tried to deal with our living here, so I thought this book might help make it a little easier."

- Simple gestures can also go a long way toward making life more pleasant for everyone. How about getting up a little early one weekend in order to make your parents a special breakfast? Or why not complete that extra chore that makes the house look especially nice? Have you considered hiring a babysitter and taking your parents to a movie or to some activity that they might really enjoy?

- Keep in mind that sharing a home with your parents will be a temporary solution to your housing problem. However, if it turns out to be successful through your combined efforts, welcome the knowledge that you and the children will have the privilege of living with all the benefits of an extended family under one roof.

- Always pay something toward rent or barter or trade in exchange for living with your parents. Have a written contract that is agreeable to all of you.

- Be open to change. Your parents may decide they need to live in a warmer climate or nearer to their friends for part of the year. Be prepared for any change in your living arrangements by having a backup plan.

to your parents some version of, "Thank you for being here for us. You're really helping me save money I couldn't afford to spend on a higher rent or mortgage elsewhere. If I get a place for myself and the children, I'll always know you helped make it possible."

Another tip: Do choose your battles carefully. If your mother wants to tell your son that socks and underwear should never be placed in the same drawer, so what? But on the other hand, if she makes constant ethnic or racial slurs, abuses substances, or hits your children, you need to work these issues out because this is not the message you want your children to receive. You will want to come to an immediate understanding about who will discipline the children and what means are acceptable to you, and determine house rules with which all of you can live.

THE DOS AND THE DON'TS OF HOUSING

+ Do stay where you are if possible to minimize the disruption in your children's lives, particularly if they are in school.

+ Do childproof or childsafe your home. If you've lived in a place for a long time before having your baby, you'll have to make some changes in your home. This means checking your home for safety every so often to accommodate the stages of your child's development. To be truly safe, get a copy of *Raising Children Toxic Free: How to Keep Your Child Safe From Lead, Asbestos, Pesticides, and Other Environmental Hazards*, by Dr. Herbert L. Needleman and Dr. Philip J. Landrigan (Avon Books, $12.50).

+ Don't be tempted to pay more for shelter than you can afford.

+ Don't try to hold on to a life style that is no longer emotionally or financially possible for you. Embrace the positive aspects of a scaled-down life style, and use the energy left to make your life more creative and sustaining.

+ Do find affordable housing and use your creative touches to make it homey.

+ Do keep the fear of homelessness in perspective. In all likelihood, this will not happen to you. If it does, keep in mind that it is a temporary situation.

+ Don't be afraid to ask for help if you need it. Contact a crisis or emergency center in your community to learn what's involved in getting temporary help with utility and other household expenses.

+ Don't allow banks and other lending institutions to intimidate you. Without you they would be out of business. Conduct yourself like the valued customer you are.

+ Do investigate all housing options. Unless you have thoroughly investigated these choices, don't dismiss the possibilities of homesharing or joint ownership.

+ Do make an effort to make living with your parents a grown-up experience. Keep communication flowing, treat your parents' efforts to welcome you with respect, and make that little extra effort to make this transition time better for all concerned.

PART 3

GETTING THE CONFIDENCE TO RAISE TERRIFIC KIDS

12
Child Care

CHOICES AND CONSIDERATIONS
WHEN SELECTING A CAREGIVER

Many moms don't have the luxury of nonstop income, a spouse's generous paycheck, or handsome dividends paid monthly through lucrative investments. Those who have to work at a job outside the home find headlines like "Stay-at-Home Moms Under More Stress Than Those Who Work" quite comforting. And they're true. Even career women who left dream jobs to stay home with their children for a while often ask themselves (after they return to work), "What on earth possessed me to give up my job?" In fact, in article after article in magazines and newspapers, many mothers talk about how their illusions about the joys of being a stay-at-home mom were shattered once the reality set in (the days spent baking cookies or drawing together just didn't happen as they had imagined), how their self-esteem took a dive without their work routine and the rewards that accompany productivity, and how they discovered what many stay-at-home moms already know: that raising children full-time means having no time alone for yourself. Even moms who can afford to stay home often put their children in some

kind of child-care program, such as "Mothers' Mornings Out," because they know the importance of attending a fitness class, meeting friends for coffee, or simply feeding their own souls by visiting museums or art galleries.

Still, most of us harbor some guilt about letting someone else raise our children. Next to financial and emotional issues that confront most single mothers, child-care concerns are probably the most stressful. However, with more and more women entering or already in the work force with children at home under the age of six, the need for child care is greater than ever before. The good news is that you don't have to feel guilty about leaving your child with a provider so that you can go to work or attend school. There are many resources to answer these needs, and you have a number of options when seeking quality care. Plus, study after study is showing that children who spend time in a good child-care situation develop better social skills than those who don't. True, the ideal situation is to be able to work part-time, up to thirty hours per week. If you have that kind of arrangement, you can lose the guilt now. If not, consider at least shaking some of the old myths that have surrounded child care to assuage some of your guilt and help you feel better about something that can't be avoided.

THOSE CHILD-CARE MYTHS

MYTH #1: *Day Care Means Putting Your Child in the Hands of Strangers.* You may recall the 1994 headlines surrounding the case of Jennifer Ireland, a young single mom who won a scholarship to the University of Michigan and kept her daughter in day care while she attended classes. The child's father had been out of the pair's lives for the entire first year, and then reappeared to fight for custody. When Miranda was three years old, she was taken away from her mom to be given to her father, Steve Smith, because the judge in the case felt that Ireland could not attend school and tend to her daughter's needs at the same time. Macomb County Circuit Judge Raymond Cashen wrote, "There is no way that a single parent, attending an academic program at an institution as prestigious as the University of Michigan, can do justice to their studies and the raising of an infant child."

But this was not about whether Ireland was an adequate mother but more an argument about whether or not she was "putting her child in the hands of strangers." The judge felt Miranda would fare better living with the father, who lived with his mother, even though the father had no job and also attended school.

It's unfortunate that too many old-fashioned and ultraconservative folks like Judge Cashen believe that child care causes children irreparable damage. Imagine the idea that having a chance to paint, draw, play, count, sing, take field trips, and laugh—not to mention acquiring social skills such as interacting with others and learning conflict resolution—could be harmful to a child. Experts say not so. They say that a quality child-care center can actually help a child get a head start on learning to live in the real world.

MYTH #2: *Professional Providers Can't Offer What a Relative Can.* In April 1994, a study by the Families and Work Institute looked carefully at in-home child care offered by relatives and nonfamily providers and found that half the children surveyed showed a lack of trust for those who cared for them, including relatives.

A family tie is not always the best indicator of good child care. Experts found that children did not necessarily form stronger attachments to relatives than to nonfamily providers. In further research, it was found that relatives see themselves as helping a family member, not as professional baby-sitters. Moreover, trained caregivers often provide more enrichment and activities for young children than do relatives.

MYTH #3: *The Next Best Thing to Mom Is Grandma.* Those who are guilty of watching too many *Andy Griffith* reruns may have the idea that the ideal single parent's child-care provider is a full-time grandma who stays at home. Not every child's great-aunt or grand-mother is an Aunt Bea. A child-care provider who is stable, loving, and consistent in his or her routines and expectations of the child can promote positive self-esteem in the child of a working single parent and also teaches young children that there are many caring adults who can be trusted. Proper training is even more important in caring for children than "old-fash-ioned" experience. Warm, loving, attentive caregivers provide the best environment for young children.

MYTH #4: *Day Care Can Lead to Long-Term Insecurity.* On the contrary, a stable environment that offers structure yet permits the child to advance at his or her own rate of learning can be a boon to a child's sense of well-being and security. As stated above, not only is the caregiver's relationship to the child not an important factor, but a group setting offered by professional day-care centers can be emotionally and intellectually stimulating for children. Research proves that toddlers and preschoolers who have greater interaction with other children excel in verbal and social skills, enabling them to gain an increased sense of independence.

THE DOS AND DON'TS OF CHILD CARE

+ Do research your child-care options long before you need them. For example, if you are pregnant, plan for child care now.

+ Don't let headlines make you paranoid about every child-care facility you visit. The majority of child-care situations are safe. Be cautious, but not panicky. You'll be more apt to make good judgments if you are calm and reserved.

+ Do ask questions, and then ask more. Then ask and check the answers again! You can never investigate a child-care provider or center too much or exhaust a list of questions too soon. Even though child and sexual abuse exists in only a minority of cases, don't take any chances.

+ Don't dismiss male providers because you think they pose too much of a threat or risk to your child (you should thor-oughly investigate the person regardless of gender). Even though this chapter refers to caregivers primarily as "she" and males are not as readily found as women in this field, qualified young or mature men who have elected to pro-vide caring, activities, and enrichment for children often bring to the job a sense of adventure, creativity, and a dif-ferent point of view—particularly ideal for boys seeking role models.

+ Do check licensing requirements for providers in your area. Even though hav-ing a license is no guarantee of quality child care, if your state requires a license for a home with five or more children, and the caregiver has six children with no license, be wary. Likewise, if a center is licensed and has significantly fewer children than the allowed staff/child ratio, be cautious, too. Maybe other par-ents know something that you don't.

+ Do keep at it. With perseverance and research, you should be able to find a workable solution.

MYTH #5: *Your Child Won't Be Sure Who Mommy Is.* Nonsense. Your child may feel like he has a number one mommy and a number two mommy (the child-care provider), but there is nothing wrong with a kid thinking that there are many adults who care for him. It's simply impossible to care for a child too much. You may feel sad if you are not there when your child experiences major breakthroughs such as taking his first step, losing his first tooth, or eventually mastering the potty-training challenge. You may berate yourself for having to work or even for choosing to work, and think that if you could be a stay-at-home mom, your child would thrive better. But staying home is no guarantee that you will be focused on your child's every move. In fact, some studies suggest that stay-at-home moms share less than thirty minutes one-on-one quality time each day with their children than working moms do.

REVIEWING YOUR CHILD-CARE OPTIONS

What is the difference between a preschool, a day-care center, and a child-care center?

Actually, most places that keep children for a fee before the child is eligible for public school are referred to as child-care facilities, whether or not they have particular preschool programs and activities. Day care is another term commonly used to describe an environment where children are kept while the parents are at work. Here is a description of the most commonly available child-care options.

In-home Care. This includes nannies, au pairs, roommates, sitters, housekeepers, and friends or relatives. In-home care is ideal for the new mom with an infant because the baby stays in his own environment, receives individual attention, and does not run the risk of picking up infections from other children in a busy day-care center. Because babies need special care the first few months, a one-on-one relationship with a care provider is preferable to that of a facility where there are many providers. Yet due to the controversy stirred up by the film *The Hand That Rocks the Cradle*, many new moms think the only safe nanny is a grandmotherly type who only changes diapers and sings nursery rhymes all day. Actually the ideal in-home provider might be a new mother who needs to earn extra money and will come into your home to care for your baby while caring for her own.

Family Day Care. This is the oldest and most widely used form of child care. It attracts many women who not only need child care but are considering their own at-home child-care service. Many women with young children who either can't afford child care or simply do not want to return to the corporate work place until their children start school have found this to be an ideal solution. It's a way to earn money while caring for their own children. One advantage of family day care is that there are fewer children in this kind of environment because licensing may often be easier for a small home-care business to acquire than a larger center. In addition, this type of arrangement may be more affordable than larger centers. However, certain drawbacks exist.

BEST BET: CHILD CARE RESOURCE AND REFERRAL AGENCIES

In 1980, there were only sixty Child Care Resource and Referral Agencies (CCR&Rs) in the United States; ten years later, there were over three hundred, and more are popping up each year.

What Is a CCR&R? A CCR&R can point you in the right direction to address your particular needs, whether you are seeking day care or night-time care, have a child requiring special attention, or have need of funding or other information. Most CCR&Rs are supported by a combination of funding from city, county, or state budgets; federal dependent-care funds; businesses and corporate foundations; United Ways; universities; and charitable organizations. Some are housed in state or other public agencies, but most are community-based organizations that have been created by parents or child-care advocates in response to local needs and are run by a small staff and volunteers.

Why We Need CCR&Rs. CCR&R organizations are becoming increasingly important for their unique ability to address the needs of both parents and child-care providers. CCR&Rs help parents make informed choices in selecting care and help develop and maintain high-quality child-care programs that are responsive to local needs.

What Do CCR&Rs Do? A CCR&R gives a parent complete information about the full range of local child-care programs and current openings, and supplies guidelines for public subsidies and other financial aid. The staff should counsel you and offer guidance about the care that is best for your child. They might offer options you may not know about and will also advise you on what to look for in the programs you visit. And because they do not provide child-care services themselves, they have no vested interest in promoting a particular form of care or care program. Facilities recommended by CCR&Rs are usually safe choices because the CCR&R provides caretakers with reliable training, technical assistance, and support to help them remain committed to their demanding but often underpaid and underrewarded profession. CCR&Rs stay abreast of all available resources to respond to shifting patterns of families' child-care needs.

Who Is Eligible? CCR&R is a service that is universally accessible to all families, regardless of income level, and has few eligibility requirements.

For more information on how to choose child care or how to become a child-care provider, call or write to:

National Association of Child Care
  Resource and Referral Agencies
1319 F Street NW, Suite 810
Washington, DC 20004
202-393-5501

The National Association for Family
  Child Care
1331 Pennsylvania Avenue NW Suite 348
Washington, DC 20004
800-359-3817

The Child Care Action Campaign
330 Seventh Avenue, 17th floor
New York, NY 10001
212-239-0138

For one, the home-care provider may not be experienced in child care or may not be prepared for unexpected crises. Additionally, this person may become burned out, decide to return to an office job, move away, or close down her business for a number of other reasons.

Workplace Child Care. Imagine being able to take your coffee or lunch break to be with your child, who is only minutes away from you when you are on the job. As ideal as this situation sounds, it is still evolving too slowly to satisfy the needs of the majority of mothers in the work force. Yet more and more corporations are realizing the benefits of having child care that is conveniently located to their employees. To find out if a company has on-site child care, contact the chamber of commerce in the area where the company is located. Also, pick up a copy of the annual *Working Mother* magazine's "Top 100 Companies" issue. This feature provides information on places that offer on-site quality child care.

Franchised or Private Preschools or Child-Development Centers. Like all child-care environments, professionally run day-care centers have their pros and cons. One problem many mothers encounter in this kind of environment is too rigid a structure. For example, because preschools and child-development centers prepare young children for kindergarten, children are moved from activity to activity at a pace that some may not be ready for. Also, you may not find the flexibility you need if your job demands you stay late at times, or if you have erratic hours during a seasonal crunch. These centers usually open and close at a fixed time and charge costly late fees, while an individual caretaker or in-home center may be

willing to work around your schedule. The bright side of franchised or private child-care facilities is that the staff is usually well-trained and the facility is equipped with state-of-the-art children's play and learning equipment and furniture.

Nonprofit Day Care. Usually affiliated with churches, synagogues, or community service agencies, these child-care settings offer reasonable rates, trained and licensed providers, and a host of activities to keep little ones occupied. Like many professionally run for-profit businesses or day-care franchises, nonprofit child-care facilities may also offer preschool programs. One thing to keep in mind when considering a church or neighborhood-run nonprofit child-care arrangement is that often these places have long waiting lists. Be sure to sign up early in your pregnancy to ensure a slot in this type of facility. Check with your local YWCA, community Head Start program, or local United Way agency for help.

Employee-Run Child-Care Co-ops. One of the brightest solutions for the future of child care is the on-site employee-run co-op. Many small- to medium-sized businesses are opting for this arrangement, for two reasons. First, they are not large enough to offer employees company-owned child care, nor are they able to provide benefits or credit toward outside child care. Second, as with larger businesses, most medium-sized corporations know that a happy worker is a productive one. And because the work force consists of a majority of women with small children at home, the needs of this group simply must be met in order to ensure production in the future.

The employee-run co-op is a child-care arrangement in which company staff using the facility donate hours to help run it. In a sense, it is like job sharing because you trade off with other employees to help manage the cooperative, plus you share job tasks with others on days when a company position is unfilled because that employee is working in the co-op. To present a proposal such as this to a prospective employer, you need to have a detailed plan of how this arrangement would operate. Remember, the bottom line to your employer is how this situation can improve overall production on the job. And don't forget to look at other concerns about starting an on-site child-care co-op. Investigate the licensing requirements in your state, and ask an attorney about any legal ramifications.

School-Age Child Care. School-age child care includes almost any program that regularly enrolls children from kindergarten through early adolescence during the times when schools are traditionally closed. This includes programs operated by schools, family day-care providers, recreation centers, youth-serving organizations, and child-care centers. Also known as extended-day programs, before- and after-school programs provide enrichment, academic instruction, recreation, and supervised care. An array of drop-in and part-time programs also serve an ad hoc child-care function.

HOW TO FIND CHILD CARE

Finding child care can be a formidable task. Parents often don't know where to turn for help and quickly become overwhelmed by high costs, varying quality, the confusing array of programs, and the shortage of openings. Most working mothers seek child care that is convenient to their home or office, has extended hours, is affordable, offers a highly trained staff or individual, and, above all, provides parental peace of mind. Following are some ways to go about seeking quality child care.

Talk with Other Parents. Because first-time mothers, particularly single mothers, have not been in the mainstream of "parent talk," finding referrals from friends and neighbors may not be the easiest method of locating an ideal placement for their child. But referrals are one of the best ways to find a child-care arrangement because not only are you being pointed toward places you may not have known existed, but at the same time you are getting information about the quality of child care. Get a list of mothers in your neighborhood who have used the services of a day-care center or preschool and call them to ask questions. You'll want to know where they found desirable arrangements, what the going rate is in your community, precautions to take, and if they know of any openings.

Read the Ads. When you can't find anyone to recommend a good child-care environment, check the ads in your local newspaper. Don't overlook the free parenting publications now becoming popular in most cities and larger communities. These freebies rely on ads targeted toward those interested in anything to do with children, families, and parenting. You could also place an ad in these newspapers or magazines stating exactly what it is you are seeking.

Post Notices. You can also post notices in your local supermarket, laundromat, post office, elementary school, children's store (if allowed), hospital and community health bulletin boards, and apartment complexes (where notices are permitted) to announce your search for a child-care provider.

Use the Phone Directory. Larger centers that are professionally owned or operated will be listed under child care in your phone directory. Some in-home centers and church- or religious-affiliated child-care programs may also be listed in the Yellow Pages of your local phone book.

Use Referral Agencies. All methods for seeking child care should be used, but if it is available, be sure to seek the advice of resource and referral agencies who can help you find a child-care facility that is right for you.

Dependent Care Reimbursement Accounts. Your company may offer dependent care reimbursement for its employees. This means that as part of your job's benefits, your place of business may pay part or all of your child-care costs. Check into this by speaking to the director of human resources or the work and family coordinator at your place of employment.

THUMBS UP

Here are six signs that your child is receiving quality care:

1. Your child shows you lots of artwork or projects he has been working on.

WHAT TO ASK BEFORE HIRING AN IN-HOME CHILD-CARE PROVIDER

- Even if you are using an agency, don't leave it up to them to investigate a nanny's references. Find out why she left her last job and ask if her former employer would hire her again.

- Ask the agency how long they have been in business and their process for screening their nannies or sitters. For example, if the nanny is from overseas, did the agency check her criminal and medical records?

- Don't hire a caregiver until after an extensive interview, with and without your children present. If your kids feel uneasy around this person, go with your gut feelings and do not hire her.

- Always ask about the caregiver's feelings on discipline. If she shows signs of impatience or rudeness, appears physically or emotionally abusive, or confesses that she makes children stay in a corner or chair for extended periods of time, say, "No, this one's not for me."

Note: Be aware of the "nanny tax" (taxes you pay for an in-home caregiver). New rules suggested by Congress would simplify the filing procedure, making families file their own 1040 forms once a year rather than quarterly as current law dictates. For information on paying social security and other taxes for nannies or other domestic help, contact a reputable accountant or your local IRS office.

Not only does this mean he's busy, but it means he's being supervised.

2. Your child is so involved in what he is doing that he doesn't want you to take him home.

3. The provider asks you numerous questions: where you can be reached, who your child's doctor is, what kinds of allergies your child has, whether your child requires a special diet, and so on. Also, the provider is not necessarily being nosy if she queries you about your relationship with your child's father. Smart sitters don't want a disgruntled, estranged ex scouting around their property. (Be sure you feel comfortable enough with the provider to disclose your situation.)

4. The child-care center has the following combination: low staff/child ratios, small group size, recommended caregiver qualifications, and well-planned activities and enrichment programs.

5. You feel you have established a rapport with the caregiver. Because a single parent does not have the other parent as a backup, the most important backup person in your daily life is the caregiver. It's a good sign when you and the caregiver are able to work together.

6. Television is used as a learning tool only, and the set is only tuned in to a public television station or a cable channel specifically geared toward kids.

CHILD-CARE CAUTION

Following are nine warning signs that may indicate a problem:

1. The baby-sitter makes you drop off or retrieve your child at her doorstep. The day-care center does not allow drop-in visits.

2. The television set is always blaring (most likely in in-home care centers).

3. The children look tired, forlorn, confused, or sad.

4. The place has an unpleasant smell or is dirty and cluttered. True, children should be able to have their things visible, but there should be a reasonably warm and tidy appearance.

5. There seem to be few toys, play equipment is broken, or play areas are unsafe.

6. The staff is smoking or chatting among themselves rather than interacting with the children. If your child stays in a sitter or caretaker's home, make sure there are no domestic issues. Your child should not be in a situation where the provider's spouse has a drinking or drug problem, or where domestic violence occurs.

7. The routines for hand-washing and overall cleanliness are less than perfect. Pay particular attention to where and how diapers and other soiled clothing are changed.

8. Your child acts differently around the in-home nanny or sitter or responds negatively to the provider at a child-care center. A baby who screams every time the caregiver appears is showing fear or dislike. If children complain frequently about a caregiver, it's more than an adjustment phase.

9. You notice changes in eating and sleeping patterns. Watch for unexplained bruises, cuts, burns, or other injuries.

THE COST OF CHILD CARE

Not only do single parents pay the same child-care costs as married or partnered parents, but more often than not single parents pay higher fees. The reason is that the child-care provider has to back up and support the single parent in the same way a second parent would and has become someone upon whom the solo parent has come to rely. However, because of the dual earnings in a two-parent family, which allow more choices in child care, the single parent often has to make do within her budget. Generally, full-time child-care costs range anywhere from $50 to $250 weekly, depending upon what part of the country you live in and the quality of care.

DEALING WITH SEPARATION ANXIETY

Leaving a child at the sitter's or a day-care facility the first few times can be extremely upsetting for a new mother. However, if you can accept these temporary separations in a matter-of-fact manner, the separation will go more smoothly for you and your child. In fact, if you treat the subject like any other routine that is part of your day-to-day parenting activities, you'll find that your child will learn to separate from you more easily. Although some experts disagree as to whether it is best to discuss the separation beforehand (many discourage any discussion, saying that it creates more problems), most agree that you need to reassure your child that "Mom is going to work now and will see you later." Try not to stress your child by telling him or her to be good or to behave. Rather, wish your child a good or fun day, and always let your child know that you love him.

Parting with Less Sorrow

I have a three-and-a-half-year-old son. Suddenly, he is clinging and crying every time I leave him with his regular sitter to go to work. Forget telling me to leave him with anyone else—now he's afraid of everyone, including his grandmother, whom he usually adores.

THE DOS AND DON'TS OF SEPARATING WITHOUT ANXIETY

• Do plan ahead. Have all of your child's belongings packed in one bag ready to hand to the caregiver so you won't be dragging out the event.

• Do be quick and straightforward about the separation. When it is time to leave, do so without hesitation and without giving your child reason to worry. Don't hug and cry excessively, or your child will suspect something is wrong with the whole scenario.

• Do have a few practice runs if parting is difficult for you. For instance, ask a friend or relative if you could drop your child off at his or her house a couple of times until you and your child become comfortable with the idea. You don't have to stay away long—maybe grocery shop, take a walk, or slip in to a movie. Make each time a little longer. In only a few weeks your child will be secure knowing that the routine always means mommy is coming back.

• Don't call your child at day care every time you get a break, or at lunchtime, asking if he misses mommy. It's okay to call once a day to say, "Hello, hope you are having fun," if you can handle this, but be sure that the time you call is okay with the center's director.

• Do develop a ritual for saying hello and goodbye. For example, leaving your child with a lipstick kiss is a constant loving reminder of your presence. Cover your lips with lipstick and then kiss your child on the hand or wrist where she can see the lipstick imprint. Long-wearing lipstick works best because it does not wash off easily. Or let your child keep a family photo in her bag or knapsack.

• Don't show how upset you are at leaving your child. Remember that children take their cues from their parents. If you handle the separation with confidence and trust, this will be absorbed by your child. If you do well, chances are, your child will do well, too.

• Do consider making audiotapes or videotapes for your child if you are going to be separated from him for more than several days. These tapes can be played to reassure your child of your presence in the world and, most importantly, of your continuing love. Try reading a favorite book on tape, telling a family story, or talking to your child about what you are doing while you are away and what you will do together when you return.

Assuming the caregiver is someone in whom you can place a lot of trust, this is probably separation anxiety. Separation anxiety means fear of losing the bond to the parent as an individual. Sometimes separation anxiety manifests itself as a fear of "outsiders," a category that includes not only strangers but everyone who does not live in the house—even close relatives like Grandma. A child dealing with separation anxiety isn't so much afraid of the outsider as he is of the possibility that the outsider might come between him and his mother. All children experience separation anxiety to some degree. It is a normal response.

Talk about what you will do together when you return—the more specific, the better because then your child will have a sharper picture left in his mind. Just make sure that you live up to your promise and do whatever you promised as soon as you return. Create a ritual way of leaving and returning. Say the same special goodbye phrase every time you leave—preferably make it the last thing you do—and the same hello phrase every time you return—preferably the first thing you do. This predictability and special attention will be reassuring to your child. Expect some distress—you cannot eliminate separation anxiety entirely. Be careful about communicating that what he is experiencing is wrong or upsetting. It's okay to comfort your child and reassure him the first couple of times this happens, but then pick yourself up and say goodbye. And leave.

I have just taken a great job. Previously I was temping for an agency, so my four-year-old daughter was in a part-time day-care program only a few times a week. I now have her in their wonderful all-day program, but she seems to be having a harder time with my new job than with the old one. Now I feel like this new job was a bad idea since I'm having such a hard time leaving her. Is something really wrong?

Sounds like you both have a touch of separation anxiety. It is natural to miss your child, but don't allow your own separation anxiety to feed hers. Don't make a big deal out of how much you'll miss your child. Parents are especially likely to experience separation anxiety of their own when the tables are turned and their child leaves them for an extended period of time, such as to go to nursery school or day care. Avoid making the transition more difficult for your child by putting off leaving your child behind, oversentimentalizing the occasion, or behaving differently from the way you normally behave.

13

Parenting Those Ages and Stages

THE EARLY YEARS

While parenting is one of the most difficult challenges any woman can face, it also is supposed to be among the greatest joys in life. And often it is, when a parent can not only guide and teach her children, but learn valuable lessons as well during this life-long process. However, for the single parent facing this challenge alone, the task seems more intense than it does for two-parent families.

Yet, when the real goal of parenting is more closely examined—that of raising a child to go out into the world as a productive, participating, and caring member of the human race—we find that all families in our country face pretty much the same child-rearing issues, such as providing a quality education; dealing with behavior and discipline problems; balancing work and family; and teaching kids to avoid drugs, crime, and heartbreak. It isn't so much a question of how one individual can raise a child alone, but rather how we as a culture are raising our children.

That is why the old proverb "It takes a whole village to raise a child" has never been more meaningful than it has been in recent years. You can raise a child successfully with one parent or two, as long as you build a network that connects your family to the rest of society by engaging others to serve as models and mentors, either directly or from a distance. Not everyone welcomes children as the gifts they truly are, and appreciates the fresh perspective their innocent eyes have to offer. But there are people out there who can become part of your community if you are willing to look. It's important to remember that you can't have too many adults loving a child, but don't buy into the rhetoric that "children must have two parents at home." As Tipper Gore, who

197

was raised by a single mom, once remarked, "A child only needs to know that he or she is the most important thing in the world to at least one adult." America's favorite "daddy," Fred Rogers, of *Mr. Roger's Neighborhood*, agrees: "Here's what I think: the roots of a child's ability to cope and thrive regardless of circumstances, lie in that child's having had at least a small, safe place (an apartment, a room, a lap) in which, in the companionship of a loving grownup, that child can discover that he or she is lovable and capable of loving in return. If a child finds this during the first years of life, he or she can grow up to be a competent, healthy person." Letting your children know that they were meant to be here means you have already started off on the right track.

YOUR BABY

Feeling Unloved by Your Baby

My baby is acting different. She was so cuddly and sweet the first year, but now she screams, fusses, and seems generally uncooperative. I feel like she doesn't love me as much as she used to. I've been working outside the home since she was four months old, so it couldn't be because I can't stay at home with her all the time, could it?

Maybe the "love affair" that new mothers and babies experience during the first year has ended, but this doesn't mean that a stronger, more unconditional love can't flourish. And it certainly isn't that your child is mad at you because you have a job.

Babies don't do too much during the first year, so there are few problems with behavior that need to be dealt with. But now your child is ready to move ahead toward greater independence and autonomy. When you have had a cooperative, easy baby, this burst of autonomy and negativity comes as a shock! Try to ride with the changes, as these are all a natural part of your baby's development in trying to explore her world while lacking the wherewithal to deal with it. Coping is a skill children develop as they grow.

"My Baby Won't Let Me Touch Her ..."

My baby doesn't want to snuggle as much as she used to. In fact, she yells when I grab her and she doesn't want to be held. She gives me grief when I try to do anything with her. I get embarrassed thinking people will judge me a bad mother because my child doesn't want me to touch her.

Infants of this age have a fear of being invaded. Intrusions into her personal space by staring too intently or standing too closely are typically met with shrieks or screams of protest. This is only your daughter's self-protective instincts at work. Embarrassing for you, but perfectly normal and to be expected from her!

Your baby seems irritable and gives you grief over the simplest requests because she is at the beginning of her journey toward independence. You have not created a monster but are merely entering a whole new phase of your child's development. All this is good news because it means your baby is moving ahead developmentally in the appropriate and expected way. Remain calm and go with it. This stage won't last forever and before you know it, other stages will bring other behaviors.

Overcompensating for Father's Absence Can't Spoil Baby

My baby is beginning to act up. I feel I may have overcompensated for her not having a father and in the process spoiled her during her first year. I'm afraid I've made a mistake by "overparenting."

Put aside your fears because it's pretty difficult to spoil a young baby. An independent one-year-old is not spoiled. The behaviors we call "spoiled" are simply children's way of asking for what they instinctually know they need—limits. Spoiled behavior occurs when a child does not know his or her limits or when to expect limits from you or others. Consistent handling and setting limits will help your child, but this does not ensure relief from the turmoil brought about by the changes occurring at any stage of growth. The beginning of your child's second year will be cause for even more change, and your child can become confused by what's happening. Maintain consistency by letting your child know what is acceptable and what isn't. Things will improve, but you need to hold on, because this is what the motherhood ride is all about!

TODDLERS

Changes After the First Birthday

My sweet little girl's first year was blissful. She ate and slept well. She smiled and laughed. I knew she was happy, and I felt like I was doing a good job. Right after her first birthday, I began to notice changes. She screams when anyone looks at her. She wakes up every four hours all through the night. Every time I want her to do something, she resists. She seems irritable. What is causing these changes? What have I done wrong? Will I ever sleep again?

What actually is happening is that your sweet, cooperative baby girl is growing up! All the behaviors you described—including being up every few hours at night—are normal, anticipated behaviors in one-year-old children. Disturbances in sleep patterns typically occur whenever the baby achieves a new developmental motor milestone like walking. More acceptable sleep patterns will return. What you need to do is have faith that one day, you will sleep through the night again.

It's Okay to Sleep with Your Child After a Nightmare

Last week my eighteen-month-old must have had a terrible nightmare or something. He woke up screaming. I was so tired myself that half-asleep I carried him to my bed, and we both fell asleep. I told my mother what had happened and she warned me that I was ruining him. What is so terrible about sleeping with your child for part of the night every so often?

Nothing. There are few issues about which mothers are made to feel greater unwarranted guilt than bringing a young child into their beds every once in a while. We have enormous taboos in this society about children sleeping with their parents.

Single mothers seem particularly suspect as awareness of child abuse sometimes crosses the line into witch hunting. All parents—even your mother—have comforted a child in their own beds from time to time. The key question is whose needs are being met. In your case, your son woke up crying hysterically and you comforted him in your bed. You did not wake up your son to comfort you. If you are the one needing comfort, then it is your needs being met, not your child's. In such circumstances you need to look for more appropriate means of comfort. You are not a terrible person if you need comfort, but your child should not be expected to comfort or take care of you.

Child Acts Up for Mom Only

Not that I expect praise, because I think this is what I should be doing and what I want to be doing, but I make incredibly complicated arrangements in order to spend the most time possible with my eighteen-month-old son. I think about him all day and look forward to a loving reunion at the end of the day. When I pick him up, he lies on the floor kicking and screaming. The caregiver at the day-care center says he never behaves that way for her.

The caregiver is right. He does not behave that way for her because she is not his mother. An emotionally healthy toddler saves his most intense feelings for his mother. This means that it is to be expected that when you pick him up he will scream or cry pitifully. He will not cooperate in efforts to dress him to go home. His behavior will lead you to believe that he hates you and

that you are the last person he wants to be with. This is not true. As part of the normal developmental process, your child must let negative as well as positive feelings surface. Otherwise your son will become passive and confused.

As your child grows older, these same patterns persist but in more subtle ways. Simply stated, children save the bad stuff for mothers because they are most closely connected to us emotionally and with us they feel safe. If we understand this, it puts things in perspective and helps us feel much less defensive and confused when we observe how many strong emotional messages from our children have only our names on them.

The best way to handle these strong reunion messages is to realize that your child needs to be comforted, not reprimanded. It is also helpful, no matter what the age of your child, to establish and stick to routines so that your child knows what to expect when you arrive to pick him up. These routines will help him learn self-control and establish trust. And don't try to accomplish too many domestic chores when you first arrive home. Your child needs your full attention and comfort. Having things as organized as possible when you get home at night and keeping things like dinner menus simple are lifesaving ideas.

It is important to remember that just as there is sometimes unconscious competition between mothers and fathers, there is sometimes the same kind of competition between mothers and caregivers. It would have been much more helpful if the caregiver had told you that your son had been waiting for you all day, rather than give you the impression that your son's behavior was directed to you in some kind of negative way. The caregiver might have wanted to reassure you that your son had been happy and well cared for. When you are feeling vulnerable and frazzled, however, it is hard to interpret her message as other than a put-down.

PRESCHOOLERS

Can My Son Learn Potty Training Without Dad Around?

Whenever I pull out the potty chair, my two-year-old son balks. My helpful but nosy neighbor thinks it's because there is no man around to show him how to do it. She says I'd better hurry and teach him before it's too late. Why is my son so disagreeable?

Many parents feel real pressure from day-care centers and preschools that want children toilet trained as a condition for enrollment. Others get well-meaning but inaccurate advice about when a child should be completely potty trained. As for not having a father around to teach your son to use the potty, that is totally unrelated to why your child balks.

Several developmental steps will need to come together before your child is ready to be toilet trained. Negativity is a hallmark of this age, and it tends to come and go. The closer your child is to three, the less likely the natural negativity of this stage will prevent successful toilet training. Your child will be more ready to be trained when he is ready to understand concepts like "This is your potty chair" and is able to follow two-step commands. He will be over the excitement of walking and ready to sit down. Many children after their second birthdays show great interest in imitating adults, and this interest in imitating can be used to spark their interest in toilet training. Children ready for toilet training are beginning to understand orderliness and putting things where they belong. The desire to put things in their proper place can be transferred usefully to urine and bowel movements.

Biting, Hitting, and Other Worries

My three-year-old son is in a play group. One of the other children bites, and I overheard the mothers say that he's acting out because his dad recently left. I felt personally offended because I'm a single mother, too. Will my child act out? Also, I was afraid to speak up when I saw one of the parents biting the child back to prove how this hurts.

Children normally communicate with each other and imitate one another, and often behavior like biting or hitting is included. However, blaming it on the dad's absence is simply a way for others, well-meaning as they are, to find an answer to a question that could just as easily plague them. Don't be surprised if your child doesn't act out at all. Do keep in mind that biting or hitting another child back is never acceptable. This overreaction sets a pattern for more of such behavior, rather than eliminating it. Children bite, hit, or pull hair at this age when they are overwhelmed and lose control. They are frequently as horrified and shocked as the child who got bitten or hit. The intent was not to hurt another child. Never bite the child back so he knows how it feels. Not only is this degrading to both, but it reduces the adult biter to a toddler level of behavior.

Instead, comfort both the biter and the child bitten. Tell the child who bit, "No one likes to be bitten. Next time you feel that way, please tell me. I will help you." Give the child an acceptable substitute, such as a toy to punch or a rubber dog bone to bite. The less adult interference, the more quickly children learn the give-and-take skills necessary to all relationships.

Teaching the Joy of Accomplishment

My almost-three-year-old son loves to be helpful. Is it too early to begin to teach him to do simple chores?

Absolutely not. Teaching your child to do useful things is a wonderful gift. As a single mother you will appreciate the help, and your son will bask in the glory of his accomplishments. It is important to keep the tasks appropriate to his age. Right now, good chores for your son might be putting the newspapers on the recycling pile or

sweeping up little piles of dirt with a hand broom and dustpan. If you're having company for dinner, perhaps he could put the napkins through little wooden or plastic rings. The time that you spend teaching your son to do his assigned chores will be richly rewarded. Responsibility and trust well earned are key to building healthy self-esteem. You could not be spending time in a more productive or useful way.

SLEEPING

I'm exhausted at night and can't stand the bedtime battle. Any ideas for promoting a more hassle-free, less fearful bedtime for a four-year-old?

Around the age of four, a child is sufficiently independent in spirit to appreciate having a big bed and an emotionally satisfying bedroom environment. Make the child feel safe and reassured by giving him special bedclothes (for the financially strapped, this does not mean fancy— recycled T-shirts are great) or a favorite sleep blanket. Although putting children to bed in their underwear can be a time-saver, especially for school-aged children, it can be confusing to preschoolers, who need the separate identity of day and night. Be sure to hang reassuring pictures on the wall, and arrange the furniture in the child's room to help create distinctly different areas for playing and sleep. Also, add to the sense of security by leaving the door slightly ajar, having the radio playing softly, or keeping a night-light on.

Nightmares Don't Mean Emotional Disturbances. Nightmares are perfectly normal, even once or twice a week. Each specific nightmare should be taken seriously, because that approach will help the child resolve any real-life issues that caused the nightmare. If the child has the same nightmare a number of times (more than six) in close succession, you might want to speak with a professional. Whether or not the cause of a child's nightmare is a troubling issue or event in daily life, the effect of the nightmare all by itself can be very emotionally upsetting.

When your child complains about a nightmare, here are some steps you can take to alleviate its effects and possibly eliminate its cause:

1. Allow your child to wake up naturally. Try not to jolt her awake—that can be as upsetting as the nightmare. Jolting her awake may prevent your child's dreaming mind from reaching its own creative "solution" to the nightmare. A nightmare that is strong enough to cause moaning and thrashing will usually provoke a child to wake up on her own.

2. Don't play fantasy games. Don't pretend that you chased the monster out of the closet or the wicked elf out from under the bed. This technique will reassure your child for the moment, but it will come back to haunt you, because the monster or the wicked elf could always come back—otherwise why would you have chased him away in the first place? Instead, show your child that there is no monster in the closet, or let her look under the bed to make sure there is no wicked elf. Do not suggest or deny that there ever was one in the closet or under the bed.

3. Do not insist that the nightmare was not real. To your child, the nightmare was very real. Assure your child calmly and reasonably that she is sane and that what happens in a nightmare can never really hurt her or bring harm to anyone.

4. Encourage your child to describe the nightmare in as much detail as possible. If your child is allowed to talk it out without being distracted by your reactions, chances are the nightmare will lose its power to terrify. Asking her to draw a picture of what was scary in the nightmare is a great idea. Also, you will learn about how your child's dreaming imagination works, what scares your child, and what may have triggered the nightmare in the first place.

5. Ask your child to describe what she could do to make things better if the same experience were to

occur again. This request will cause your child to rehearse coping strategies, both consciously and subconsciously, that will help her to manage this specific nightmare if it happens again, as well as similarly upsetting nightmares and real-life situations.

6. If your child wakes up from a nightmare and is especially upset, consider letting her sleep the rest of the night with you. It's perfectly okay.

The Difference Between Nightmares and Night Terrors

I'm a single mother who is going through tremendous guilt wondering if something happened at day care because my child has terrified me a couple of times with night terrors. Actually, they may be nightmares, but how can I tell and what should I do? I feel like such a lousy parent.

Night terrors (also called delta parasomnia) are not psychologically induced, but *can* be dangerous, as some children sleepwalk while having them and can hurt themselves or get lost.

The way to tell if a child is having a night terror rather than a nightmare is that during a night terror he will not respond appropriately to outside stimuli even though he looks awake. Thus, your child may be screaming "Mommy, Mommy, where are you?" even though you are holding him and reassuring him that you are there.

Here are six tips to follow if your child has a night terror:

1. Don't wake him up unless it is absolutely necessary. The episode will last a few minutes, and your child might return to normal sleep with no ill effects. If you wake him up, you will panic him.

2. Hold your child gently and do not resist any strong efforts to break free. Remember, your child does not realize you are there. If your child gets out of bed, follow him and do what is necessary to prevent accidents.

3. If you can and he does not resist, pick him up and put him back in his bed. Obviously, if you think he is going to hurt himself, wake him up. This is the exception to the don't-wake-him-up rule. Wake him up gently—a warm washcloth on his face is good.

4. Your child will not remember having a night terror after awakening. Remain calm. Night terrors are developmentally okay at this age. They do not mean that you are a bad mother or that your child has deep-seated emotional problems or has had a trauma.

5. If you feel that your child's night terrors are dangerous, talk to your health-care provider about how your child's difficulties might best be handled. Some physicians recommend avoiding caffeine at night by eliminating snacks of chocolate or soda, as one way to lessen the night terrors.

6. Stop telling yourself that you are a lousy mother and instead pat yourself on the back for following these steps. You did the right thing.

EATING

My daughter used to be a hearty if somewhat messy eater. Now, my four-year-old is finicky about certain foods, refusing to eat and misbehaving while eating. Are these behaviors signs of an early eating disorder like anorexia?

Not likely. Children younger than six seldom suffer from eating disorders with psychological roots such as anorexia or bulimia. Children do have a wide range of problems in coming to terms with the eating schedules, diets, and contexts that are imposed on them by the outside world. Each child has a unique set of eating habits and tastes. It is impossible to make general statements about what is normal, when to expect problems, or what to do in troublesome situations.

I worry that my child is poorly nourished because he sometimes refuses to eat anything, at home and in day care. What's more, I'm concerned that others will think I'm neglecting my child because I already feel scrutinized by my neighbors about my single mother status. They are always hinting that

I probably am too busy to feed him. Yet he seems so active and healthy.

First, you don't owe your neighbors any explanation other than that you appreciate their concern, but since your child is giving every other indication of good health, he is probably getting proper nutrition. That is probably the best guideline to go by. Remember, too, that after the age of two, most children experience a natural reduction in their appetites. If you really are worried, however, write down everything your child eats for one week and ask the caregiver to do the same. Consult your child's health-care provider and listen to his or her judgment.

Guidelines for Feeding Your Child

1. Be patient and avoid making a big

MOST CHILDREN USUALLY EAT WITH JUST MOM

According to a study by the Department of Child and Family Studies, Syracuse University in New York, in the *Journal of Divorce and Remarriage* (1990), mothers in married homes and those in single-parent homes eat with their kids with the same frequency. The fathers were absent from the table in many of the dual-parent households, since they arrived home from work after mom and the kids had already eaten. Another study, at Biola University in California, noted that single moms catered to their kids' eating preferences, while married moms catered to their spouses'. However, single mothers tend to eat out more with their kids, so be careful if you are on a strict budget.

deal out of children's poor eating habits, such as picking at food or pushing away vegetables. If children get a lot of attention—even negative attention—the poor eating habits will be reinforced, which means they will persist and get worse.

2. Determine at what times and under what circumstances your child eats best. If your child eats better after a bath or a story, feed him then. Maybe breakfast is the big meal, so play up this healthy habit. See when you can devote the most time and energy to meeting this need, even if it isn't your own best eating time.

3. Take note of when and what your child eats when under the caregiver's supervision. This information will help you to ensure good nutrition by knowing what "gaps" need to be filled in by meals at home. For example, if your child refuses to drink fruit juice with the caregiver, you need to make sure he drinks his orange juice in the morning.

4. Some children do best eating alone, away from others. Mealtimes should not last longer than thirty minutes. Children should learn to eat meals when they are served. Try to provide a calm atmosphere.

5. Introduce new foods singly and in a pleasant, low-key manner. Don't be overly enthusiastic when introducing a new vegetable. Children notice and appreciate when food is presented in an attractive way. Nice-looking eating utensils and

manageable-looking portions can go a long way in getting a child to eat. Even if you are a time-stressed single mom who serves cold pizza for breakfast, cut the portions out with cookie cutters in the shapes of dinosaurs or stars or triangles. Not only are the portions the right size and very appealing, but you could throw in a few words about the differences between geometric shapes. You'll know it's time to quit when your teenager demands that you cut apple slices into trapezoids!

6. Do not force your child to eat against her will. Don't override a "no" by shoving the food into her mouth. This will only aggravate the problem. Give the child a set amount of time to eat most of what is on her plate. However, if an hour goes by, and only half the meal is eaten, don't expect her to sit there the rest of the night in order to clean her plate.

7. Do not offer your child dessert until she has eaten something of more nutritional value. This is an effective, time-honored technique—do not abuse it. Use this technique only once a day, at the meal where the most nutritional value is offered. Always stick to the bargain without theatrics on your part.

8. Do not worry about table manners until your child is around seven or eight—table manners are a sophisticated skill. Don't make the table a further battleground by insisting on good table manners before the child is ready.

TOILET TRAINING

Toilet training should be an accomplishment for the child, not for the parent. All mothers tend to want to rush this stage because it's such a noticeable milestone in their child's development. Moreover, many day-care centers like children to be potty trained at around two and a half to three years, which makes single mothers particularly vulnerable to the potty-training rush.

Don't Rush Potty Training. Because tight budgets are often common in a single-mother household with young children, the temptation to skimp on diapers looms large, steering moms into trying to potty train too quickly. Don't cave in to it. If you need to ration out the diapers, make sure you don't let the baby stay soiled too long, because this can lead to rashes. Or you may want to consider cloth diapers, which are the cheaper alternative and certainly the best bet for the environment.

Other Suggestions. Buy cheaper diapers and purchase in bulk packages, ask for contributions to a diaper fund, or request extras from your pediatrician. Pushing a child too soon will only result in wasted effort and frustration for everyone.

Creative Potty Training Tips

♦ If you find that your child is reluctant to potty train or balks more than necessary, why not add a little fun to the task by playing "sink the Cheerios"? This helps to motivate your child while saving on diapers, too. Simply put some ring-shaped cereal such as Fruit Loops or Cheerios in the potty and ask your child to sink them. Soap bubbles (for playing "bust those bubbles") or cat food shaped like fish work just as well.

♦ Many children are fascinated with the new underwear that accompanies potty training. Certainly less cumbersome than diapers, "big boy" pants or "fancy" panties for little girls are often a terrific incentive to use the potty. Make a big deal out of this new clothing and stress how these items signify "big kid" status. Your child will not only have fun but may actually look forward to using the toilet, rather than diapers!

FEARS

Why is my five-year-old so fearful? It makes me feel inadequate that my child doesn't feel secure with me as her mother.

The child under the age of six lives in a world so baffling that it is difficult for adults to understand. Everything is new and potentially unsettling—capable of causing fearful reactions. It is hard for young children to differentiate between what is real—the death of a pet, for example—from what is not real—the death of a character on a television show. Children of this age are well aware that they are small and powerless, and they routinely feel shocked, puzzled, and surprised by what is happening. Naturally, children of this age experience many different fears as well as individual incidents of fear. Big message: This is normal five-year-old behavior. Second big message: Parents should not overprotect in the face of fears at this age. Fear teaches. Fear of dogs teaches a child to develop safer, more respectful, more appropriate ways of treating all animals. Fear of separation can teach a child to appreciate being taken care of, to manage anger, and to feel empathy for others in need of human contact.

Managing Your Child's Normal Fears

♦ Listen respectfully to what your child is saying, but do not respond with a shower of concerns. That not only rewards being afraid with attention but also scares the child more.

♦ Do not belittle or dismiss the fear either—then your child will not discuss fears with you, and what remains unexpressed will hurt your child emotionally far more.

♦ Be patient and allow the child to confront and overcome fear at his own pace. Help your child devise constructive ways to cope with his own fears.

♦ Praise his efforts, even if they consist only of petting the senile dog down the street in his first attempts at overcoming a fear of dogs. Honestly reassure your child about his own coping skills. Say, "I have seen you pet that big dog down the street and you were not afraid."

♦ Encourage physical play, drawing, painting, and performing small tasks—all activities that demonstrate to children that they can exercise control and master their own little worlds.

♦ Set a good example by not communicating your own anxieties to your child. Perhaps you were afraid of bugs as a little girl, but your child may find them interesting if you don't project your fears.

♦ Anticipate frightening situations and prepare for them. This is not the same as overprotection. For example, if your child is afraid of scary-looking faces, it may not be a good idea to have him greet the trick-or-treaters who come to the door. Better yet, make the ghouls and goblins take off their masks and show your apprehensive five-year-old their real faces underneath.

Could Fears Be Related to Not Having Dad at Home?

My kindergarten child always has one fear or another. Now he is very reluctant to go outside because he tells me that bugs will get him. His teacher reports the same fears at school and wonders if he is excessively frightened because we have no "daddy" at home to protect us. Could she be right?

It's very unlikely. A more probable explanation is that he generally needs to explore things with reassurance. It's good that he talks about these fears. Ask your child what kinds of bugs he fears. The next step would be to find a simple book or video about insects and ask him to indicate which ones are scary and which ones are okay.

Another possibility is that your child is very creative. Like Calvin from the comic strip *Calvin and Hobbes*, he imagines these critters changing into"megamorphasaurs" or whatever and needs help putting the fear into perspective.

Trap a few of the kinds of insects your child fears in a drinking glass, and let him look at them safely from a distance. Arming your child with this new understanding will go a long way toward eliminating this fear. Let the teacher know that you appreciate her concern but feel very capable of protecting your family whether or not a father is present.

DISCIPLINE

My five-year-old daughter is making me a frazzled lunatic. You wouldn't believe the scenes she makes in front of other people whenever I take my eyes off of her, even for a second. It's like she wants to be the center of attention. I give her everything she asks for and spend a lot of time with her (although sometimes I'd like to hop a freight train and leave), and yet she complains incessantly that I never do this and I always make her do that. I don't have a moment to myself! Don't tell me to let her visit her father. He's been out of the picture since birth.

Your daughter is the center of attention and will remain there as long as you allow her to behave this way. Right now, you need to decide that you are going to make time for yourself, because your life needs to revolve around you. You were here first, you are the mother, and you get to make the decisions. Ask yourself, too, how anyone as little as a five-year-old can drive you nuts. Children can't make us crazy

unless we let them play on our guilt.

Why on earth would you want to give your daughter *everything*? Won't this be setting her up for some future shock when she has to mature and meet the real world?

Stop spoiling her now. But remember, it took a while for her to get like this, so be patient.

Invest in a kitchen timer. Announce to your daughter that you will spend, say, thirty minutes of uninterrupted time with her. While you're together playing or reading, don't answer the phone or allow other distractions. Let her know that this is her time and she is to make good use of it. If she wastes it, that is her choice.

After you've spent some quality time together, set the timer for another twenty minutes and explain to your daughter that now it's your turn for some private time. Make sure she has a quiet, safe activity and inform her that she is not to bother you until the timer goes off.

If she balks, give her a choice of either coloring or reading books. If she keeps acting up, send her to her room and tell her to have her tantrum in there.

I feel so guilty every time I punish my four-year-old son because I feel his not having a father (he left right after our son was born) is punishment enough. But he won't go to bed when I ask, throws tantrums in public if he doesn't get everything he demands, and is generally driving me loony. Is it too late to unspoil him?

It's never too late to unspoil a child, but first you need to figure out why you equate "loss" with "punishment."

What you may see as a gain, such as giving in to your child's demand for candy or staying up late, does not necessarily replace a particular loss, such as a parent leaving. Loss is the way we learn to grow, and it cannot be avoided by anyone, whether it is the loss of a loved one, a job, a limb, or even a dream.

One particular way of looking at this comes to mind through the writing of single mother and author Anne Lamott. In her book *Operating Instructions* (Pantheon), which is a journal of her son's first year, Lamott laments that her son, Sam, does not have a father to toss him in the air or teach him manly things like fixing the toaster. At the same time, she's thinking of friends who are expecting a boy named Sam in a few months who will be born with only one arm. She pictures the two baby Sams hanging out together while she and the other Sam's father are teaching a workshop. Her Sam is studying the other Sam and says, "So where's your arm?" and the other baby shrugs and replies, "I don't know; where's your dad?"

The point here is that loss is not punishment. Loss is loss. One kid doesn't have a father, the one across the street doesn't have a pet, the little boy on the corner doesn't have his own room because of the new baby, and the little girl in 2A has a physical abnormality. There is no perfect person, perfect family, or perfect life other than what is falsely depicted on television. But we can all strive for the best for ourselves. First, accept that this is the way things are and then go from there. Stop spoiling your child by trying to provide everything because you think he is deprived. You will be giving him more by setting limits and saying yes less.

I've yet to go through a grocery checkout line without purchasing gum, candy, and other junk for my hysterical, demanding daughter. Should I just stop taking her shopping and avoid seeing friends and doing other things? I work all week and must accomplish shopping and other errands during the weekend. Plus, I don't have extra money for baby-sitters and really don't feel right being apart from her just to go get the dry-cleaning, etc. I'm beginning to dread weekends and wish I were back at work, but I feel guilty there too, thinking that if she had a father, she wouldn't need so much.

It's true that if she had a father, you would have someone to take her when you need a break, which is why work on Monday morning looks so appealing. But having a father at home does not guarantee that she wouldn't be spoiled or demanding—that is based upon what you have allowed her to get away with.

As for making the errand time run more smoothly, try this: Ten minutes before you leave for the store, discuss the purpose of the trip and what kind of behavior you expect from her. This will give your child enough information so that she gets into the right mood.

"We are going to the grocery store to buy milk, bread, and onions, and you may choose the flavor of ice cream we are going to buy," you might say. Agree also on one thing your child may buy, and stick to the agreement. Your child then has a limited opportunity to control some aspect of the trip.

If your daughter pulls a stunt at the grocery store after you have given her two warnings, simply put all the items back on the shelf and leave the store. You may think this is inconvenient, if not impossible, but it works, especially if you say, "I will not take you shopping with me if you behave that way again."

Maybe if she behaves extra well the next time you go out, you can give her a reward such as a sugar-free sucker. But mostly encourage her with praise.

Remember that toys, gifts, and candy do not a father make! Break the cycle now and don't expect results overnight. Be persistent.

COPING TOOLS FOR DEALING WITH ANGER

While parenting is one of the greatest joys in life, it can also be stressful. This goes double for single parents. If you

THE DOS AND DON'TS OF DISCIPLINE

- Do discipline with consistency and fairness. The punishment should fit the crime and should not change or be arbitrary. If timeout is how you handle throwing things, or no television is the result of failing to do chores, then stick to these.

- Don't spoil your child. Single parents, contrary to misconceptions, are not only less abusive but actually tend to spoil their children, largely because many solo parents feel they must overcompensate for the lack of the second parent. Purchasing candy at the checkout line in the grocery store or buying toys or games every time you go to the drugstore does not make up for a missing spouse.

- Don't think only dads are disciplinarians. This doesn't mean you should spank or hit, but it does mean that a mother can be just as firm as only fathers were thought to be by previous generations.

- Do try to remember the benefits of single parenting, particularly if you came from a volatile household where you spent much time dealing with an argumentative spouse. Don't continue this style of communication with your child. Instead, teach negotiating skills and be grateful for the peace that you've acquired.

- Do take periodic breaks so you don't overreact to something minor. If you're stressed out, things will seem bigger than they really are.

- Don't forget that there is no greater gift you can give your children than the ability to cope and to live in loving cooperation with others. Negotiating fairly and teaching them to accept "natural consequences" for their actions, such as having no ice cream if they forget their snack money, is far better than constant struggling and teaches them coping skills.

could use some suggestions for releasing family tension or expressing negative feelings in a controlled manner, read on.

1. Learn how to communicate your anger in nonjudgmental ways. In other words, rather than telling a child who has misbehaved, "I'll wring your neck" or "You are a rotten kid for doing that," try saying, "This has made me very mad" or "I don't like what you are doing right now."

2. Put your child in a timeout chair or send older school-age kids to their rooms or a special timeout place. For toddlers and preschool children, experts advise estimating about one minute in timeout for each year of their age.

3. Don't return hurtful feelings by saying "If I die, no one will care for you" after your child may have screamed, "I hate you, I hope you die!" All children get these feelings every now and then. Remember, it's okay for your child to have feelings of anger, rage, and "hate," but it is not okay to express those feelings with physical violence or abusive words.

4. If your child really needs to "feel those feelings," put her in a safe place—her room, a play area, or a "tantrum tent" (made by throwing a sheet over a couple of pieces of soft furniture). Explain that she can grovel on the floor like a wild thing if she wishes, but you prefer not to watch. Never strike or punish your child for having feelings.

5. Encourage your child to take a run around the block, do jumping jacks, or throw a ball against the side of the house. These are coping strategies that he will be able to use both now and in the years to come to handle negative feelings appropriately.

The Family Primal Scream. One way to get bottled-up anger out of your system and help your kid express negative feelings while under control is to organize a "scream." This really works if you find a special place for this. One single mom who lives in a rural community rounds everyone up in the car and cruises an uninhabited street or country road. Then she rolls up the windows, and on the count of three, she and her daughter and son simultaneously scream, with the dog howling in harmony.

The first time you do this, your child may look at you like you're nuts. Just say, "Mommies get angry, too," and then have a contest to see who can scream the loudest.

Laughter Is Another Way of Releasing Family Tension. See who can laugh the loudest and longest. In fact, just smiling can bring with it positive physiological changes because of the number of facial muscles that are pulled into action.

If a little one is acting horribly, and filled with miserable discontent, try "squeezing the meanness out of her" with firm but gentle hugs. Tell her you'll stop when you get a giggle. When all else fails, tickling works wonders.

IT'S HEALTHY TO BE SELF-CARING

Think the best parents are the ones who dote excessively on their kids? Think again. Single mothers who have an interesting, active personal life are actually setting a more positive example for their children.

No one feels the pressure of the supermother syndrome more than single working mothers. Not only do single moms think they have to devote twenty-four hours a day to entertaining, stimulating, educating, and caring for their children, but they think they have to do this with double the gusto. Because they've also been led to believe that their children are "at risk" for all sorts of emotional and academic problems, they erroneously assume that they must provide more attention and perform these child-rearing tasks exactly as would two parents. Nothing could be further from the truth. Single mothers deserve a break. It is not that you don't know that, but that a break never seems to be in sight.

Do Your Kids a Favor—Ignore Them a Little. Unless you tend carefully to your own needs, some needs of your children won't get met as optimally as they should. Now you ask, "But what need of mine could possibly be more important than feeding when hungry, warming when cold, bathing when not clean, not to mention what goes into providing an education and the constant watching and worry?"

Children who have mothers who pamper themselves actually learn how to take the needs of others into consideration and understand that they are not always the priority or the center of attention. Let's face it: Nothing is more annoying than an adult who whines, attempts to manipulate, and genuinely feels that the world should accommodate him or her at all times. So, the next time you worry that you're doing your child a disservice by not being there for every whine and whim, think about this.

The more attention you pay to yourself, the more your child will realize that you are worth paying attention to.

Seize the Moment—Take a Nap! There are plenty of single mothers, from Hollywood to the housing projects, who paint simply for the joy of it, have taken up piano, do crossword puzzles, and, yes, actually nap while getting their nails done! One single mother, a nurse, worked a ten-hour shift, after which she picked up her children and a neighbor's daughter from day care and school promptly at 3:30 every day. She learned that she needed a nap every afternoon at 4:45 when she fell asleep on the couch one day in spite of trying desperately to stay awake. Even though she awoke refreshed and ready to deal with what the evening had in store, she still felt a little guilty until she realized that her children looked forward to these moments, which they affectionately referred to as playing "funeral."

Make a Game out of Rest Time. It started when her seven-year-old son asked what was wrong when Mom collapsed on the couch, and she replied that she was just too tired to move. He saw that this was not the moment to ask her if she wanted to play a game. He knew she would probably tell him to do his homework anyway, which he was supposed to do before supper. When his precocious four-year-old sister and her five-year-old friend asked if the weary mother was dead, she looked into their little faces and whispered, "Almost." The little neighbor girl's face lit up as she delightedly exclaimed, "Let's play funeral!" Mom was instructed to close her eyes and lay still while the two little girls proceeded to the backyard and lovingly picked dandelions from the lawn. They laid them carefully on the now-sleeping mom's chest, put kitchen towels on their heads, and marched around the couch quietly humming. While the "procession" mourned, Mom, who was having no trouble holding up her end of this game, was deeply relaxing and rejuvenating herself. As long as she kept her eyes shut and did not move, the girls were happy. In fact, the older one commented on what a nice mommy she was because "you are such a good dead person!" In the meantime, her son was doing what he was supposed to be doing and her daughter was playing happily. This thirty-minute mini-nap soon became a family ritual. During the winter months, single sheets of toilet paper became the substitute for fresh flowers, but no one objected. Even though the children are now grown, the phrase "playing funeral" has retained a special meaning for this family because it reflects the intimacy of a shared experience. And this is what being part of a family is all about!

Sure, there will always be another room to dust, a load of laundry to be done, a kitchen counter to be wiped. Your child will always be ready to say yes to one more story, ten more minutes at the playground, or just one more round of her favorite board game. Children are typically marvelous negotiators and will not hesitate to demonstrate this skill. You have that same privilege, so why not learn from them?

SPECIAL CONCERN: TEACHING HERITAGE TO BI-RACIAL CHILDREN

I recently became a single mother when my daughter's father left me a couple of months before I was due to give birth. I am white and he is black, and I am uncertain how to bring cultural richness to my bi-racial daughter's life. I have another dilemma: My mother refuses to have anything to do with me or the baby. I feel like a single mom dealing with a double whammy. Any ideas?

Single parents in similar circumstances suggest seeking out local churches, schools, community centers, and if your community has one, the African-American Resource Center for support.

Although your daughter's father has chosen to be out of the picture, his family doesn't have to be. Establishing a relationship with a member of your ex's family—aunts, uncles, cousins, grandparents, siblings—can not only help teach your daughter about her cultural heritage but may provide you with some emotional support as well. They may very well want your daughter to be a part of their lives, but you'll need to make it clear to them that this isn't an effort to get your ex-boyfriend back, or to make him pay child support. (Deal with him directly if you choose to obtain child support.)

Your mom's inability to give herself to the grandmother role may change with time. Her attitude may improve with each visit. One mom of an Asian-American daughter now has the support of both her parents. Eventually, her father's love for her helped him see his granddaughter as part of him rather than clinging to the idea of bi-racialism in an abstract sense.

But if this doesn't happen, you have time to prepare your child to face her grandmother's prejudice by explaining that your mother's ideas about race differ from yours, which is, remember, your interpretation of your mother's actions.

When your child is old enough to understand racial differences, you might say, "Even though my mother raised me, she has different ideas about race than I do." It's important that your child know that she was not the cause of her grandmother's shunning her. It is her grandmother who suffers from intolerance and bigotry.

Tips for teaching pride to your bi-racial child:

◆ Educate yourself. Reading books such as *40 Ways To Raise a Nonracist Child*, by Barbara Mathias and Mary Ann French, and subscribing to magazines geared to specific cultures can teach you a lot.

◆ Prepare your child for sticky situations. Overt racism often can be a lot easier to explain than subtle prejudice because of the mixed messages that are perceived. For example, your Anglo sister-in-law may think Michael Jordan was the best thing ever to happen to America, but she'd hate the idea if her daughter was married to him. On the other hand, telling your child that a perpetrator of a race crime is a sick individual is pretty straightforward. Keep your eyes open to different kinds of racism.

◆ Expose yourself and your child to a variety of literature, theater, and films. It's important for you both to see a broad spectrum of culture and talent but don't stop there.

◆ Get out and make friends. Learning about your child's heritage only through a screen or a book can be limiting, so find people of color or the same ethnicity as your child who can be positive role models. Better yet, create a supportive community of friends of many different backgrounds.

◆ Consider how you talk about beauty in your household. Do you typically admire only European or Anglo features? Then your child needs to hear praise regarding the appearance of other types of beauty.

◆ Keep maps and globes in your house and let your child "visit" his or her homeland often.

◆ Frequent restaurants or shops that specialize in food or other items from your child's birth father's region. An Italian mom from Los Angeles practically lives in her favorite Korean restaurant, not for the food as much as the family-type atmosphere offered by the owners who adore her Korean son.

◆ Don't try too hard. Recognize your limitations. You can never become a different race, but by inviting people into your lives from many diverse backgrounds, you can enrich your life and your child's future with acceptance.

14

As Your Child Grows

SCHOOL-AGE CHILDREN AND TEENS

As your child grows, parenting doesn't get easier; it becomes, as many mothers say, "different." Demands that young children make are no longer placed upon you, but newer challenges arise. Your child's needs are not any less or more important, but they have evolved to a new level. For example, you don't have to remember to feed them all the time because they are quite capable of knowing when they are hungry and fixing themselves a snack. But they may need guidance and reassurance about making decisions regarding school, friends, and others, and becoming comfortable with who they are along the way. They are becoming young adults, people who are beginning to show responsibility for their actions.

There are so many ways for gauging your child's success according to different child development experts. Some say if you raise a child who is liked by other people besides you, you've done a fine job. But one single mother found the following in an old newspaper column and has shared it with others:

You can use most any measure
When you're speaking of success
You can measure it in fancy home,
Expensive car or dress.
But the measure of your real success
Is the one you cannot spend.
It's the way your kids describe you
When they're talking to a friend.
　　　　　　　　—MARTIN BUXBAUM

WORKING WITH YOUR CHILD'S SCHOOL

It is the responsibility of all types of families to work conscientiously to make sure that their child receives every possible benefit from the educational opportunities available.

The greatest all-consuming challenge for some single parents is to ensure that their child with special educational needs is provided with appropriate services. This challenge will be no different and not any less difficult than for parents with a different family set-up. Each of us, no matter what the family background, will meet with situations less than ideal for our children, and it will be our responsibility to negotiate around and through these circumstances. The difficulty is that these less-than-ideal circumstances can take many forms. It is virtually impossible to prepare parents for each and every situation that may come along.

Handling Insensitive Remarks at Parent-Teacher Conferences

My seven-year-old son is entering second grade. Last year, he entered first grade shortly after my partner and I split up. Because my son is energetic and restless, he has trouble sitting still and paying attention. His first grade teacher blamed this on his being from an unstable home. She says this behavior is common among "fatherless boys from broken homes." I was so devastated. How can I make sure that nothing like this happens at the next parent-teacher conference? It's none of the teacher's business, but the truth is Brian is actually behaving better since his father moved out. I just don't think I could go through this again.

Despite the fact that there are more than 11 million single-parent families, many schools still stereotype the children from these families as being "at risk." Teachers who are inexperienced in dealing with single-parent families often rely on the quickest explanation for a problem, suggesting that the blame lies with the facts of the child's home life. They normally wouldn't comment on the personal life of married parents, but this is a way that the staff can be excused from

further responsibility and effort on behalf of the child in the classroom.

Your Child May Have ADHD. Restlessness, inability to focus, and difficulty shifting form one activity to another may indicate that your child has Attention Deficit Hyperactivity Disorder (ADHD). If you suspect that your child's difficulties in school have less to do with your marital status than with behaviors your child is not able to control, discuss your observations with his teachers and, if possible, the school psychologist. There are no specific psychological or medical tests to determine if a child has ADHD. In fact, many mental health professionals and educators feel that this label is being placed on far too many children. Generally speaking, this diagnosis is not made until a child is seven years old, since distractibility, hyperactivity, and difficulty focusing are hallmark behaviors of all toddlers and preschool children. Before concluding that your child has ADHD, you will want to rule out any possible medical problems that might be contributing to your child's difficulty. At a minimum, you will want to be satisfied that your child's hearing and vision are okay. Psychological testing is also recommended since some behavioral problems are explained by mild, undiagnosed learning disabilities.

If you suspect that your child might have ADHD based on your observations or if other members of your family have been diagnosed, ask his classroom teacher to record her observations or provide you with a written statement of what is observed in school. Take these observations and comments to your health-care provider. Discuss the specific behaviors observed both at home and at school. If you, the school, and your caregiver observe that your child exhibits the same behavioral problems in all settings, then the diagnosis of ADHD needs to be strongly considered. In this case, some parents have found stimulant medication therapy very helpful. Discuss this option with your health-care provider. Also, just as important, educate yourself by attending parent support groups and by reading the many books available on helping ADHD children to cope more effectively.

Allergies or Immaturity Are Common Causes for Problems in School. There might be other reasons for your son being fidgety. He might be a little too immature to sit still for long periods. Or he might have certain allergies, need more sleep, or simply require more exercise. Perhaps a combination of all of these may be the cause. These are things you can look into now. Discuss your concerns and observations with your health-care provider.

Be Prepared for the Next Meeting. Before meeting with your son's teacher this year, be prepared. Inquire about the exact reason for the conference. Don't schedule the meeting on an already hectic day. You might want to jot down beforehand some questions you have for the teacher and also include what you are currently doing to help remedy your son's problems. For example, you might tell her that you are limiting Brian's television time and enforcing rules about snacks and bedtime in addition to encouraging him to ride his bike in the morning so he's not as restless when he arrives at school.

Keep the Meeting Focused. If the teacher strays from the topic, you can say, "I understood we were here to discuss my child's difficulty sitting still and paying attention. Let's stick to this subject, please."

Keep in mind that you only have to answer the questions that you are comfortable with. Inform the teacher that most married parents probably wouldn't respond to such questions and neither should you. However, it is important to let her know that you want to work together as a team.

Establish Boundaries. You should set boundaries between your personal life and your son's education, but at the same time you should strive for cooperation between school and home. Not only will you be helping your son throughout his education, but by your own example of successful single parenting you just may help to educate the teacher.

FILLING OUT SCHOOL REGISTRATION FORMS

I'm an unmarried mother who absolutely hated filling out the form

to register my child for kinder-
garten. Every time a question asked
about father's date of birth, or
employment, or who to contact in
an emergency, I went to pieces. I
know my son wants to join Cub
Scouts soon, but I don't think I can
handle those forms again.

Every time you register your child
for day care or school you will be
handed a mountain of forms to fill
out. This is routine for every parent,
so try not to take it so personally. But
maybe you need a few tips to help you
get through this the next time you
have to fill out those inevitable information questionnaires:

- Identify the reasons why this is a
  source of discomfort for you. Does
  seeing the word "father" on the reg-
  istration form remind you of your
  loss or make you feel that you are different or that you are the only single
  mother in the world? Or do you feel
  you are being judged by the school
  secretary? Try to remember that
  these forms are geared to all families
  and are not a test but simply procedure, and in most cases, school staff
  really aren't interested in prying into
  your private life.

- Be aware that you must produce a
  birth certificate whether or not the
  father's name is on it in order to register your child for school. Some
  school districts also require proof of
  residency, such as a copy of your
  lease or utility bill. Save time and
  energy and come prepared.

- Decide ahead of time what information about your home situation you
  are going to share with the school.

- When asked for information about
  the father—date of birth, name,
  place of employment, etc.—feel free
  to leave this space blank.

- Ask the staff to consider redesigning
  the forms (if possible—for example,
  at smaller, private schools) so they
  don't automatically assume that
  every mom is a Mrs. or that every
  child comes from a two-parent
  household.

KEEPING YOUR SCHOOL-AGE CHILD SAFE

Unfortunately, safety in schools has
become a major concern in recent
years, and not just at high school level.
In fact, every year more than 3,000,000
crimes are committed, over 9,000 fires
break out, and hundreds of thousands
of students are injured in schools.
While you probably shouldn't resort to
sending little Joey off to school in a bul-
letproof vest, you can take several steps
to keep your child safe—and help you
sleep a little better at night:

- Do not give children large denomi-
  nation bills for school lunches. They
  might be seen getting change, followed, and robbed. Give them the
  money they need one day at a time.

- Tell your child not to resist if robbed.
  No amount of money is worth getting
  hurt. Children should be encouraged
  to tell you if they have been assaulted,
  whether in school or not.

- Show your children the safest walk
  home from school, one that avoids
  seedy or wooded areas. Remember
  that children often love to find back

roads. Explain to them why you don't want them to use shortcuts.

- Organize a buddy system with children of neighbors for the daily walk.

- Consider a block parent program. Parents designated on each block display a sign in their windows indicating to passing schoolchildren that someone is at home and available if anyone frightens or accosts them.

- Know the school bus drivers and crossing guards. Encourage children to greet them by name every day, so they will be well-acquainted with them. Tell your children that if they are frightened, they should stay with the guard until they feel it's safe to continue.

- You can help make schools safer if you know what is happening and want to do something about it. Get *Safe at School: Awareness and Action for Parents of Kids Grade K–12* by Carol Silverman Saunders (Free Spirit Publishing), a comprehensive guide that covers every school safety problem you can think of and offers step-by-step action plans.

HELPING YOUR CHILD ACHIEVE SUCCESS IN SCHOOL

Students achieve greater success in school when they have a good relationship with their teachers. But, like any relationship, the student-teacher relationship is a two-way street. Help your child develop positive relationships with her teachers:

DID YOU KNOW...?

Yellow paper is a great study aid. Children see information better on yellow paper. That is why people use yellow highlighters or yellow self-stick notes. The best way to help children to learn new words or facts is to print them on yellow paper with black ink.

- Let your child know that you value education. Research indicates that a parent's encouragement is more important to a child's eventual success than family income or background. Show your child that you think learning is important every day by reading together, watching educational programming, and helping her with homework.

- Talk positively about teachers in front of your children. If you have a negative attitude, so will your child. If you have a problem with a teacher, speak directly with that teacher.

- Reward your children's efforts, not just the results. When your child tries to read a more difficult book than usual, praise him for this new interest. Do not criticize him for the words he is stumbling over, but emphasize all the new things he is learning. If your sports-minded son suddenly picks up his sister's watercolor paints and tries his hand, don't devalue his first efforts and thereby give him the message that he should stick to football. Children who are praised only for their successes can become afraid to try new tasks. Or they might try only once and give up.

This kind of behavior is very discouraging to teachers.

♦ Encourage communication. Children who have learned to express themselves at home with parents and siblings have an easier time talking with their teachers. This means taking the time to listen and not interrupt. Tell your child that you respect his feelings or point of view and demonstrate respect by being a good listener. The best way to help your child be a better communicator is to encourage a home atmosphere where everyone's feelings are accepted and respected. It does not work to set aside time for family meetings if nobody talks to anyone else at all other times. Shouting, name calling, or deliberately hurtful remarks have no place in a home where respect for one another is valued, and certainly will not be tolerated in most classrooms.

♦ Practice good manners at home. Children must not only be encouraged to express themselves but must also be taught to have good listening skills, to follow directions, and to work cooperatively in a group. These skills are best mastered by children whose experiences at home incorporate these expectations. Start to teach these skills well before your child begins school. For example, when your baby is sitting in his high chair watching you cook, say out loud the steps you are following to make that pot of spaghetti. Routines at home are also important. Tell your baby the plan even if you feel a little silly reciting a list of errands or chores to a three-month-old. Working cooperatively in a group might begin with simply letting your toddler watch older children work or play together. Tell your little one what is going on by saying something like, "See how nicely Joey and Philip are working together building that sand castle," or "Look how Sally waits for Jessie to finish before she takes her turn." These kinds of experiences alert early on to what the expectations will be when they begin school.

♦ Teach your child how to wait his turn. Teachers cannot always give immediate attention, so learning to wait your turn is an important school skill.

♦ Give your child the opportunity to know that everything in life is not instantaneous. Many teachers complain that children reared in the era of video games and TV come to think that everything should happen right now. Life does not work that way. Provide your child with the opportunity to learn patience. Grow plants from seeds. Do jigsaw puzzles together as a family project. Share with your children activities such as furniture refinishing or needlework, which require time and patience. Create and display proudly a lifelong collage that each of you adds to as the years progress.

Problems with Teacher. It is possible that a child could be singled out for verbal abuse or scorn from the teacher because he is from a single-parent home. But it is more likely that he could be given this dubious distinction because he is creative, belongs to a racial or ethnic group for which the teacher harbors extreme prejudice, or reminds her of someone from her past.

If you suspect that your child is being singled out for any reason, ask for a conference with the principal and teacher. Be prepared with specific examples that illustrate your concerns, such as that the teacher makes embarrassing comments about your child's clothing or hairstyle, or anything else that can damage self-esteem. If, after this conference, you feel that your fears were well justified, ask that the child be transferred to another teacher. If you sense that the principal is not taking your concerns seriously enough or you are aware from other parents that this teacher has a history of picking on children, write a letter to the superintendent of schools or the principal's immediate supervisor detailing your reasons for asking to have your child transferred.

The best strategy when your children encounter such hurtful people is to listen and to help them understand why the teacher may be behaving like this toward them. You cannot run interference for your children with teachers once they reach high school except in cases of sexual or physical harassment or other such serious breaches of ethical conduct. Again, the principal is the person to contact because he or she is legally responsible for what goes on in the building. Hold the school accountable and make it clear that you will be an active team participant in your child's education.

CHILD CARE FOR THE SCHOOL-AGE CHILD

Changes in family structure and values have altered the way in which many children are cared for. Because more families are headed by single parents and fewer relatives are available to care for children, increasing numbers of families are looking for ways to care for their children in before- and after-school programs.

There are many options for school-age care. Each offers advantages and disadvantages, and none is right for all children under all circumstances. Some children may benefit from the slower pace and smaller environment of family day care, while others may need the larger physical and social setting of an after-school program. Children with special talents may enjoy a narrowly focused program that allows them to improve their skills, while other children may require highly varied programs that help them maintain their interests.

Advantages of after-school programs also include the use of community resources as much as possible. They usually provide indoor and outdoor space for active play and places for socialization and private time, not often available in someone's home.

Supportive Services for Self-Care or Latchkey Kids. In addition to adult-supervised child-care programs, some communities offer supportive services for self-care. These include educational materials and curricula that provide information for latchkey children and their parents; telephone reassurance lines staffed by phone counselors trained to provide a friendly voice and occasional advice; and block parent programs using trained volunteers who make their homes available during after-school hours in case of emergency. These programs are designed not to address the day-to-day needs of children after school, but to reduce the possibility of serious trouble confronting a child.

WHAT YOU SHOULD KNOW ABOUT
PUBLIC SCHOOLS AND YOUR RIGHTS

Managing your child's education will be easier if you are able to live somewhere where the values and standards are compatible with your way of thinking. But you need to remember that even when you don't see eye-to-eye with your child's school, you not only have rights, but the school staff is in your employ. Never forget that your tax dollar is helping to pay for classrooms, curriculums, and salaries.

◆ Remember that you are not a child to be intimidated when you enter the school—you are an equal. If you act like a victim, are overly apologetic, or are defensive about your circumstances at home, you are giving the school license to act on this information, to chat about it in the teachers' lounge, or to use your circumstances to justify or explain any problems your child might have. Expect accountability.

◆ Seek out the helpful people—the school psychologist, principal, guidance counselor, or a teacher your child might have had with whom he worked particularly well. Use the resources available to you.

◆ Be aggressive about finding out about programs for creative or gifted children. Call the district or county school board office. Ask about magnet programs or special summer programs. Request information about scholarships or funding that might be available. There are people sitting in those offices waiting for the phone to ring to give out just such information.

◆ If you have a child who is physically or mentally challenged, know that your child has guaranteed civil rights under federal legislation. If you are getting the runaround from your local school district, contact your state or congressional representative's office to find out which advocacy groups can assist you. Elected officials love to help. This is how they build constituency loyalty, which is how they get reelected. All this help is free of charge, as are the services to which your child is entitled. Sometimes districts try to see how little they can do—meaning how little money they can spend. If the school knows that you know your rights, they will quickly stop the game and your child will get the services he needs.

◆ Stay in touch with other parents. If PTA meetings are held during the day and you are not able to attend because you work, then find someone who is able to attend and ask her what was discussed. Many times stay-at-home moms enjoy being able to share their information. Read carefully the PTA newsletter and other information that comes home in your child's book bag. When you attend Little League games or school events, share your concerns with other parents, listen to what other parents are focusing on, and get involved. You are not the only mother who works and certainly not the only single mother, although sometimes it feels that way. You are more empowered as a group.

◆ Remember that it is the principal of the school who has both the authority and the responsibility. Hold her accountable by keeping her informed or meeting with her to discuss problems or concerns. Do not think she is too busy or you are not important enough.

Few studies have measured the impact of self-care on children over time. One study of former latchkey children found that negative reactions to unresolved stress did persist into adulthood. A handful of studies indicated that children in after-school programs did better in terms of academic performance and social adjustment than peers who were not in care.

Unsupervised Latchkey Arrangements. Self-care arrangements do not meet the developmental needs of all school-age children. Because some of these children are still struggling to make the transition from childhood to adolescence, they need opportunities to make friends, play, develop skills and initiative, and receive attention and appreciation from caring adults. Most children caring for themselves do best when there is a supervising adult on hand, but children who are not quite as mature certainly aren't ready for any kind of unsupervised self-care arrangements.

Is Your Child Ready for Unsupervised Self-Care? The National Child Care Survey conducted in 1990 by the National Association for the Education of Young Children and the United States Department of Education found that 44 percent of school-age children with working parents have no supervision after school. Numerous other studies have shown that many parents are forced to let their children fend for themselves at young ages, either because good child care and after-school programs were unavailable or too expensive, or because their parents were isolated from other members of their community.

A good rule of thumb is that children below the fourth grade are not ready to be unsupervised at home. Setting absolute guidelines for older children is difficult because so many factors must enter into this important decision:

◆ Do you have neighbors upon whom you can depend in the event of an emergency?

◆ Is your child fairly obedient? For example, if you make rules about not turning on the stove or other appliances, is your child likely to obey or will he have to test the limits?

◆ Is your child able to occupy himself in your absence with safe, quiet activities like watching television or, better yet, by reading or working on other independent projects?

◆ Does your child enjoy the quiet respite and the responsibility that comes with being alone or does he find it scary and intimidating?

Think through your own situation carefully. You might want to begin by orchestrating some trial runs during which you leave your child alone for short periods of time so you can determine how well he handles the situation and how closely he obeys the guidelines that you set.

What Can I Do with a Summer Latchkey Child?

Any ideas on what to do with a latchkey schoolchild who is home for the summer? Two hours a day after school was manageable—homework, talking with friends, and doing a little yard work or straightening up around the house occupied my daughter's time. She'll be thirteen soon, and pretty responsible, but I'd hate to see her wandering around aimlessly all summer, or spending days watching TV. I can't afford these expensive camps that some of her friends are attending.

With a little ingenuity and some scouting around, you should be able to locate some alternatives to your daughter's just "hanging out" all summer. A good place to start is with your child's school. A number of school systems offer summer activities through after-school programs or in cooperation with your county's department of parks and recreation. The difficult part might be the transportation factor—coordinating your working schedule with your daughter's plans. One way of handling this would be to initiate a car pool. Exchange phone numbers with other parents whose children will be attending the programs you are considering.

Other suggestions for creative outlets that are reasonably priced include the following:

◆ Many community arts centers feature courses and workshops in pottery, dance, painting, music, and acting. Don't forget to look into scholarships that these cultural centers and programs often make available to lower-income children.

◆ County parks, state and national parks, and recreation facilities usually have activities for kids and teens all summer long. Check in the government section of your local phone book. Also, community pools offer

swim classes. Better yet, if your daughter is a good swimmer, see if she can qualify for free admission by working as a junior lifeguard.

◆ Day camps run by the YMCA or YWCA or the Boys' Club of America are affordable and can fill your child's afternoons with arts and crafts, swimming, boating, and sports. Again, inquire about available scholarships and sliding-scale options, and consider your child's working as a junior counselor to earn her fee. Investigate the possibility of her earning school credit by either taking summer classes or serving as an apprentice in programs or camps that need helpers. Many churches and synagogues offer inexpensive summer fun. Your daughter might volunteer to help out during these planned events in exchange for available or free transportation.

◆ Public libraries not only host storytelling hours, film and video showings, puppet shows, lectures, and writing classes, but also have countless brochures, flyers, and other

HOME ALONE: TIPS TO KEEP YOUR CHILD SAFE

◆ Know Your Child: Is your child comfortable being left alone? Never force your child to handle this responsibility if he is frightened or emotionally unready.

◆ Make the Rules Clear: Evaluate your particular home situation and your child's maturity and capabilities to determine the rules of the house in your absence. Clear, specific rules are needed regarding having friends in the house, leaving the house once your child has come home, use of appliances, activities that are permitted, and whether homework must be done before you return home.

◆ Children are Always Hungry! Prearranged, safely prepared snack foods are a must for those hungry after school hours. Teenagers and their friends eat practically all the time.

◆ Review the "What If Emergency Plans" Often: Make sure your child knows what to do in case of fire, sickness, accident, or other unexpected happening.

◆ Get to Know Your Neighbors: With fewer stay-at-home mothers or fathers, it might not be possible to rely on the constant presence of another parent with young children as your back-up or emergency plan. Seek out older neighbors as the more reliable source of back up. Consider bartering services like helping with heavy chores, meal preparation, or some special skill in return for asking older neighbor to keep a watchful eye on your children "just in case."

◆ Consider Installing Caller ID: If you are concerned that your child may tell unexpected or unwanted callers that you are not at home, caller ID can be an inexpensive protection. Instruct your

child to answer from only "pre-approved" callers allowing unknown calls to be picked up by the answering machine or left to simply hang up.

◆ Wear a Beeper: Beepers can enable your child to let you know he is home safely or to alert you to call home immediately. Equipping yourself with a beeper is particularly smart if your workplace is less than "child friendly" about making or receiving personal calls. Consider using prearranged codes to convey specific messages.

◆ Give Your Child a Beeper: If your child is old enough to be allowed out of the house in your absence, a beeper will allow you to contact her and keep abreast of her activities. If your pages go unanswered or are not responded to within a reasonable period of time, find out why. Consider if your child can responsibly and safely handle the amount of freedom you are allowing.

◆ Consider a Cellular Phone: It takes a very responsible child not to overuse or misplace a cellular phone. Consider all the possibilities before bestowing this potentially expensive privilege. If you equip yourself with a cellular phone be aware that even the best of cellular phones can be finicky and vulnerable to black out areas and weather disturbances. Cellular phones are banned in many work places like hospitals and schools. Older cellular phones able to dial only 911 or other similar emergency numbers are offered at nominal charge as a public service by local telephone companies. Investigate the availability of this service if you feel your child (or you) may need to have the protection of being able to summon the police at any time.

information on the various goings-on in your region during the summer months. And the library's community bulletin board is a great place to advertise your car-pooling needs. You'd be surprised at how many other parents are in the same situation.

◆ If your daughter is a Brownie or Girl Scout, don't overlook the summer camps that might be offered in your area. The 4-H program is another excellent source of summer fun. Many children enrolled in after-school programs during the school year are automatically members of 4-H. Call your county's department of human services to see what camps and activities are available for children of parents on a limited budget.

◆ Check now with your child's teacher, guidance counselor, or principal to see if any of them would be interested in setting up a part-time summer program that might include facilitating field trips. Some young teachers are interested in supplementing their income and would be a good source of names of other parents who are seeking similar options for their summer latchkey children. With everyone chipping in an acceptable amount, the benefits to teacher, parents, and kids would be enormous. This type of networking might also lead you to high-school or college students who are looking to receive extra school credit by tutoring or caring for younger children.

◆ Contact your local chapter of AARP or a senior citizens' center. Elderly people who don't have relatives nearby often welcome the opportu-

nity to spend time with children. "Adopting a grandparent" could be a mutually rewarding experience.

◆ Don't rule out the idea of starting a baby-sitting co-op at your place of business. Talk with your employer and other parents about establishing a co-op supervised by older teenagers and a parent. Business owners are aware that working parents are more productive when they know that their children are safely cared for. Try to work out a schedule where each parent rotates time supervising the co-op. And don't overlook the school credit that the older children can earn by working as child-care providers. Reward the responsible pre-teen or teenager with a night out of pizza, roller-skating, or a movie.

◆ Keep in mind that there is no rule that says kids should be completely and thoroughly entertained at all times. Sometimes a little boredom spurs creative behavior. Just remember to limit TV and keep a large supply of books and other reading materials on hand.

THE TEENAGE YEARS

Until the twentieth century, there were no "teenagers." There were merely young members of farming households. The transformation of youth from members of farming households to teenagers occurred during the last hundred years and was ignited by several forces. Before the Industrial Revolution, youngsters went from childhood to adulthood. It was not uncommon to be married by fourteen, start a family, and work on the family farm where you had worked alongside

your parents as a child. But then came child labor laws creating a class separating children from adults. Cities and public schools were built, men went off to war, and all sorts of major cultural changes were in the works. Slowly, there emerged a group between children and adults that had no name or identity. But little by little, they began to relate to things that neither children nor adults could claim. Music like rock and roll and clothes that seemed to look good only on their bodies became their trademark. Still, they had no

identity. Were they children or were they adults? Their biological structure wasn't too different from their counterparts at the end of the nineteenth century, but they began to mature a little more quickly.

These are today's teenagers. A group of people making the transition from childhood to adulthood and living in a nether world of confusing expectations. Inadvertently abandoning teenagers to their own culture is seen by many as one of the social costs of our changing world. Teenagers may be difficult to understand not because they are rebelling or evading us, but rather because the adults around them have become absent. With the absence of significant adults, teenagers turn to unreliable sources for information, guidance, and emotional support.

BELIEVE IT OR NOT: THE TEENAGE YEARS ARE AN EXCITING OPPORTUNITY NOT TO BE MISSED

When your children are young, a moment of privacy in the bathroom is an unheard of luxury. A trip to the supermarket unencumbered by restless, demanding children seems the impossible dream. More quickly than you could have imagined, however, the toddler who never gave you a moment of privacy is now the sulky teenager who acts like she does not want to be seen with you. Your bathroom suddenly has real-man shaving equipment. There are more kinds of shampoo positioned around the tub than you ever thought existed. Instead of exhausting solo trips

THE DOS AND DON'TS OF RAISING TEENS

♦ Do choose your battles carefully. Arguing over everything is fruitless. Pick what's really important, such as responsibility in calling when promised or feeding the dogs if that is his job. Issues like hairstyle, clothing, and loud music are time-honored ways for teenagers to show their independence and are best ignored if at all possible. Body piercing and tattoos on the other hand are clear health risks. Funny smelling rooms and clothes that walk themselves to the hamper often respond best to simply closing the door.

♦ Do be involved. Attend your child's school activities and sporting events. Volunteer to be a chaperone or volunteer for the concession stand. Start early so your child gets used to having you around. Shared activities and experiences give you and your child common ground for conversation and mutual interests. It is also a great way to network with other parents and keep abreast of happenings in your community.

♦ Do get to know each other. Knock on the door and ask to visit in your child's room. Save the lectures on the value of neatness for another time. Act like the guest you have asked to be. Share information about your day or your feelings. Communication is a two way street. Kisses and hugs during your private time together let your child know that as much as some things are changing, your love for him never changes.

♦ Do be alert to emotional changes in your child. If she suffers mood swings, eating disorders, or depression or has a violent temper, consult a mental health professional immediately. This is a tough time for kids and you need to let them know that you are on their side.

to the supermarket, you have an eager young driver who would happily drive twenty miles for a loaf of bread. Your child is taller and stronger than you. Your child has skills you do not possess. Interests and activities are often separate from your own. Passionate beliefs are expressed which you do not share. Your child cares deeply about his friends.

It is so tempting to think that the hard work of parenting is now nearly complete. Being able to leave your child for significant hours during the day is a great relief to the time pressured single mother. In addition, many single mothers report that having a teenager in the house prompts a midlife crisis. Regrets, self-doubt, the desire to recapture our youth confront many single mothers as their children enter this defining life stage. Issues and goals in your own life may take on an accelerated sense of urgency. Even the most dedicated and responsible single mother may wish nothing more than to get out of the house leaving behind the twenty-four-hour-a-day cares, demands, and responsibilities of raising children solo.

While no human being can be complete without dreams, desires, and goals of their very own, your children's teenage years are not the time to lessen your involvement and participation in your children's lives. Remember those years from birth to age two? Every day your child was growing, changing, and learning more about the world around him. The teenage years incorporate nearly as much physical, social, and emotional change as those first critical two years. The teenage years can be just as memorable, joyful, and rewarding as those unforgettable and endearing "baby times."

The teen years are your last opportunity to have a real and lasting impact on your child's life. Your teenagers need your time and attention. Just being there, your physical presence is the best guarantee that your children will make safe, healthy, and appropriate choices. Single mothers, who typically nourish closer relationships and more open communication with their children, should continue to use this well-earned advantage. We need to know what is really going on in our child's real life, not just what we think, assume, or hope their life is all about. No teenager is going to accept advice or guidance from any adult who does not have a genuine understanding of what really goes on day to day in his or her life.

This is also a time when important life skills that will equip your child for a smoother transition to independent life can be taught. Time and money management are the keys to self-reliance. You, as a successful single mother, are a master of these skills. Share your knowledge directly with your child. Teach essential skills like check writing and keeping track of receipts. Under your guidance and supervision, allow your child to schedule her own routine doctor and dental appointments so

that she is able to take care of these needs when she no longer lives at home. Your teenager should be guided toward responsibly managing everyday chores like shopping, kitchen cleanup, and errands. Things will not always go smoothly. Resist the idea that it is easier and quicker just to do it yourself. When responsibilities are unmet or mistakes are made, sit down with your teenager and review what went wrong and how different choices would have led to a more successful outcome. Emphasize that with the privileges of growing up come added responsibilities. Actions, not words, demonstrate that your teenager is ready for a later curfew, greater access to the family car, a part-time job, or whatever your teenager feels he wants to do. A young man who protests that he can't figure out how to use the vacuum cleaner is obviously not ready to be trusted with the infinitely more complicated family car.

Most importantly, teenagers need the gift of our time. Teenagers may not need us round the clock like a newborn, but they need us "on demand." Let your teenager know that, without meaningful exception, you are available for them at any time. Make it true even when you are dog-tired and can think of a thousand things (sleep number one!) you would rather be doing at 11 o'clock at night.

TEENAGERS NEED LIMITS: BE THE ADULT THAT YOU ARE

Your teenager requires firm limits. He will secretly appreciate the love and concern setting and enforcing such limits demonstrates. Set curfews and enforce them by staying awake until your child returns home. Keep informed about what she is doing and whom she is doing it with. If your daughter says she is at Sue's house, then dropping by Sue's house to check will be no big deal. If your daughter is not telling you truthfully where she is going, you need to exercise more control and greater supervision.

If a party is planned, call the host's parent to make sure that this parent will be home all evening to supervise. Remember that the last minute phone call asking to sleep over at a friend's house is most often the cover story for all night partying or other rule breaking activity. Insist that sleepovers be planned a day ahead. It is important to be neither gullible nor intimidated. Practice saying, "I'm not concerned about what the other kids are allowed to do. I'm concerned about you. These are the rules in this house." You are, after all, the parent. And as much as teenagers act like they know everything, the truth is they do not have your hard-earned experience, maturity, and wisdom.

You are going to have conversations about topics never whispered or imagined about during your own teenage years. We live in times where the unimaginable is regularly seen on the 6:00 news. Be genuine with your own feelings. If you are confused, admit it; if you are appalled, say so. Your example is the strongest message. Tell your child what you believe about sex, drugs, and alcohol. Do not expect the school to do more than teach the facts. Your child's values and subsequent choices about sex, drugs, and alcohol will come largely from what you have taught and the behavior you have displayed.

What Teenagers Ask of Their Single Mothers. Like young children, teenagers may repeat the same questions over and over again even though you have been openly discussing certain family issues for years. But their questions may mask the real issue: Am I going to turn out just like my father? Very few teenagers have the insight to know and to express that this is really their deep-down worry. You need to say to your older children, "I bet you worry that along with those beautiful blue eyes you also somehow inherited your father's tendency to hurt and disappoint." It does not matter what your child calls an absentee dad, but do not be surprised if your teenager stops referring to him as "Dad" and starts calling him by his first name. As your child grasps the degree of emotional distance, this may seem more authentic to him. Teenagers may worry about their own romantic relationships and ask themselves if they are holding on to an "over with a long time ago" boyfriend or girlfriend because they just can't handle another abandonment. Teenagers may need the experience of volunteering with younger children to prove to themselves that they can be of value to younger children. Often teenagers choose to volunteer with children who are precisely the same age as they were when their own father more or less left. This is an important healing experience and should definitely be encouraged. Tell your teenagers that their life experiences have only made them more sensitive and aware of the pain the kind of behavior they have experienced causes. They are less likely than most to repeat the mistakes both you and their father may have made. Tell then straight out—because it is true—that they are better, stronger, and wiser people for all the things they have experienced, survived, and, indeed, triumphed over.

My son is starting to date, and I am concerned that he may treat young women badly because of behavior of his father's that he has witnessed. His father was a notorious womanizer, which makes me that much more worried that if my son copies him, he will risk AIDS.

Rest assured that very often children who have had the opportunity to see over time the results of boorish behavior of a parent or older brother or sister actually strive hard not to make the same mistakes. Your son, no doubt, is aware that his father was unfaithful to you and has probably lost track of the number of girlfriends who spent the night while he was visiting his father. None of this was very appealing at the time and is probably an even less appealing life-style choice now. It is more likely that your son will want to take an entirely different path. It may even be that you will have to encourage him to date many girls before he gets too serious.

Encourage your son's participation in group activities and sports so that dating does not become the exclusive focus of his free time. Discuss drugs and alcohol use with your son. Establish clear rules and enforce them. Remember that curfews are not just for girls. Remind your son of the need to practice safe sex. Make sure he has condoms, even if you buy them and leave them in his dresser drawer. Make sure he knows, also, that it's OK not to have sex if he doesn't feel ready. Thinking of our children as sexually active is always a jolt, but we cannot be good mothers if we are in denial about the realities of our children's world.

WHEN IT IS TIME FOR A MOM TO HAVE THE BIG TALK

My daughter and I have discussed openly for many years that she was conceived well after my first divorce with a man I barely knew. Despite such incredibly lousy romantic choices, my daughter and I have created a happy, stable family life. It is now time to have serious talks about sex during which any good mother stresses responsible behavior and the need for careful choices. How can I possibly have these kinds of talks with my daughter when she knows my own behavior was the total opposite? I want her to avoid the mistakes I made, but I certainly do not want her to think that I feel she is a regret or a mistake.

It should come as no big surprise but many woman, even those who end up happily married with 2.2 children, have sexual histories that they are less than eager to share with their own daughters or sons, for that matter. Most of the time, however, these mothers do not exactly lie, but rather spread the truth differently about their own past (or current!) sexual behavior. These women typically think of themselves as "good mothers." You should think of yourself no differently.

Glossing over certain things or spreading the truth differently is not options for you. With just a few possible exceptions, the whole truth are your greatest ally in helping your daughter make the critical life choices ahead. It is likely that some of your less than wonderful choices were influenced by a lack of self-understanding. Tell your daughter how important it is to know what she is doing and why. Girls are often influenced to dress up their sexual appetites and activities in romantic clothing pretending that hormonally driven lust is really true and lasting love. Help her to know the difference. Now that your daughter is older, you can certainly discuss in a limited way not only the joys, but also the heartaches of single motherhood. Your success as a single mother has involved compromises like any important life choice. Make your daughter aware of these compromises. You certainly want to stress the greatly increased health risks of sexual activity. Keep the lines of communication open. Our children expect us to be less perfect than our fear and confusion make us imagine. Make your experiences valuable teaching tools to counsel and guide your daughter as she enters the sometimes-scary world of relationships.

WHEN PETS BECOME ALL IMPORTANT

During my son's freshman year in college, he adopted an abandoned kitten and named him Leland after his lacrosse coach. When my son moved into an apartment, he was more concerned about the apartment being right for the cat than right for him. He buys dry cat food in fifty pound bags so that Leland can never go hungry. He has a special blanket for the cat and buys the cat toys. He takes pictures of the cat, which he carries in his wallet. He tells me that each meow has a different meaning and, if your listen closely, Leland meows "out" when he wants to go outside. I don't think this is normal. My son acts just like a proud father, but Leland is a cat not a child.

Could this have anything to do with the fact that my son has seen little of his father since he was about seven years old? Should I worry that my son goes so overboard with this cat?

Obviously, some people really love cats but, more likely, your son is taking important steps toward healing the wounds caused by his father's abandonment. Along the way, your son has asked himself whether he has the capacity to be a loving and committed father. Your son has something to prove to himself. In taking such loving and devoted care of this cat, your son is practicing the responsibilities, joys, and, yes, drudgery and worry of parenthood. Every day your son is proving to himself that he can be the kind of "daddy" he did not have. It is probably not the time in his life when he should be assuming the responsibility of a "real baby" so he has, in essence, done the next best thing by caring for Leland. Naming the cat after an important male person in his life is no accident. This choice of name signifies that the coach is an important role model in your son's life on and off the athletic field.

Perhaps you are not ready quite yet to be called grandma, but cherish the opportunity to watch your son preparing and practicing for the joys and responsibilities that parenthood will eventually bring to his life. Stop worrying and congratulate yourself for giving your son the emotional stability and courage to heal himself while taking exceptional care of one very lucky cat.

15

Where's Poppa?

HOW TO TALK ABOUT AN ABSENT PARENT

We know that the number of ways that women become single parents are many—from initiating a divorce to finding oneself abandoned; from accidentally becoming pregnant after a brief fling to choosing anonymous donor insemination; from staying in a relationship just long enough through the childbearing years to conceiving a child with someone you thought you knew better but realized you knew nothing about. And even though moms mothering without their child's biological father may emphasize many different concerns, most place a pretty strong focus on one particular area: how to handle the "daddy" questions.

ARE YOU READY TO TALK ABOUT DADDY?

Make sure you are ready to discuss this vital topic with your child well before he brings it up. Know that his questions will come at the most unlikely moments—while you are waiting on line at the supermarket, dropping him off at day care on the day of your big presentation, twenty minutes before your big date arrives for the first glamorous, romantic evening you have had in months. This is all the more reason to be prepared.

If you feel you are not ready, if the thought of discussing your child's father makes you angry or upset, then address your feelings first. Write down exactly what thoughts get you going or bring tears to your eyes. Better yet, write a letter to this person without the intent of mailing it, and state all your disappointments, regrets, and sadness over how your expectations were never

ANSWERING THESE THREE ZINGERS:

"Why did you and Dad split up?" Avoid statements suggesting that you "fell out of love." Then children may think that it is also possible for you to stop loving them. Let them know that this can never happen. It is okay to say that you and your child's father don't love each other as moms and dads should anymore. Assure your child that a mother is always a mother and that you will always be there for them.

"Will Dad ever come back?" Hope is the magic that sparks everyone's life in a positive way. However, falsely suggesting that a father who has no intention of returning will come back, or stating that you would like a father to return with whom you have no intention of ever becoming involved, makes way for more loss. It's better to say, "I hope that you and your father can find happiness and peace together as the special people you are." But for now, he will just have to occupy a place in your child's heart, if he can't be there in person.

"Can I live with Dad?" This question has a totally different meaning when asked by a toddler and by a teenager. Older children may be thinking about living with Dad when their values and life plan are in place and they are able to take care of themselves. But when a little one asks, try not to feel threatened or unappreciated. Tell your child that it's okay for him to think about living with Dad when he is older. Just remember that in all likelihood this will never happen. But, again, a little bit of hope is a healthy feeling.

Keep in mind, too, that you wouldn't be the first single mom to have adult children develop a kind of friendship with a long-gone dad. If this remarkable event happens, your strength and loving spirit, which has enabled them to forgive the past, has helped make their father some small part of their lives. What a tribute and a triumph for you!

met. Keep in mind that you want to purge these feelings, not necessarily find fault with or blame this person. To add a healing, ritualistic touch, why not burn the letter, tear it to shreds, or continue a long-held tradition of bottling it up and sending it out to sea? If you find no relief on your own, seek help through a support group, friend, trusted minister, or a mental health professional. It will be difficult work, sorting out these feelings and leaving the anger and otherwise destructive emotions behind you. But these steps will ensure success in answering any questions your child may have.

What to Expect. Most little ones begin asking questions about Daddy around the age of four or five. Before that, children think that all families are just like theirs. At the preschool age, children become more aware of the world around them and start to see themselves as part of that bigger world. Children also observe other kinds of families by participation in day care or by attending church or synagogue activities. We know that what children see on TV influences them greatly. Children also by this age become keen observers of simple day-to-day living around them.

How to Begin. Start your talks about Daddy by discussing the differences in families your child may have observed. Comment that a friend at school does indeed live with her mother, father, and both grandparents or that another friend has her married sister and her husband living with her. Take every opportunity to tell your child that these differences in families are to be celebrated. Talk about the positive things that happen, for example, when a grandmother might be living with a family. Mention that the grandmother can share stories of the family that others cannot remember or were not alive to see. Such celebration and acceptance of differences in other families sets the stage for your discussions of your own unique family and how you came to be. It also teaches children that diversity can be beautiful.

Remain positive, even upbeat, if possible. Especially if their father is neglectful or abandons his responsibilities to them in a major way, keeping your words positive will be emotionally demanding. Children neglected or abandoned will express rage, hurt, or anger. Comfort them as only a mother can. Say, "I know you are feeling hurt. I am sorry. I wish I could make things better for you." Resist the urge to say things like "Now you know why I left the bum!" or "What do you expect from a jerk like your dad?" This will require every last ounce of maturity and strength you have. Every time you succeed, your child will gain an added measure of happiness and self-esteem. Make this effort a life priority.

Every positive comment you make about their father becomes in the same way part of how your children view themselves.

Think about your words as sharp, deadly arrows. Protect your children from wounding words just as you would protect them from physical danger.

WHY THE DADDY TOPIC IS SO SCARY

Children learn their view of the world from the messages and values taught them at home. If mommy says that some children live with both a mom and a dad, others live with either a mommy or daddy, and still others live with a grandparent or relative, children will accept this with little difficulty. The problems arise when children sense that Mommy is uncomfortable or anxious about their own situation. We know that children take their cues from their parents on any subject. If it is clear to children that we are comfortable with a discussion, our comfort will translate into comfort and reassurance for them.

Remember that there is nothing so unusual about single mothering to make us feel isolated or different from what many would like to think is mainstream society. The fact is there are more children today living in single-parent and blended families than there are those who spend their entire upbringing in their biological parents' home. Your children need to know this and should be encouraged to realize early that they fit in just as well as anybody else—whatever their family background. One mom, to give herself some moral support, taped a cartoon to the bathroom mirror that was captioned, "Normal people from traditional, two-parent families." It shows an auditorium with a banner spread before hundreds of empty seats reading, "Welcome Adult Children of Non-Dysfunctional Parents," and two self-conscious participants looking around to see that they are the only ones who showed up!

Another mom recalls a television sitcom where a boy wonders if on his first day at a new school he'll be the only kid with two parents at home. He cringes, hoping he finds another outcast! She reported that her attitude allowed for a bit of levity. When we can laugh at different kinds of situations, it brings a sense of normalcy to them. Maybe one way to look at it is to see single mothering as "normal." Stepfamilies, two-parent families, single-parent families, adoptive families—their makeup, size, and structure may be defined differently, but they are certainly all "normal."

MISTAKES TO AVOID WHEN DISCUSSING DADDY

Sometimes we tend to jump in too quickly with words of reassurance or with too much information because we are trying to convince ourselves that everything is okay. But, by doing these things, we discourage the child from expressing his feelings.

Don't Change the Subject or Try to Avoid Listening to Your Child. It's most important to allow him to express freely whatever feelings or thoughts are on his mind.

Keep Your Discussion Age-Appropriate. We also sometimes forget that our explanations need first and foremost to be appropriate to our child's developmental level. For example, there is no way a four-year-old understands what commitment, trust, or intimacy means. The explanation, "Your father and I were not able to live together," rather than details about how he was never able to make a commitment to you, would be more easily understood by a preschooler.

Don't Give More Information Than Necessary. Sometimes we are so apt to share every detail regarding our children's birth with them, we forget to keep our conversations age appropriate. Surely you will recognize this new interpretation of a dusty old joke: A woman who had been inseminated with donor sperm was asked by her five-year-old son the long-awaited question, "Mommy, where do I come from?" Priding herself in being quite a liberal parent, this mother engaged in an elaborate dissertation regarding eggs, sperm, basal body temperature, and so forth. The child's eyes glazed over, and after about fifteen minutes he pleaded with her to stop. But being a no-nonsense kind of woman, she kept right on talking. Finally, he interrupted her with, "No, Mommy, I mean, Johnny comes from New Jersey. Where do I come from?"

The lesson here? Stick to the basic facts first and keep your explanations simple.

WHY DO CHILDREN ASK THE SAME QUESTIONS OVER AND OVER AGAIN?

I am satisfied that I have answered my eight-year-old's many questions about her father, who left us while I was still pregnant, honestly and

MAINTAIN YOUR CHILDREN'S TRUST IN YOU

In today's very small world, where the information superhighway will soon make everyone more or less next-door neighbors, keeping secrets will seem almost impossible. Lying to your children doesn't work because you simply won't be able to sustain the lies. Most children, as they mature, will eventually find out the truth, even if they wait until after they become adults. Rather than have them suffer another loss—loss of the ideal image they may have cherished in their minds and hearts or worse, jeopardize your future relationship with them by risking their loss of trust in you, be as open as possible.

♦ Reveal more and more information about their father as they mature.

♦ Assure them that their father's behavior does not mean that they are burdened with any of his less-than-desirable characteristics.

♦ Let them know that they don't have to repeat their father's behavior. If he broke the law, he wouldn't want them doing the same thing. Even if he was a lifelong counterfeiter, your children can still emerge the most honest on the block.

♦ Every positive comment you make about your children's father becomes in the

same way part of how your children view themselves. Be truthful, but try to remain positive. Tearing their father down in no way affects him but could cause serious consequences for your children. Positive comments about their father help to build their self-esteem. This is tricky, but possible. The secret is to share the information, but without personal judgment. For example, "Your father is a selfish, womanizing creep who wakes up drunk every morning in some bimbo's bed" just isn't appropriate! Try, "Your father was unable to act the way I expected a husband to behave." If your child asks why, it's okay to say, "I just don't know why or what he was feeling. But that's how it was."

As children get older it is less necessary to have the answer and more important to give them the opportunity to discuss their observations and feelings about what they have experienced. As they mature, their experiences and observations will influence their feelings and perceptions about their father. Their world becomes more complicated and things are less black and white. The good news is that as your children grow, you will do more listening and reflecting and less explaining and comforting.

thoughtfully. Maybe I am wrong, because my daughter tends to ask the exact same questions over and over again. What am I doing wrong?

In all likelihood, nothing. Children ask questions over and over again partly because they can't initially grasp all the information given them. Sometimes they are told too much too quickly, or their own learning styles

prevent them from absorbing completely all that was told them. Remember, for example, you probably did not understand multiplication the first time the teacher discussed it. She reviewed it many times while you practiced. This is how learning takes place. Understanding of what has been shared about your child's father will be no different. It will take time and repetition.

Children also ask the same questions over and over again to see if the answer remains the same. Little ones take comfort in the security of repetition the same way they like hearing the same bedtime story or eating some familiar food. However, the most important thing to remember is that if you are comfortable with your feelings about your single-mothering experiences, chances are your child will be, too.

SHOULD YOU EVER LIE?

You're told over and over again how important honesty is when talking to your child about why the other parent isn't around. But it can be terribly tempting to lie about a former partner, particularly if the movie title *Dirty, Rotten Scoundrels* comes to mind whenever you think of him. Maybe he considers prison a home away from home, or he's never seen a sober day in his life. Or maybe you thought you were really connected to this person only to learn that he had a harem of others who felt the same way.

Do you gloss over certain painful parts when talking to your child, or allow some little white lies to creep into the talk? It's okay to tone down the truth, but creating a whole fictional person, even though it seems the kinder and simpler thing to do, just doesn't work. Don't do it, no matter how huge the temptation. You may think you are sparing your children the heartache you underwent, but fictionalizing means being untruthful. Being diplomatic and sophisticated in your choice of words is better. No matter what the circumstances are that helped create your single mother status, don't stray too far from the truth.

IF YOU ARE DIVORCED OR SEPARATED

For divorced or separated single mothers, the challenge is that the daddy questions can change depending upon the circumstances, or may simply focus on the same painful issues throughout your child's growing up. For some fortunate children, while divorce may mean some adjustments, not all of them easy, Dad remains an active coparent who is involved in their lives. For other children, their father is around a lot initially, but then gets into a different life style and may see them less and less. One or both parents may remarry or be seriously involved with another partner. Sometimes a father moves to a different part of the country, and the loss of his attention is devastating. The divorced single mother must be ready to answer a host of different questions in response to whatever life path the father of her children has selected.

Remember, being able to talk about things isn't enough by itself. Establishing a fairly predictable household routine is important for all families, but it is particularly helpful in a recently divorced situation. Children need structure and a sense of order—from getting dressed in the morning, to regular mealtimes and bedtime—especially since the usual household routine has already been altered or disrupted.

When Dad Acts Like He Still Lives with the Family

My husband was routinely unfaithful, and after a lot of therapy I got my own act together enough to ask for a divorce. He readily agreed, obviously eager for his freedom. I did everything I could to make the transition easier for the children. Just as we were getting our lives together, we started seeing more and more of Dad. Apparently, freedom was not as much fun as the sneaking around. The children are asking me why Dad is around our house so much. What should I tell them?

A good question—why is he around the house so much? Part of getting your lives together is establishing boundaries and house rules. Boundaries in your case mean that your ex-husband is not allowed to come and go in your house as he pleases. It is not a good idea for anyone, particularly for the children. It is confusing and sends the wrong message.

Calmly tell your former husband that he is welcome to visit if he calls first. If he balks, insist in a firmer tone of voice. Tell him you are sure he would not want you to drop by his new apartment unannounced, particularly on a Saturday night, and this is just how his behavior feels to you. Tell him it is confusing to the children, particularly since you are working so hard to help everyone get their lives back on track. It might be a good idea to change the locks on the door and, for now, not to give him the keys.

When Dad Comes Out. This scenario might be what viewers of sleazy talk shows want, but when marriages or relationships end because the man finally accepts that his sexual preferences are homosexual, it can be a very poignant experience. Difficult as this revelation may be for a number of reasons, one of the toughest tasks for the mother of his children is explaining to them why Mom and Dad are no longer together.

Your children should be told what will be publicly known for now. If your partner or husband is really going to "come out" and announce his homosexuality publicly, then the children have to be told, assuming they are old enough to understand. For children under ten, this information is not appropriately shared. For young children or in cases where your former partner will choose to keep his sexual orientation private, simply saying that you could not love and support each other any more is enough. If the children ask why, tell them that this sometimes happen between grown-ups— never with parents and children—and that when they are older, it will be easier to understand.

When a No-Show Dad Breaks Promises

I try to give my ex-husband frequent and regular visitation. My children adore him. The trouble is that he is very irresponsible and often hurts their feelings by not showing up when he promised. I am often left with two crying, disappointed children. When I confront him about this, he just shrugs his shoulders and tells me that something came up. How do I lessen my children's hurt?

The best way to handle this situation is to prepare. The next time he is scheduled to take the children somewhere, talk to them about what the plan will be if their dad does not show up. Say very specifically, "Your dad is planning to take you to the movies on Saturday. He told us he would pick you up at 12:30. What is going to be our plan for the day if he does not arrive?" To minimize disappointment, the alternate plan should probably be something more fun than vacuuming the car or washing a few windows. Suggest, for example, that you do a few errands and then see the movie later in the afternoon. If your finances are tight, decide together on a fun and low-cost activity like kite flying or a trip to your local museum. Do not let dad have control of the day and charge of everyone's feelings when past experience has taught you that he may suddenly and for no reason decide not to show up.

Why Does Dad Pay More Attention to His New Girlfriend?

My ex-husband is like a scene out of a bad movie. He had a mid-life crisis of mind-blowing proportions. He has a new hairpiece and a girlfriend half his age he showers with lavish gifts and nonstop attention. The children are puzzled by their second-class status with him, and I suspect they are deeply hurt. He has not seen nor spoken to them in several months. What do I say when they ask me why dad likes his new girlfriend more than he likes them?

It will not help to tell them it just is not so when all the evidence points to her over them on their father's priority list. Begin by telling them that you certainly know and understand that they feel hurt. Explain that sometimes grown-ups have difficulty knowing what is most important in their lives and can get off track—just like when children "forget" to do their homework so they can watch TV. Further explain that this is someone with whom their father is fascinated because she is a different type of person than he usually spends time with or spent time with when you and he were

together. No doubt that is true in more ways than one!

Tell your children that sometimes we just need to be patient and see what happens. There are some things over which we have no control, and other people's behavior is certainly one of those things. Tell your children that, much as you would like to, you cannot make their father pay attention and spend time with them. This is something he must want to do himself.

Remind yourself that mid-life crises typically end with the big hangover of reality. It is likely that in your case things will be no different. He will wake up and realize that the girlfriend is gone, the children have moved along nicely without him, and he is not only lonely but alone.

If Dad Is Getting Remarried. Few children are thrilled by Dad's impending change in marital status because it deals the death blow to the cherished "reunion fantasy." You need to be alert that this news may impact the kids in a number of ways, but you may notice mild depression. They may also may be "acting out," especially if Dad just blurts the news out or they stumble on the fact when they spot wedding invitations lying around Dad's apartment. So be prepared first. If you suspect wedding plans are being made, ask your ex for the specifics about when and where, and discuss the best way to tell the children.

Why Does Dad Lie to Me?

My children are ten and twelve years old. Their father has a long history with illegal drugs. I am sure he is now dealing crack to support his habit. He is an advertising executive with plenty of income but, nonetheless, a cocaine addict. His visits with the children are few and far between, but when he does visit, he promises them all kinds of things. Sometimes he arrives with presents as though it were Christmas, giving them some of the things that he has promised in the past. For this reason, my children tend to believe his promises, although their trust and belief are wearing thin. What do I say when they ask me why Dad lies?

Your children have reached the age when they are very conscious of truth and the difference between right and wrong. Begin by telling your children that dad has the disease of addiction. You will be supported in your explanation by the fact that children are being taught at school about substance abuse and this information will not be new to them. Obviously, it is painful to discover that your own father is an addict. Explain his lying behavior in terms of his addiction. Explain that he is lying not because he does not love them, but rather because his addiction makes it impossible for him to behave toward them as he would choose to if he were well. Tell them that addiction is like having a broken leg. It makes it impossible for that person to walk or run normally. That is what addiction does—cripples the addict and prevents him from being able to do things that would normally be expected of him.

Before their father visits the next time, remind the children that Dad will make many promises. Remind them gently to remember to put the words "I wish" in front of whatever their father tells them. For example, he may promise to take them camping or on a trip to the mountains. Your children should listen to his words and think to themselves, "Dad means he wishes he could take us camping or to the mountains." This is truthful. Their father does wish these things, but he is weakened by his own addiction. Moreover, lying is a defense the addict uses to avoid acknowledging his own addiction. In a sense, he is lying to himself intentionally, but lying unintentionally to others.

Why Is He Always with Different Women?

My children, ages twelve, fifteen, and sixteen, see their father about once or twice a month on a schedule convenient to him. Every time they see him, he has a different woman with him whom he introduces as his girlfriend. This is nothing new to me. I left him because of his nonstop womanizing. The children are curious and ask me why Dad has so many girlfriends. What am I supposed to say?

Probably the most appropriate thing is to tell your children that this is a good question to ask their father. If they are uncomfortable doing so, tell them you can only guess at why there are so many different women in his life. Since your children are older, the point to make here is that you do not have all the answers to why anyone behaves in a certain way. Again, since they are older, ask them to try to guess why their father behaves the way he does. They may guess that he likes to be with different people, that he has never found someone he wanted to be with all the time, and other similar responses. Any or all of these could be right, and you should tell your children so. Their observations and your discussions of the possibilities are a good lesson for them about the complexity of human behavior. These discussions can also open the door for you to further communicate your own values about the importance of commitment and honesty.

Why Does Dad Love His New Kids More Than Me?

My former partner is uninterested in the nine-year-old daughter who resulted from the twelve years we were married. He left several years ago, has remarried, and turned into Superdad not only to the child he fathered with his new wife but also to her three other children. What do I say when my daughter asks why her father loves his other children so much and does not love her?

This kind of abandonment is really heartbreaking. Begin by telling her that although adults seem to know how to do everything well, this is not always the case. Some adults learn to show love and concern in stages, just as people learn to play the piano a little at a time. When her father was with you, he did not have the skills to show the kind of love that each of you needed.

Explain also that he has probably come to realize that unless he behaves in a loving way toward others, he will never receive love in return. His new children are not in some way better or more lovable than your daughter, but are rather on the lucky receiving end of changed behavior on his part. Simply stated, tell your daughter that her father has changed. She will ask, no doubt, why if he has changed he cannot be different

---

THE DOS AND DON'TS OF TALKING ABOUT A DEADBEAT DAD

- Do recognize that children are aware when fathers do not pay child support, if only because finances often become critically tight.

- Do consider different methods of answering questions about dad's failure to pay. For example, if dad's lack of support is due to sickness or unemployment, share these facts.

- Do point out that their father may be angry for a number of reasons, some of which he may not understand. However, point out that not paying support is a poor way to express these feelings.

- Don't say that dad's failure to pay is because he never really loved his children or that he's a lifetime member in the low-life club. These words will wound your children and will certainly do nothing to make the checks arrive any sooner. Better to explain gently that his behavior is sort of like a grown-up temper tantrum.

toward her. Tell her honestly that you do not know, but again these differences have nothing to do with her and everything to do with what her father is capable of doing. Tell her that you wish things were different, acknowledge and comfort her in the pain of rejection she is experiencing, and give her the extra measure of attention and support that she needs.

If you have any kind of relationship with her father, take the opportunity to meet with him and discuss the feelings your daughter is experiencing. He honestly could be unaware, immersed as he is in his new life. Encourage him to set aside some special time on a regular basis to spend just with your daughter.

If Dad Left and Hasn't Returned

About four years ago, my children's father left one Friday evening and never came back. I am sure he will never return. My two boys, eight and ten, still talk about him and refer to him as their father. We were never married, and I am sure that is why he left. They still hope he will come back, and it breaks my heart. I do not even know where he is. How do I answer their questions about why he left?

In many ways this is tougher than losing a father to death because his choice to leave is so final, like death, but is obviously his deliberate choice. Acknowledge what a terrible loss this is for your boys. It is okay to tell them that you do not know exactly why he left, but his decision was definitely not about them. He did not leave because they were bad boys or unlovable or in some way not good enough, but rather for reasons that he himself may not

even understand.

Help your boys come to terms with the loss of their father. Transitions in life like marriages and death are commemorated in our society with rituals and ceremonies. This is what you need to organize for your boys. Choose a quiet evening. Give each of the boys an opportunity to give a little speech about their father—kind of a eulogy for the living. You can also talk about your good memories of their father. You can set aside photos and other mementos in a special place. Light candles and prepare special refreshments. Irish Americans would recognize this as a good old-fashioned wake with tears and laughter. Most importantly, there will begin to be some kind of closure. The loss will be acknowledged and mourned. This is critical for all of you. Your boys can hope that Dad will someday return. On his birthday, light a candle and express the hope that he will return, but remember that these hopes cannot dominate any of your lives. The ritual of lighting the candle once a year keeps the hope in proportion to the probability of his return. Wish Dad well on his birthday as the candle is lit, but at the same time tell the boys that it is time for all of you to move on with your lives just as Dad is moving ahead with his.

Will Dad Ever Come Back? Life is meaningless without hope, and this is precisely the reason that children will continue to express the hope, long past any reasonable expectations, that dad will return. Many children ask frequently if they will be able to find their father when they are older and go live with him.

Many single mothers find these questions deeply disturbing, for a number of reasons. Many of these long-absent dads have given their children nothing but disappointment, and mothers fear that their children's quest for these men will lead only to more heartbreak. Other mothers know that their former partner's addictions, habits, or deep personal flaws make it unlikely that their children will ever be able to establish a parent-like relationship. These are not men upon whom to depend, nor are they appropriate for their children to trust. Many single mothers, weary from the conflicting and demanding roles of single motherhood, feel resentful that their children are so interested in a man who has provided nothing and lives responsibility-free.

IF YOU WEREN'T MARRIED TO YOUR CHILD'S FATHER

If Your Pregnancy Was Unplanned

I feel a little guilty when I hear other single mothers who chose to become pregnant talk about all the soul-searching and planning they went through. My pregnancy was an accident. I chose to keep the baby because it seemed like the right thing to do, and it has been the best decision of my life. Do I tell my child he was an accident?

No. Tell your child he was a delightful surprise. Many single mothers report that their pregnancies were accidents, but many experts believe that there are fewer contraceptive accidents or failures than there are unconscious desires to have a baby. More than you may be able to understand or accept now, your decision to have a baby may

have been more planned than you realize. It may have felt like the right thing to do because in ways you still may not fully understand, you were ready to become a mother. The best parts of life are often the delightful and unexpected events. For you, a seemingly unplanned pregnancy may have been one of these events. Emphasize with your child the joy and surprise. Save the word "accident" for events like crumpled fenders and spilled milk. And never forget that some people "plan" themselves out of a lot of joy. Don't be one of them.

Special Concern: If You Were Raped

My child was born as the result of my being raped. It was not an attack that occurred in a dark alley or in my home. I knew the person casually, and this took place as he drove me home from my job one evening. I have no idea how to talk about this to anyone.

If your pregnancy was the result of a rape, you cannot begin to discuss this event with your child until you are at peace with how this traumatic event shaped your life. Counseling has probably been an essential part of your healing. Even if your need for counseling support has long ended, it is now a good time to seek some professional assistance in helping you explore and discuss your child's violent conception as he begins to ask the expected questions about how he came to be brought into this world. This is especially important if your rape was publicized and members of your community are aware that your child resulted from this violence.

Didn't Dad Want Me?

My child's father left when I was pregnant. He lives nearby, although we never see him. He is completely uninterested in my son, who, frankly, receives a lot of attention for his handsome appearance and great athletic skills. Now that he is twelve, he is beginning to ask with more seriousness why his father rejected him. What do I say that I have not already said a thousand times before?

You have no doubt assured your son that his father's lack of interest has nothing to do with him and everything to do with his father's limitations. Your son has asked this question time and time again because he has probably thought about this a lot. Now that he is approaching adolescence, you can begin to give him more information that you might not have appropriately offered in the past. For example, his father probably has a problem with commitment in all areas of his life. If this is the case, you might now be able to say to your son that dad has real troubles committing to most other people—not just him. As an athlete, your son is familiar with what coaches demand: dedication and commitment. Emphasize that he has not

inherited his father's limitations. Give him examples of how he has shown commitment, and reassure him that you are there to help him develop into the kind of man he wants to be.

"My Daughter Makes Up Stories About Her Father …"

Despite my best efforts to positively and realistically discuss my decision not to marry her father, who incidentally had a major drinking problem, my six-year-old daughter has created elaborate fantasies about him that are so far from the truth it's scary. What should I do?

Your concerns are shared by many other single mothers who express worry and fear when their children conjure up detailed, unrealistic portrayals of their biological fathers, even if they have never met them. But don't become overly concerned, because it is quite normal that fantasy plays an important part in every child's life. Young children have vivid imaginations that they use to provide themselves with the entertainment and stimulation they need. This is why children of this age may have imaginary friends or pets or talk about taking trips to places like the moon or Candy Land.

Become Interested in Your Child's Fantasy. Rather than immediately trying to correct or change your child's story, try adopting an interested and accepting attitude. When your child claims that her daddy is an ice cream man and drives all over town giving children ice cream, respond with, "You are pretending what a fun job your daddy has! Wouldn't it be great to ride on an ice cream truck all day long and get to eat all the ice cream you want!" She doesn't need to know for now that her father is a CPA with so many drunken driving convictions he's not permitted to drive a car, let alone an ice cream truck!

As time goes on and your child matures, her interest in fantasy naturally becomes replaced with a growing interest in day-to-day reality. This is when your child will want to learn more facts about her biological father.

"My Daughter Pretends Her Father Was in a Car Crash ..."

I overheard my teenage daughter tell her friends that her father was killed in a car accident in California. We recently moved here from out of state, so everyone believed her. The truth is we really don't know where her natural father is. I doubt he has ever been to California. What would prompt her to make up a story like that?

There are probably many reasons your daughter told her new friends this untrue story. First of all, she is new in town and probably is trying hard to impress her new classmates. Possibly she feels awkward and insecure. When the subject of her father came up, probably very innocently, she made up a story designed to impress and to quash any further questions on that topic, which proves what a quick thinker she is! Remember, too, that teenage girls have something of a flair for the dramatic, and this story certainly would rate four stars for drama.

Yet you do not want to encourage her to go through life making up "interesting" stories about herself. At a quiet moment when you can be reasonably sure you will not be interrupted, talk to your daughter about what you overheard. Assure her that you were not eavesdropping, but you think that her new friends' questions probably surprised her and she most likely did not know what to say. Explain to her that these other young people probably did not mean to embarrass her—they were just curious.

Seize the Opportunity to Discuss More. Your daughter would probably welcome the opportunity to learn how to deal with this the next time questions about her dad arise. Tell her that many of her new friends are being raised in single-parent homes and nobody would have been shocked or surprised by the truth. Help her rehearse or practice responding with something like, "My mother and father could not stay together happily." Or let her know that saying, "My father has lived in a lot of places and we really do not see too much of him" would have been perfectly all right.

Reveal More Information as the Opportunity Arises. Your daughter might also welcome knowing some new information about her father in order to feel more comfortable. Make sure you share what you can remember about his interests, early family life, or work life. This information will give her a feeling of connection—for example, when you let her know that her fabulous math skills obviously come from her father (particularly when you're still counting on your fingers to balance your checkbook).

Child May Be Angry at Dad for Being Absent. Consider the possibility, too, that your daughter made up that story about her father being dead because she is really angry about him not being around. If, when you speak to her, such anger is apparent, you must help her find ways to come to terms with the absence of a father in her life. This may mean just talking it out quietly or having her speak with a counselor. Often, schools have staff-facilitated support groups that allow children to discuss their family situations or crises with their peers, so check into this, too.

"My Son Pretends His Dad Died in the War ..."

My six-year-old son told his teacher that his father was killed in a war far, far away. Absolutely not true. I think he made this up from all the stuff that was on TV recently about the Persian Gulf war. I have never even mentioned his father to him because he has never asked. What would make him create a crazy story like this?

By not discussing his father with him, you have created something of an information void. Your son's story is his way of filling this void. He needs to know about his father, and since you have not brought the subject up, your son has tried to meet his need for information by creating what sounds to him like a perfectly logical explanation. Maybe now is the best time to start talking with your son about his father.

You might break the ice with something like this: "I'll bet when you go to Paul's [here you would name any friend who has a father living at home] house and his daddy plays football with you,

you wonder about your own father." From this starting point, you can explain how you and your son came to be together as a family.

When Your Child Never Brings Up the Subject

My seven-year-old daughter has never once asked me about her father. He left us when she was a baby and I was devastated. I try to bring the subject up because I know she must be curious. Why do you think she never wants to discuss her father?

Some children are not as curious about certain topics as others. Maybe because you've attempted to bring this up in the past, she doesn't sense any secrecy and has enough information to satisfy her. On the other hand, children are wonderfully intuitive, and your daughter may perceive that this is a painful topic for you. For this reason, she denies to you that it is important to her. Tell her, as you have been doing, that you know she must be curious about her father. Look for opportunities to bring her father into the conversation. For example, as you flip around the television channels, casually remark how much her father loved westerns or football or whatever is accurate. These simple remarks let her know that it is okay for you to talk about Dad, that you won't burst into tears, and that it is definitely okay for her to have questions about him. Keep things as positive as possible, stressing his good qualities. She will no doubt ask why he left. Explain to her that raising a little girl is a big job and that her father was not ready to take on such an important job. He left her with you knowing that you would always love her and take good care of her.

Can't Dad Get Better and See Me Too?

My son is seven years old. His father is now living in a halfway house thousands of miles from us in recovery from alcohol and substance abuse. He met our son once several years ago, but his addictions have kept him from having any relationship with our little boy. I have explained to our son that his father's illness keeps him from being here for him. My son wants to know why dad can't get better and still be with him, if only for visits?

This is a pretty logical question from a seven-year-old boy. He sees you doing many things even when you have a cold or the flu, so it just seems natural that someone could recover from addiction and still watch TV with him or come to his Little League game. Explain to your son that addiction is not like the time you were sick with the flu and still packed his lunch and made sure his homework was done. Tell your little boy that addiction makes it impossible for adults to do the things they are expected to do and want to do. Recovering from addiction, it should be explained, takes every bit of energy adults have. Emphasize that his father really wishes he could be with him, but now he just cannot. Your little boy should be made aware that his father's residence in a halfway house is a hopeful sign that his father is trying to get well. Encourage your son to communicate with his

father by letter or an occasional phone call if this is possible. If not, your son can keep a box or scrapbook containing things he would like his dad to see or know about when the time comes that Dad is well enough to be some small part of his life.

When Children Want to Search for Their Birth Father

My sons' natural father disappeared about five years ago. He has many problems, including substance abuse. We have not heard from him since my younger boy was nine. Both my sons are suddenly obsessed

HEREDITY ISN'T DESTINY, BUT WATCH FOR RED FLAGS!

If your child's father has a history of substance abuse, even if he is completely out of your lives, it is important to remember that his history may have given your child a genetic predisposition to substance abuse. You need to instruct your child explicitly and with great care about the dangers of these substances. You need to set a good example by drinking responsibly and abstaining from all drugs that are not prescribed or recommended by a physician. Routines and structure are key life skills for children whose hereditary makeup includes the potential for such serious problems. Your responsibilities are greater than for other mothers whose children's past do not include such dangers, but it doesn't guarantee that your children will also abuse drugs or alcohol. It means that you need to establish strong communication—carefully, openly, and honestly—with your child.

with finding him, and they talk about this all the time. I don't know if I would want to find him if he even wants to be found, or what the boys and I would do if, indeed, we did find him. What do you think is really going on in their minds?

More likely than not, your sons' interest in finding their father has more to do with curiosity and concern than anything else. They are both now at an age when they realize the hazards of their father's substance abuse and, with good cause, probably worry about his safety and health. They are also at an age when they are beginning to think of themselves as young men and are naturally curious to know more about their father as a man.

Launching an all-out search would probably be expensive and unproductive. Not only that, your sons could be hurt if you found their father and he was unable to see them because of his addiction or unwilling to see them out of embarrassment or denial. Compromise with your sons by contacting relatives or friends of your sons' father and asking if they know of his whereabouts. If they do, perhaps it would be best if your sons

wrote to him rather than trying to arrange a visit. If their father's whereabouts are not known to family or friends, you can at least alert these people to your sons' interest in a reunion of some sort. You can certainly assure your sons that if they still want to find their father when they are older, you will support their decision no matter what. But finding someone who may not wish to be found is an adult decision and one they can make only when they are grown-up and on their own.

When Your Child Calls Someone Else Daddy

My children's natural father drifts in and out of their lives. They call their natural father by his first name, Howard. They call my boyfriend, who has lived with us for the past three years, Daddy. This has just sort of evolved, and I am wondering if I should let well enough alone or whether I should insist that they stop calling him Daddy. It is not very likely that we will get married, although I think we will continue to live together.

Your children have given your boyfriend the name that probably best describes his role and place in their lives. He is obviously more of a daddy to them than their absent, neglectful father. He is the one who tells them bedtime stories, plays with them, eats meals with them, washes their clothes, helps provide for them, and performs other "daddy-type" duties. You are right to be sensitive, however, to what this name might mean to them.

There is no reason for them to stop calling him Daddy, but do explain to them that this is a pet name for this very special person in their lives. In most situations, children call their biological father Daddy, Dad, or Pops. Calling your boyfriend Daddy as their pet nickname does not necessarily make him their father. And since it is uncertain whether or not your relationship will lead to a permanent commitment, it is also important to tell the children that their relationship with "Daddy," although wonderful, might not last forever. You don't need to share the details of why your relationship may not be a lasting one. He did not help make them, which in itself is not a definition of daddy either. But what's important is to let them know that if this relationship is not permanent, it is okay for them not to assume he will be a part of their lives forever.

Why Can't Daddy Take Care of Me?

I had a long relationship with a man who has a serious drinking problem. I left him for good after my son was conceived because I did not want this alcoholic chaos in my child's life. This man's life is still in a shambles, and he can barely take care of himself. When he is well and able, I encourage him to visit our four-year-old under my supervision. My son adores him and asked me the other day why his daddy cannot be around more and help take care of him. How do I begin to answer my son's questions?

Begin by telling your son how much his father cares for him and how much he wishes that he were able to spend more time with him. Inform your

child that his father has a disease called alcoholism that makes him too sick most of the time to take care of a little boy. When your son asks if his father will ever be better, tell the truth by saying that you hope so but do not know for sure. Encourage your son to hope for his father's sobriety while at the same time reassuring him that you will always be there for him.

Why Doesn't Daddy Show Up When He Says He Will?

I am a single mother outside of marriage. The father of my child refused to have anything to do with me after he found out I was pregnant. I wanted a child more than I wanted him, so I kept the baby and dumped him. Now that my daughter is almost two, he suddenly contacts me and wants to see her and me. The first time we arranged a meeting at the local park, he never showed up. The next time he was an hour late. I would like my daughter to at least meet him and have some relationship with him. How do I handle his irresponsible behavior?

The best way to handle irresponsible or inappropriate behavior is to respond to it as responsibly and appropriately as you can. The next time your child's father calls, remind him of the importance of being on time as he promised. Allow him a thirty-minute grace period and then leave and implement Plan B. Plan B is whatever you decided to do ahead of time in case he did not show up or was ridiculously late. Try meeting him one more time. If he is a no-show but calls again, suggest that next time he call you from a nearby restaurant or coffee shop when he arrives. Then he can wait the five or ten minutes until your arrival. If you do not hear from him within a half hour or so on the day and time you both selected, leave your house and go enjoy the sunshine. Do not wait by the telephone for him to call.

When Dad Suddenly Appears

My child was conceived with a man who, despite my pathetic and desperate pleas at the time, left us for parts unknown. I had explained to my daughter, now age eight, that he was simply not ready for the big job of taking care of a little girl. Suddenly he appeared on our doorstep one day announcing that he was ready to be "everything a daddy should be." What do I do now? How do I explain when she asks why he has suddenly returned?

Before you explain anything, insist that you and your daughter's father meet alone and discuss exactly what he means by "everything a daddy should be." Assuming that you have established sole custody, his rights to spend time with your daughter are under your control. Your concern should be to

allow him to develop a relationship with your daughter, becoming a special adult friend to her, without inflicting the double whammy of abandoning her again. He will need to understand that there may be now or in the future other men in your life who will also be important to your daughter. You have not been in suspended animation waiting for him to return. He will need to abide by the house rules and support the values you have been working hard to teach.

This relationship should begin with the three of you spending an hour or two together sharing an activity like visiting the zoo or seeing a movie. You need to know for yourself that this man is reliable in both his judgment and behavior before you allow him time alone with your daughter. In many ways, he is a stranger and you should exercise the same care you normally would if any other new person wanted to be part of your daughter's life. It is not unheard-of for fathers like this to decide to take ownership of their children and literally kidnap them. Better to be overly cautious than risk exposing your child to trauma and danger.

At the same time, you need to explain to your daughter that adults sometimes realize that they have made mistakes and try to correct those mistakes. In her father's case, he now feels that he made a mistake leaving her and is trying to make things right. Explain gently also that sometimes adults can know they made a mistake but not be able to fix it. Tell her that both of you will try together to build a relationship with dad, but it is up to him to show by his behavior that he would like to be part of your lives. Make sure you also let her know that you are aware that she must feel quite confused and surprised by what has happened. Assure her that you understand and share her surprise, but at the same time you will do all you can to make sure that she is well taken care of and protected.

IF YOU DON'T KNOW THE FATHER'S IDENTITY

My child was conceived during a time in my life when my behavior was not exactly exemplary. Fortunately for me, my three-year-old son was born healthy, and I am lucky enough not to have gotten AIDS or killed myself with drinking and drugs. But soon my child will ask who his father is. I do not know. It could be either of two men. What should I tell my child?

You need to decide for yourself who the father was and appoint him in your mind and heart as the "designated dad" before you can discuss this with your child. Presumably, your former sex partners are long gone, and the chances of one claiming paternity are slim. Maybe a good start is asking yourself whom you would have chosen as the biological father. If you spent considerable time with one man and had only one or two encounters with the other, it is most likely that your regular lover was the father of your child. Of course, without a test there are no guarantees, but based on your son's appearance and disposition, who is the more likely candidate? Does your son's sweet nature and pitch-black hair allow you to discard as the candidate the ill-tempered blond surfer with whom you spent one very unforgettable night?

Make your best decision and stick with your choice. When your son begins to ask about his father, tell him what you know about his "designated dad."

But add, too, that you and this person did not love each other the way grown-ups who parent together should. It's okay to say that you didn't know him very well. Assure your son that your meeting was special because your son was the result of this event, but point out that his dad was not destined to have a larger role in either of your lives.

When Dad Was a Forgettable One-Night Stand

I conceived twin girls with a man I met in a bar at a convention in Las Vegas very soon after my divorce. At the time I was bored and a little down and thought I was treating myself to a little fling because I had no intention of seeing him again. When I realized I was pregnant, I knew that I had not let this happen by total accident. I had had real longings for children for many years. My girls are the greatest, but now that they are four the daddy questions are starting for real. How do I explain to my children that Dad was nothing more than a pickup in a bar?

Begin with the most obvious—tell them how very much they were wanted. You can tell your girls that sometimes grown-ups do not know exactly what they want until it starts happening to them. Tell them you were far from home and feeling lonesome. You met a man and shared a very special adventure and made two beautiful babies together. Tell them that things in life happen for a purpose and that you met this man for one and only one purpose—to create the little girls you love so much. Discuss him more as a useful part of getting your heart's desire rather than the lounge lizard he most likely was. When they push for more information, it's okay to tell them that you really don't know that much about him. Do emphasize, however, that you know that the most important thing about him was the part he played in helping you to make them.

IF YOUR CHILD WAS ADOPTED OR CONCEIVED VIA DONOR INSEMINATION

My three-year-old daughter is adopted. I have used this word with her since the day I brought her home at nine months. When she asks me why her parents gave her up, what am I going to say?

All adopted children ask this question in one form or another many times over. At your child's age, simply say that some mommies and daddies are not ready to take on such a big job as raising children. This is a good beginning. Also, be sure to let your child know how important birth parents are and how they help those who are physically unable to have children become parents. Emphasize over and over that their help makes many people—especially you—very, very happy. But more importantly, because some adopted children were given up by single mothers, be sure to let your daughter know that you want to be her mommy always.

What Is a Father? Many thoughtful single mothers have answered the question "Who is my father?" in unexpected ways. Yet most moms—whether donor-inseminated or impregnated by someone they know—reject the notion that providing sperm in whatever way automatically makes a man a father. To them, "father" is a title to be earned by love, devotion, sacrifice, and plain hard work. In response to the "daddy" question, some tell their children that they have no father. In answering the question, "What would you say to those who think it's wrong to tell your child he or she has no father?" one donor-inseminated mom suggested teaching a child the definition of the word *father*. Then she would tell her, "I wanted you, this is what I went through to have you, so this is what you've got. Be grateful that you are here and loved very much."

Others respond differently, depending upon the circumstance. For example, some refer to the child's grandfather as a father because he has been a loving, guiding, nurturing man in their lives and will continue to be until the day he dies. Still other women might tell their children that their new husband or partner is the children's father because this is the responsibility that he has freely chosen.

If you were donor-inseminated, it is important, just as when children are adopted, to incorporate this important piece of information into the fabric of your child's life literally from the day you bring the baby home from the hospital. You can never say too often or too early how much you love your child and how much you wanted him. Emphasize the planning and care that went into his conception.

Who Was My Daddy? When your child begins to ask questions in earnest at about age three, tell him that you knew you wanted to be a mother more than anything else, so you went to a doctor who helped you have a baby by using the seed from a specially selected man. As your child grows older, you can give more information on the donor's background, which is furnished at the time of the insemination. Some artificially inseminated mothers use special, affectionate terms for this donor like "miracle maker" or "special helper" when discussing with their children how they were conceived.

When the Donor Sperm Came from a Friend

My son was conceived using donor sperm from a friend of mine. There were so many qualities, not to mention good looks, that I admired about him. I wanted to have his child but knew we could not make each other happy as husband and wife. My son knows that Jake is his father as well as a special friend of the family. But now that he is eight, he is beginning to ask why Jake and I are not married. What should I say?

This is a perfect example of how practical and easy it is to tell the truth. Your son can be told exactly what you have just told us. There are many things about Jake to admire, and it is beneficial to your son to elaborate on these at every opportunity. Mention

Jake's honesty, sense of humor, or whatever qualities you like best. Tell your son that you think Jake is a handsome man. Mention his terrific smile and big muscles. It is then important to explain that not all grown-ups who like and admire each other love each other in the special way husbands and wives do. Tell your son that both you and Jake knew that you could not make each other happy as a married couple. Tell your son also that you and Jake are glad that you realized this before you tried to be married and made each other unhappy.

"My Daughter Tells Me She Is a Freak ..."

I was donor-inseminated by an anonymous donor because I was ready to be a mother but had not found the right man to share my life and the big commitment of parenthood. My daughter, now age thirteen, has been told all of this over the years. Suddenly, however, she is very upset. She tells me she is a freak of nature and she hates me for ruining her life.

Every mother who has ever raised a daughter has been told countless times for countless reasons that mom has ruined her life. The reasons range from not being allowed to get a tattoo to insisting that she do her homework. Forget the "ruining her life" barb. This is normal teenage-girl stuff and is best ignored.

Just as you have let her know the facts of life as they relate to how she came to be, it is now time for a few more lessons in reality. Teenagers, like all children, need limits and boundaries. You need to tell her exactly how it is and not get caught up in the turmoil and drama many teenagers like to create.

Tell your daughter that having her was the most important thing in your life. You decided that donor insemination was the best way for you to bring her into the world as your child to love. This is how it is and you are certainly not going to debate the wisdom of your choice or listen to her refer to herself as a freak of nature. Tell her straight out that she should just be glad that she is here. You certainly are.

I Want a Dad to Beat Up That Bully's Dad!

My seven-year-old came home from school very upset and sporting a black eye. The boys on the playground were bragging about whose dad was the toughest, and the bully said he'd beat up my son because he has no dad to protect him. Rather than walk away, my son went for him. Suppose there is a next time?

"Bully" is a good word to describe this kid, since this situation has little to do with your home situation. Use this as a learning experience for your son so he will know what to do next time.

Explain to your son that a bully is someone who feels unhappy or unloved, which makes him want to hurt others. Compassionate as your child may be, let him know that this still is unfair because the victim of the teasing or roughness could begin to believe that he or she deserves this treatment, which isn't so. No one deserves to be treated that way.

Rehearse with your son for the next time by letting him play the bully's role

while you play your son. When he gets obnoxious, stare back at him fiercely and announce, "Stop this nonsense, NOW!" and walk away. Encourage your son to try reversing roles.

Don't turn this event into a major crisis, but for added measure you might want to add, "I wonder if that boy has a dad at home who is mean to him" to engage empathy on your son's part while letting him feel good about himself.

IF YOUR CHILD'S FATHER HAS PASSED AWAY

Talking to a child about his deceased father can be extremely difficult, even if you have come to terms with your own sense of loss. Take heart: while many mothers find this process emotionally wrenching, they also find it healing. If you are still grieving, be sure to read Chapter 6 for advice on how to deal with the loss of your spouse or significant other before you attempt to explain it to your child.

The following tips should help you help your children understand the truth when those "daddy" questions arise.

♦ Give your children a sense of their father as a person. For example, share with them his likes and dislikes of simple things like food or recreation. Tell them stories that reveal positive aspects of his character and beliefs. If you need to be selective, that is okay. Emphasize positive qualities like his love for animals and minimize flaws that are meaningless now anyway.

When You Were Married

♦ Share the details of your courtship and marriage with your children in ways that make them feel the joy you both experienced. Include the mundane details like who wore what to the wedding. A full description of Aunt Sophie's purple chiffon dress is what family history is all about.

♦ Give your children a clear understanding of how their father died while supplying them with socially appropriate ways to answer questions others might ask. For example, if he died of AIDS, it would be perfectly acceptable for them to say he had a terminal illness.

♦ Emphasize that, no matter what the circumstances of their father's death, his choice was not to leave them. Whether true or not, let them know that he loved them very much.

♦ Don't be surprised by occasional episodes of inappropriate behavior or outright defiance. This may be your children's method of expressing their feelings about their father's death. It is natural for them to feel not only sad but angry and abandoned as well. Encourage them to use healthy outlets for these emotions. Younger children may benefit from using a punching bag, while older children may enjoy keeping a diary or journal.

When You Weren't Married

♦ Share with your children the happy details of your relationship. Talk about how you met and the kinds of things you enjoyed doing together.

♦ Don't portray their father as a complete loser even if he left you without as much as a goodbye note or died while in prison. This man is still your children's father. They need to have a positive view of him, so try being creative by pointing out his most interesting or redeeming trait. If he had numerous tattoos, emphasize to your children these may have reflected his interest in medieval art.

♦ Try to keep some small mementos of him so that the children have something tangible by which to remember him. You may need to create these. For example, if he loved the circus, you might think about having a circus poster or a small statue of a clown in your home.

♦ Give your children reasons why you two did not marry. Practice with them ways to answer questions that might come up about who their father was and where he is now.

16

Mothers and Daughters

GIVING THE GIFT OF SELF-RELIANCE

It's not uncommon to hear kids, particularly teenage girls, complain about their parents. But two decades ago, it was rare to meet a young girl who didn't insist, "There's no way that I'm going to grow up to be like my mother!" Clusters of them swore they wouldn't be caught dead dressing or acting like their moms, and many have stated they were often embarrassed that their mother's position in the home seemed about as significant as a doormat.

More and more often, however, experts who work with families and girls are noticing a major change. Girls are no longer panicking at the prospect of turning out like mom, but rather are finding their mothers' lives interesting and exciting. With more and more mothers working outside the home, young girls are not only admiring these women and appreciating them, but they are more likely to model themselves after their behavior. Today's mother is also mentor.

PREPARING YOUR DAUGHTER FOR THE FUTURE

Raising a daughter to take her place in the world is a daunting challenge no matter what your family circumstances might be. It may be tempting to think of your job as infinitely more difficult because you are a single mother. Your perspective really depends upon your answer to the age-old question: Is the glass half empty or half full?

HOW BIG A LOSS IS IT NOT TO HAVE A DAD AROUND?

It is true that your daughter won't experience the love, support, and validation that comes from having a loving father at home. She will never be "daddy's little girl." Yet, judging from the confusion many young women express today about topics ranging from career choices to sexual preference, it is hard to believe that all the problems facing young women are somehow more easily faced and more quickly solved when their childhood was spent with Dad close by. Having a father at home, just physically present, does not guarantee that he will be a good parent. Some dads are just there like another piece of furniture or, worse yet, are emotionally demanding, uncaring, and in some cases abusive. So before you lose heart and begin to worry that your household is less healthy for your daughter than one in which both mother and father are present, be sure you are seeing things as they are.

When Daddy Does Not Seem to Be Missed

My ninth-grade daughter came home from a friend's house very upset the other day. At first, all she could say over and over again was how lucky she was not to have a father. Apparently this friend's father is quite abusive verbally and really did a number on my daughter's friend with all her friends watching in terror. I am glad that she is not terribly sad about her father's absence from her life, but this is going a bit too far. How should I handle this?

First of all, tell your daughter that she is not lucky her father has chosen to be out of her life, but that she is lucky she does not have a father in her life who behaves the way this father apparently did. As she describes what happened in greater detail, use the words "verbal abuse" and tell her the kind of damage this kind of behavior

creates. Tell her that people's self-esteem and pride in themselves are often severely damaged by contact with abusive people. Use this sad experience to alert your daughter to the dangers of abusive relationships. This father is a sort of negative role model, and you should identify him as such to your daughter. Tell her that this kind of behavior should alert her that she is spending time with someone who can potentially hurt her a great deal—in short, not the stuff of which great boyfriends are made.

WHAT HAPPENS TO GIRLS DURING ADOLESCENCE

Any kindergarten teacher will tell you that when girls begin school they are miles ahead of boys. They are taller. They are better coordinated and much better able to hop, skip, and run than their male classmates. Their fine motor skills are also much better. Girls color, cut, paste, and learn to write much

more quickly and certainly with greater neatness than boys. They usually learn to read more quickly. Girls more often bring home the proud-to-hang-on-the-refrigerator report card, while boys seem to need their mothers to come to endless conferences with the teacher to discuss the latest snag in a non-too-illustrious elementary school career. All told, little girls are the stars of elementary school, while it's not uncommon for little boys to struggle.

All these advantages seem to come to a crashing halt as adolescence begins. As one exasperated mother put it, "What happened to my daughter? One day she was the star of the sixth grade, and the next day she was a mess! Where did all these problems come from?"

This mother's lament reflects the changes girls experience as adolescence begins. It is not the bodily changes in and of themselves, but rather how society's expectations influence how girls view themselves as their bodies naturally change.

The confident, accomplished sixth-grade girl begins to grow and develop as does her somewhat less stellar sixth-grade male classmate a few years later. Abruptly, this once-confident little girl is subjected to a whole new standard—how she looks. Grades, interests, accomplishments all take a back seat to appearance, and particularly concerns with weight. It is society's obsession with appearance that makes the journey into adulthood so perilous for girls. For boys, however, who are applauded loudly for simply letting their bodies do what they are expected to do—grow taller and get heavier—the trip is much easier. The changes girls can expect naturally are not always changes society welcomes. Girls can expect a temporary awkwardness in movement, mild skin eruptions, and the inevitable addition of fat, which is necessary for menstruation.

Television and Other Sources of Mixed Messages. Television and other media exploit normal female adolescent

---

CHORES AS CONFIDENCE BUILDERS

It's important to give your daughter responsibilities at home:

♦ The youngest child is capable of doing simple chores like putting the napkins on the table or stacking up old newspapers. Be sure the chores you give are age appropriate, and also make sure they are not gender identified. For example, don't limit tasks to cooking or cleaning activities. Have your daughter put tools away.

♦ Don't view your daughter's doing chores as "helping you." It's better to think of these chores as ways she is helping herself to develop the confidence to tackle bigger and more complicated tasks independently. Confidence is the first step toward self-reliance.

---

concerns about body image and development by creating characters like those on the hit show *Beverly Hills 90210* who are portrayed as teenagers but are, in reality, played by actors in their twenties. The message is clear: Be pretty, and, above all else, be thin. We harp on good grades and worry that they will not be able to go to a good college or get a well-paying job. Meanwhile our daughters are reading magazines geared for them that feature articles like "Rating Your Buns—How Does Your Fanny Compare?" or "15 Can't-Miss Ways to Make Boys Really Like You." There is little wonder girls are confused.

This confusion all girls experience as adolescence begins has less to do with the part their fathers play in their lives than with how suddenly their bodies are in conflict with society's unattainable ideal of teenage beauty—perfectly clear skin, waif-like thinness (skip the breasts and hips), and the grace of a ballerina. Perfect SAT scores as well as being president of the student council, head cheerleader, and part-time model would also be nice touches!

What's a Mother to Do?

My fourteen-year-old daughter is really unhappy. She is going through that very awkward stage. Her skin is a mess. Maybe if her father were around she would feel better about herself. How can I help her? I am particularly concerned about the weight she has gained. I have always watched mine carefully, and I am nuts that she might get fat.

First of all, too many mothers are tempted to view their daughter's bodies as extensions of their own. Your daughter's body is not your body, and how she looks is not a reflection of you nor under your appropriate control. If you choose to try to control your daughter's body through ridicule, nagging, or constant mention, the result will be that she will rebel even more than is typical. She may begin to show you how much she is in control by seriously overeating or by experimenting with drugs and alcohol.

As for her father, who is to say what part he would play if he were around? The point is that he is not around, and giving your daughter what she needs is up to you. According to a number of developmental psychologists, what your daughter needs is good old-fashioned maternal warmth. Daughters need Mom to be Mom. Girls need their mothers to express their love with hugs and kisses. Girls need their mothers to be genuinely involved in their concerns and interests—from what they are now washing their face with to what they are

planning to do for their science project. Maternal warmth means being there for them always and without reservation. This does not mean you cannot express an opinion or even forbid them from doing something. It means that always in your every word and action you are telling them that they are loved and accepted for who they are now.

LOOKING FOR ROLE MODELS

While girls are being shown physical role models who resemble survivors of a death march, they are also aware that life holds more promise, opportunity, and expectation for them than to be wives and mothers. As women's roles have expanded, ironically, the pressure has only increased. Now you need to be not only beautiful and thin but accomplished and talented as well. But who are today's young women supposed to look up to as models for how to fashion their lives so that they can take every advantage of the opportunities and expectations placed before them?

When Successful Women Are Seen as Unfeminine. Many young women admire Hillary Clinton. Before becoming First Lady in 1992, she was known as one of the country's top lawyers. There certainly is much there to admire. She is a woman of accomplishment, principle, and strongly held beliefs. It is difficult, however, for even the youngest girls to overlook the unrelenting criticism and personal attacks Mrs. Clinton has endured. Jokes about her husband have been pretty popular, too. Many members of the press have suggested that his alleged rendezvous with other women resulted from the fact that his own wife was too busy in the office and not attentive enough in the bedroom. But what these messages say is that maybe society wasn't quite ready for a First Lady who was not only attractive, but also intelligent, accomplished, visible, and outspoken. Unfortunately, this makes it difficult for young women to start their search for role models they can admire and identify with.

Looking First at Home. Whether you feel up to the challenge or not, your daughter will first look to you as a source of inspiration for her own life. You can be the inspiring woman she is looking for, despite what you feel to be your failings, shortcomings, and mistakes. Just as you are strong enough to appreciate all the uniqueness of your daughter, she is also, given the opportunity, strong enough to embrace your weaknesses, faults, and failures. Give her this chance to know and understand you better!

How to Be a Role Model. Honest communication is the key. For example, if you feel you married too young, short-circuiting what might have been promising opportunities in a career you loved, say so. This will not be interpreted as a rejection of what came to be your daughter's eventual place in your life, but an honest recognition of the costs any choice entails. If you feel you were influenced by what you felt everyone else was doing or what your parents wanted, tell her so.

At the same time, tell her about women who have influenced your own life in a positive way, and why. Since there are so few complete role models for any of us, most of us wind up taking for ourselves selected characteristics or beliefs of people who have influenced and shaped our lives. Tell your daughter, for example, about your fifth-grade gym teacher, who taught you so well what real sportsmanship was all about. If you admire someone now, share this feeling with your daughter. You may admire someone who is able to decorate on a shoestring or give terrific parties on a budget. Tell your daughter so. Point out women of accomplishment and discuss their contributions toward making this world a better place.

Sharing Your Goals. Not only is it important to share with your daughter your past, but it is equally important to share with her your goals and aspirations for the future. Your goal does not have to be becoming recognized as a world-famous oil painter. It is wonderful enough that you would like to expand your creative side a bit and try oil painting. Perhaps you would like to go back to school. Your goal does not have to be medical or dental school in order to be worthwhile. If your plans begin with simply getting your high school equivalency certification, your daughter will be pleased to share in the events of your life and help you to plan. Involving your daughter in this way will give you a common bond of shared experiences and encourage her to share more easily her own thoughts, plans, and dreams.

Giving the Gift of Self-Reliance. Being able to take care of yourself and depend upon yourself, without question, is a priceless life skill. Self-reliant individuals, both men and

WAYS TO TEACH SELF-RELIANCE

Look for Opportunities to Show Your Daughter that She Can Take Care of Herself. Camping is a terrific opportunity to demonstrate independence, confidence, organization, and self-reliance. If your daughter can be part of an organization like Girl Scouts or Camp Fire Girls, see if you can get her involved. If no such organized opportunities are available, think about a camping trip for the two of you. The equipment does not have to be fancy (try borrowing from a friend to begin with), and the destination does not have to be exotic. Just sleeping under the stars while taking good care of yourselves is a terrific way to begin.

Encourage Your Daughter to Fix Things. Knowing how to do simple household repairs lets your daughter know that she is capable of taking care of her own little world. Knowing how to stop the squeaks, leaks, and drips is an empowering set of skills. If you cannot teach your daughter such skills, maybe this is something you both can learn together. Men were not born knowing these skills—some-

one taught them or they read about how to do them in a book. You can do the same. Consider it a mother-daughter project

Make Your Daughter Smart About Money. Dispel the myth that nice girls do not discuss or worry about money. Teach her money managing skills early by giving her an allowance and helping her learn to budget. As she gets older, allow her to participate in family money decisions. For example, if you are able to make investments or buy life insurance, explain to her how you came to make these decisions.

Encourage Your Daughter to Be Strong. There is little opportunity for self-reliance when the physical body is not strong and healthy. Encourage and, if possible, show by your own example by abstaining from smoking and taking illegal drugs. If social drinking is a part of your life, do it with moderation and responsibility. Encourage healthy diet and regular exercise. Further encourage your daughter to participate in sports. Help her to know that she is strong and capable.

women, will have a great edge on those more dependent, less confident types as the challenges and opportunities of the next century draw closer. People in the coming century will be expected to have more than one career and will certainly be expected to juggle many different responsibilities simultaneously.

Single mothers are fabulous role models of self-reliance. Your daughter will remember how courageously you juggled many tasks, often with little to rely on but your own ingenuity and strength. Begin to give your daughter this precious gift of self-reliance by offer-

ing her the opportunities to develop not only the skills but also the confidence in herself needed to face any life challenge.

ISSUES ABOUT SEX

Studies conducted by researcher Shere Hite indicate that even though discussing sex with their daughters is one area in which mothers still could use some liberating, most mothers are doing a fine job raising girls and many are bravely treading new ground in this arena. Yet a dark cloud still remains over families headed by single mothers as far as sex and raising daughters are concerned.

The Myth About Girls from Single-Parent Homes. Research conducted in 1995 and sponsored by conservative fathers' rights groups such as the Institute for American Values and the National Fatherhood Initiative has suggested that girls from single-parent families become sexually active at a younger age than do daughters with a father at home.

This claim is disputed in the twenty years of study results from the various Hite reports noting that girls as young as seven have touched themselves or masturbated and are very aware of their bodies. There is little truth to the myth that girls from single-parent homes are more sexually active than girls from other family structures.

A better explanation for what may be happening is that girls from single-parent homes who are experimenting with sex may be more apt to discuss this subject with their mothers than daughters of more traditional families.

Will My Daughter Be Promiscuous?

I was very promiscuous when I was my daughter's age. By the time I was sixteen, there had been too many men in my life for me even to count. Do I share these mistakes with my daughter? If I tell her that I was sexually active at her age, doesn't that just give her permission to be the same way now?

No, not necessarily. In fact, it actually may open up the lines of communication for you to be able to talk about sex with your daughter. You may want to tell your daughter that at her

age you made foolish and reckless choices. And you were fortunate back then that most of what it took to deal with the results of permissive sexual behavior amounted to nothing more than some visits to a health clinic for a few shots of penicillin. But today such choices could be lethal because of the threat of AIDS.

Tell your daughter your honest feelings. These sexual experiences were not exciting, satisfying, or even fun. They were probably your way of finding affection and comfort in a world that was not offering you too much at the time.

Of course, telling her this won't guarantee that she may not have to make a few of her own mistakes along the way. At the same time you are telling her of choices you regret, make sure you are telling her that if she chooses to be sexually active, birth control and safe sex practices are musts. This information can and should come from you. Do not rely on her teachers or friends to give her the information she may need to save her life.

Where male sexuality is often a source of pride, it takes most women ten years or more of experience to accept themselves sexually. Take pride in knowing that you are one of the pioneers in bringing mothers and daughters closer by not keeping secrets and by allowing your daughter to be open and honest.

Should My Daughter Know I Am Sexually Active?

I am unclear about how much I should share about my dating life with my eight-year-old daughter. I am concerned that she will become sexually active way before she is ready if I give her any indication that I have a lover now and have been sexually active my entire adult life.

You are right to be concerned. Your daughter does not need to know that you have a lover, but you certainly can let her know that you understand what it means to be curious about sex and that you understand what it feels like to be sexually attracted to someone. What is most appropriate to share with your daughter is that sex is a wonderful experience—for adults. Emphasize with her that becoming sexually active means being able to take responsibility for birth control and for protection from disease. Most children are really not interested in hearing too many details of your private life, but it is your job to teach the information your daughter needs to make safe and responsible choices in her own life. However, as she matures, keep the communication open and more honest. You may bring up the subject, for example, when you are getting ready for a dinner date by saying out loud to yourself, "I wonder if I should let him kiss me goodnight? He's such a great person and I really like him." Your daughter may be speechless, but after a few more "talks" she may respond. Never burden her with your problems about men, but at the same time you should let her

know that she can discuss anything she wants with you.

When Your Little Girl Seems Too Interested in Men

My six-year-old daughter seems to be obsessed with men. Her father has not been with us since she was two years old. She is affectionate with everyone but seems particularly interested in flirting with every man who crosses her path. Of course, she gets a lot of attention when she blows the postman a kiss or waves an enthusiastic goodbye to the gas station attendant. How do I know if things are out of hand?

Your daughter's behavior sounds like natural six-year-old stuff. Since she is getting so much positive attention for her antics, it is very likely that she will continue to blow kisses and wave. When people stop paying attention, she will lose interest.

What you might be worried about is whether or not her attention-getting behavior has something to do with her father not being around. It is possible that it does, but not necessarily in a harmful way. Your daughter wants male attention and is finding age-appropriate ways to get this attention. Her behavior should alert you to this possible need and suggest to you that she may need more male figures in her life. You might want to speak with the school principal and request, if possible, a male teacher for next year. You may want to seek out more male friends, not necessarily romantic companions for you, to include in your extended family circle. Enroll her in activities like soccer or other sports where she gets to be with other children and their fathers.

A male coach would be a terrific idea for your daughter.

When Teenage Daughter Has Dates and Mom Doesn't

My daughter has started dating. Instead of being proud and thinking how my little girl is growing up, I feel resentful. I've been critical about the boys she picks and don't like anything she chooses to wear on dates. Could I be suffering from sour grapes because there is no one in my life at this time?

It is natural for you to experience some jealousy and resentment. Your daughter has more options than you do, and that is an enviable place to be. You have already taken the first big step by acknowledging these feelings. The next big step is not to let these feelings get in the way of your relationship with your daughter or cloud your vision when it comes to helping her navigate the treacherous teenage social scene. Much as you might regret the choices you made in your life, chances are that deep down you would not want to be a teenager again. The envy you feel is not the desire to relive the rejection and uncertainty, but rather wanting a chance to be part of things in a new way. This is a choice open to you. Happiness for a single person requires action. You need to build up your social support network and actively seek out intellectual challenge. Your daughter's maturity and independence give you added opportunity for just such positive actions.

Your daughter needs your guidance and support. If she does not get these things from you, she will seek sources of information elsewhere, and these sources of information may be nothing more than shared ignorance. If you have delayed talking to her about sex, delay no longer. Your daughter needs the facts about sexually transmitted diseases and birth control. If she is sexually active—and there is no use putting your head in the sand about this—she needs appropriate medical care. More importantly, you need to share your beliefs, experiences, and values with her.

THE DOS AND DON'TS FOR MOTHERS WITH DAUGHTERS

- Do take your daughter camping, mountain climbing, and fishing, and have her participate in activities that were traditionally considered more appropriate for boys.

- Do teach your daughter to fix things. Even if she's a toddler, let her watch you repair household items or witness your attempts at tightening the bolts on a swingset.

- Do attend self-defense classes together.

- Don't harp on looks or focus on topics such as dating and marriage. Concentrate instead on what makes your child's personality sparkle, her strengths, and her likes and dislikes.

- Don't give her too many mixed messages. For example, don't say things like, "It's not that important to have boys like you" and then in another breath tell her she looks dumpy in a certain dress. Beware of telling her how important studying to be an electrical engineer might be and then criticize her for not behaving in a ladylike way or for eating too much.

17
Raising Boys

TAKING THE TESTOSTERONE CHALLENGE

Today a number of mental health professionals dispute the notion that boys require constant male companionship and male guidance in order to grow up healthy. These professionals believe that boys can be successfully raised by either parent. In fact, having a father at home who does not provide the necessary qualities of a healthy male role model can do more harm than good, according to the experts and authors Olga Silverstein and Beth Rashbaum. In their book *The Courage To Raise Good Men*, the authors write,

"The assumption that the world is full of good men, or that any man is better than any woman to help a boy, is ridiculous. To saddle boys with the wrong kind of men will simply help create the kind of men we now deplore, men who are overly competitive and unable to form intimate ties."

THE OEDIPUS COMPLEX AND OTHER THINGS YOU SHOULDN'T OBSESS ABOUT

I read that boys go through a stage where if they don't work out their feelings with mom and dad, they will suffer from the Oedipus complex and grow up gay, wanting to marry their mother, or hating women! I'm worried because I'm five months pregnant, and I know already that it is going to be a boy and that his father is not going to be in the picture.

Before you start worrying needlessly, you should know that current research findings suggest that one in ten people is gay and that this may be a

YOU, TOO, CAN RAISE GOOD MEN

Did you know that actor Tom Cruise, TV journalist Ed Bradley, former White House chief of staff Alexander Haig, economist and head of the Federal Reserve Alan Greenspan, actor Bill Cosby, world-renowned pediatric neurosurgeon Benjamin Carson, physicist Sir Isaac Newton, writer Victor Hugo, and TV talk show host Les Brown were all raised by single moms?

natural part of their biological or genetic structure and has nothing to do with the kind of parents they had. You also need to know that the Oedipal drama is not like the terrible twos, nor is it like weaning or toilet training. It is not a stage through which every boy passes, nor is it a developmental milestone when this so-called drama is concluded.

According to Freud, the Oedipus complex emerges when a child develops a wish for an exclusive, vaguely sexual union with the parent of the opposite sex and feels a hostile rivalry toward the parent of the same sex. In a nutshell, Freud contended that a little boy wants to marry mommy and has desires of killing daddy, and that if the son doesn't resolve the issue of daddy winning both the battle and mom, he will have years of therapy ahead.

Many psychologists discount Freud's ideas because his claims were based on his work with a very small number of neurotic, wealthy people who came to him for help with their problems in pre-World War I Europe. Freud did not observe large numbers of children, nor did he conduct the kind of psychological research common today.

A More Modern Version of "Romantic Behaviors." Behaviors that traditionally have been thought of as part of this so-called drama, such as a son telling his mom he wants to marry her, are thought of today as simply an attempt by boys to identify with their same-sex parent. What often resembles "romantic behavior" is nothing more than a young boy's attempt to mimic and try out behaviors they see male relatives, friends, even TV heroes do. Nothing unhealthy here. Jealousy and the desire for undivided attention from mom are also part of the scene.

After all, to the boy, smothering your mother with kisses and telling her you want to live with her forever will get you, at least briefly, undivided attention. Boys will do this over and over again, since this behavior gets them what they want—hugs, kisses, and Mommy professing her love.

The romantic behavior may be played out differently, perhaps through play, dreams, or behavior where your son may fantasize that he is a warrior taking you to his magic kingdom or playing different versions of "house." Again, this is normal because vital play activities are how children grow emotionally as well as learn. The business of children is play! Your job is to reassure your son of your love but make it clear that you love him the way a mommy loves her son.

The Oedipal Stage Is Simply a Part of Learning. Today's mental health professionals believe that the Oedipal stage is simply part of your child's learning. For a little boy, discovering that Mom will not be his wife is part of figuring out how the world works and what his place in the world will be. However, it is important that you make it clear to your child when he enters the "romance with Mommy" stage that mommies love their sons differently than grown-ups love each other. It is also okay to let your son know that one day when he grows up he can marry someone like you if he wants to, but mommies and sons do not have the same relationship that married people do.

A Mother's Gentle Detachment Might Be Healthier Than a Father's Rejection. If there is no man in the household, the advantage might be having a son who does not compete for

THE DOS AND DON'TS OF RAISING SONS

◆ Do expect that most boys grow and mature at a slower rate than girls, so be patient about your son's development.

◆ Do teach your son values but let him express them in his own masculine way, which may mean not showing his feelings about things the way you do.

◆ Don't worry that he won't learn manly things without a man at home. Half the population is male, and he is certain to pick up social skills from other males he comes in contact with.

◆ Do believe in yourself and try to encourage self-esteem in your child as well. Let your child know that you are confident as a parent.

◆ Don't avoid talking about his father even if you didn't know him well. Give your son someone to think about with whom he can identify. Point out positive traits your son may possess that remind you of his father.

◆ Do teach your son to show respect for both males and females and to cultivate friendships with both.

◆ Don't ever make your son the "man of the house." He can have responsibilities and chores, but they shouldn't be representative of what is expected of grown men.

◆ Do help him seek healthy male role models. Point out the positive qualities in men you see on a day-to-day basis, including the helpful shoe salesman, the friendly pharmacist, or the talkative neighborhood patrolman.

◆ Do limit the amount of violence your son witnesses. Let him know that what is shown on television is not always the way healthy men should behave.

your attention and does not have to harbor guilt feelings for wanting bad things to happen to "he-who-takes-my-mommy-away." Moreover, the child may not have to experience the rejection and belittling that often accompany the man's vying for mommy's attention.

No Dad at Home Is Better Than an Incompetent One. Poor relationships with their own fathers may be the root problem for a lot of men. Consider all the magazine articles, countless books, and talk shows dedicated to understanding why some men can't commit, or why certain men cheat, are aggressive, avoid responsibilities to their families, are afraid to marry, or beat their wives—the list goes on and on. A large number of these men, unable to form intimate bonds although they had fathers living at home, state that they had or have some problems relating to their fathers. Feelings of being inadequate, betrayed, ignored, or humiliated by their fathers were the most common complaints. These men also said that when they were boys, they felt pain and ambivalence at being expected to cut their emotional ties to their mothers and "start acting like a man."

If a single mother is aware early on that her son's behavior and opinions may be somewhat different from hers and yet affirms and accepts them even if she can't understand them, she has a good chance of raising a man without a lot of the baggage that these other men carry around. Be positive. It can be done!

WHEN THERE'S NO REGULAR MALE ROLE MODEL

What happens when boys don't have one single, constant male to do things with and fashion themselves after?

This might actually be a good thing. Your son will not have only one role model but will be given the opportunity to have many. He will pick and choose and take for himself the behaviors, habits, and beliefs of the men he encounters during his growing-up years. The men from whom he selects will be influenced, in part, by the kind of men you allow into his life. Some men, like coaches and teachers, are the luck of the draw. Some will be friends you introduce him to.

If you are there to guide and be supportive, the best parts of the men in your son's life will become part of your son, like a lovingly pieced-together patchwork quilt. Some of the pieces are tiny—like how your son's band teacher may be the one to teach him how to knot his tie. Other patches are part of a larger design where the influence of many men can be seen—like your son's views on sportsman-ship. This piecing together gives your son a richness of experience and opportunities that many men lack. Your son will be conscious of this process as he matures, although he may not talk to you about it. By the time he reaches the early to middle teen years, he will begin to share with you why he admires those who have impressed him.

BOYS DON'T NEED FATHERS BUT DO NEED MEN

Why does my son need any man in his life? I have four brothers who turned out great, and my single mother didn't have any men around us.

True, men and boys come from women, and women and girls come from women. To many, this would seem to make it preferable to have a planet with nothing but moth-er-headed households. And in some cultures of the world this works, because the men of those societies take part in helping young boys become initiated into manhood.

Because your son will become a man influenced by Western society, he also needs another point of view in his life, the male point of view, which is his ini-tiation or "rite of passage." He doesn't need a father living at home, although our culture has always maintained a patriarchal system claiming the reverse. But he does need to come in contact with men. As he matures, let him have his unique male relation-ships, just as you have special relation-ships with your female friends. Don't worry too much about finding male role models—men make up about half of the population! He is sure to have many options. Just be there to guide him and help him make wise decisions.

WHAT A GOOD MALE ROLE MODEL DOES

There are five important benefits from letting boys bond with adult members of the same sex. In order for a good male role model to help teach a boy to become a man, he should:

◆ Encourage independence. Because men generally are bigger "risk-takers" and less protective than women, the benefit might be that boys will be more open to exploration and assertive behavior.

◆ Broaden the child's world. Male role models can be a link to the outside world through their jobs, leisure activities, and interests or hobbies. A young boy's horizons are expanded when he gets the male perspective on issues and ideas.

◆ Improve overall parenting. The quality of mom's parenting can be greatly enhanced when the male role model serves as a sort of alternate or supportive "parent," just as other members of an extended family would. Stepping in during times of stress can help avoid a crisis at home and give mom a well-deserved break. Additionally, the "rough and tumble" that males desire can be fulfilled through playing with other males.

◆ Discipline firmly but gently. Men seem to accept fewer excuses from

kids and seem to demand the most out of them. Although men can often seem too rough on boys, sensitive men know what boys are and aren't capable of, based on their own feelings surrounding their experiences at that age.

◆ Invite the boy to "join the club." Sexist as this sounds, when a boy feels he belongs to a club where there are no girl members, only others just like him, he can separate more easily from the mother by accepting his differences in an understanding and compassionate environment. Moreover, because girls learn and mature more quickly than boys, boys as a group can overcome feelings of inferiority to girls. Although their interests may be different, boys can learn to respect girls as equals and ultimately grow up to get along well with both males and females.

WHERE TO FIND ROLE MODELS

Your community may have local programs where men can serve as mentors to young boys. Big Brothers/Big Sisters has chapters in many cities and towns. Your local Y, athletic club, and community center are also good sources. Be sure your child gets involved in school- or community-related activities where men help coach ball teams and sponsor other events, including music clubs, Little League, 4H clubs, and scouting, and where boys can find wonderful teachers. The neighborhood policeman might also be involved in kids' activities and can serve as a role model to teach your child why it is important to respect laws and rules. Additionally, don't

CAUTION!

Although Cub Scouts and other clubs for boys usually have caring, honest, and reputable people running them, beware of certain group leaders if your instincts suggest foul play. Men who molest children have been known to volunteer for such activities. Speak to other parents in the community about how they feel this person is working out, and maintain the contact whenever a new volunteer arrives. You don't want to falsely accuse anyone of unacceptable behavior, but you do want to keep the lines of communication open with the other boys' parents, and as busy as you are, you want to stay involved in what your child is doing. If you are certain a man is abusing boys in some way, and you are not the only one who feels this way, speak up. Let the authorities know. You may be saving the life of a child.

overlook friends, relatives, or neighbors who have something special to offer. The man down the street who routinely feeds homeless animals, or the pilot next door who explains the principles of flying to young airplane enthusiasts, could very well be role models you might otherwise not have noticed.

WHAT TO DO IF YOUR SON LIKES TO PLAY DRESS-UP

Playing dress-up is normal for young children, so you don't need to worry. However, if you'd like to keep your child out of your closet, take a trip to the nearest thrift shop or attend a yard sale and buy lots of big shirts, baggy suits, and ties for your son to play dress-up with. Uniforms are great, too, especially because little boys love to pretend to be policemen or soldiers. For a few dollars, you can fill a box with stuff that will keep your son busy for hours.

While I am putting on my makeup for work in the morning, my two-year-old son Kevin stands next to me applying lipstick, powder, and anything else he can get his hands on. Do I need to be worried that he'll be gender confused or something like that?

Not at all. Kevin is mimicking your bathroom routine in the morning—combing hair, brushing teeth, and in your case, putting on makeup. All children do this at an early age because this is how they learn. By the time he reaches kindergarten, he will naturally outgrow this, even though it's not uncommon for first and second graders to find amusement playing around with Mom's makeup. However, if you want to get a head start on defining the differences between male and female secondary sex characteristics, try this:

◆ Explain to your son that little girls grow up to be women or mommies and little boys grow up to be men or daddies. Daddies and men don't wear makeup, but they do have "guy stuff."

◆ Set out a little basket of male toiletries for Kevin to use in the bathroom while you're fixing your face. Fill it with a mock razor, shaving cream, comb, toothbrush, and maybe a bottle of "after-shave" (two drops of cologne mixed with water and a drop of food coloring). Place it on the sink or counter next to where you keep your cosmetics. Announce to your son that he is to use this stuff and not yours.

♦ Stop worrying and enjoy your child's antics. Be comfortable with your parenting abilities. Besides, you never know if there will come a time when grown-up Kevin will be too busy to visit his mom and will need to be blackmailed with all those old make-up stories!

RAISING A HEALTHY SON

Following are fourteen surefire tips to help you raise a physically, emotionally, and spiritually healthy son:

1. No matter how hard it is for you to understand your child, accept your son's differences from you, such as the way he views things, plays, or responds to problems. Boys grow and mature at a slower rate than girls, so be patient, too, about his development. Teach him your values, but let him express them uniquely. He's a male and may respond to emotional situations somewhat differently than you might.

2. Give up worrying about whether your son is missing out on anything by not having dad around. Stop wishing his father or any father was around to see his antics, and start enjoying your baby, toddler, or school-age child now!

3. Believe in yourself as a strong and confident guide for your son. Your high self-esteem and positive attitude can be contagious.

4. Teach your young child that it is okay to be raised just by Mom. Reading to a preschool boy from the many children's books featuring animal families raised by mommy mice, cows, or chickens is an easy start. Later, you can point out other single-mother families you come in contact with.

5. At the same time, try not to avoid "daddy stuff" totally. It's okay to read stories about all kinds of families to your child in order to give your child a realistic perspective of the world and to allow him to become tolerant of diversity. It is also important to place a high value on male/female relationships because it is a necessary fact of life for everyone on the planet that we must learn to get along with each other.

6. Regardless of how you became a single mother, never make your son the "man of the house." True, you want to teach him to grow to be a man, but there is a distinction between being the little man and being responsible for things that adult men are supposed to do. Your child is not your confidant, your knight in shining armor, or your rescuer. His job is to be a child.

   Especially important for the newly widowed or divorced, correct others if they ask your son, "Are you taking good care of Mommy?" or "How does it feel being the man around the house?" Tell them, "Just because there is an absence of an adult male, this doesn't mean the oldest child should take on any adult

GOOD NEWS ABOUT MEN WHO WERE RAISED BY SINGLE MOTHERS

Findings published in 1995 from *The Hite Report on the Family: Growing up Under Patriarchy* (Grove/Atlantic) have found that men raised by single mothers tend to have better relationships with women later in life. Moreover, many boys from mother-only households did not have to "abandon their mothers" or "side with men" if they wanted to be accepted into male society, whereas those in a patriarchal family often developed a guilty conscience about this betrayal of their early bonds with their mother. The research also concluded that boys who grow up with "only" their mothers are better off— particularly those who were close to them during their teens—by having an emotional and psychological head start: They are not so fearful, are not so closely bound to patriarchal stereotypes, are more sure of themselves, develop better relationships with men and women, and are generally more comfortable with change.

responsibilities. Children have a right to be children for as long as they can."

7. Try not to have negative attitudes toward men even if you became a single mother as a result of the most excruciating circumstances. Be sure you have resolved any issues about men and relationships. If you are still angry at men, find an appropriate outlet for venting those feelings. When you look at your child and see his father's face, it's okay to get a little emotional. After all, if your ex gave you anything of value, you're looking at him. Let your son know how important he is to you regardless of how you feel about your ex.

8. Point out the positive qualities in men you see on a day-to-day basis. This means that if you're buying your son baseball cleats, and the salesman is especially attentive, point this trait out by mentioning what a helpful person he is. Even if you can hardly find anything nice to say about your son's own dad, find something. For example, if you know that his father liked vanilla ice cream, you might mention something like, "Isn't that neat that you like vanilla ice cream? Your father's favorite flavor is vanilla, too!"

9. Help your child learn "guy stuff," but don't sweat the details. For instance, many single mothers report concern over their son's using the potty while sitting. Chances are your child will outgrow this when he realizes that it's easier and more fun to urinate while standing.

10. Role models are important and will be found in every aspect of your son's life. Help guide him toward men who can teach him important life lessons.

As your child matures, investigate local boys' groups or clubs he could join, such as nature societies, 4H, Cub Scouts, and Explorers. In male-dominated activities, don't be intimidated by such sponsored events as father-son boat races or picnics. Let the group leader know that with the number of single-parent families these days, it would be a nice idea if the organization would consider sponsoring parent-child events.

However, joining a "males only" club has its advantages, according to many young boys. They feel special during the initiation ritual that welcomes them into the group. The ritual might remind you of reruns of *The Honeymooners*, where Ralph Kramden and Ed Norton did that contortionist version of the Raccoon Lodge salute—but try not to laugh. This is an essential boost to the self-esteem of little boys—that feeling of belonging to a group with whose members they can closely identify.

11. Make expressing your feelings an essential part of family life. Do not give boys the message that it is okay to shut people out. Do not disparage your sons when they tell you they are feeling frightened or vulnerable. Let boys cry when they feel they need to.

12. Exercise is critical for all children, but in cases where boys can't seem to center themselves as comfortably as girls, they might need some other means of releasing excessive energy. Remember, testosterone is an active hormone! If your child is really energetic, get a chinning bar for his room for rainy days. Check out your local hardware store for an expandable closet bar, the kind that has suction cups on the ends. Install it between the door jambs of his room, and when he gets rowdy,

have him "do ten." Make sure you install the bar correctly to avoid accidents. Start low, but raise the bar higher as your son grows. Inexpensive stair steppers, step-up benches, or even jump-ropes are also wonderful alternatives to outdoor activities.

13. Encourage your son to have girls as friends. Girls are socialized to be more collaborative and less focused on dominating others. Boys are typically trying to compete; girls are more likely to be cooperative.

14. Limit TV viewing and exposure to violence in movies. TV tends to promote artificial heroes, and your son needs real heroes to model himself after, not false ones. Seeing too much violence can desensitize boys to the terror, pain, and trauma that these actions bring and can convince a young child that this is the correct way to resolve a conflict. Reinforce mature conflict-resolution techniques such as negotiating and discussion.

PART 4

RELATING JOYFULLY TO OTHERS

18

Custody and Coparenting

PARENTING TOGETHER SEPARATELY

A minor child must be in the legal custody of someone who serves as his or her primary caregiver, whether that person or persons are the child's parents, guardians, or the state. Generally, shared physical custody was the standard in the past for traditional families consisting of a married couple with biological children. However, because of the rise of multi-defined family types including single-parent families due to divorce or out-of-wedlock births; stepfamilies and blended families; foster, gay, extended, and adoptive families, there are a number of custody scenarios.

JOINT CUSTODY

Joint custody means the child's mother and father (or other legal guardians) have equal control of the decision making and responsibility for a minor child's life. Although the common routine has the primary parent, usually the mother, having the kids most of the school or business week and the father taking the kids on weekends and occasional week nights, problems arise when mom hates being the heavy while dad is the fun and vacation guy. For single mothers through divorce who become the primary custodians, this is often frustrating, because the major burdens and responsibilities of child-rearing are hers, but the ex can veto almost any decision—decisions like whether the children should attend camp or undergo therapy.

Joint custody is whatever is agreed upon at the time the papers are drawn up. It could mean the child spends the school year at mom's and summers with dad, or it could mean that you can live wherever you choose with your child if your ex is agreeable. If you and your former partner see eye to eye on most of the child-rearing decisions, this solution is workable. In cases where the father and mother plan to coparent (see the section on Coparenting), joint custody can be extremely successful and rewarding. However, if you know that you will be seen as the "drudgery parent" while dad only reaps the

benefits of having his kids occasionally, joint custody is not a good idea.

SHARED PHYSICAL CUSTODY

Joint custody is often mistaken for shared physical custody, but the definitions are quite different. Shared physical custody means exactly that: Each parent has equal physical responsibility and access to the children. Neither family receives child support because each is paying for the care of the children. This arrangement is gaining in popularity, particularly in places such as California, where the child can live part of the week with one parent and the remainder with the other and still attend the same school because the school districts are so large. But be warned that even though your child may not have to leave his or her school, this kind of arrangement can be stressful and may upset the normal routine that children, especially young children, require to feel secure. Many mental health professionals believe the shuffling back and forth from one parent's house to the other is not consistent with setting patterns of routine stability, predictability, and security. Think about it. How many adults do you know who would want to possess two sets of

everything, in addition to toting a suitcase around a few times a week in order to return comfortably home at the end of a day? Unless extreme circumstances dictate this type of arrangement, shared physical custody is frowned upon by many experts.

PERMANENT SOLE CUSTODY

Permanent sole custody with generous visitation rights for dad is usually the ideal solution for single mothers who have an ex who may be somewhat or sporadically involved with the child but is not reliable or responsible about finances and decisions about the child's future well-being. For example, your child's father may have a large family from whom your child could benefit by remaining connected, or he may be the apple of your child's eye but often is unpredictable, unaccountable, and irresponsible. He may suffer major career lapses, indulge in frequent relationships, or even harbor emotional problems. This doesn't mean he's bad for your child to be around. It just means that you don't want him making any major decisions for your child and his future.

TEMPORARY CUSTODY

Temporary custody is sometimes given to one parent or other custodian during an unresolved divorce or when further investigation is warranted to determine who should gain permanent custody. Although any custody decision can be contested, temporary custody always means that there will be a court date in the future to settle the custody issue once and for all.

WHEN TO DETERMINE CUSTODY

The safest bet for avoiding a custody fight is to have all the details of custody drawn up in your divorce or separation papers. Don't wait, because it's in the best interests of the children to plan this now. If your father's child opted out of the picture, file for sole custody immediately.

When You Weren't Married to the Father. If you were not married to the child's father, it is still necessary to establish custody because biological fathers have rights in almost every state, whether or not they were married to the mother. New MOMs (Mothers Outside of Marriage) often make the mistake of assuming that they automatically have sole custody of their child because the father was uninterested or simply disappeared at the time of birth. In some states this may be true, but it's best to check with an attorney, family court clerk, or legal clinic to avoid a custody battle later on if the father should suddenly reappear on the scene.

TERMINATING PARENTAL RIGHTS

I have heard stories about men suing for custody for all kinds of crazy reasons and winning but then not wanting to continue raising the children. I want to avoid any problems with my son's father, whom I do not wish to be part of our lives. Besides, I haven't seen him in two years.

In many states there is a statute of sorts that says that if the father did not show parental responsibilities for a certain period of time, his rights can be terminated. In Virginia, for example, this can happen automatically. But in most cases, you need to petition the court to terminate the father's rights. Keep in mind that you need to think this out clearly because you can never expect him to be obligated to pay child support. If you are okay with that, then this is what you should do. Of course, he will have a chance to oppose this, but chances are he won't show up for it.

Your best bet is to get an agreement signed by the father relinquishing his rights to the child. However, if he is willing to contribute child support but agrees not to fight over custody and other important issues, you should outline his obligations in this agreement in detail. The two of you can draw up this agreement and have an attorney draw up a contract. Keep in mind, too, that contracts are not impossible to break. Still, this will provide the leverage you may need in the event of a future custody battle.

WATCH OUT IN COURT! JUDGES DISLIKE:

- When you request sole custody simply because you are angry at your child's father.

- When you try to limit visitation.

- When you use lack of child support as a wedge to prevent visitation.

- When you move or make major changes without consulting the other parent.

WHY FATHERS SEEK CUSTODY

A small percentage of men seek custody because they know they are the better parent for the child. Their spouses may not want the children, or they may have serious addictions or other emotional or medical problems. There is no question that many children would thrive being with their father as the primary parent. However, joint custody is more common for fathers who want to be active participants in the child-rearing process.

LEARN YOUR RIGHTS REGARDING CUSTODY

Your best bet if you are strapped for money is to request a consultation at your local Legal Aid or Legal Services office, or at your county's bar association-sponsored legal clinic. For about $30 (this varies from state to state), you can learn your options for establishing sole custody. Be sure to make a list of all your questions and be very specific. For example, ask if an attorney is necessary or if you can petition the court yourself, how much a custody order would cost, and what time frames, if any, there are in order for the father to waive his rights. Keep in mind that many legal clinics that service lower-income clients are unable to handle custody issues unless there is an immediate threat of danger to the children.

CHILD CUSTODY BLACKMAIL

I'm not a single mother but am seriously considering getting divorced. In fact, the only thing preventing me from going to an attorney to file separation papers is the fear that my husband will get the children. We have no relationship. We rarely do anything together, and when my husband is around, all we do is yell and argue, which upsets the kids. But he has said—more than once—that if I try to leave, he will take the kids and not only won't I get a penny, but I'll have to pay him child support. My job does not pay as well as his, and he couldn't and wouldn't care for the children the way I do. This seems unfair, because I feel incredibly trapped, but I don't want to waste my life in this dead-end marriage. Can he really get the kids? He probably doesn't even know that the youngest one has allergies, or that the children need lunch money or a meal packed for school!

Custody blackmail is something many attorneys report seeing much of these days. A father will sometimes threaten to take the children in an effort to get the mother to give up certain financial rights. Many attorneys will tell you that fathers sometimes threaten to seek custody as a way to

avoid paying child support. Some men actually think it is cheaper to raise the children themselves than to pay child support.

Most lawyers agree that the father usually has no intention of following through on his threat, but many mothers, especially working mothers, often relinquish what is rightfully theirs—for example, part of the house, profits from investments, or a car or a beach house—for fear that this threat will become a reality.

In almost all divorce cases, the factors that come into battle are children and money. Because women in these cases are typically more concerned with what will happen to their children while men are usually motivated more by money and property, it is not uncommon for many fathers to use the fear of taking the children as a weapon to achieve financial gain.

Evaluate where your husband places the emphasis in his threats. For instance, if money and property are repeatedly stressed, as in, "I'll see to it that you lose the house and everything unless you let me have the kids," chances are he won't follow through because he is using the children as a wedge to force you to sacrifice what you are entitled to. Learn what legal rights you have and what your chances are of winning custody before you sign anything giving up any material goods.

Punishing a spouse with threats regarding the children is usually an attempt to try to control that person and, in many cases, a way of prolonging the relationship. Always consider the children's needs first. Whichever parent can provide a loving home with nurturing and unconditional love should be the custodial parent, whether it is the father or the mother.

In the meantime, do not make any concessions without talking to an attorney first.

When You Can't Agree About Custody

My husband and I are divorcing after years of drifting apart. My ex is Mr. Mom—sort of. He takes care of the children after school and sells insurance. I have worked my way up from secretary to vice president for marketing at a software company. The hours are grueling and the traveling gets exhausting, but I really love it. No doubt about it, my hard work is what makes our comfortable life style possible. I spend as much time with the children as I can and try to attend all their school functions whenever possible. My husband wants custody of the children and has made it clear that this is not a negotiating tactic. My attorney tells me that losing custody is a possibility. How could a judge take the children away from me and let them live with my less than ambitious ex? I thought only drug addicted or prostitute mothers lost custody. How is this going to be resolved? Who is going to decide which of us gets custody?

In all likelihood the judge assigned to your case will order an Impartial Evaluation of Comparative Custodial Fitness. This means that a mental health professional, often a psychologist, and typically called the evaluator, will interview and observe you and your husband as well as the children. Psychological testing is often administered. Questionnaires will also be completed that give the evaluator additional information about you and

KIDNAPPING ALERT!

Never leave your child alone with a parent who has come back after a long disappearance. The risk of kidnapping is enormous. In fact, the majority of kidnappings in this country are committed by an estranged parent.

Children are also at great risk for abduction by the noncustodial parent if the custodial parent sues for child support. Children are often snatched as a means of revenge and to scare the parent away from making further efforts to collect child support. Therefore, if you are in the process of suing to collect unpaid child support, extra precautions are necessary:

◆ If your former spouse has made threats to abduct your child, do not ignore these threats. Threats should be taken with greater seriousness if your ex has recently quit his job, sold his house, or done similar things that suggest he may flee. Ask the police to contact your ex and remind him of the possible consequences (i.e., arrest and possible imprisonment) that would follow from the abduction of your child.

◆ Teach your children their full names and telephone number.

◆ Make sure your children know how to use the telephone. Practice making collect calls at a pay telephone.

◆ Tell them you will always accept a collect call.

◆ Instruct them to call you if they get an uneasy feeling about where they are being taken or what is happening.

◆ Tell them they should always call you if someone tells them you are dead, sick, and unable to care for them, or do not love them anymore.

◆ Make sure your children understand that you will always take care of them and share your life with them.

your husband's background, interests, and perceptions of the children and one another. Share with the evaluator any documents or information you feel are relevant. The evaluator prepares a written report that is sent directly to the judge and reviewed by your attorneys. This report is not a public record. In some jurisdictions, even the parties involved are not permitted to read it. Sometimes the evaluator also testifies in court. The costs for this evaluation are paid according to what the judge orders or the attorneys agree upon. The evaluator also makes recommendations regarding visitation schedules. The judge has the final say, but most often

the judge considers the evaluator to be the expert most able to determine what is in the best interests of the children.

In the past, the courts invariably ruled that children belonged with their mothers except when the father could prove that the mother was grossly unfit. Most states now, however, view a husband and a wife in an impending custody dispute as equals. The evaluator will look closely at which parent has the greater psychological bond with the children. A mother with a successful career achieved by hard work, sacrifice, and extended work hours may find herself at a disadvantage in a custody dispute when the children's father has

(continuation)

♦ File a certified copy of the custody decree with the clerk of the court in the county where the noncustodial parent lives. This is especially important if your former partner lives in another state. By filing this decree you will be notifying the courts that a valid custody decree has already been made and must be honored and enforced.

♦ The best protection is to include in your custody order a provision prohibiting school authorities, day-care centers, and baby-sitters from releasing the child to the noncustodial parent without your prior consent.

Preventing International Abduction

♦ Avoid joint custody in families with citizenship in more than one country. If your former partner abducts your child to his native country and there is a custody agreement specifying joint custody, officials in that country may interpret this custody arrangement as permission to keep the child in their country.

♦ Do not allow a United States passport to be issued to your child. If you have sole custody or if there is a court order forbidding your child's removal from the United States, send a certified copy of the court order and a written request for denial of a United States passport to your child to the office of Citizenship Appeals and Legal Assistance, Office of Passport Services, U.S. Department of State, 1425 K Street NW, Room 300, Washington, DC 20522-1705.

♦ Ask the court to order the noncustodial parent to surrender his passport along with the children's passport to a designated person, like the clerk of the court, prior to exercising visitation rights with your children.

been the "hands-on" parent. Despite the obvious financial contribution, the father may have been more available to parent. Obviously, this is not the only factor upon which an evaluator bases his recommendation, but which parent is available to do the work of parenting and has achieved the closer psychological bonding with the children are two critical issues.

My ex and I cannot come to any agreement about custody or visitation and the judge has ordered an Impartial Evaluation of Custodial Fitness. I want to say and do the right things when I meet with the psychologist the judge has assigned.

What exactly should I say or do?

Understandably, the custody of your children is of overwhelming importance to you. You are anxious to make a good impression on the person who will be making recommendations to the judge. The best advice is to be you. Of course, like for any important meeting, you want to be on time and prepared. You will want to bring with you any documents the evaluator has requested or any other documents you think are important.

You should keep in mind that children who are given psychological permission to maintain an active relationship with the noncustodial parent are in the long run happier and more well adjusted. The evaluator is going to be sensitive to a willingness on your part to cooperate with your former partner to ensure that your children have the opportunity for a meaningful relationship with their father.

During the interviews, it is not wise to try to pretend that you have no personal deficiencies or shortcomings as a parent. First of all, the evaluator is typically a highly trained individual with a lot of experience, so your less than truths are going to be quickly exposed. The evaluator will also be obtaining information about you, your former partner, and the children from other sources to verify and to crosscheck what he has been told. These efforts will quickly let the evaluator know if someone has been less than honest. In addition, your former partner or husband is also going to be interviewed and will be asked, as you will be, to discuss the other person's weaknesses and shortcomings. It is better to be up front about your life experiences and current situation rather than to allow your former partner to give out information about you. A plan to address your shortcomings is usually seen in a favorable light. For example, if you have a lot of trouble disciplining your children, let the evaluator know. It would be helpful if you were attending a parenting class or attempting some other way to improve your disciplinary skills. Do not confuse wishing or planning to do something with actual accomplishment. Pretending or lying is harshly viewed.

Drug and alcohol addictions are certainly investigated because their effects are so devastating to children. Other health and safety issues are also examined. The known effects of second hand smoke may put a parent who smokes at a disadvantage. Evaluators may take into account which parent actively encourages safety measures like bicycle helmets and wearing of seat belts.

VISITATION

Visitation is almost always allowed for the noncustodial parent except under the most dangerous circumstances. Although most states require that a child in custody cases has a right to emotional and/or financial support of both parents, visitation has little or almost nothing to do with child support. In other words, the state can enforce child support but can't force a person to visit his child. Likewise, if you are supposed to receive child support but don't, you can't withhold visitation either. They are two separate issues. However, statistics tell us that the majority of men who pay up have reasonable access to their children.

Visitation for the "Sometime Dad." You can establish that you will be the sole custodial parent for your child and still offer a reasonable visitation schedule for the father. In fact, this is encouraged, for a number of reasons. First, men who can see their children usually will pay child support. Second, you will have less explaining to do about who your child's father is if the child can see and know him firsthand. And third, the child will benefit from whatever interaction they have while you may gain some free time.

When child support payments are chronically overdue, less than the amount the court ordered, or nonexistent, the temptation for many mothers is to restrict or deny their former partner's visitation rights. Difficult as it is when you are barely scraping by, it is important to treat visitation and child support as completely separate issues. You cannot deny your ex visitation rights if he is not paying child support.

Supervised Visitation. If you suspect foul play or worry that the father abuses alcohol or other substances, you can request that the court recommend supervised visitation. If you've already had unsupervised visitation, you will have to show the court reason for wanting to suspend it. Bring documents, witnesses, and as much information as you can if the father won't agree to this outside of court. Although not as hard to prove as in a custody case, you do need to prove to the court that supervised visitation is warranted.

DROP-OFF CENTERS

If supervised visitation is needed, investigate using a drop-off center. Drop-off centers provide safe havens where children can visit the non-custodial parent. Particularly when there has been a history of violence, exchanging the children in this "neutral zone" is far less likely to escalate or incite violence than if the children are exchanged in a parking lot or fast food restaurant.

These drop-off centers are also available for parents who have been accused of mental or physical abuse or neglect, as well as parents involved in custody disputes. Non-custodial parents impaired by mental illness, alcoholism, or mental retardation who still want to maintain relationships with their children in safety can also be serviced by drop-off centers. Funded primarily through federal money, these drop-off centers are typically a better alternative than private, and often costly, supervised visitation facilities.

Breastfeeding and Visitation

My daughter is still nursing. Her father, with whom I agreed to coparenting but not to marriage or a relationship, is trying to keep her overnight because the drive is so long for him. Should I wean her or talk to him about postponing visitation for a while?

Talk to him about postponing visitation until she is off the breast and at least onto a bottle, if not a cup. Of course, if he still wants to come for the day, fine, but let him know that babies who breastfeed often reject the bottle, and he may be at a loss about what to do should she spend the night at his place. If you don't work this out with him, you may be the one making long-distance, late-night trips in your car!

Unpredictable Visitation

The father of my child was very supportive the first two years of my son's life. But now he visits infrequently, popping in and out of our lives whenever he pleases. What can I do about this man? I think it is wrong for someone to just come and go as he pleases. Maybe I should keep my child from him, but my son enjoys him. Besides, how is this going to affect my son later in life?

Just because his father sees your son sporadically doesn't mean that your son will automatically suffer problems later in life. But if you prevent him from seeing this man totally, you are asking for trouble. Your son, as he matures, will have to decide whether or not he wants his father in his life. It's clear that the father is not making the wisest choices regarding his method of visitation, but this is how things are for a great many single mothers. The best thing to do is to give your son a consistent and predictable home life. If his dad shows up and it's okay with you, let them spend time together. If not, then just go about what you were doing before he interrupted you. Be sure to let your son know it is nothing about him that keeps his father away. Tell him that you don't know why his father isn't available to him more, but that is the way it is.

From Visitation to Custody for Mom

Although I felt I was the more suitable parent during our divorce, my husband had the lawyer with the higher price tag and the more convincing mouth, and he got custody of our three children. Actually, he is an excellent parent and the children have been living with him for five years while visiting me often. Recently the oldest, my twelve-year-old daughter, has come to live with me and things have been going very well. Her father agreed with this decision, particularly because she's going through "womanly stuff" and he felt my input would be beneficial. However, he hasn't given up sole custody. How can I parent like this?

Since your daughter is living with you full-time right now, you need the authority to make decisions regarding school, health care, and other issues concerning her welfare. In light of future situations where you will need full legal custody, you should discuss the need for a transference of custody. It sounds as if you can have a mature discussion with your ex about this and point out the benefits to him.

EXPLORING COPARENTING

Coparenting simply means cooperating, regardless of the intensity of the interaction between the ex and the children. Coparenting is an activity for grown-ups, with little or no room for immaturity because the well-being of the children is the primary goal. Keep in mind that each parent will come up with a different set of expectations for one another and a different way to negotiate the rules, but they never abandon the keys to successful coparenting, which are cooperation, respect, and flexibility.

Successful coparenting is what happens when you both realize that divorce may have ended your marriage, but not your roles as parents. Sadly, the majority of couples who have separated have no idea that they can raise their children together successfully even though they no longer live together. There are basically six steps toward coparenting successfully, and although it may seem that coparenting is impossible, keep in mind that there are degrees of cooperation. In other words, you are not jointly parenting, but rather trying to cooperate with each other to ensure the most consistency in your child's routine.

The Six Steps of Coparenting

1. Agree on who is the primary parent. The primary parent is the one who shoulders the majority of the responsibility for all aspects of child-rearing, including health issues, education, financial support, day-to-day challenges, and routine activities. Although being primarily financially responsible is often unfair for the custodial parent, particularly because she is less able to advance along the career track than one with fewer home responsibilities, this parent usually does shoulder the majority of expenses. Unless you make substantially more than your ex, if he is not contributing his fair share financially, then coparenting is not happening because you can't honestly cooperate with someone who is systematically cheating your children!

   The best time to be thinking about coparenting should be while the separation or divorce agreements are still being negotiated. However, if you decide after the agreement is signed that you want to coparent as the "bottom-line" parent, additional time and energy to rework the agreement will be necessary. Be aware that much of what men may want in agreements when they are not the custodial parent has to do with control and not with concern over the well-being of the children.

   If your children's father resists this notion of you as the "bottom-line" parent, point out that it simply must be this way since the children are living primarily under your supervision. Because most of the day-to-day responsibility is yours, you need the authority to make plans and decisions without fear of being contradicted or undercut. Explain that you will certainly listen to his views and respect his opinions, but that this arrangement gives the children the consistency they so desperately need in their lives. Be sure to let your ex know that just because you are the "bottom-line" parent, this doesn't diminish his ability, attributes, and contributions as a person.

   Although we are told that relationships should be equal in order for them to work best, the truth is there is no such thing as a purely egalitarian relationship one hundred percent of the time. In the healthiest of relationships, there is often a subtle shifting of power, not in an intimidating or controlling way, but rather in an "on-call" kind of way. Look at relationships you may have with family or friends who are extremely close and comforting—you'll find that each of you experiences times of need when the other is more powerful. It is trust in the process of give-and-take that makes apparent the real meaning of relationships. For example, if your ex loses his job and can no longer pay child support, perhaps with his extra free time he can help out more dropping off or picking up the children at their various activities.

   The task of coparenting requires different styles of participation in order to be accomplished. Don't expect the father of your child to behave exactly as you do, but rather enjoy the fact that he is contributing something different yet useful to the business of coparenting. You can learn something even if you are the primary or "bottom-line" parent.

HELPFUL TIPS FOR THE WEEKEND DAD

The noncustodial dad sees his kids an average of fewer than six days a month. Maintaining a close relationship with children during such a short time span can be difficult. Here are some guidelines for the father who is facing the challenge of trying to enhance his relationship with his kids:

◆ Stay abreast of your child's activities. Attend parent–teacher meetings, class functions, games, and club outings and participate in music, sports, and swim lessons whenever possible.

◆ Plan in advance for special occasions. Arrange to spend time together with your children on birthdays and holidays if this does not interfere with activities their mother may already have planned.

◆ Plan special outings. The quality time that you spend together doesn't have to be expensive, like going to costly theme parks. If you just look in your local paper you'll find some great recreation spots and other cheap activities, including museums, zoos, beaches, historic places and monuments, fishing, hiking, camping in national parks, library events such as storytelling hour or puppet shows, and films and spectator sporting events. Discuss the options with your kids and let them help choose the weekend activities. Just reading books and talking with your kids is a way of ensuring quality time together.

◆ Make videos of your time together. If you don't have access to a video camera, keep a photo album. Include pictures of outings with your children as well as birthday parties, holidays, and special occasions such as when a tooth falls out at your house.

◆ Don't spoil your kids by lavishing them with presents during their visits. Not

2. Vow to keep your feelings about each other out of your children's hearts and heads. No matter the extent of the pain, betrayal, or anger you are harboring, if you can't put a lid on it in front of the children, then you are not ready to get down to the business at hand. These feelings have to be worked through at least to the point that the times when you are dealing with your ex do not become the outlet for them. Coparenting requires that you act with maturity and dignity, and often this means putting other feelings on the back burner. Although you shouldn't hide these emotions, you need to find appropriate outlets for them since your ex is most likely only interested in the day-to-day matters regarding your children and doesn't want to hear intense anger or rage.

(continuation)

only does this confuse them because they will continue to expect gifts each time they visit, but they may start to think this is the only way to show love. Surely you can find other ways to show your love for them. Besides, this is one thing that really ticks Mom off!

♦ Participate in the current program for discipline. This does not mean punishment or any other kind of punitive treatment, especially without the mother's approval. Rather, this means that you should reinforce the child's expected behavior at home such as maintaining good table manners and eating habits and showing a respect for others.

♦ Stick to the normal routines as closely as possible. Insist that your children adhere to personal routines such as bathing, brushing their teeth, and taking any vitamins or prescribed medication they may have. Even though you may not have them stick to their usual bedtime because they may be allowed that extra hour of TV on the weekend, try to limit the amount of viewing, and don't let them sit too close to the television set. Also, avoid giving your children excessive junk food, such as colas, candy, food laden with chemicals or preservatives, or food that consists simply of empty calories. Monitor their cleanliness routines, their diet, and what they watch on the tube.

♦ Above all, reinforce your love through your words and your actions. Simply saying, "I love you," or a gentle hug is often the best. But when you are away from them, keep in touch by making "in-between" phone calls, or if your job requires you to be on the road a lot, send them postcards of places you've been. By maintaining contact through phone calls or the mail, you stay tuned in to their activities and emotional needs.

When communicating to your ex that you still have leftover feelings regarding the breakup of your relationship, try not to use an accusatory tone, but rather say something like, "I still feel so much hurt over your affair that I hope I don't let it get in the way of working with you." Saying, "You did this to me" or "You were the one who didn't want to stay together" only signals to the ex that it is time for the walls to come up. Words like that also mean that you are stuck and not ready to move ahead. And it's impossible to work together when one person is stuck and the other person is hiding. Do

say, "I am working to deal with my feelings of anger that we are no longer together."

3. Assure each other that you are doing the best job you can on behalf of the children. Maintain a respect for this person if for no other reason than that he is the father of your child. Even if his involvement with coparenting amounts to daily telephone calls but not much more than occasional weekends and holidays with the kids, if there is a benefit in his contact with the children, let him know. He might need to be motivated, and the carrot has

always worked better than the stick. One of the earliest determining factors in whether or not you will coparent well is being able to praise and show appreciation and respect for the other person.

4. Always keep the lines of communication open. If you think about any relationship, communication is the core. Without communication, forget it. That's why it is so important to listen to your kids, to your ex, and most of all, to yourself. Many marriages and relationships suffered from lack of communication. If yours was one of them, resolve for the sake of the children to find a way to communicate. If you can't come to an agreement about effectively dealing with the children, or find that you chronically disagree, or either of you claims to have been uninformed regarding new rules or changes, then you need to establish clear rules and procedures. Schedule a regular weekly meeting during which planning problems and concerns are discussed. You can keep these meetings informal and on neutral territory where you are likely not to allow the discussion to escalate into a yelling match. Keep in mind, too, that these meetings don't have to take place in person. For example, if you're both up on the latest computer networking software, why not take advantage of e-mail? Or if you're still on the off ramp of the infor-

mation highway, the telephone message service or voicemail is an excellent way to keep each other posted on behalf of the children.

There has to be both the commitment and the tools by which regular communication takes place. Divorced and separated people, especially if the parting was a particularly bitter one, do not have the desire to talk with one another as friends. Communication will take much effort, but this communication is not unlike the kind that any successful partnership requires. Remember also that your feelings are important and deserve no less consideration and attention than those of your former partner. You will be unable to meet your children's emotional needs during this tricky time if you yourself are emotionally adrift, so be sure to stay in touch with how you are feeling and respect the power of your own emotions.

5. Allow for change and scary feelings. There is nothing as certain in life as change. Changes will most likely occur in your life as well as in your ex's. New jobs, new careers, perhaps a return to school, an illness, a promotion, or even a move to a different neighborhood or another part of the country might be some of the changes you both need to deal with. Your ex may remarry, posing the problem of your children having another adult to deal with when their father is in charge. Your ability to coparent successfully depends largely on your willingness to accept that circumstances will change and that each of you will need to accept the inevitability of change.

True, change of any sort can seem terribly scary. In fact, it is the very fear of change that explains why so many people stay in relationships that are no longer satisfying or remain in households that are abusive. Your agreement to coparent represents another change on top of the big change everyone experiences in a major family disruption such as divorce. It's okay to be scared, because it means that you recognize the power and potential in creating a whole new life style that includes cooperating with someone to perform the most important job in the world, that of child-rearing. Anyone facing such a formidable challenge would be less than realistic if they did not feel at least a little bit scared. Remember that a healthy bit of stage fright can produce the most astounding performances of a lifetime!

6. Talk to and listen to your children. Your children need the opportunity to express their feelings about how their lives have changed and how they feel about the new parenting arrangements being negotiated on their behalf. A child might balk at certain decisions, but you are still the parent and he or she is still the child, which means that you have the final responsibility and final say. However, it is important to respect children's feelings and to listen to their fears and worries. Some of their fears, like who will take care of them when they are sick, can be easily assuaged by giving them the straightforward facts. You can explain to them that if you're called away during a bout with the sniffles, Aunt Linda or your best friend Jean may have to cover for you.

Your children will want to know the nuts and bolts of how their lives will change. Younger children will want to know at whose house they will be trick-or-treating or how Santa Claus or the Tooth Fairy will find them. Older children will want to know who will attend parent conferences and sign their report cards, and be there to cheer them on at soccer games. Will friends be allowed to sleep over at both Mom and Dad's house, and can the dog come, too? Be ready with the answers. If you don't know, it's okay to say, "Right now I just don't know, but as soon as I discuss this question with your father, I will let you know." Don't expect every single detail to be ironed out in advance. Allow your children's input and suggestions to be heard by their dad. Better yet, if at all possible, have family meetings occasionally, where everyone gets a chance to be heard.

The Good Ex—A Head Start at Coparenting. There are many kinds of exes, but only one is heaven-sent. He is: Devoted; Enthusiastic and energetic; Appropriate in his actions; and Reliable (DEAR). If all exes could be classified as DEARs, divorce and separation in themselves wouldn't be played up as the culprit in causing problems for children. It would be recognized that it is the disruptions that arise when there is a need to move, a sharp decline in family income, and possible changes and adjustments in school that cause complications. Coparenting with a DEAR can ensure that these problems are kept to a minimum.

The DEAR Is Devoted. This man never lets his children doubt his love for them. His children know that their parents' marriage has ended, but his love and devotion have not wavered. This child will say that despite the divorce her dad was always there for her. When the class makes Father's Day gifts at school, this child doesn't need to wonder if he will see his dad to give him the gift or if his father will even care.

He's Energetic and Enthusiastic. This means he has time for his own new life as well as the physical and emotional energy to drive his son to hockey practice at 6:00 A.M. or be there for the less than glamorous moments of parenthood, like middle-of-the-night trips to the emergency room. He's enthusiastic because he's not just there for the recitals, performances, and games out of politeness but is really involved.

His Actions Are Appropriate. This kind of ex does not violate your privacy by looking under the beds and checking the house like a general on an inspection tour. He doesn't interrogate the children about what you have been doing and with whom. Other appropriate behaviors are: does not open drawers and look through your checkbook or other private belongings; doesn't have his bedmate of the moment spend the night when it is his weekend to have the children; tries to keep the children on an even keel during his visitation, giving them regular meals and some semblance of bedtime. He is not King of the Land of Do As You Please while you are the Wicked Witch of Homework, Toothbrushing, and Other Dreaded Routines.

He Is Reliable. Most important of all, this ex shows up when he promises to and doesn't make the children wonder if they are indeed going to the Saturday afternoon outing he promised, or if they should just go with their friends to the park. His word can be trusted. He pays child support and other financial obligations without constant reminding, nagging, threats, or coercion.

There are a number of blessed women who have DEARs—former husbands and/or significant others who continue to support their children financially, emotionally, and with practical assistance. Even in cases where the father is unable to contribute financially, he still participates in the child-rearing process through other kinds of assistance. These men who continue their financial or emotional commitment—or both—to their children do so without legal threats, intimidation, or an attitude of patriarchal superiority. They not only love their children with full and giving hearts, but they respect your privacy and independence and do not seek to control or belittle you. These fathers know that children function best when the rules and expectations are firm and consistent. You are never the "bad mommy who makes them take baths and do homework" while he is the "best daddy in the world who takes them everywhere and buys them everything." These men have agendas that don't include bad-mouthing you to the children or using the children as messengers or spies. In short, we're talking about grown-up men who, despite any other weaknesses or failings, deserve to be respected, prized, and admired.

Regardless of why you separated, if you find yourself with an ex who shares the love and care of children with you, then coparenting will most likely be a successful venture that can only serve to benefit your children and enhance the future for all of you.

THE TRANSITION FROM HIS HOUSE TO YOURS

You take care of the kids all week, cooking, cleaning, working, schlepping them to and from ball practice, and listening to their stories ranging from hating the new teacher to having a crush on the little girl next door. Friday comes around, and you actually find yourself excited to see your ex because the freedom you are going to experience this weekend fills you with visions

---

THE DOS AND DON'TS OF VISITATION

In all probability, you are your children's primary role model. They look up to you to learn appropriate conduct so that one day they too can become mature, responsible adults. Although at times you might find it tempting to point out your ex's shortcomings or argue with him in front of the kids, you should avoid it at all costs. By following these simple suggestions, you can set a positive example for your children, even if you're the only parent acting like an adult:

♦ Do not poison your children's minds by discussing the other parent's shortcomings with them. This hurts kids because a little bit of that other parent lives in them. If something is wrong with the other parent, then kids think something is wrong with them, although they may not verbally or actively demonstrate those feelings.

♦ Do not expose your children during overnight visits to any member of the opposite sex with whom you are sexually involved. (See Chapter 23 for the right time for your kids to meet your lover.)

♦ Do not use your visitation as an excuse to continue arguments with your spouse.

♦ Don't visit your children if you have been drinking or taking any kind of decision-impairing substance or narcotic.

♦ Don't visit your children at unreasonable hours.

♦ Don't fail to notify your spouse or ex as soon as possible if you are unable to keep your visitation date, as this is unfair to your children, who are expecting you. Be mature, responsible adults and work out another agreeable time for visitation.

♦ Don't continually question your children regarding the activities of your former spouse.

♦ Don't make extravagant promises to your kids that you know you will not or cannot keep.

♦ Do prepare the kids. The parent with whom the children live must prepare the children both physically and mentally for visitation and have them available at the time mutually agreed upon.

♦ Do negotiate fairly. If one parent has plans for the children that conflict with the visitation and these plans are in the best interests of the children, be mature, responsible adults and work this out together.

♦ Do always work for the spiritual well-being, health, happiness, and safety of your children.

or pampering yourself, doing a little shopping, or—even more luxurious—sleeping till noon!

The kids are happy, too, because they know that they are getting away from the daily grind of school, chores, and homework. Saturday and Sunday to them means eating pizza, watching cartoons when they get up in the morning until they pass out on the sofa, and going to bed without taking a bath!

But now it's Sunday evening and here they are, desperately needing a bath, a decent night's sleep, and a hot, healthy meal. They are strung out, and guess who has to endure their withdrawals—not unlike drug addicts coming down off a high. That's right, it's good old Monday-through-Friday mom!

You try to get them settled back into their routine, but pretty soon they are screaming at you, "I hate you! I'd rather go live with dad." Before you can run out into the street to catch him so you can pummel him for bringing back these children-turned-monsters, he's revved up the engine and is gone.

There's no question that you're now getting pretty mad at yourself, but first think about this. Your ex probably had as much trouble with the kids over the weekend as you do when they are returned to you. Maybe that's why he gives in to their whims, because to him it is simply easier. After all, they had to make the transition into his life and only had two days to accomplish that. You can pretty much count on Monday coming around and things settling back into place.

Try not to lose your temper or exhibit hurt feelings when your children tell you everything that transpired over the weekend. Most likely they are not trying to hurt you but are simply finding a way of sharing their weekend lives with you. You don't want your children tiptoeing on eggshells around you because you well up with tears if they say, "Dad's girlfriend came by and he treated us to ice cream sundaes."

Even with the best intentions and an acute interest in coparenting by both of you, transitions from one place to another are inevitably going to be bumpy. Try to make the change go a little more smoothly by:

♦ Establishing some kind of ritual. This ritual can be a signal to start getting back on track. You might have them take a bath or a shower—wash that dad right out of their hair, so to speak.

♦ Remembering that your kids see the weekend world as one without the responsibilities that they have Monday through Friday. Let your kids know that whether they live with you or Dad, there will ultimately be responsibilities for them to endure, even if it means accepting the consequences for being irresponsible at times. For instance, if your daughter won't brush her teeth at Dad's, chances are the next visit to the dentist will cause a consequence that will be her responsibility to shoulder.

♦ Talk to your ex about trying to set up mutual expectations for your kids, so that there is some kind of routine despite the transition.

When Your Ex Sets No Rules or Limits at His Place

My six- and eight-year-old sons visit their father every other weekend. Although I look forward to the break and the opportunity to pursue my own activities, when the boys return, the free time hardly seems worth it. Their father's house is vacation city to them—no set bedtimes, eating lots of take-out food, and constant snacking. The boys will frequently tell me that I am mean and too strict because when they visit Dad they are allowed to do so many things I do not permit. Do not suggest that he and I sit down and negotiate. If we had been able to work complicated and important issues like this out, we would not have gotten divorced. It seems like my children's lives will always be in turmoil because of all the transitions they must make due to our divorce.

Instead of thinking about your sons' need to make transitions as a negative experience, remember that everyone needs to learn to behave differently in different settings. We are not allowed, for example, to speak loudly in church or in libraries, but it is fine, and in fact expected and encouraged, to shout and make noise at a football game. Helping your boys to make the transition from one household to another—households with different rules, standards, and expectations—is an opportunity for you to teach your children a valuable lesson in life.

Hold a family meeting where you sit down and have a talk with the boys. Acknowledge that there are different rules with Dad than with you. Talk about these differences in terms of context, not personality. For example, tell your children that because Dad sees them only on weekends, bedtime can be flexible because they do not have to get up for school the next day. Since they are not at their dad's all the time, the kind of food they eat there can be an occasional treat. If they lived there all the time, different food standards would probably apply. Avoid discussing differences in terms of personality, such as saying that "your father allows you to eat take-out food because he is too lazy to prepare nutritious food." Although this might be perfectly true, you will only make the situation worse by badmouthing your ex and exposing his shortcomings.

Even though kids often want to see their parents together, they have a natural instinct to divide and conquer, because this manipulation helps them get their way. By making this a personality issue, they will seize the opportunity to pit you against each other in a kind of twisted "who-loves-them-more" or "who-is-the-better-parent" contest. Stick to the simple reality that different rules and expectations will prevail at each house because there are different life circumstances at each house. At your house, bedtime is important because school cannot be missed. Nutritious food is eaten because you are responsible for their good health. Occasional lapses are okay, and those lapses will take place at Dad's. This does not make you the "mean mother," so refuse to accept this role. This makes you the consistent, caring, dependable parent every child needs. Anybody can be a playmate to a child; it takes a grown-up to be a parent!

Can I Withhold Visitation?

I'm tired of being Ms. Nice Guy to my ex and Ms. Bad Mom to the kids. My ex-husband and I had a fairly civil divorce, and he agreed wholeheartedly to my being the custodial parent. But now, after I had been pretty generous about his visitation rights, he's keeping the children later and later in the evenings and even sometimes overnight on Sunday. He thinks he can make up for not being with them all the time by spoiling them. Because he recently got laid off from work, he stopped paying child support, but says it is only temporary. It's amazing how he can take them to any restaurant they want, buy them toys and clothes without having a job, and give them money whenever they want for video games. Can I withhold visitation, especially because he is not contributing financially right now?

There is no connection between support and visitation, other than the statistics that tell us that the majority of men who do not see their kids don't pay any kind of support. Legally, there is nothing you can do about withholding visitation strictly on the grounds of not receiving child support. But if you really believe the amount of time your kids spend with their dad is detrimental to them, you could request that the court modify the visitation order. However, it would certainly be better for all involved if you could come to an agreement since there will be so many years of coparenting ahead. As calmly as possible and not in front of the children, explain to your ex that his child support obligations have not stopped because he is unemployed. A portion of his unemployment compensation should be going to the support of the children. If he anticipates that he will be out of work for a long time, it is up to him to get his child support obligations reduced in a civil court. Until his child support is reduced by court order, his obligations remain the same and back support keeps accumulating. He is not helping himself and certainly not helping the children by being Mr. Big Shot with the unlimited supply of money for video games and other toys and treats. If you are not able to work this situation out between you, contact your local child support enforcement agency or discuss this situation with your attorney.

Explain to your ex that the kids being late for school Monday morning or arriving unprepared is only going to cause grief in their future, not necessarily in yours or his. He might be feeling very inadequate right now, after losing his job not long after losing his family, at least in the traditional sense. Generally, spoiling is nothing more than an inconvenience to moms perpetrated by grandmothers, rich aunts, and guilty exes. But if major consequences result from the kind of attention your ex is lavishing on the kids, then certainly a revised visitation order would make sense.

19
Child Support

WHY, HOW, AND WHERE TO GET IT

Child support is money to be paid per order of a court, most often as part of a divorce or dissolution of a marriage. Child support is also awarded at the time paternity is established. The purpose of child support is to make sure that children enjoy the same comforts and opportunities they would have enjoyed if their parents were together. Child support is not intended to financially subsidize the mother as an individual or another adult with whom she might choose to live. Single mothers, whether they receive child support or not, must be aware that their long-term survival depends upon becoming financially self-sufficient. Even ample and regular child support will end when the child reaches maturity. A life built upon the illusion that child support will continue indefinitely will be in crisis when the payments stop.

Along with an agreement about child support, the court order typically includes stipulations about custody and visitation, and other matters related to the care and upbringing of the children. Many fathers fulfill child support and other such obligations freely and responsibly. Some men go beyond simply "what is ordered" and provide willingly a better life for their child. These

men deserve the respect of their former partners. These men rightfully have peace of mind because their child is secure and stable. These men are committed to their child and keep their promises. If your former partner is one of these admirable men, count your blessings.

Too Many Broken Promises

Unfortunately, too many men have walked away from their child support obligations, effectively deserting their child. Many men justify this financial and emotional abandonment with anger toward the child's mother. Lack of personal responsibility and a "me first" attitude underlie most excuses. Many men feel it is beneath them to take a second, and often low paying, job—in other words, to do what many

---

MAKE THIS PHONE CALL!

Contact the non-profit Association for Children for Enforcement of Support (ACES) at (800) 738-ACES for helpful information about child support.

single mothers do to make ends meet. Deadbeats never compromise their own desired life style and consider themselves entitled to spend their money as if they had no other obligations other than to themselves. Typically, deadbeats feel the children can have what is "leftover" after they have all the grown-up toys and leisure activities they desire. This sense of entitlement can take many forms, but it almost always means that children are left out in the cold, sometimes quite literally.

Times Have Changed
Lack of child support has been one of the primary factors contributing to the disgraceful number of children and their mothers living in poverty. The latest figures available from the Census Bureau reveal that about 32 percent of parents with custody who were owed child support but did not get any lived below the poverty line. About 22 percent of parents who received only partial child support were poor.

In light of these sobering statistics, child support enforcement has become a hot political issue. Conservative, liberal, Democrat, or Republican, each group supports the need for non-custodial parents to bear financial responsibility for their children. Lack of child support has gone from a shameful

family secret to a topic of public debate and concern.

Arising from this public debate and outrage, landmark federal legislation has been passed to assist custodial parents, overwhelmingly mothers, to collect the literally billions of dollars owed in unpaid child support. The number of mothers who are receiving child support is increasing. The good news is that with careful effort and perseverance it is likely that you will be able to collect child support. Begin by figuring out if trying to obtain child support is the right decision for you.

Should You Collect Child Support?
Some mothers feel that it is easier to raise a child alone than to hassle with the problems of collecting child support. Here are some reasons you should consider opening a child support enforcement action against your child's father:

♦ Eighteen years is a long time. Who know what your financial circumstances may be in the future? Are you being totally realistic about your ability to handle all the expenses involved in raising a child? Remember that your expenses increase as your child gets older.

- All children are entitled to support from both parents whether or not their parents were married. This is the law.

- Men who pay child support are more likely to involve themselves in other aspects of their child's life and be more willing to help out with other medical, educational, or recreational expenses.

Here are some reasons NOT to open a child support enforcement action against your child's father:

- You know that is best for your child's father not to be in your child's life at all because he is violent, mentally ill, and/or an alcoholic or substance abuser.

- You want parental rights terminated (which waives your rights to child support).

- Your child's father is dead and no action can be taken against his estate.

- The birth father cannot be identified.

- The father is in prison, institutionalized, or has a permanent total disability.

- You purposely got pregnant by deceiving a man who was repeatedly very clear about not wanting children. In this case, you should assume sole responsibility for the care of your child.

HOW TO BEGIN

Get a Legal Order for Child Support

It is necessary to have a legal order for child support that spells out the amount of the obligation and how it is to be paid. Many states have arrangements for establishing the support order by an administrative procedure or other expedited legal procedure. The hearing may be conducted by someone other than a judge, like an administrative hearing officer, master or referee of the court. An agreement made between the parents and approved by this type of agency generally has the same effect as one established in court. It is legally binding on the parties concerned.

How Is the Amount of Support Determined?

Every state has guidelines for determining the amount of child support to be awarded. When granting support, the judge refers to these guidelines, which take into account the income of each parent, and various other factors like the number of children in a family and costs like medical expenses and child care. Even though support orders are now computed using state guidelines rather than the old-fashioned and faulty method of "gathering receipts" from the custodial parent to justify every expense, you should still compile a list of all the costs involved to raise your child. Consider expenses like shelter, food, education, and clothing, but do not overlook hidden costs or the need to save for large expenses. Future college expenses, special medical or dental needs, summer camp, school field trips, vacations, and memberships in organized programs and clubs are real expenses that will add up!

If a non-custodial parent attempts to get their child support reduced, the judge may grant a reduction for legitimate reasons like serious illness or long-term unemployment. Typically, however, judges are prohibited by law from reducing the support obligation retroactively—i.e., future child support may be reduced, but he is still liable for the full amount of past support owed.

IF YOU NEED HELP

Get in Touch with Your Uncle Sam. Title IV-D of the Social Security Act passed in 1975 established a local IV-D child support agency in every state in the union. These local IV-agencies are federally funded and must help you collect child support if your children are under 18 or if you apply for help before your child reaches 18 years of age. Find your local IV-D agency by contacting your local Child Support Enforcement Office. Look in the telephone directory under the state or county social services agencies. These agencies go by different names in different states.

The maximum application fee that can be charged for services through a IV-D agency is $25. Some states charge slightly more for child support services. There are efforts underway to eliminate the dubious practice of charging fees to victims of non-support. Check with your local agency for a fee schedule.

Your state's child support enforcement program is available to help you to find the non-custodial parent,

WARNING!

Private support collection organizations make claims they cannot prove, often preying on financially desperate women. The private organizations are not regulated by any government agency, but will use government resources and collect steep fees or percentages for accessing these no-cost government services. Investigate carefully before signing any agreement!

establish legal paternity (fatherhood), establish the legal support order, and to collect child support payments. You can also obtain help to establish and enforce medical support. IV-D agencies can enforce alimony if it is in the same order as the child support. IV-D agencies can also enforce court orders though wage withholding, contempt proceedings, judgments, and liens. IV-D agencies can attach unemployment compensation, military wages, retirement benefits, or V.A. benefits as well as federal and state tax refunds. IV-D agencies can also assist if a modification or change is needed in the existing child support order. Other legal issues like custody, visitation, and property settlements are not, by themselves, child support enforcement issues so child support enforcement programs cannot intervene in such matters.

When the Threat Is Bankruptcy. Child support payments generally cannot be discharged in a bankruptcy. This means that your ex cannot escape his child support obligation by filing for bankruptcy. Bankruptcies do not act as a stay, or hold, on actions to establish paternity or to establish or modify child support. Back child support is never canceled in bankruptcy proceedings. This means that once child support is owed, it will always be owed until it is paid.

When You No Longer Know Where He Lives. To obtain a court order or to enforce a court order for child support, legal documents must be delivered to the absent parent notifying him of the legal action that will

take place. This is a constitutional right which protects all of us from having legal obligations imposed without an opportunity to tell our side of the story. If you no longer know where your ex lives, you can obtain help in locating him through your IV-D agency, but you can speed things along by doing a little simple detective work yourself.

Send him a letter at his last known address. Write FORWARDING ADDRESS REQUESTED on the envelope. The post office will send you back the letter with either a little yellow sticker on it with your ex's forwarding address or let you know that there is no forwarding address. Your ex will not be notified by the post office of your attempt to locate him. You can also contact the Department of Motor Vehicles and for about $3.00, the DMV will provide you with an address and a list of vehicles registered under his name. You can do this even if you live in a different state. Contact his high school or college alumni office and see if they have a current address on file. You need not tell the alumni office exactly why you are asking for his address. Just say that you are interested in getting in contact with him. This is certainly not a lie.

When You Must Establish Paternity. There are two ways to establish paternity. The father can voluntarily consent, which means he admits he is the father. Sometimes men may not be so eager to admit paternity. They may be angry at the child's mother or be jealous that you may be in another relationship or simply no

YOU SHOULD KNOW

Recent changes in federal law make paternity acknowledgements the equivalent of court orders usually within 60 days. This means that voluntary establishment of paternity is simpler and faster than in the past. Before a mother or alleged father signs a paternity acknowledgment, each person must be informed both orally and in writing of the legal consequences, rights, and responsibilities arising from the paternity acknowledgement. Unless a father signs a voluntary acknowledgement of paternity, his name cannot appear on the birth certificate.

longer want to be a father. The father may himself be in a new relationship and now wants to avoid the anticipated child support obligations from a prior relationship.

If he is unwilling to admit paternity, you will need to arrange with either a private attorney or your local IV-D agency to serve him with a summons to appear in court to either acknowledge or deny paternity. If he tells the judge or administrative hearing officer that he is not the father or he is not sure that he is the father, then a genetic blood or tissue tests will be ordered.

This is the second way in which paternity can be established. Paternity is now based entirely upon the results of increasingly sophisticated genetic and blood tests. Allegations and denials, once the substance of many paternity disputes, have been replaced with beyond-any-reasonable-doubt laboratory test results.

What About Getting an Attorney?

All the IV-D agencies have attorneys who provide services for child support matters. There are no income eligibility requirements. To use a IV-D attorney, you simply have to fill out a IV-D application. Obviously, this low-cost /no-cost legal representation is a critical benefit, particularly if the lack of child support has led to financial hard times. You need to remember, however, that you are going to be one of probably hundreds of cases the IV-D attorney will be handling. There will be little personal attention and you will need to be organized and active in keeping your case moving forward.

Representing yourself or appearing pro se may seem like a good idea. You have control on actions taken or not taken and can be sure that paperwork is filed in a timely manner. There are major drawbacks to being your own legal advocate. You will not know all the legal ins and outs and may miss opportunities to place in evidence key information. Child support hearings are emotionally charged events. Think about facing someone in court whom you used to love. Emotions can cloud judgment; this is why even the best attorneys do not represent themselves.

Pro bono attorneys, meaning non IV-D attorneys, who will take your case for free are few and far between. If you find such an attorney, you will probably find yourself a low priority in her or his schedule. This means even more delay and longer waiting to get the outcome you are working toward. You will still be responsible for filing fees and other court costs.

Private attorneys charge by the hour and are the most costly option, If you are fortunate enough to be able to afford this route, make sure you choose an experienced individual— this is not the time to be paying for someone else's education. Be clear what you expect to gain from court proceedings. Make sure that your expectations are realistic. Understand what the expected fees and costs will be. Look for someone with whom you feel comfortable and who makes the process easy for you to understand. Above all else, remember this person works for you. There is no reason to be apologetic or ashamed of the circumstances which have led you to seek her or his services.

WHEN YOUR FEELINGS THREATEN TO OVER-WHELM YOU

Counseling Is Not a Luxury. In addition to legal assistance, if your single parenthood status is the result of a devastating circumstance (your husband's death, his abrupt departure, his disinterest in his child) counseling for you and your children is essential. Do not allow limited finances to be an obstacle. Investigate what mental health services are available in your community. This is an excellent time to find out what your health insurance benefits cover. You and your children need a safe place to sort out and deal productively with the conflicting and painful emotions that each of you is experiencing. In some cases—e.g., if your husband has left you and your teenaged child for another relationship—you may need to know how not to get your child mixed up in

unhealthy emotional reactions or your child may need help in understanding how to be involved with both of his parents without hurting one or the other.

The work ahead is difficult. There is nothing more frightening than the prospect of major life change. Each of you is now confronted with enormous life changes that probably were neither positive nor welcome. You can rebuild your life and your children can thrive, but you must take charge of your life by confronting and working through the powerful feelings that every woman in your circumstances has experienced.

Let Go of the Role of Victim. Only your own heart can guide you in matters of forgiveness. If you do decide to forgive your ex husband, you would not necessarily be doing it for his benefit nor would your forgiveness imply that negative actions were morally acceptable.

Constant anger is easy to understand, but will only drain your energy and be destructive to your own life. You are not hurting him, but are hurting yourself and the children by letting your anger make you bitter and resentful. Your energies are better focused on creating a better life for you and your children. Strive toward having your ex as emotionally absent as he is physically absent from your life.

HELP IN THE TOUGHEST CIRCUMSTANCES

When Your Ex Lives Out of State and, so far, NO LUCK! The dismal record of child support enforcement,

KEEP IN MIND

Making these laws work for you and your children begins with application to a IV-D agency. United States attorneys who will be prosecuting these felony cases will coordinate with the IV-D agency to obtain a referral package with all the information needed to begin the investigation and prosecution. Cases are typically accepted for federal prosecution only when other remedies have been exhausted.

particularly when fathers move to a state different from where their children reside or even move to a foreign country prompted passage of the Child Support Recovery Act (CSRA) in 1992. It was recognized that many of these out-of-state moves by a non-custodial parent were simply to avoid child support obligations. Interstate child enforcement had been notoriously difficult, expensive, and time consuming. Typically, mothers were frustrated by the time delays and costs and often gave up the fight. The Child Support Recovery Act (CSRA) made it a federal offense to willfully fail to pay a past due support obligation for a child who lives in another state.

The CSRA was recently amended to create the Deadbeat Parent Punishment Act of 1998. These amendments create two new first offense felonies that may now be prosecuted under the CSRA. Deadbeat dads (or moms) can be now be sentenced to a two-year maximum prison term and a fine for traveling to another state or foreign country with the intent

to evade a child support obligation, if the obligation has remained unpaid for longer than one year or is greater that $5000. Deadbeats can also be charged with a felony for willfully failing to pay a child support obligation for a child who resides in another state, if the obligation has remained unpaid for longer than two years or is greater than $10,000. Willfully failing to pay means that you must be able to prove that the child's father knew about his child support obligations.

When He Threatens to Cry Poor. The Deadbeat Parents Punishment Act does not require you to prove that your deadbeat ex has the ability to pay. The deadbeat parent must now prove he is unable to pay. This is a subtle but important difference and a great victory for child support enforcement.

This is the practical result of the change in the law. There is no need for you to obtain bank records, pay stubs, back tax returns or any other type of financial information in order to collect back child support. The

deadbeat must supply the records to prove that he is unable to pay. This important change addresses what many single mothers have learned from painful experience. It is difficult to prove hat the deadbeat dad is earning or acquiring income or assets. Child support offenders are notorious for hiding assets and failing to document earnings. Obviously, if you have any access to such records or can somehow show evidence of the deadbeat's opulent lifestyle, this is helpful information.

The law now makes the assumption that if the deadbeat parent had a legitimate change in circumstance after the court order for child support was put in place, like prolonged sickness or job loss, he would have had his child support order reduced in civil court. If a deadbeat has not tried to have his child support reduced, the law now requires that he puts forth evidence that he cannot pay. Substantial and complete financial records and other documentation are needed by the deadbeat to prove he has an inability to pay. Failure to keep records does not get the deadbeat off the hook. In fact, it may get him in even deeper trouble.

When He Is Not Just a Deadbeat.

Priority is given to cases where a pattern of flight from state to state to avoid payment can be demonstrated. Federal officials are also giving priority to cases where frequent job changing, concealing assets, or using false social security numbers show a pattern of deception. Failure to make child support payments after being held in contempt and failure to make child support payments in connection with or related to activities like

---

COLLECTING CHILD SUPPORT MADE EASY

Delinquent child support payments can be withheld from a non-custodial parent's wages just like payroll taxes even if he lives in another state. Check with your local IV-D agency for updates on how exactly to get the process moving for your children. Be prepared with three certified copies of the original court order and any changes, three certified copies of the withholding order or petition to withhold; a sworn affidavit from you that states how much you are owed; and, if possible, a copy of the payment record from your Clerk of the Courts or child support agency that may have collected or distributed payments.

---

bankruptcy fraud, bank fraud, or tax evasion are of particular interest to federal prosecutors.

When He Would Rather Be Unemployed.

Unemployment compensation can be attached for child support under federal law. Working

THE DOS AND DON'TS OF
CHILD SUPPORT

◆ Don't give up because the paperwork seems tedious or because you think you will never find a missing dad.

◆ Don't refuse child support because you feel guilty about the relationship ending. Your child's needs are a separate issue.

◆ Do remember that child support is not a favor; it is the law.

◆ Do remember that you are your own best advocate. Stay informed and take an active role in gathering information and asking questions.

◆ Know your rights and be persistent when you deal with attorneys and agencies.

◆ Do get organized by keeping copies of every document in a safe place.

◆ Do not use your children as spies or confidants.

◆ Do take the time to take care of the business of seeking or enforcing child support orders. Try to see these efforts as business rather than as a reminder of the pain your ex is continuing to cause.

◆ Do not let attempting to collect child support drain the joy out of every day living or stop you from pursuing other goals and dreams. Let these efforts be only one facet of your life.

---

through your local IV-D agency or with a private attorney, you can also ask for a contempt hearing and request that the court order your ex to seek employment and provide proof to the court that he is looking for work.

This is called a "seek-work order." Ask the court to order your ex to report to the court on a different day each week with signatures and telephone numbers of at least ten places where he has sought employment. If he fails to provide this weekly report or the names of the prospective employers on the list cannot be verified, he can be sent to jail after the second contempt hearing is held to show that he did not comply with the seek-work order issued in the first contempt hearing.

When His Wages Are Off the Books. You can arrange through your IV-D agency or private attorney to do a credit check to determine his assets. The court can issue a judgment for back child support. Sometimes you can even collect interest. Once you have an order for the back child support owed, any asset you discover, for example a house, car, or boat, can have a judgment executed against it.

If he claims to be unemployed while earning money off the books, you can also obtain a seek-work order. Violating this seek-work order will mean that he is in contempt of court and could face jail time. Be aware, too, that if the non-paying parent is receiving income without declaring it while accepting unemployment benefits, this is viewed as fraud by the unemployment office and is punishable by law.

When He Suddenly Owns Nothing. Not only is it unfair, it is also probably illegal to put assets in someone else's name to avoid paying a valid debt like child support and can be a fraudulent conveyance. If you can prove that he is living in the house or driving the car and is the one making the payments, these assets can be attached to pay back child support. You must also prove that these assets were transferred to another person when the child support payments were due. New federal laws require that states have laws under which fraudulent transfer of assets to avoid child support can be investigated and prosecuted. Speak to an attorney or check with your local IV-D agency.

20

The Ex from Hell

HOW TO MANAGE AN UNCOOPERATIVE EX

Coparenting with a cooperative, considerate, and reliable ex can be heavenly. Attempting to coparent with an ex with whom communication was difficult enough when you were together can be worse than impossible ... it can be the nightmare from hell.

True, you're better off having an ex from hell than a partner from hell, but it would be best for you, your children, and everyone around you if you could learn to manage a difficult ex.

In cases where you find yourself with an ex from hell, it's best not to fantasize any charming coparenting scenarios but rather to simply try to survive with as little disruption as possible in your children's lives and yours.

IF YOUR EX IS OUT OF YOUR LIFE

Maybe you are fortunate enough to have no troublesome ex at all to contend with. But even if you weren't married or know you'll never see your ex again, the simple presence of your chil-dren is a daily reminder. If you are like many women who share a positive outlook, your child can be a reminder of what was best in your relationship with the significant other rather than what was strained. Look at your children and be grateful for what their father contributed, if only helping to create them. And if that doesn't help, keep reading, because you'll be grateful for what you're avoiding!

THOSE CRAZY, HAZY POST-DIVORCE DAYS

No matter what twists and turns, advances and setbacks appear in most of the stories of divorce and separation, there is one thing you should never count on—that your previous relationship will improve by the mere act of removing yourself. Most likely, the post-divorce days will be a continuation of the same problems that ultimately killed the relationship in the first place. Often, things can get worse. For example, once you were able to depend on his financial contributions; now you may not even see that. If your husband or significant other was emotionally unavailable, you can be fairly sure that his emotional ties to the children will remain distant or even evolve into nonexistence. If he was financially irresponsible and left many of the significant responsibilities to you, such as keeping creditors away, keeping the lights turned on, and paying the rent or mortgage, you can pretty much count on assuming these burdens solo.

DON'T SHOOT— IDENTIFY HIM FIRST!

The good news, although we don't hear enough of it, is that even if you have an impossible ex, there is hope. There are steps you can take to ensure that you can relate to him without killing him. Too many women limit their efforts to cope with an ex from hell by fantasizing a murder, such as electrocuting their ex by flinging the hairdryer in to the tub after luring him into a cozy bath. This is great but only for writing a brilliant mystery novel. But on a serious note, the only way to deal with an ex from hell is to stop the "murder" fantasies and get clear about why he is such a problem.

Is there anything you can modify in your own behavior that might at least enable the two of you to avoid major clashes? As in most situations in your life, you need to recognize what you are dealing with before you can survive it.

Try to identify the emotions at play. Ex-husbands/significant others generally fall into recognizable groups within two basic categories. He's either a RAT (Really Always There) or a variation of a MAD (Minimal Access Dad). Work

on strategies to counter the negative energy he may bring to you. Then you can focus on what is positive and build from there.

THE RAT (REALLY ALWAYS THERE)

The RAT is simply around too much, but always on his own terms. Rather than simply providing adequate child support and spending time with their children, RATs consciously maneuver their former wives/significant others into circumstances, financial and otherwise, that work best for them. The needs, wants, and desires of their former partners are never given any serious consideration. All the behaviors of the RAT can be explained by their need to keep their ex dependent and to maintain control over the family. In all likelihood, they chose to leave their children.

Often there is some kind of dance between former spouses that maintains the connection between them way beyond the point of appropriate cooperation on behalf of the children. The father may see his ex-wife as having a very specific place in his life. Her role in life is to be the mother of his children. Although he would give ready lip service to her entitlement to a life of her own, this man constructs and manipulates the shared parenting responsibilities in such a way that her freedom and decision making are minimized while his power and control over the children remain unchallenged.

Accepting this place as ex-wife may serve the needs of this woman, particularly if she is in denial that the relationship as she would have liked it to continue is over or if she would

rather have half (or less) of this relationship than none at all. The result is
that both the man and woman are
stunted in their emotional growth by
this unspoken pact between them.
Such a man, while probably a loving
and involved father, is not emotionally
available to another woman or other
relationships. And the ex-wife certainly
won't be, either.

Keeping the RAT Under Control.
It's tempting to keep a RAT around,
because he appears to do so much for
his family. But little traces of his visits
linger long after the RAT is gone, causing contamination of the home. Total
extermination isn't the answer, but
RAT control is. Firm boundaries must
be set: The RAT needs to call first, or
have set times for communicating with
the family. Expectations must be made
clear: He's visiting, not living in your
home. And finally, the temptation to
ask him to help you needs to be resist-
ed: When the faucet is leaking, fix it
yourself or call a plumber. RATs don't
go away by themselves but will stay
away for longer periods when they
aren't so welcome.

*I've been dating a guy who seems
devoted to his kids, but something
weird is happening. Even though
he's been divorced for ages, I feel
like the other woman! He's constantly at his ex's house doing something, while I pull teeth just to get
him to go to a movie with me. I care
about him, but this is hurting me.*

That's because you are dating a RAT.
You may at first be impressed with
his love and concern for his kids. He
may even, in what he sees as a noble

THE DOS AND DON'TS OF DEALING WITH YOUR EX

- Do recognize the kind of ex you have. If you are among the lucky few with a devoted, energetic, appropriate, and reliable ex, count your blessings now.

- Don't let his negative energy dominate your life.

- Do minimize his power in your life by planning ahead and strategizing.

- Do resolve to come to terms with the jealousy, feelings of betrayal, anger, and rage that might have been the bag-gage from your marriage. These unre-solved feelings will only interfere with your happiness and the well-being of your children.

- Do make your children's well-being your highest priority at all times. Ask your ex if he would make a pact with you to the same effect.

gesture, blame himself for the dissolution of his marriage. He may say the
divorce was his idea, and because he
admits the marriage ended due to his
vague reasons of discontent, you may
think, "Hey, this guy's got his priorities
in order because the issues with the ex
are largely resolved." Hold on! As you
get to know him, you'll see something's
out of place. You'll hear more about his
ex than you care to know and may be
struck by the intricacies of the arrangements between them. For example,
they may still have their insurance policies for their cars tied together even if
they have been divorced for ten years.

He's aware of how much money she makes and where she spent her last vacation, and he may even be in a position to veto any home repairs or remodeling in her house.

Some RATs are free to come and go in their ex's home, or his ex may do his laundry or care for him when he's sick. Why? He probably feels guilty about the effects his leaving had on his kids. If his identity and self-esteem are tightly linked to his children, but he didn't want to stay married, then he is trying to maintain his role as father and head of the household.

As nice and devoted as the RAT appears, he's really a controlling kind of man who deals with his guilt by keeping his former home's activities close to his standards and expectations, maintaining a distorted kind of tie with his ex.

The ex-wife needs to set clear boundaries for this person—no comings and goings uninvited, no veto power in homemaking decisions. You need to have your expectations met, too, even if it is just getting him to a movie. If you can handle the relationship for what it's worth and enjoy him in the here and now, that's fine. But if what you want is a committed union, it would be better to look elsewhere.

MEET THE MAD (MINIMAL ACCESS DAD)

Besides the RAT, there are six other variations of exes, which fall under the category of the MAD (Minimal Access Dad). A MAD typically provides only the bare minimum, whether it is financial support, emotional giving, or both. For him his children are psychologically and physically in a convenient, safe niche far from the practical realities of his everyday life.

When a Rich MAD Makes You Mad

I recently visited a college friend who is the divorced single mother of two teenage boys. She is really struggling—financially, emotionally, and professionally. There is not a nickel to spare, and her family often does without much of what they want and need. Her former husband, a lawyer, has all the trappings of major success—big house, lavish vacations, expensive car, country club memberships, trophy wife. And my friend is the one who put him through law school! How can this man not give a damn and offer only the bare minimum of child support, knowing his children need winter clothes? I'm enraged!

There is more social injustice and unfairness in the world than we are sometimes able to face. This story is a sample of that injustice. However, without rage, social injustice continues, since rage is what powers social change. In spite of recognizing the low priority our society assigns to the welfare of children, it sounds as if you are trying to understand how this becomes an all-too-familiar family situation. And, of course, you would like to offer your friend some kind of practical help or advice.

This man can appear not to give a damn about his kids because he simply does not think about it at all. MADs are not even aware of, let alone troubled by, the fact that they are taking lavish vacations while their children

WHAT TO DO IF YOUR EX BAD-MOUTHS YOU TO YOUR KIDS

Why is he bad-mouthing you? Is he angry because you are building a new life, perhaps with a new and improved partner? Or is this just a continuation of patterns in your previous relationship? Whatever the case, rejoice that you are on your own. Perhaps his new bachelor life is not all that he imagined it would be. No matter what the reason, here's how to respond:

◆ If your children are under the age of eight and report, "Daddy says you are something bad," reply, "I am sorry to hear that Daddy feels that way."

◆ If your children are older, add, "I've noticed that people who bad-mouth other people usually feel bad about themselves. I am sorry your father is feeling this way."

◆ Employ nonemotional responses. Your children will lose interest in reporting these remarks to you. Dad may learn

that they did not mention his comments, and the bad-mouthing will lessen because he isn't getting any reinforcement.

◆ Never bad-mouth him back. If you blow your stack, your children will share this information with him when he asks and the dialog will continue.

◆ If he persists and the children are upset by his words, you can try speaking to him privately and let him know that his words do not hurt you, but do hurt the children very much.

◆ If he really has to get stuff off his chest, he can send you a letter, which you can burn without reading if you choose. (Just make sure you remove the enclosed support check first!) Allowing him to vent would be very generous of you, but it would certainly be understandable if you did not afford him this luxury.

may not, for example, have sufficient warm clothing. If this inequity is pointed out to them, they may grudgingly take some action, but typically they don't. MADs will be unable to do whatever it is that is begged, pleaded, screamed, or threatened of them to do.

How the MAD Plays the Game. MADs lack the essential emotional connection with their children. The identity and self-esteem of a MAD are simply not linked to the happiness and well-being of his children, but rather linked with other aspects of success in his life. This is why MADs can take

lavish vacations while their children may not have enough warm clothing. One thing simply has nothing to do with the other—because his children have nothing to do with his daily life.

Give Up Thinking It's Your Fault. Don't waste too much energy trying to understand why a MAD is a MAD. Conversion of a hard-core MAD, particularly by his ex-wife, is not realistic. Perhaps Dr. Seuss said it best when he described the Grinch: His heart is simply two sizes too small.

You can be a good friend by making sure that your girlfriend doesn't blame herself or harbor a sense of wrongdoing. Her first step should be to look back at her marriage with a sharp and realistic eye. Most likely, this now-obvious lack of emotional connection with the children is part of a long- standing pattern. It probably had a lot to do with why her relationship ended in the first place. Because, like many MADs, her former husband may insidiously communicate that she got what she deserved, she may believe that her current situation is the result of something she did or didn't do during the marriage. Not true. Sure, we all have to look back on our marriages and come to terms with our part in the difficulties that ended the relationship. But remember, the post-divorce life style is rarely, if ever, a fair judgment of what went on during the marriage.

When the Kids Are Mad at You

I think it is destructive to bad-mouth or even criticize a child's absent parent, but doesn't there come a time to sit my teenage sons down and tell them that the reason they can't play hockey, join the soccer team, or go away to summer camp is because their father supports them only minimally? It bothers me the way both boys complain about the run-down house and the lack of money to buy clothes, criticizing me while thinking their father is the best thing since sliced bread. But maybe if I wait it out, they will one day realize the truth.

Relentless bad-mouthing of the non-custodial or absent parent is harmful. However, you understandably have strong feelings of rage, anger, hurt, and disappointment. These feelings need to be expressed but not directed at your children.

Conversely, when we refuse to make any comment regarding the conduct of our former spouse, strong emotions are also at work. The opposite of bad-mouthing the other parent is denying our feelings, which is harmful to you. Many women do this because they fear that if they stated how they really felt, they would become totally out of control, a scary feeling for most of us. When we repress our anger, the result is often depression. And here's the catch-22: Depression makes us more vulnerable to the inequities MADs perpetuate. Depression also gives permission to your ex-husband to dish out as truth the idea that you are somehow to blame for your present circumstances.

Your children are clearly angry, but they are not exactly sure at what. Because you are their only emotional anchor, guess who hears it? The energy you expend repressing your feelings, coupled with the energy your boys spend complaining, could be put to better use by holding a family meeting and getting to the point regarding your financial situation. Forget the fantasy about some future magical moment of enlightenment when the kids recognize and praise you for your many years of silent sacrifice. Even if it did happen, nobody is comfortable around martyrs. Let them know that they are deserving, wonderful kids, and that they really have nothing to do with their father's neglectful behavior. This is just how it is.

Resolve to Forgive your Ex—For the Sake of your Child

I have raised my son alone for the past eleven years and have done a fine job according to teachers, doctors, and our minister. My husband ran off with someone else when I was pregnant and has rarely had any contact with me or his child. No birthday presents, no Christmas cards. Other than a couple of phone calls asking to speak to his son (I refused) and one hospital visit when Trey had surgery, he has really not shown any interest. Now he wants to see Trey more often and actually sent a very expensive Christmas present, which I have not even told my son about. What nerve to try to worm his way into our lives now! Where was he when the going got rough? Why on earth should I let this selfish bum give anything to my son now?

Why should you let this person give anything to your son? Because your child has a right to know his father—shortcomings and all.

You need to take responsibility for your bruised feelings about your ex before you can even discuss his father with your son. Whatever happened between you and this man has nothing to do with who your child is—rarely do people run off or get divorced specifically for the purpose of harming a youngster. What generally exists is a situation where a father cannot handle the responsibility of raising children, or suffers from such low self-esteem that he has very little to offer a family. Or maybe there is a drug or alcohol problem, or the irresponsible parent lacks coping skills. But whatever they can give—whether one phone call a year, or an expensive present every ten years—might be the only thing this person is capable of giving and should be recognized as the best they can do.

It sounds incredibly complicated and painful, separating your emotions from the current situation, but any good therapist will tell you that it is the only way to move on. After all, what's done is done. Why should your child be deprived of any information about the other parent because you still harbor angry feelings toward him? What's painful for you may not be unpleasant for your son. In fact, experts have been saying for years that some knowledge about the absent parent, good and bad, is more beneficial to a child than unanswered questions.

Want to know what resolution you can make to start the New Year off right? Try forgiving this person for his failings and inadequacies. This doesn't mean giving up the struggle for child support, if that is an issue, or anything else your child is entitled to, for that matter. It also doesn't mean letting this person into your child's life without establishing ground rules, or dismissing your own emotions toward your ex. It does mean, however, that you are willing to let your child form his own relationships with others without imposing your feelings on him. This is not the only relationship whose painful and joyous moments he will have to weather—life is a series of uncertainties, and people have a right to experience situations in their own personal way.

THE STRAFE BOMBER

Remember those old World War II black-and-white movies? The unsuspecting civilians would be going about their everyday life and suddenly, without warning, a squadron of bombers would swoop down from the sky.

Boom! The countryside was in flames and ruin. The civilians were left to rebuild while at the same time hardly knowing what had hit them or when these same attack bombers might return.

This sad scene pretty much describes life with the strafe-bomber ex. You go along doing the best you can for yourself and your kids, trying to hold everything together, and suddenly, without warning, he swoops in with a big noisy show, leaving nothing but emotional destruction in his wake.

A perfect example is the ex who rarely visits with the kids and is otherwise a good-time Charley. When you try to discuss things like homework, rules, and routines, he turns a deaf ear. He simply seems to take no interest, and when he does, his reactions are always dramatic and, of course, lack any kind of follow-up.

Strafe Bombers Are Deaf But Not Mute. Women with this type of ex learn to handle more on their own because they know that involving the ex only leads to headaches. One such woman reported that when her younger son was diagnosed with Attention Deficit Hyperactivity Disorder, her ex was the last person she turned to for help and advice.

Because her son was more distractible than most seven-year-old boys, his attention span, except for video games and TV, was short. He had trouble staying in his seat and listening to directions and suffered a disastrous kindergarten year. Through hard work and lots of reading, this mom became something of an expert on children with ADHD. She worked cooperatively and closely with her son's school to make sure first grade was a better experience for him. The teachers began to see the child in a whole new light, acknowledging his creative side and encouraging his willingness to learn to read. Everyone regarded this particular crisis to be at least under control.

Spending one weekend with his father, the child was accused of being a "space cadet" because he was unable to perform requested tasks. As you might guess, the ex accused this mother of not spending enough time with her son. One thing led to another, and she found herself discussing ADHD and all the reading she had done and all the meetings she had attended.

Strafe Bombers Don't Respond, They React. The strafe bomber only hears what he wants to hear and reacts immediately, inappropriately, and dramatically. In this case, the father decided he was going to the school the very next morning to "have a serious talk with the teachers and straighten this thing out." He arrived at school like a bull in a china shop, intimidating, criticizing, and belittling all involved, and managed to undo at least some of the work the mom and school staff had done to get the child on track.

The strafe bomber will position himself by declaring, "I am the father," as if that gives him the power to attack.

The Shelling Can Happen Anytime, Anywhere. The bombing can happen any day or every day. The strafe-bomber ex may be one of those guys who still feels that the marital residence, now occupied by you and the kids, is still his house. The "bomber attacks" may simply be his frequent unannounced visits when he takes the opportunity to make some comment or criticism that leaves everyone present just a little less—less happy, less content, less at peace— than before he arrived.

Strafe-bomber exes have short, selective memories coupled with the need to make grand entrances. Even if he is well-off, when asked for financial help such as for college expenses he might reply that he is tapped out. No matter how many jobs you or your kids have, or how many loans you've taken out, watch what happens when graduation day joyfully arrives. The strafe bomber will show up big as life with a video camera and proceed to document the whole event as if it were his idea and responsibility from start to finish.

Damage Control for the Strafe Bomber. There are ways to control the damage caused by the strafe-bomber ex. Above all else, set boundaries and edit the information and access given to the strafe-bomber ex carefully. Your children will need more careful instruction and guidance regarding what is appropriate behavior and what is not. For example, in the case of the bombing caused by the ex when he showed up at his child's school, mom should be prepared to explain this to her son. "It was inappropriate for your father to come to school after never having come to any other school event and begin yelling at the teachers. It hurt your teachers' feelings and embarrassed me. A better way would have been for him to come to conferences all along and listen carefully to all the ideas everyone had." Your children will need you to set a good example of the value and importance of day-to-day consistency and the true meaning of commitment.

THE "BACK-FROM-THE-DEAD" EX

Similar to the strafe bomber, the back-from-the-deads suddenly arrive and decide they want to be part of things. Often their sudden arrival corresponds with your legal demands for child support. These men will sometimes go so far as to try to sue for custody—a real explosion. The difference between a strafe bomber and a back-from-the-dead is that there was always a slight hum in the distance from the strafe bomber, making you aware that he was still alive.

But you won't have heard a single word from this other type of ex for several years. Then you begin to grow tired of shouldering all the expenses yourself and maybe take advantage of the improved laws on child support enforcement and locate him. This kind of ex might want to be back in his child's life not only because he is paying support, but also because his son or daughter might be at "more of a fun age" than when you all lived together. He might even try to persuade your kids to move in with him.

The common thread that binds bombers and deads is the lack of emotional maturity needed to be a productive, contributing, consistent presence in the lives of their children. These men see their "bombing runs" as proof positive that they are good fathers, when actually these runs are their attempt to atone for their lack of consistent involvement with their children. Their typical reaction is to blame you. When pressed about their lack of involvement with their children, typically they will say that their ex-wives kept the children from them. In the companionship of their children, they seek to meet their own emotional needs. They may even describe their children as their best friends. For an older child, the reappearance of Dad and the opportunity to live with Dad and to have a fresh start in a different part of the country can be very enticing.

THE COWBOY

The cowboy really isn't such a bad guy, he just needs to ride into the sunset every now and then to find himself. Cowboys need room. They need space. They need a change. Like the back-from-the-deads, these are men your children barely hear from for years at a stretch. But when they return, they are all glitter and glamour, electric horsemen with stories to share about adventures on the long and lonely road. The bad news, however, is that every time they show up, there is the hope and expectation that somehow things will be different. Kids think that maybe this time their father will stay. When children are much older, they will understand the pattern and with support and reassurance will see that it is the limitations of their dad, and not anything they have done, that has caused Dad to pursue the great unknown.

These guys aren't purposely harmful unless their mystique seems to attract your kids to the point of running off with a rodeo. But even then, things usually turn out okay, amounting to nothing more than the kids, like the ex, watching too many Clint Eastwood movies. However, to avoid stepping in his cow patties, stress to your kids that his stay is temporary. Saying, "Daddy is just visiting" helps reduce the fantasy that maybe this time it is forever. When their father promises things like a fishing trip or a chance to visit him in his own home on the range, share the children's excitement by affirming that it would be wonderful if they could visit Dad where he lives. But when he gallops off, be ready to give your children an extra measure of love and reassurance.

If your ex has any kind of permanent address, older children should certainly be encouraged to write to him. You could also create a daddy box where things they would like to show Daddy are stored until the next time he moseys into town. In fact, the daddy box is a terrific idea for any kids who have some variation of the Minimal Access Dad.

WHEN HIS FAMILY BECOMES THE ONLY FAMILY

I am a 39-year-old mother of two. Immediately following the divorce, my husband disappeared for parts unknown. Although we hear from him occasionally and sometimes he even sends child support and a rare birthday gift, he basically has a noncommittal relationship with his kids. Would you believe he's discovered parenting since remarrying and becoming the doting stepfather of four-year-old twins? On top of this, his new wife (who was pregnant when they married) recently had a baby, and they are both utterly delighted. Our children seemed to take the discovery of their father's new-found interest in parenting in stride and even think it is kind of neat to have a little stepbrother. I am so angry I can't describe it.

It's justifiable to feel anger for an ex who had so inadequately provided for his children and involved himself so little in their lives and now seems so committed to this new set of children.

Most likely, this new development made it necessary for you to think back on why you and your husband divorced in the first place. In situations like these, many women find that at the time of their marriage their husbands were emotionally impoverished and immature men. They had few emotional resources left after always placing themselves and their needs first.

Maybe, life for your ex had been a progressive lesson in learning how to love. Men like this have been dumped more than once by women unwilling to put up with immature and selfish

behavior. One day, the light dawns on them that they have to make some changes or remain alone.

Your ex needed intensive and ongoing tutoring and his new wife is apparently willing to be his teacher. You, and maybe others, either have been unwilling to be his teachers or are simply burned out trying to teach the unteachable.

Your children are able to accept their father's situation for what it is because you have provided them with the emotional strength to accept his limitations.

Dealing With Things as They Now Are. When a former partner remarries or becomes involved with a new partner as an energetic parent to his new children or stepchildren, it is painful. The pain is greatly magnified when his care and concern for the children you share has been less than adequate. Remember that things are not always as they seem. Some men want you to think that they have become standout dads as a way to hurt or further reject you. They can do little to you directly but can still hurt you through the children. Demonstrating love and concern for a new set of children often brings the emotional pain and expressions of outrage these men want.

What's Ideal for Her Is Not for You. Some men have been transformed into the picture of paternal involvement by women equally willing to parent them as if they were their children. This guy may show up if asked and baby-sit if directed, but the real feelings of attachment and commitment are just as absent for the new set of children as they are for yours. His new wife or partner is simply more willing to put effort into creating the ideal picture than you were.

Maybe It's a Miracle. Some men do change, evolving slowly into the kind of man we hoped they would be when we married them. If this miracle has actually occurred, it probably took many years and a lot of hard knocks. It is unlikely that if you had stayed with him he would have changed in the same way. You are certainly different than you might have been had you stayed married. The same thing has happened to him.

Accept the Changes. Things are different now. He has changed, his circumstances have changed, and his experiences have made him different. You know that you are different and in many ways better. Accept this change in him. Release the anger and resentment so you can continue to move ahead by telling yourself in the form of an affirmation that his "improvement" is a wonderful gift to you and your children. This improvement allows you to feel better about having your children away from you, leaving you to pursue your own interests without worry or guilt. Tell yourself, "His growth is my gain."

Allow your children to be involved with their father and his new life. Make good use of this unexpected break from daily child-care responsibilities to relax.

THE UNDER-DOG (UNDER DARLING'S ORDERS TO GROVEL)

When a former husband commits to a new relationship with someone else, you may find the shaky alliance you previously forged as coparents greatly changed. This new wife or girlfriend is clearly calling the shots. The child support checks now bear her signature and arrive late. There is clearly no room to negotiate for one penny more, no matter what unexpected circumstances arise. When your ex calls you from the office or workplace, he is talkative and interested in hearing about the children. But calls made or received from his new home are abrupt. You always get the feeling that you or the children have called at the wrong time.

This Puppy Was Never Weaned. Your children's visits to Dad become crises. Your daughter announces that Dad's new wife says that you are fat or a slob or sucking Dad dry. Your son may tell you that Dad is not allowed to do certain things anymore, like have a beer before dinner or see some of his old friends. She yells at your children frequently. You wonder why she does not take the weekend off and visit a girlfriend instead of spending time with children who so clearly annoy her. The change in your former husband's behavior is hard to understand. He seems to have turned into kind of a sissy.

Look beneath the hurt and this is what you find. Your former husband has been looking for and found what he needed—a mother. He is not able to function in a relationship as an equal partner. He wants to be taken care of, and these needs are so strong that he is willing to sacrifice his relationship with his children in order to get the care he needs.

The Controller and Under-DOG Are Sickly Compatible. The new woman is the type of person who feels adequate only when she is part of a couple. She is controlling and insecure. She does hate having your children visit, but she could never go off and visit girlfriends. She has to be there so she can continue to be in control. She is insecure in his love and feels jealous and resentful of his attachments to his children and his past relationship with you. She sees you as a constant threat no matter what the reality of your feelings are.

This is a tough situation. The more you try to intervene, the more controlling she will be and the more hostile he will be. By trying to keep things on an even keel for your children, you are interfering with their disturbed little dance. Try to stop the music and you will know how deeply enmeshed they are. He mistakes her control for the love he never got from Mom. She wants to edit out his children so that she can have him all to herself. There is no maturity or stability here. Attempts to change either one will not meet with success.

You're Equipped to Play by Her Rules. Try to play by the new rules while still keeping your children and yourself relatively sane. If you are able to call him at work, do so. Try to keep your children's visits to him short, with activities planned. Talk to your children about how Dad's new wife may react to what are pretty typical behaviors for their age. Make sure they bring lots of "quiet-time" activities, like games and puzzle books. Do not overreact to the comments made about you, which your children will dutifully report to you. If she could see you laugh off her rude insults, it would make her nuts. That fact alone should give you strength. Show your children how mature adults behave. The lesson will not be lost on them. It will comfort them to know that she does not have all that much power over you.

Do not dignify her name calling or petty remarks by responding to them. Calling her names and making snide remarks about her in front of the children will not help. If you feel comfort-

able having your former husband in your home, see if he will visit the children there. She may be more at ease knowing you are not there during his visits, so use this free time to pursue your own interests and activities. Resist the urge to share your insights about how screwed up this relationship is. Nothing will be improved for you or your children by telling your former husband that he is a mamma's boy or acting like a sissy. Be glad that while the music plays and they dance their little dance, you are conducting your own orchestra.

RUN!
(REALLY UGLY NEWS)

Members of this group include active alcoholics, the substance addicted, bigamists, con artists, men serving repeat jail time, and men who disappear for several years at a time without a trace. Your children may see these men only once every several years or may see them often but never for the right reasons. These men may never be sober or capable of recognizing any degree of responsibility toward their children. They can be counted on for nothing.

Contacts with these men almost always bring great emotional pain. There is always the hope that this time things will be different, but somehow things never are. See and accept the truth. Failure to accept the truth will cause your children's hopes to be continually dashed, making it hard for them to trust other people. Help your children to separate what he is from what they are and are capable of becoming. Explain their apparent abandonment in terms of the father's inadequacies or addictions, not theirs. Say, "Your father is not able to care for you because he is always breaking the law and ends up spending a lot of time in jail." Or, "He has a problem with drugs that makes him very sick. This is why he is not able to help to take care of you." Be vigilant about establishing healthy habits at home, particularly if the problem is drugs or alcohol. Consistent, predictable routines are especially critical for your children. Know that your children may continue to have a need to keep contact with him. Do not be threatened by this need. Their feelings are no more than simple curiosity.

WHEN YOUR EX'S BEHAVIOR WITH THE KIDS IS UPSETTING

My ex-husband infuriates me. He takes the kids once or twice a month, but he's always late picking them up. (I think he does this just so I can't plan my weekend.) He usually shows up with one of his idiotic chain-smoking friends, knowing that the little one has allergies. He forgets to make the children put on their seatbelts, and when I insist that they wear seatbelts or he can't leave with them, he mutters and grumbles with a cigarette sticking out of his mouth while adjusting and tightening the kids' belts. Then he takes off like a bat out of hell while I'm handing him their medicine or other essentials. To make matters worse, I'm convinced he parties and takes drugs while the kids are at his apartment. I can't believe he's taking good care of them. He's fairly regular with child support payments so I can't withhold visitation, but sometimes I swear I could kill him right on the spot! Any ideas?

It would be surprising if this obnoxious behavior were not the main reason you two are no longer together. But then again, this might be his coping mechanism for dealing with the divorce.

There are some steps you can take to deal amicably with your ex. The key is to establish a groundwork of communication. Let him know that you will give him a chance to speak while you listen, and that you would like him to listen to you when it is your turn to talk. Many successful negotiators are firm believers in setting time limits. Kitchen timers are ideal for this purpose and also are great for disciplining kids. Allow five to ten minutes for him to explain the weekend schedule. When the buzzer goes off, it's your turn. If you have trouble and it turns into a yelling match, you might consider a neutral third party to help mediate.

When your ex comes to pick up the kids, see that they are not waiting outside so he can just pile them in the car and peel out of there in a flash. Invite him in for a cup of coffee or soft drink (no alcohol) and tell him, very politely, that you need to go over a few things with him regarding his plans for the weekend. Allow him to speak and then say your piece, requesting that no drinking or drugging is to take place while the children are in his custody. Also explain that the law in most states requires children to wear seatbelts. Remember to let him know that you would like it if you could cooperate with each other. Above all, stay calm, and don't let him push your buttons. As difficult as this appears, try to be pleasant, since this might help prevent his walls from coming up, blocking out any communication you might need to share with him for his information and for your own peace of mind.

IF YOUR EX POSES A THREAT TO YOUR CHILDREN

If you're convinced that his behavior is a danger to your children, you will need witnesses or proof of his neglect to present to the court. Are the children injured or sick when they return home? Do you know for a fact that he abuses dangerous substances?

If a complaint is brought before a judge, the court most likely will issue a warning, which might be enough to make your ex take notice of your concern and, more importantly, of your children's activities. The next step would probably be supervised visitation, rather than total revocation. If the court, however, is eventually convinced that the children's lives are in constant danger, revocation would be in order.

KEEPING YOUR CHILDREN SAFE

◆ Seek an attorney's advice immediately if you believe your ex is putting your children's lives in danger. Or have a friend of the court, child advocate, volunteer at a battered women's shelter, or even a police officer advise you on how to get a court order barring this person from you and your children.

◆ Don't let your children ride in a car with an ex who has been drinking or taking drugs. If your ex is impaired and insists on taking your child in his car with him, don't upset him. Call the police or 911 immediately, explain the situation, and give the police all the details, such as the license plate number and the direction he was heading. In a 1994 case, a woman was convicted of homicide because she "allowed" her drunken ex to take her daughters with him in his vehicle. He had an accident, and he and the two girls were killed. Protect your children and yourself!

◆ If your ex has been unsafe to be around but is in some kind of treatment program, investigate the safe visitation havens that some cities offer. These are supervised facilities where a parent and his children can meet on neutral territory, thereby sticking to a visitation agreement. Check with your local department of social services or county health department.

◆ Don't negotiate anything with your ex directly if he is unsafe. Have a mediator, law enforcement officer, attorney, or magistrate or court official handle any dealings. Have this person express either verbally or through your written communication that you don't want to hurt your ex or deprive him of his children, but you feel that at the present time it would be unsafe to let your children be around him. Let him know that as progress is made, you will agree to modifying the visitation order.

21

Dealing with Your Ex-relations

HOW TO MAINTAIN A RELATIONSHIP FOR YOUR CHILD'S SAKE

Your former spouse's or partner's family may previously have been so involved with you and your children that you considered them your family, too. If you've established a relationship with members of his family, maybe his mother or a favorite sister, and you've managed to maintain this connection, you have made great strides not only for yourself but for your children. The connection to a group of people who were previously linked to their lives can be tremendously therapeutic for the children whose parents are undergoing a breakup.

For the majority of estranged couples, however, the separation also brings with it a parting of the ways of other family members. After the breakup, you may notice a sudden change. Where once you and your ex's sister yakked on the phone for hours, shopped together, and complained about the male species with a secret camaraderie, you now find that you are being snubbed, overlooked, or worse, even made the target for attacks and complaints. And of course, this will affect you because these rejections come at a time when you are most vulnerable and are in need of friends and family support more than ever before.

FIGHTING REJECTION

It certainly would be understandable for you to want to defend yourself or at least show your disappointment at being rebuffed by people who were once so close to you and your children.

But women who have been through this strongly advise against it. The reason? Even though these people may no longer be a part of your life, your child still has a right to remain connected to them. Of course, if they choose to disappear totally, you can't force them to remain family to your child. But you can try to arrange time to discuss this issue and let these individuals know how you feel about their keeping contact with your children. Why not send a letter expressing your hope that a relationship with your children be maintained? Your willingness to help should be expressed, as well as how you feel this arrangement would be beneficial both to your children and to the members of your ex's family. A letter makes it impossible for you to be misquoted or misunderstood or for you to say things in the heat of the moment that you might later regret. You may also want to show your children the letter you are sending, or you may wish to keep a copy of the letter to share with younger children at a later time.

HOW TO DEAL WITH FORMER FAMILY MEMBERS

If your desire is to help your children be able to trust other adults and count on them despite any change in the makeup of the family structure, then you not only deserve to feel proud and capable, but you might be able to teach these other adults a thing or two.

Here are some tips to help you face your ex's family with pride, self-respect, and an assertive yet friendly demeanor.

- Mentally go over who you are most likely to run into from your ex's family and what it is about them that causes you to experience anxiety or fear. Try not to let their opinions of you affect your opinion of yourself.

- Try to be as physically presentable as possible. This doesn't mean going out and having your hair done or investing in a new wardrobe, it simply means looking pleasant enough so you won't overly concern yourself about your looks and what they will think.

- Review what it is you want from these people. If you feel like a motherless child because you have no family of your own, then you may need to develop an extended family apart from these people. Additionally, if you are dependent on these folks, this will only perpetuate your falling prey to their verbal attacks or faultfinding. But if you want these people to remain in your child's life because it would benefit your family, let them know.

- Rehearse what you would like to say to them. Your ex's father may have taught your son how to bait a hook or use a grass trimmer. Let him know how important you felt his contributions were by saying, "It would really mean a lot to Kevin if you would continue to take him fishing every now and then. Regardless of how you feel about what happened between me and your son, your grandson loves you and would miss you if he couldn't see you." Be aware, too, that even if some of your former family members are receptive

THE DOS AND DON'TS OF DEALING WITH YOUR EX'S FAMILY

- Do keep in mind that divorce or the end of a relationship will affect your relationship with members of your ex's extended family.

- Don't discuss the personal aspects of your relationship with your ex with his family, unless you have a particularly strong relationship with a family member that would endure whether or not you knew your ex.

- Do remember that your children's lives will only be made richer by keeping ties with your former partner's family.

- Do remember that a family is simply people who support and love one another. Feel free to create your own family of choice.

- Do try to put yourself in the place of your children's stepmom and ex's new girl-friend. It is not always an easy place to be. Don't waste precious energy thinking about how much you hate her. Get over it.

- Don't forget that you are the number one adult in your child's life. Do not feel crowded out by new stepmothers or girl-friends. Do not use these relationships as an excuse to give your child less than one hundred percent of you.

- Do try to avoid fighting, blaming, and confrontations with the ex-in-laws. Remember that those in traditional marriages such as your ex's parents' may still hold the notion that something they did wrong is to blame for your marriage dissolving. Be aware that they just may not know how to behave.

to the idea of continuing their relationship with your child, you may be the one to have to initiate the visits, the phone calls, and the discussions. However, if their responses are more of a noncommitment, it would be better to spend your energy trying to create an extended family of your choice.

- If a family member seems receptive to continuing a relationship with your child, by all means invite her to join you at a family celebration or outing. Explain again your desire to have the relationship continue and express your willingness to do the driving or whatever legwork is necessary to make it easier for your child and this special adult to remain close. Sometimes the adult is not quite grown-up enough for this. In these cases, you need to explain this loss to your child so that he understands that the adult was unable to continue the relationship and that it was not because of anything your child has or has not done.

WHEN GRANDMA WAS YOUR NUMBER-ONE SITTER

If your former partner's or husband's mother baby-sat fairly regularly, let her know that you would love for her to continue to do so. Explain that although she might have offered her services because she wanted to see her son get some free time, and you can understand her resentment in doing something extra for you, the benefit would really be for her and her grandchild. It would enable them to maintain their relationship in spite of what transpired between you and her son. She may not realize that her feelings toward you, should she choose to handle them by ignoring you, could be upsetting to your child. Moreover, the longer she stays away from her grandchild, the greater the sense of loss will be for your child.

If, however, your former mother-in-law seems unable to control her feelings of anger, resentment, or bitterness toward you and cannot keep these feelings separate from her relationship with your child, then you may need to rethink this arrangement of letting her see the children without you. If it is likely that she will speak poorly of you to the children, serve as your ex's secret agent, or be unsupportive while you and the children forge a new life, it may be best, for the time being, to include her instead on a family picnic, a trip to the beach, or a day in the park.

FACING AUNTS, UNCLES, COUSINS, AND OTHERS

Other family members on your ex's side may feel similarly. For example, suppose your ex came from a long line of "forever married," or grew up enmeshed in a family unit consisting of aunts, uncles, cousins, nieces, nephews, and other distant relatives. Maybe they resembled the 1950s type

of traditional family, and they think theirs is the only "normal" one. Although divorce may occur in this group, when it does, there seems to be a deep sense of disappointment and failure. But who shoulders the responsibility? Often in families of this structure, there is a sense that if a member's marriage dissolved, something went wrong in the system. But blaming the outsider, the person who married into the family, is one way they can remove themselves from any responsibility for the divorce. Additionally, divorce may unnerve some of these family members because it forces them, however briefly, to look at their own lives honestly.

If You're Bound to Run into Them. Even if you find it easier to simply stay out of their faces and keep them out of your lives, chances are there will come a time when you are all thrust together—during visitations or school functions, because of health-related matters, or simply because you all live in close proximity to one another. If you are suffering guilt feelings over the ending of your relationship to your child's father, you may not be comfortable facing any of these people—at least, not any time soon. But try to remember that regardless of the circumstances surrounding the breakup of this relationship, you are not an evil person or the sole destroyer of men as they may have you believing. In fact, accepting full blame for this split shows that you are shouldering responsibility far and above the call of duty.

HOLIDAYS AND CELEBRATIONS

Holidays like Christmas or Chanukah, and how and with whom they will be spent, are typically part of the divorce agreement. Again, the spirit of the occasions should prevail. It is hardly appropriate to use the spirit of the holiday season as an opportunity to keep your children from people whom they have grown to love. Remember that what you give to your children with respect to generosity and empathy toward others will be returned to you many times over.

Occasions like graduations and weddings mean a gathering of family—from both sides. And it's special functions like these that separate the grown-ups from the not-so-grown-up. In other words, even though the graduation ceremony or the wedding preparations should belong to the scholar or the bride and groom, their wishes regarding who is invited and who sits where are commonly challenged by the relatives displaying some level of immaturity. If your ex's mother threatens not to show up if you do, don't fall prey to this nonsense. True, you don't want to hurt any-one, but if you are invited, and you feel like going, go. Have a good time.

Who Pays for What? As far as footing the bill for these occasions goes, there are no hard and fast rules. Issues such as who pays for what should be discussed well in advance of the occasion and everything written down so there is no room for misunderstanding. Many fathers who did little in the child support arena do like the show of being the father of the bride. Accept this as further proof of his limitations and enjoy the party.

WHEN YOUR CHILD'S FATHER'S FAMILY REMAINS A MYSTERY

Suppose you recently exited a relationship with a mate or husband whose family you would barely recognize if they came to your front door. If no family members are available to your child, that's okay if that's the way it is. After all, this isn't such an obvious loss as, for example, having a cousin your child's age with whom your child spent many hours and then that cousin is never heard from again.

If you do have any information on your ex's family, you might want to share this with your son or daughter. Let's say your ex has fathered other children that you know of, or he himself is a grandparent. Furnish your child with a photograph, if possible, explaining that, "Although we may never get to meet Kimberly, she actually is a half-sister to you." Or you may have a trinket or something your

HOW TO HELP YOUR KIDS' NEW STEPMOTHER

Regardless of how you feel about this person, it's important to recognize that when you help her, you help your kids. Here are some ways:

- When her new partner (your ex) has his daughter every other weekend, they may wind up clashing even if they got along great when she and Dad were dating. Instead of gloating and telling yourself, "I wouldn't want my daughter around that person anyway," tell yourself that as long as your ex has visitation rights and as long as he is involved with her, your child most likely will be a part of her life, too.

- Don't tell your ex what a worthless parent and person his new girlfriend or wife is if the kids complain that she doesn't do anything right. Chances are, he still won't appreciate you any more for all that you have done.

- Be aware that kids tend to harbor a lot of guilt about trying to be nice to a new stepparent because they think it means taking away love from the biological or custodial one. Don't add to their guilt. By promoting a positive relationship between your children and the ex, you are setting an example that the more love you have to share, the more you can produce.

- Don't refer to her as the wicked stepmother. This gives permission for her and the children to give you a not-so-flattering title, too. Put an end to the name calling.

- Avoid setting her up for failure. For example, if she is the manager of a seasonal store that gets busiest around the holidays, don't expect her to take the kids on Christmas Eve.

- Let her know that she needn't take your kids' behavior to heart too much when they are giving her a rough time. Explain that this is their way of expressing their loss and that they want to be sure they don't lose their dad to her.

- Try letting their dad know what is going on and suggest that he ask the kids straightforward questions like, "Do you feel disloyal to Mom?" or "Do you feel bad that your mom and I aren't together or resent having to share me?" Once these feelings are identified, both of you can assuage the kids' fears. You can help by allowing them one-on-one time with their dad and reassuring the new stepmom that eventually she and the children will form some kind of relationship. Tell her to try to set reasonable limits on their behavior and, above all, try to be patient.

ex gave to you that belonged to one of his family members. Mention that "this bracelet is something your Aunt Meagan wore when she was young. I don't know much about her, but this sure is a pretty bracelet." Giving your child a sense of connection to others is enough to allow him or her to feel like a member of a very large family indeed.

RELATING TO YOUR EX'S NEW SIGNIFICANT OTHER

At the other extreme from the stories you hear about ex-wives and new girlfriends dealing with one another like a pair of mud-wrestlers are the tales of the new wife and the discarded one becoming buddies and even confidantes. You've heard them. Especially the one where the two women start to console each other on what a rotten choice of mate he was to begin with, and why didn't they think they deserved better than this. So they both dump him for good and start hanging out together, only to start fighting over a new man.

Is there any middle ground for accepting the new partner of your former partner, even including her in your world and your child's, without borrowing each other's underwear? You bet.

Looking at How She Might Feel. First, consider what a thankless job— even if only on weekends and other occasions—a stepmother's role must be. She might hear nothing other than, "Mom only does it this way," or "Our mom would never put cinnamon on those," or "Our real mom would know the answer to that question." It's enough to make her want to pack her bags and head toward the nearest retirement home.

Okay, so you're having a little chuckle to yourself, and deservedly so, knowing that you've wished to get even with this man-stealer for years. But never let this reach your kids' ears. They need to know that they are safe and sound when in her care and that she is going to be a part of their lives as long as their dad is involved with her. The best thing is to forgive, let go, and move on. Any energy expended on hating her is wasted.

If She Is a Danger to Your Children. Clearly if she is physically or mentally abusive to the kids, don't just sit around. In this case, you need legal advice to change the visitation agreements, or if you suspect harm, to take immediate legal action. But if she is like the majority of stepmoms, trying to be civil to the kids, try to work with her, at least to the extent of communicating important information on behalf of the kids. If, for example, your child wins an award for a project he accomplished while staying with her and your ex, why not invite her along with Dad to congratulate the child and to witness the award ceremony?

When the New Girlfriend Is a Barrier Between Your Child and Your Ex

I am the single mother of a wonderful seven-year-old daughter. Her father lives out of state, so she does not get to see him as much as she did when he lived down the street. When he changed jobs and acquired a new girlfriend, he decided to move. Every few weeks, when my daughter tries to call him, her father tells her rudely not to call him because these calls upset his girlfriend. How do I ease this hurt and explain to her not to call him anymore? My daughter is such a sweet, loving child, and it angers me to have him be rude to her.

Maybe the best thing for now is to explain to your daughter that at least temporarily she should not try to talk to her father on the telephone. It's obviously not such a good idea. Every time she attempts to call him, she is met with rudeness, so why allow this scene to be repeated over and over again? Not because these calls upset his girlfriend, but rather because they hurt your daughter.

The best way to explain to a seven-year-old girl that her father has chosen to be more concerned with his girlfriend's feelings than with her own is by stressing that this situation is the result of what her father is unable to do. In other words, it isn't that your daughter is less loved or less important than the girlfriend. On the contrary, he is probably not able to explain to his girlfriend or even understand himself why he is having confused feelings right now with all that is happening in his life—his new job, new relationship, and a move. Emphasize to your daughter that "even grown-ups sometimes feel angry, ashamed, mad, and sad all at the same time. And although none of his feelings have anything to do with you, maybe talking to you makes him miss you that much more. You are a wonderful child and, in the best way he can, your father loves you." You can't repeat this last sentence too often.

Your daughter should maintain contact with her father. Perhaps the best way for the time being is for you to contact him by telephone at work, since you know he cannot handle calls like this at home, or to write him a note. Because your daughter is too young to be caught in the middle of all of this, you need to accept responsibil-

ity. Let him know that his daughter wants to stay in touch with him and ask how he would like this to happen. But be careful not to place blame, even though you think his girlfriend is behaving like a total idiot. By maintaining a matter-of-fact approach, you have a better chance of success.

If the girlfriend remains threatened by his occasional contact with his daughter, then perhaps the phone calls could be replaced by letters or cards sent to work or even to a post office box he rents for this purpose. If, however, he states that he wants no contact with his daughter, either written or verbal, have your daughter keep writing, but save these notes and other special things in a box labeled "For Daddy Later On." The most important thing is that you allow your daughter to have some way to keep a relationship with her father even if he doesn't respond. Assure her that his behavior is the result of his own limitations and has nothing to do with what a sweet, wonderful child she truly is.

SHARING DISCIPLINE WITH STEPPARENTS

When my kids spend time at their father's place, his new wife's kids complain constantly about how they hate the visits. I thought they were just jealous, but their mom says that my children run around like maniacs, get special treatment, and never have to pick up a scrap of paper, toy, or item of clothing. In fact, they don't have to do anything, she says, and wonders if they behave this way at home. I don't buy this, but I'm still not sure what to do.

First, buy it. Most likely, this situation, common to new stepfamilies adjusting to a new routine, is exacerbated by your ex not enforcing house rules and his new wife not feeling comfortable enough to discipline effectively. In fact, some say it can take up to two years for a stepparent to feel comfortable about sharing discipline (never, ever physical) and even to receive respect from the children.

It's not your house, so it is up to the two of them to establish rules. Your ex needs to determine if he is indulging his children's every whim and letting them rule the roost because of guilt feelings he has regarding the divorce. Maybe he can come to grips with this by spending more one-on-one time with the kids. Even though it is also up to the adults of that household to spell out what happens when rules aren't obeyed—for example, loss of TV privileges—you can still talk to your kids and explain that this is not how you taught them to behave in other people's homes. Just because the home belongs to dad mean they have license to behave as if no one else who lives there matters. Make it clear to them that you don't want to hear any more unpleasant reports about their behavior.

IF YOUR EX IS REMARRYING

Attendance at your ex's wedding should be optional for the kids because this may be a rough time for them. Hopefully, the ceremony will be low key and tasteful. However, if this is a first-time marriage for the bride, it can be a full-fledged affair just like the one you and he may have had. Good taste and sensitivity dictate that:

♦ Children do not serve as maids of honor or best men (this is what adult friends are for).

♦ Boys are not expected to propose toasts or be ushers.

♦ You should avoid having your daughter or son be the flower girl or ring bearer if you think this may give them the opportunity to "act out" any negative feelings they might have. (One woman reported that her little girl urinated all over the floor just as the wedding march began.) If your children have gotten through their anger or seem to be handling this well, you may consider letting them have roles in the ceremony.

- The best roles for your children are as honored guests, with particular attention paid to making the event as comfortable as possible. Some dads make incredible issues out of their kids attending and participating because in this way the dads reassure themselves that "we are just one big happy family." You both need to respect your children's feelings.

YOU'RE STILL THE MOM

Don't worry, you are not being replaced. To children, a new stepmother often is considered an additional person in their lives, and not a substitute mom. As long you remain involved with your child, that relationship won't change. However, the danger lies when you worry that this new person will have influence over your kids, and will probably replace you, so why bother being a parent anyway? Don't withdraw from your child's life! Doing so will actually be setting your children up to turn to the stepparent for the concern and love that you seem to have suddenly withdrawn. Maintain the same physical and emotional involvement in your child's life you've always had.

22

Sex and Dating

REENTERING THE WORLD OF ROMANCE

It is a very wise woman indeed who is able to recognize the difference between wanting a relationship and needing physical companionship. For years, leading sociologists and anthropologists have known that physical closeness is a need, not unlike eating, sleeping, and exercise—perhaps not as urgent in the short term, but necessary for physical and emotional well-being. However, through miseducation, religious dogma, and the media, our popular culture has us convinced that sex and love are synonymous, a myth most Americans cling to. One problem with this belief is that it pressures people into entering relationships that may be wrong for them simply because they need to justify the sexual aspects of the relationship. For example, people all too often marry sex partners with whom they have nothing else in common in order to validate the union as something more significant than it is. It is okay to pine for physical closeness occasionally as long as you don't mistake sexual desires for true love. Loneliness that stems from being in an unfulfilled relationship is far worse.

HOW TO FEEL LESS LONELY

There are subtle yet recognizable signs in a person who is feeling unfulfilled. Because at certain times healthy humans need fulfillment emotionally, spiritually, intellectually, and physically, we mistake a lack in one of these areas for general loneliness and tend to fall in a slump. Many of us were taught that this feeling means we need to find romance.

But this doesn't mean that you should run out and find a lover immediately. On the contrary, you need to find out what you can do for yourself to instill that sense of balance most of us feel when those four needs are being met. In fact, the best time to seek out a relationship with the potential of becoming partnered is when you are feeling fulfilled and have a lot to share and offer another, not when you are feeling empty.

Humans who are creative and empathetic and indulge in a love affair with themselves often state that although they experience times of true solitude, they do not necessarily feel lonely. This doesn't mean avoiding friendships and even romantic encounters with men, especially if you have been living alone for a while or have been through a series of dead-end relationships. It means engaging yourself physically, spiritually, and intellectually, in order to be ready for the emotional challenge of entering a relationship.

OBSERVE YOUR SEXUAL FEELINGS

Pay close attention to your sexual feelings. When you feel anxious, lonely, or bored, could you be just plain horny? Sometimes when people are under chronic stress, nagging physical needs can seem so overwhelming that many feel the lack of a sexual partner more strongly than usual, leaving them with a sense of utter loneliness. Women ask themselves, "How can I have sex?—I don't even have a boyfriend!" Yet sexual activity may be just the prescription because, as scientists have pointed out, sex is a great stress-buster. Masturbation may be frequent at times like these, which is perfectly normal. Or you may have a friend with whom you indulge in sexual play, and this is okay, too, provided that you use precautions against disease and unwanted pregnancy. After all, you're single, not dead. Equally important as asking yourself if it's physical satisfaction that you're missing, you also need to investigate whether you receive enough emotional support. If you find that you are lonely and need nurturing, see if you have enough loving friends, family, and peers in your life to give you support, empathy, unconditional caring, and acceptance. At certain times, a hug or back rub, a touch of the hand, or a nod of the head is more beneficial than what a sex partner can give.

FIND A CREATIVE OUTLET

Ask yourself, "Have I been creative lately?" You may be surprised to learn that many cultures believe that sexual energy and the creative process stem from the same center of the body. In all the latest books that explore the duality of women's nature—the civilized persona and the wild woman within—the wild woman has been revealed to be a passionate artist who needs to express her creativity. Because she demands expression, and because time constraints— "I don't have time because of my kids ... my job ... my dirty house"—often are used as an excuse to avoid painting, writing, dancing, making music, and re-creating nature, the woman within often confuses her passion for creating with romantic passion, or, bluntly put, horniness. Because these feelings stem from the same center of our being that produces the urge to create, including the urge to reproduce, women need to recognize the difference between their sexual desires and the need to create something from within themselves.

During part of your life as a single mother, your sexual needs won't be as readily met as they might be if you were in a relationship that includes sex. Use this time as a gift to reveal your creative potential.

Any time that you spend alone finding yourself feeling dry, exiled, depressed, or empty, you must create. Keep a journal on your nightstand, a cassette player at hand, or a sketchbook on your dresser. Don't let the notion that you can't afford to sabotage you. Whether you are working two jobs to make ends meet, or your extra cash is going toward your child's piano lessons, it doesn't cost much to sing or dance and bring a little joy into your life. Keep in mind, too, that you are meeting two challenges with a single effort: You're utilizing your creative energy, and you are also setting an example for your children on how to explore their own creativity, which has been touted by parenting experts as a way kids can boost their own self-esteem.

So now you can relax a little by seeing how much you can accomplish simply by allowing the artist in you to emerge. Try inventing software for children if your job as a computer programmer gets boring. Or start a newsletter for women artists in your community. Create interesting meals, take up photography, or paint a shelf turquoise. The possibilities are endless.

IF YOUR KIDS WORRY THAT YOU'LL BE AN OLD MAID

My daughter has actually tried to fix me up with her science teacher, but I'm not interested. I'm content with my life, but she acts like something is wrong. I wonder if there is something wrong with me because I don't feel like dating right now.

People do not have to be in tandem with someone else to experience joy and contentment in their lives. This is a big myth to which we are all exposed, and it has been bought into big-time, especially by girls. Maybe you don't feel like dating because you were involved in an emotionally draining relationship and now you need time to regroup. This could be a good time for you to do something for yourself that you did not have the time or energy to do when you were in a committed relationship. How about taking a cooking class or reading those books you had promised yourself you would someday read? Your children may need your full-time attention now, leaving you little energy to pursue or maintain a romantic involvement. Being temporarily uninterested in romance is not a bad thing. It leaves you able to focus your energies elsewhere, and that is good. If your lack of interest is fueled by anger or other unexpressed pain or hurt, then it is time to work toward resolving these feelings in ways that work for you. The romantic respite may simply be your time to heal.

Why is your daughter so interested in your having a boyfriend? Perhaps, particularly if she is a teenager, she feels responsible for your happiness and guilty about leaving you alone to be with her friends or participate in activities or sports. Your children, no matter what their ages, cannot be the sole focus of your universe. You need to give your children permission and encouragement to lead their own full and happy lives.

THE FEAR OF BEING INEPT AT DATING

I haven't dated in ten years. I feel like a female Woody Allen with sweaty palms, too much cologne, and not enough confidence. How do I even begin to talk to another adult, it's been so long? I feel like I only know how to talk to children. Plus, where do I find an eligible man?

The cliché about being yourself probably won't help you at this point. If you are uncertain about what to talk about because you have spent the last few years conversing only with children, then listen first to what the other person has to say. This doesn't mean you have to sit there while he bores you with his recital of every stock listed on the exchange, but it may prompt you to ask him how he plans to use his investment profits. If he responds that he'd like to build children's hospitals, well, you've got an in. If he says he wants to purchase a car with a name you can't even pronounce, then maybe you'll figure out that your values are not compatible. The best way to start talking to another person is to hear what is important to that person.

As far as where to meet men, you have many options. See the section on "Best Bets for Meeting Men" later in this chapter for ideas.

REENTERING THE DATING WORLD

I'm thirty-five years old and have been raising my eight-year-old daughter solo for seven years. During the first four years, I did not have much interest in forming new relationships with men, or even in dating for that matter, since my experience with my daughter's father was emotionally abusive, and I felt I needed time to heal. This period also allowed me to devote more time to my child and more time to learning about myself. The few encounters I've had with dates were disappointing. But now I think I'd like to meet a nice man, although I'm uncertain whether I'm ready for a relationship or if it's physical companionship I need, since it's been a long time, if you know what I mean. I feel confident at times, but doubtful and confused other times. Any suggestions for sorting out these feelings?

Congratulations. It sounds like you've been examining your feelings and are getting to know yourself pretty well, which is probably the most critical thing one can do to ensure an honest, productive, and meaningful life. You're already doing a great job sorting out your feelings. Maybe it's a combination—occasional release from sexual tension and the pleasures that a committed partnership can bring—that you are now seeking. You seem ready for both.

IT'S OKAY TO WANT A BOY-TOY

This cannot be said often enough: You are single, not dead, and deserve a personal life. And a personal life means, among other things, sex—doing it, thinking about it, planning for it, dressing or undressing for it.

Having sex does not mean first that you must pledge or feel undying love. As long as you practice safe sex, the kind of sex you choose and with whom is entirely up to you. This may be a time of major experimentation for you. This may be the first time you ever felt "the earth move" even though the guy may possess the IQ of an eggplant. Right now, you may not want or be capable of involvement or commitment. You may just want sex and then to go about your life without entanglements or interference. It is perfectly okay to have a boy-toy with whom to play sex games.

WHEN IT'S PLATONIC— BUT YOUR KIDS WISH IT WERE MORE

My best friend, Robert, is handsome, intelligent, and good with my kids. However, we have never been attracted to each other in a romantic way. My kids feel disappointed that we aren't going to marry.

There is little here that is a problem. Introducing your children to healthy men who have much to offer in terms of experiences, affection, and support is a positive thing. As the saying goes, "One can't have enough friends." Keep up the good work. There is probably no better way to prepare your children for our changing world than to show by your good example men and women sharing and giving to one another as friends and equals. Explain to your children that Robert is one of the most valuable things any human being can have—a friend. Describe the qualities that make him a good friend. Tell your children that husbands and wives need to be friends above all else, but that not all men friends become boyfriends or husbands and not all women friends of men become their girlfriends or wives. When your children become teen-agers, explain to them that people who think of members of the opposite sex only as potential bed partners limit themselves significantly. This is a one-dimensional way to think about people.

BEST BETS FOR MEETING MEN

On a first date, arrange to meet on neutral territory, such as a coffee shop. Never invite someone to your home before you get to know him. If you're actively looking to meet men, bring a friend who is looking, too. Not only is there safety in numbers, but you can give each other a reality check now and then. Try attending functions or gatherings that would hold an interest for you whether or not you plan to meet someone new. If you're the outdoorsy type, join the Sierra Club. Or you may meet men in places you would take your kids, such as sporting events and fairs. Other places to meet men include:

Air Shows: Even if you know nothing about planes, stunt flying is fun to watch and can turn you into an enthusiast. Your kids will love it, too. Often a local Civil Air Patrol (CAP) will sponsor these shows for a small admission cost.

Baseball Games: And not just major league! Almost every community has

---

THE DOS AND DON'TS OF DATING

♦ Do try painting, drawing, dancing, sculpting, or writing when you feel an urge surfacing somewhere in the lower belly and groin area. Some of the world's greatest artists produced their finest masterpieces during periods of celibacy. Remember, the sexual urge stems from the desire to reproduce offspring. Creating art is also a way of creating life.

♦ Do keep in mind that although you may be ready to date, your child may not be ready for you to date. Some children are not ready to be confronted with your having a significant other, so be patient.

♦ Don't give up on having a private life simply because you fear hurting your children. By using discretion and wise judgment, you should be able to have a fulfilling personal life and still be a good mother.

♦ Do remember that you are single, not dead. Do enjoy sex, even if the relation-ship you are in is only for physical grati-fication. Just be sure to keep your sex life separate from your children.

♦ Don't refer to overnight male guests as Uncle Lou or Cousin Ed. Overnight guests in general can send troubling enough messages to your kids, without having them think you are committing incest by sleeping with relatives. This was a popular explanation for having strange men in the house during the 1940s and 1950s, but it wasn't then, and isn't now, a good idea at all. If you must have your date spend the night because he consumed too much alcohol, he's too tired, or he has car trouble, be sure he sleeps where you normally would put overnight guests.

♦ Do not make your child your confidant. Talk to a friend, minister, or peer, keep a journal, join a support group, or get counseling. A child is just not the

---

local clubs sponsoring games, and tickets to minor league games are affordable.

Beaches: Even if you don't meet anyone, it's never a waste of time just to look at different kinds of physiques. Who says women can't enjoy just looking?

Camping Trips: One single mom rescued a noncustodial dad and his son when their tent collapsed and needed redoing. She and her two daughters even managed to teach this indoorsy type the sailor's knot!

Chance Encounters: The fabulous guy next door is often met through a chance meeting in the supermarket when you both reach for the last can of beans. Remember, you'll never meet Mr. Right if you spend your spare time on the sofa watching TV. Get out there and see what happens!

Churches, Synagogues, Temples, or Spiritual Associations: This is one of the best places to meet men with the same spiritual beliefs as yours. Everyone has his or her own path to personal fulfillment, and finding someone traveling on the same road as yours allows for initial closeness on very intellectual, spiritual, and emotional levels. Plus, churches have singles

(continuation)

appropriate person with whom to share the ups and downs of the dating game.

♦ Do be sure that dating partners respect the rules of the household. Under no circumstances should they be involved in the disciplining of your child. If the relationship evolves into a committed one, then parenting would become part of your partner's life.

♦ Do expect unpredictability in your child's reaction to your dating. Children of single mothers by choice may resent the intrusion into their cozy little world. Or they may be anxious for you to marry if they are going through a phase of wanting to be like the "family next door." Even more baffling, children of widows might take your dating as a betrayal of the memory of the deceased parent or, conversely, behave as if they want an immediate replacement.

"Listen" carefully to your child's reactions.

♦ Do consider a new approach toward relationships. Before entering a committed, permanent relationship, look at it as a third entity created by two people, and not as a merger or a single union, as our culture pushes. You'll be less likely to succumb to the risk of losing yourself in this other person. If a breakup occurs, you'll still be intact because you maintained your identity as a whole being, and not as half of a couple.

♦ Do opt out of the dating scene for a while to allow yourself a long look at the big picture, to decide what is best for yourself and your children.

♦ Do allow a change of mind about the kind of man you would like to go out with. Maybe the dashing, athletic type might be better replaced by the kind of man who will bring you a cup of coffee, as in, "Honey, you sleep in. I'll make the coffee."

groups and adventure clubs where you can go camping, traveling, and vacationing on a budget.

Clubs and Societies: If you are environmentally conscious, you may meet someone terrific at the Sierra Club or Green Earth Society. If you're into nature, consider the Audubon Society or local 4H. If your exotic likes include wine tasting, tai chi, or scuba diving, consider joining a club for these enthusiasts.

Cooking Classes: There are more guys than women taking some of these cours-

es, and for good reasons. They are no longer in a relationship where a woman prepares many of the meals. They want to entertain their dates with sophisticated, home-cooked dishes. Not only is it cheaper than going to a restaurant, but a lot of men believe a cooking class is a great way to meet women!

Cruises: If you've got the money and time, go for it. Some cruises for single-parent families offer drastically reduced rates for the kids, plus baby-sitting services, which can afford a vacation full of family fun. Or take a singles cruise with a friend and leave the kids home.

Dances: Just look in your local newspaper or entertainment guide, and there will be at least a couple of singles dances held in area hotels or nightclubs on any weekend evening.

Education: Surely there are single dads attending the PTA. Or why not expand your horizons and take an adult education class, offered in the evening or during your lunch break? Many community colleges also offer on-site child care, so don't pass up the opportunity to advance your education. Learning is a never-ending process, and we should take advantage of the endless courses available to continue this process.

Fishing Trips: Fishing can be very relaxing for the whole family, and it gives a mom a sense of accomplishment when she can catch dinner with her two hands, a net, and a worm.

Fast-Food Restaurants: Almost every single mother we've met has said most weekend-custodial dads take their kids to one of these. And those pizza places where they have puppet shows and performing bears are highly rated spots. Dads are looking for something that will feed and entertain the little ones, and usually don't cook for their kids on a Friday or Saturday night.

Golf: The miniature or goofy kind, that is. Of course, if you are a seasoned golfer, by all means get up early on a Saturday morning, send the kids to a sitter or relative, and get yourself in a game.

Holiday Parties: The key here is networking. Make sure every coworker, friend, and relative knows that you are interested in meeting nice men. Help them plan their invitation list if you

know of men you'd like to meet. Better yet, have a party, and ask these people to invite all the eligible men they know. Make sure you know how many people will be attending, or request that guests bring a covered dish or drink.

Jogging, Running, or Biking: Certain parks and sections of towns and cities have jogging paths and biking lanes. Find a place where you could enjoy getting some healthy exercise.

Kite Flying: The kids love it and so will you. It's cheap, and guaranteed to get you out of a slump if you've been in one. It's also a great excuse to ask for help when your beagle, daughter, and kite are all wrapped around a tree.

Lunch: Make time to have a relaxing lunch with friends at least every other week at a regular gathering place. Befriend the staff, and they might let you know who's who from their regular single male tables. Another lunch tip: When you first start to date a guy, rather than spend money on baby-sitters, why not meet at a local lunch spot? The added benefit to this is that if it turns out that you don't click with this person, you have an excuse to go back to work.

Men's Department of Large Stores: If you have no reason other than to meet a man, we don't recommend you do this. Too desperate, and a waste of time, unless you really have a genuine interest in men's clothing.

Network: Simply put, network, network, and network some more. Let everyone know that you would like to meet an interesting person with whom you can share fun, ideas, dinner, and companionship. The lady in the apartment down the hall might have an eligible brother, or the sales rep who comes by to upgrade the office equipment may have a friend or neighbor who might be just your cup of tea. Looking for a potential partner is not unlike looking for a good job, so ask around.

On Line: The latest technology in meeting potential partners. Many services offer people forums and connections where you not only have access to millions of on-line subscribers, but you get to exchange ideas about art, health, food, relationships, and of course computers, all for under $10 a month!

Outward Bound Programs: Participation in activities as rigorous as this program can improve the quality of your life because of the strength and independence you can uncover in yourself. It's a win–win experience because upon completion of the course, you will definitely feel powerful. Wanting a man to depend on won't be a priority, and if you are still seeking a permanent relationship, you will probably have developed the guts to talk to anyone without worrying about rejection!

Personal Ads: Most singles publications and newspapers have a section for responding to ads or for placing your own. Be sure to follow their instructions or their procedures, particularly if you have never done this before. Because relationship experts liken looking for the ideal relationship to job hunting, placing an ad stating your requirements is a very logical way to seek out someone who shares your interests. Just be sure to use a post office box number or an answering service for initial correspondence. Never, ever, give out your address and telephone number to strangers.

Parks: State parks and recreation facilities are a great, inexpensive getaway for having a picnic or for hiking up the side of a mountain. Bring an extra sandwich in case you run into a hungry park ranger.

Auto Races: Great for moms and kids, but particularly for moms of grease-monkey-type boys. One single mother says this is her favorite—because her five-year-old son is addicted to anything with wheels. It's a great place for boys to be exposed to all aspects of this hobby without a mom having to tear apart her own car. There is always someone who can show your son the ropes, and it helps him get some of that male bonding little boys seem to require.

Sightseeing: You're the only adult with a camera and you wonder how to take pictures of you and the kids together. One advantage of wanting to get in the picture is that it gives you a perfectly logical reason to stop the next nice-looking guy you see to ask him if he wouldn't mind taking a snapshot of you and your children in front of the World Trade Center, Statue of Liberty, Parthenon, or wherever else you happen to be sightseeing. Single mothers with a passion for photography have a great introduction that leaves little room for rejection by the unavailables, because if worse comes to worst and his wife appears from the restroom, at least you've got a nice memento for the photo album.

Teaching: This one is in the "kill three birds with one stone" hall of fame! Get all your creative weekend parenting ideas down on paper, then put an ad or flyer in your local paper, or on community bulletin boards in your neighborhood, announcing, "Divorced Dads and Moms—Got the Kids This Weekend? Take a class on how to have cheap, creative fun without losing your wallet or your sanity."

First, you can make some extra money on weekday nights. Next, you might meet an interesting group of people. And last, you will have used your creative abilities and resources to expand your own vision, and possibly give you the motivation you need to start something different in your life, such as a career change.

Work: With all the controversy about sexual harassment in the work place, this might seem like a nowhere idea. But actually, you have an opportunity to get to know male coworkers on an intellectual level by talking about company goals, business problems, and personal aspirations. Never gossip or bad-mouth fellow workers or bosses. By becoming friends with some of your male coworkers, eligible or not, you are open to the possibility of meeting their available friends.

Zoo: Another great weekend hangout of the single dad set.

Note: Don't lose heart if your attempts at meeting someone special don't pan out right away. Just remember that every meeting holds something to be learned. Rather than seeing the times you strike out as rejection, why not view them as time spent practicing and developing a style?

WHEN YOUR CHILD EMBARRASSES YOU

Here you are, a sophisticated 29-year-old professional, getting ready for a date with Jim, a man you have been seeing steadily for six months. This is his first visit to your home. You have discussed Jim's impending arrival with your four-year-old son, Christopher, describing Jim as a special friend of yours. The doorbell rings, you look gorgeous, and the baby-sitter seems to have everything under control. Except that, despite your careful preparation, Christopher beat you to the door chattering to a startled Jim, "Are you going to be our new daddy? Ours never lived here."

Rather than slamming the door in your date's face and hiding under the bed, try not to take this so seriously. Because your four-year-old sees you only as a mommy (even though your resumé is ten pages long), it's natural for him to look upon a male as a daddy. Kids pick up on roles that adults play by observing people in your day-to-day life, overhearing your conversations with friends, and from relatives, television, and movies. You might say something lighthearted to your date, if he's still standing, like, "This is just a test to see how strong-stomached you are. Wait until you see the bathroom!" Anything more than a quick, offhand response might make you sound emotionally needy and unsure of what you're looking for. You owe him no other explanation other than perhaps agreeing that "Kids sure do say the darnedest things!"

WHEN FRIENDS FIX YOU UP

Be grateful for the attention and interest of your friends. One date is not forever, and think of the interesting stories! Turning down the opportunity to spend an evening with someone who clearly sounds strange is one of the perks of being single. Turning down every social opportunity, however, means you are letting many of the interesting parts of life pass you by. Very often, opening yourself up to new opportunities and experiences can be very healing in unexpected and positive ways.

DATING A MARRIED MAN

It is a big shock for many women to reenter the dating scene or return to work after a hiatus at home to discover that many of their single women friends date married men. Some single women find married men a convenience. Scheduling time to see each other is tricky, but this need to make appointments to see each other sometimes fits right in with the hectic life of a single mother. The sex is typically great. After all, these guys know what they are doing. Since they typically have little to offer in the companionship or loyalty department, they go all out trying to please in the bedroom.

THE DOS AND DON'TS OF DATING ANOTHER SINGLE PARENT

Following is some advice on how to comfortably mix a social life with parenting when you both have children:

♦ Do introduce the kids to each other after you have spent a reasonable amount of time with each other's children. Make sure you don't pressure the kids to like each other.

♦ Do get together for family "dates." For example, movies, ice skating, or a visit to the zoo can involve all family members. Let the kids be part of the decision-making process.

♦ Do introduce family weekend dates by having a mock overnighter in your home or the home of your companion. Make sure everyone is provided with his or her own sleeping bag and camp out in the living room. Because the kids feel included, you can eventually request a little privacy without their feeling left out.

♦ Do let the kids know that they are not going to be included in every activity. Point out that your needing another adult in your life is similar to when they just want to be with their friends and not have you around.

♦ Don't initially introduce both sets of kids on family dates that last more than a few hours. Save outings such as overnight camping or traveling for when they have known each other a while. If the kids initially feel uncomfortable or threatened, attending a movie or going on a picnic allows everyone the choice of going home to their separate dwellings.

♦ Don't be despondent if the kids don't click. Children are flexible and resilient, but they need time and patience to get used to an idea. Don't ask too much of them and don't pressure them into sharing their feelings about your friend's family.

♦ Don't expect the oldest child to begin baby-sitting immediately after she or he has met the others. This can lead to resentment and friction. In fact, avoid having one sitter watch the whole bunch until after it has been proven that these kids are really friends. Better yet, wait until you know if this relationship not only will endure but will remain long-term for the kids as well.

Affairs with married men typically begin in the work place or on business trips far from home. Many single women report that their married lovers are also wonderful mentors, interested and supportive of their ambitions and goals.

Married men are always on their best behavior when they are with you. They always look good, smell good, and sometimes spare no expense to show you a good time. It is all romance and fantasy and is clearly an escape from your responsibility-filled daily life. It is easy to lose sight of the fact that none of this is real. What is real is that you are getting a bad deal. He gets a wife and all the companionship and validation marriage entails, plus whatever extras he is getting from you—and maybe other women as well. You get whatever scraps of time and attention he feels like giving. You will never be in a position to ask for anything. You cannot call him when you are lonely or in a jam unless the crisis takes place during work hours and he is free to take your call. Forget holidays or your birthday. He'll be sorry to hear if you have been sick or hurt, but that is as far as it will go. Most importantly of all, you cannot begin to care for this person without inflicting major hurt on yourself. You can tell yourself that you are a big girl and this is just an adventure, but often it is hard to keep a tight rein on your feelings. And why should you? Don't you deserve better?

Remember that no matter how terrific this guy seems to you—how smart, how successful, how tender, how supportive—the bottom line is that he is lying to his wife every single day. How terrific can a guy be whose own wife cannot trust him?

DATING A MAN YOU SUSPECT IS GAY

There is a great misconception that men are either exclusively heterosexual or homosexual, both in their fantasies and in their actual behavior. About one in six men are bisexual, and generally they tell lovers of both sexes what to expect. Few of the approximately ten percent of men who are exclusively homosexual ever marry. Given that approximately sixty percent of men are exclusively heterosexual, this means that at least twenty-five percent of men fall somewhere in the middle. Many men live a predominantly heterosexual or homosexual life and then change their mode because of social pressures or circumstances. Many homosexuals force themselves into a heterosexual life style. Young men face enormous pressures to date and marry, and many young homosexuals want to believe that their feelings are just a passing phase. Many homosexuals want to be fathers and enjoy what they perceive to be a normal family life. Given all these pressures, it is not surprising if you have been dating a gay man. Some women marry gay men and are not even aware of it. Most women, however, do know that a man is gay once the relationship becomes deeply involved or they are actually married.

You need to be clearly aware of what you are getting into if you continue this relationship. If you have a hidden agenda for this person, such as thinking your influence will induce change, you may be disappointed. Be aware of what you can accept and live with, and be true to your own feelings. These relationships can work, but only with an added measure of communication and honesty.

DATING YOUR EX'S BEST FRIEND

Sometimes dating the brother, friend, or cousin of an ex can be a way of holding on and staying part of the family. If these are your feelings, work at resolving your feelings of loss. Do not complicate your life further by trying to bury these feelings in the excitement of a new romance. Everyone involved will be hurt.

If you are simply attracted to a friend or relative of your ex, this is not necessarily bad or wrong. There are rules, however. Respect the privacy of your former spouse. Telling your new boyfriend some less than stellar tale of your ex will charm him for the moment, but later he will wonder what secrets of his you will share for a laugh down the road. Do not frequent places where you will be likely to see your former husband. If you are looking to stick it to your ex by dating his brother or best friend, then you are in the relationship for the wrong reasons. Simply stated, you are just using this man. A little respect for your ex's feelings will be appreciated and will go a long way. Try to keep the conversation with your new love interest future focused. Although you have many past experiences to share, look for new and different things to do together.

DATING YOUR BEST FRIEND'S EX

Dating your best friend's, sister's, childhood buddy's, or college roommate's ex is one of the dating world's more complicated scenarios. So complicated and juicy, in fact, that it is the substance on which many TV soap operas and Grade B dramas of the week are based.

Careful thought is required before you take actions you may later regret. Consider what feelings you may be trying to deal with by thinking about a relationship with this guy. Could there exist just-under-the-surface feelings of jealousy or envy? Do you really believe that despite many nights of listening to your pal complain bitterly about this man, he deserves more credit than she gave him? How will your girlfriend feel about this new relationship in your life? It takes people who have genuinely put the past behind them and are ready to accept that both they and their partners have a new life. Maybe you or your girlfriend belong in this "grown-up" category, but if you don't both see eye to eye about this situation, it is important to think things over carefully, discuss these ideas with each other, and then proceed cautiously.

Keep in mind that if your best friend or sister ended her relationship with her husband with anything less than grace and humor, more than likely she will not stay your best friend too long after she finds out you two are seeing each other. Remember that boyfriends (and some husbands) come and go, but girlfriends are forever. Do you really want to risk jeopardizing your relationship for the sake of a couple of possibly go-nowhere dates?

True, many relationships flourish and continue to grow in spite of a change in partners, but it takes an extraordinary amount of maturity, acceptance, and consideration on the part of everyone involved.

WHEN TO TELL A NEW MAN THAT YOU HAVE CHILDREN

A single mother can mention her children in a factual way on the first date—"Yes, I have two sons aged eight and twelve, and they attend Parkview School." More than likely your date is asking to be polite and to make conversation. This is not the time to review toilet training woes or the fact that your fifteen-year-old got picked up last week by the police for joyriding. As the relationship progresses, you will want to share more and more about your children. Remember that your children are, of course, the most precious thing to you, but it is really premature to share every little detail of their lives with someone you barely know. A little mystery goes a long way.

If your date is interested in you, he is probably trying to figure out the "lay of the land"—Do you have full-time custody? Where is your ex? And the question he'll want to know the answer to but will be afraid to ask: Are your kids problems from hell? Remember to ask about his children. His attitudes and comments about his own children will tell you volumes about the kind of man he is. If he does not have children, wait until you are reasonably confident and secure in the relationship and are seeing each other exclusively before you ask the big question: "So, how come you never had children?" Or, "How do you feel about children?"

SHOULD A NEW LOVER BE SPENDING THE NIGHT?

It is not okay to involve your children in your sex life. It is not okay to bring this kind of interesting, one-night stranger to your home. You do not want your children to get up in the morning and ask who that is sleeping in your bed or taking a shower in the bathroom. Equally unacceptable is for your children to be introduced to every man (or woman, if that is your preference) you date. It is definitely not okay for you to encourage your children to spend time with "Uncle Bob" when you do not know or maybe even care if you will ever see Uncle Bob again yourself.

The Consequences of Having Overnight Guests. Children may have enough trouble making sense and creating order in their world without creating unnecessary confusion. Bringing the natural uncertainty of dating into their lives does nothing but create more uncertainty. Every man (or woman) they are encouraged to get to know who then is no longer a part of their lives represents a loss. After too many losses, their ability to trust is compromised. Humans who cannot trust are damaged. Nothing is worth doing that to your child. Finally, whatever you do in your personal life and make known to your children will be a message to them that they can do the same. Are you willing to tolerate the same standards of behavior in your fifteen-year-old daughter that are now working for you? Do you trust that your children will practice safe sex and not get themselves into situations that are risky or downright dangerous? Probably not.

There are so many ways to have what you need and want without compromising your children. There is always his place or the ever available hotel or motel. If money is an issue, and it practically always is, remember that you are not the only single mother with a privacy problem. See if you can swap children for a night or even for a luxurious weekend so that you can spend the night together in your own home. If you are involved with a grown-up, he will understand and perhaps surprise you with his ingenious and creative solutions to your need to maintain privacy. There is something about not being so available to men that tends to pique their interest and add an extra measure of lust and passion to a relationship. Consider your circumstances a plus, not a minus.

DON'T FALL FOR THE MYTH OF ROMANTIC LOVE

In his classic, *The Road Less Traveled* (Simon and Schuster), author M. Scott Peck, M.D., notes that one of the characteristics of "the experience of falling in love" is the illusion that the experience lasts forever. Moreover, he points out how the notion that there is only one man meant for only one woman (and this of course has been predetermined in the heavens) who can meet each other's every need is a dreadful lie.

Basically, if you subscribe to the myth of romantic love, it means you tend to enter a relationship based on what your hormones tell you, rather than your brain. You might also fall for hype such as the belief that opposites attract (great if you're a magnet), the need for a better half (as if you're incomplete before seeking a partner), and the notion that if sex is no longer new and exciting, then the honeymoon is over, or the chemistry is gone.

In actuality, the deepest love is demonstrated through empathy, true concern, and caring enough to want the best for that special person.

OUTGROWING THE BOY-TOY

I have been seeing a man on and off for two years. Honestly, the best and probably only thing this relationship had going for it was sex. But now I am bored and plan to break it off. He called the other night, and my son answered the phone. This guy gave my son his name, told him I was a friend of his, and left a message for me to call. I freaked. I have never brought this man anywhere near my house, never mind my son. All this was private and separate from my son. What am I going to say if my son starts asking about this guy?

You have done everything right so far, so why are you doubting yourself now? Obviously when you and your boyfriend were together you did not tell your son specifically where you were and what you were doing. There is no reason for any destructive bursts of candor now. Probably your son has forgotten all about this call. If he does ask, just say that he is a friend from work. If your son asks if he knows him or will meet him, tell him probably not because you know for a fact that he is looking to go elsewhere—and you know that is the truth. Tell your soon-to-be-ex to please not call you at home again. Do what is good for you and stop seeing him when you feel the time is right. Because you have not involved your child in any way, you are free to live your private life as you see fit with no worries about how your actions will affect your child. Congratulations on being such a grown-up.

23

Relationships and Remarriage

CREATING A NEW BLENDED FAMILY

After repeatedly hearing statistics about higher divorce rates for second and third marriages, you may have a gun-shy attitude toward intimacy. But those statistics usually involve people who "jump out of the frying pan and into the fire," or those who enter relationships for all the wrong reasons, such as wanting to fill a void or replace an absent father.

If you have spent your time alone wisely and productively, your chances of maintaining a successful partnership with a new mate are extremely good. In fact, because you are in control of your own life and not overly needy, you have many options when choosing the type of partner and relationship you'd like. Still, all relationships between men and women bring sticky problems that can only be resolved through strong communication, empathy, acceptance of the other person, and a willingness to accept some degree of risk.

ARE YOU READY FOR THE REAL THING?

If you think you are really ready to engage in a long-term, committed partnership, here are some factors to consider:

◆ Are you content and fulfilled by yourself? If you are, you'll have a lot to offer.

◆ Would you want someone with whom you share a lot in common? Men and women are so different by nature, it only makes sense to find someone who is practically a clone of yourself, who approaches life from the same perspective, especially if you have strong values and praiseworthy qualities.

◆ Do you view a relationship as a separate entity rather than a merging of two people into one being? Two whole beings should create a third entity, an extension of themselves that they can care for without losing the ability to care for themselves. You should be able to remain intact so that you can nurture or form other meaningful relationships, such as with your best friend, your child, your family, and your business associates.

Above all, live by your own definition. If you need to "fix" someone, or need to be taken care of, or are only in the market for a father for your child, then you are not ready. But if your opinion of yourself cannot be changed by someone else's opinion of you, you are ready not only for a relationship or marriage, but for a lot more!

RELATIONSHIP STRATEGIES

When Should Your Children Meet Your Boyfriend?

I have been dating a man for about six months and, so far, have kept the relationship separate from my sons, aged six and nine. I am not entirely certain where this relationship is going, but I feel there is the possibility for commitment. What is the right way to gradually introduce John into their lives?

You are already on the right track by using the word "gradually," as in slowly and cautiously. A good rule of thumb is to keep your children's involvement with a boyfriend a step or two behind your level of involvement with him. For example, if you are just beginning a relationship, there is no reason for your children even to be introduced to this casual date. If, on the other hand, you are seeing someone exclusively and the potential for commitment is there, it is then time to introduce your children to this new person in your life. Keep their initial meetings simple. Ask your boyfriend to join you for an afternoon in the park or for a picnic. Don't force the children on him and certainly do not expect the boys to instantly bond with your boyfriend. He should be introduced as a guest in your home and a special friend of yours. Your boys should not be your sounding boards on how the relationship is progressing, nor should they be encouraged to think of your boyfriend as a permanent part of your home life. Take things slowly and enjoy the time together.

Showing Affection to Your Boyfriend in Front of Your Kids

When is it appropriate to begin showing affection to each other when the kids are around? My boyfriend and I were holding hands when my daughter tried to pry us apart.

As far as seeing you and your boyfriend hugging or treating each other with affection, start slow and take it one step at a time. Walking arm and arm, hand holding, or having your partner's arm around you in the movie theater when you are all out as a family is a good start. Some mothers report that when they are holding hands with their significant other and their young child tries to pry them apart, they let the child know they don't appreciate this and then go on holding hands. However, it would be better for the three of you to hold hands, considering that your daughter is telling you she feels left out. If your daughter lets go, you can continue holding hands with your boyfriend. If it is an adolescent who is embarrassed by your behavior, keep in mind that at this age almost everything Mom does embarrasses them.

"My Boyfriend Should Have Warmed Up to My Kids by Now…"

My boyfriend doesn't know when he should start being a little affectionate with my sons, ages three and seven. He's very nice to them but isn't sure how to handle closeness like hugging. We have been dating almost a year.

It's time that your boyfriend showed affection toward your children by reading to them, or watching TV with his arm around the seven-year-old and maybe the three-year-old on his lap. As things progress, he can help tuck them in at bedtime, or even give them a hug or kiss goodnight. If you've all been out late at the zoo or park, he may offer to carry one of the children if they get tired. Be patient, and if the kids aren't receptive when he offers to show some affection, let him give them a little breathing room and try again. Eventually, you may want to introduce them to a "sandwich hug," where you and your companion hug with the two little ones in the middle. Just keep in mind that although this is sometimes appropriate, they need to know that your relationship with this man is at times private, too.

Should Your Kids Ever Get in Bed with You and a Significant Other?

Some single mothers feel that a level of commitment does not depend on legalities, and having a boyfriend spend time overnight in their homes feels all right to them. Such single mothers have often experienced a bitter and costly divorce and vow, if only for now, never to marry again despite their love and commitment. Even under such circumstances, unless the boyfriend has become an integral part of the family, it is not appropriate to have even your preschool children join you in bed.

Since you and your partner are not married you need to be acutely aware that events in your home that may be quite acceptable to you may cause unforeseen consequences to you and your children. For example, allowing even the youngest infant or child to bathe or shower with your boyfriend or to use the toilet together may give your children's father grounds to gain custody of your children. Even if you have no ex in the picture, children relating events like bathing with a boyfriend give school and day-care authorities grounds for concern that your child might be the victim of sexual abuse, and they will be legally obligated to file a report with Child Protective Service (CPS) for possible sexual abuse. A report of possible sex abuse will involve intensive home study over a period of time by a social services agency and, in some states, police investigation complete with blaring sirens and flashing lights. This is a humiliating experience for families.

If you feel that the advantages of having a live-in boyfriend outweigh the possible risks, it might be prudent to discuss this change in living arrangement with your ex-husband before he finds out from the children. Consider also informing your child's teacher that there will be a new member in the household. Doing so leaves less room for misinterpretation and false allegations.

If Your Kids Hate Your Boyfriend

I'm a single mother with two children, a son five and a half and a daughter who just turned four. Their father and I have been divorced for over two years. I'm now in a serious relationship (we're talking marriage) with a man I've been dating for eight months. Even though this man has tried everything under the sun to please the kids, they act like they can't stand him by being incredibly rude, even obnoxious to him. My daughter once even told him it was time to leave. How should I handle this?

This behavior is fairly typical of the things kids do and say under such circumstances. You and your boyfriend should try not to take their "dislike" too much to heart. It's really nothing personal. It's just that in their eyes, Dad has a continued existence in the family, and your boyfriend's presence brings out a strong defensive reaction from them.

Consider, too, that your children enjoyed your undivided attention from the time Dad left the scene to the time your boyfriend came into the picture. It's normal for them to have a tough time accepting that the attention that was once theirs alone is now being shared with someone else. Try to understand that your relationship with your boyfriend is a signal that you are ready to move ahead with your life.

Maybe You're Ready, But Your Children Aren't. Your children might not be ready to accept a new male presence. By being extra-sensitive to their needs, you can help them make the necessary adjustment more smoothly. For example, where once it was just you and your kids cuddling up on Friday evenings to watch a video, now you and your boyfriend join friends for an evening out. This is a loss to your children, and most likely they will resent it. But don't think this means that you are chained to the house forever. It's just a signal that says compromises need to be made.

Schedule Your Boyfriend Around Your Children, Not Vice Versa. Maybe the video can be enjoyed earlier in the evening with a picnic supper around the TV, and you two can go out later. If your boyfriend does not support and accept your children's needs for attention during this time, then maybe he is not too grown-up himself. This big change in your life means that your children will need you more now. Negotiating change is one of the biggest challenges there is in life, and your children really need your help. The time and energy you invest helping them make this adjustment now will pay off handsomely in a smoother transition and happier home life for everyone.

Children Require an Adjustment Period. Children are creative little critters and can find a million and one ways to sabotage a relationship they feel is shutting them out or causing them to lose the attention and care to which they have become accustomed. They need to adjust to the fact that you have a life outside of theirs and that although you may give them a different type of attention, you love them as much as ever.

Sit down alone with the children and allow them to talk about their feelings. Try not to invalidate their feelings. Rather, let them know that you understand how they feel, but that it is perhaps not your boyfriend they don't like, but the situation. Emphasize your unconditional love and assure them of your desire and commitment to care for them. Be sure to request that they treat any and all of your guests, including your boyfriend, with respect and politeness, as you have taught them. By allowing your children an environment in which to express themselves and their feelings, you are letting them know that they remain your primary concern and that all your life plans take their needs and feelings into account.

If the problem isn't resolved, you may have to get more assertive by letting them know that you will not tolerate any rudeness. If they choose to behave this way, they will be sent to their rooms or given time out until they decide to apologize.

If He Constantly Puts Down Your Kids. If your boyfriend is constantly criticizing or finding fault with your children, then this behavior could mean verbal abuse. Sometimes because of experiences in our own lives, we are unable to recognize verbal abuse when it is directed at us but are sensitive and aware when this abuse is directed at

our children. Take a step back and listen to what he is saying both to your children and to you. You need to discuss what you see going on with your boyfriend in a direct, nonconfrontational manner, out of the children's earshot. Put your statements to him as "I" statements. For example, say to him, "I feel put down when you criticize my ..." rather than remarking, "You are mean" or "You are abusive." This kind of dialog gives your friend the opportunity for growth and change. He may simply be replaying old childhood tapes indicating the way he was treated as a child. He may have a bad habit and be honestly unaware of how his words hurt. Make a conscientious effort to work on this together. You and your children deserve to live in a peaceable home. If your partner's verbal abuse represents yet another abusive relationship in your life, then if only for the sake of your children, seek counseling or join a support group.

No matter what the reason, the constant criticism and nit-picking about everyday stuff must stop. Otherwise your children will turn you both off and decide they might as well really misbehave since that seems to be what is expected of them.

When Your Boyfriend Can't Cope with Your Kids

My boyfriend can't seem to cope with my kids. Any ideas?

How familiar is this man with typical childhood behaviors? Does he know, for example, that all two-year-olds have one favorite word: No! Does he realize that all households have some commotion and resistance around bedtime? Does he know that teenagers are testing you every minute of the day? Does he know that all children have to be reminded about homework, toothbrushing, and picking up their rooms, and that whining develops in utero during the first month? Perhaps all that is needed is for your boyfriend's world to be widened. Take the opportunity to socialize with others who are raising children and feel free to share your war stories. Think about taking a parent education class together or joining a parent support group.

When Your Boyfriend Doesn't Want Children

My boyfriend has stated that the only obstacle to our future together is the kids. He just doesn't want children, ever.

Your companion is entitled to his own opinion about whether or not to include children in his life plan. Yet even if he does not see children in his present or in his future, it is still possible for you to continue your relationship with him, as long as you set certain boundaries and limits.

It is disrespectful to your children to invite this man to spend extended periods of time in your home. Does he treat them in a polite but distant manner? That's fine, because your children will learn the lesson that you cannot charm all of the people all of the time. But is he hostile or critical? In that case, the only lesson your children would learn is how to tolerate abuse in their own home, which is a lesson better skipped. Can you still enjoy the ballet with him or indulge your passion for silent movies with him? Yes. Might he be the best thing that ever happened between sheets? Perhaps. The point is that his disinterest in your children does not mean no relationship with you. It does mean that you have to remember that it is unlikely that he will change his mind, and that means it is unlikely that this relationship will develop into a permanent one if the total package—husband and father—is what you're after.

When a New Boyfriend Plays "Daddy". Be careful if your new boyfriend is already assuming the role of father to your kids. Why is he acting this way? Does he have great control needs and feel that he is in charge no matter what the situation?

Or do you encourage this because things may have gotten a little out of hand in your house? Maybe the normal routines became lost in the face of battles between you and your ex. Or maybe there is no ex and you are unwittingly grooming him to be Dad.

Perhaps his playing daddy is simply in response to the chaos that reigns in your home because you have been ill, stressed out, or buried in your work. If so, harness his interest and involvement by accepting his help and suggestions. This is different from letting him run things, causing conflict, confusion, and hard feelings with your children—something that is bound to happen no matter what place their natural father has in their lives. Some men like the daddy role but are unable to accept all the commitment and hard work parenting entails, so they selectively choose the part of parenting they like—kind of like ordering a la carte off a menu.

You must stay in control of your household. You are the parent and already may be in some type of parenting relationship with the children's father. It is up to you to find a place for your boyfriend in this set-up, if you so choose, and it is up to the boyfriend to decide if he wants to be included. He can participate and be a valued member of your extended family. Sometime in the future, as your husband, his role may expand significantly. But for now you need to set the rules.

"My Boyfriend Is Jealous of My Children…"

I am dating this guy who is terrific except for one big thing—he is jealous of my children. He complains that I do so much for them and that there is no time for him and for us as a couple. I think he does not realize that I have to be both mother and father to my ten- and twelve-year-old sons and that it makes me feel good to do everything for them and to make life easy for them. How can I convince my otherwise almost perfect boyfriend that I am right?

Maybe you are both right. It is possible to do too much for children, particularly when we feel that we must compensate for the other parent's lack of responsibility and involvement. Perhaps it is time to step back and see if what your boyfriend is saying better expresses your overprotection and involvement rather than his unjustified feelings of jealousy.

Doing everything for your boys now may make you feel good about yourself, but what kind of message does that send to them about their own capabilities and what will be expected of them in the world? If you are making their beds and picking up their dirty clothes before they even hit the floor, you are sending a clear message that there will always be someone to anticipate their every need. Realistically, unless they plan to wed royalty, this is not true. Your boys will not develop self-reliance or personal responsibility. There is very little room in this world for people without these skills. Down the road (shortly) your sons will resent your efforts, and your boyfriend will tire of always being in second place.

Try to step back and look carefully at your household routines and what you are expecting from your boys. Ask other mothers with children your sons' ages what their expectations are. It is likely that it is time to help your boys develop self-reliance by teaching them how to accomplish simple household chores and expecting them to do them. Having the boys pick up their own dirty clothes and do daily chores like the dinner dishes will free you up not only to enjoy more time with your boyfriend, but also to pursue your own interests and leisure activities. Remember that no one loves a martyr except in paintings.

IS THIS A MAN OR A FIX-UP PROJECT?

You've heard of him before. This guy is always out of work—has numerous allergies although he continues to smoke—spends his paycheck on vitamins but has ungodly eating habits.

You've witnessed terrible fights with his family, and maybe he drinks but just on the weekends, and he can't help flirting with any woman who isn't dead. Or he is simply afraid of commitment, poor thing, since his wife left him for a woman, and you chalk it up to bad timing. You say, "But he is nice and he loves me, and I know that if I just stick by him he will get better." He just needs someone to help him work on himself, right?

Right. But unless you charge a minimum of about $90 an hour, and don't get involved with your clients, he needs someone other than you.

Single mothers are particularly vulnerable to hooking up with this kind of "fix-up project." This is because single mothers routinely handle challenges that would overwhelm less capable individuals and often bring this "I can do the impossible" attitude into their personal lives. No money or poor job prospects—you can help him network. Major drug or alcohol issues—no problem. You hear that you can meet a lot of nice people at those AA meetings. You promise to be there for him even after he steals—excuse me, borrows—the last of your wedding silver and then pawns it to buy drugs. Poor health—you cook for him and get him to like healthy foods. After all, who can make the airplane noises as the spoonful of oatmeal nears the reluctant child's mouth more convincingly than you? Habitually tardy, forgets your birthday, does not keep promises—what can you expect from someone raised in that crazy family of his? Besides, you've cut out that magazine article about how to make your man be on time and taped it to the fridge.

Is this a man or a project? Don't you deserve better? Where are you going to get the energy to build your own nurturing, supportive network or to manage your own career? Why are you so willing to take on all this responsibility? Are you so stuck in the mother role that you cannot see that this is what this guy needs? Sometimes we get so scared of being alone that we grab and hold on tight to the first man who comes along and notices us. Let go of the fear. Work on you, and the kind of relationship you deserve—one of equals and give and take, not just give give give—will come along.

ABUSIVE SITUATIONS

If You Suspect Child Abuse. Are you allowing your children to be abused? Perhaps you were unaware until you saw the bruises or your child told a trusted adult or teacher. Is your boyfriend abusing you in the same way? Does he demean and ridicule you so your self-esteem is in the toilet? Are you financially dependent on him? Is he just one in a long line of abusive men who have dominated your life? Perhaps your self-esteem is so shot from the divorce and the stigma of being a single mother that you unwittingly picked this kind of person to punish yourself even further.

No matter what the explanation, you need help to get this person out of your family's life. You are not the first woman to be in this situation, and there is help waiting for you. Look in the Yellow Pages of the phone book for agencies and hotlines specializing in domestic abuse. If it seems just too hard for you to take this first big step, perhaps a friend or family member can be there to help you make this all-important call. But you must do it. Now.

If Your Boyfriend Mistreats Your Children

My boyfriend is mistreating not only me, but my two young sons. I feel trapped. I don't want to start over from the bottom, but I just don't know what to do.

If you are financially dependent on him, then do what you can to gain your independence now, even if that means getting public assistance. True, there is a certain type of abuse reported by women who have endured the red tape and bureaucratic debasement of waiting on the welfare line, and you may feel that trading in one type for another is just not worth it. But you must remember that you and your children are entitled to any help you can receive and that your lives are worth protecting. Also, it's only temporary.

Be aware that as you get stronger and take more control of your life, he will promise to stop the bad treatment and will profess his undying love and devotion. You will be tempted to take him back because you feel that you need him. You may also confuse love with the exhilarating feelings that often accompany abusive relationships—the highs of the renewed attraction after the lows, the letdown, and the feelings of despair. These emotions are understandable. Every woman who has been in an abusive relationship understands exactly how you feel. Many experts go so far as to say that a chemical change actually occurs, releasing endorphins in the brain, which results in a feeling not unlike a drug high. This accounts for the incredible lovemaking or dramatic romantic behavior that many women say will often follow a brutal attack. If you let him back into your life, he may treat you like a queen for a short time, but almost all abusers will begin the abuse again if they haven't gotten any kind of treatment. Friends and family might even pull away from you because of your inability to stay permanently away from him and because it causes them pain to see you in this predicament.

And the sad fact is that sources of financial and emotional support will be less available to you the more often you return to him. The children's father will certainly have every right to protect his children from this abuse and may even call the police. Your child's school or day-care staff may intervene and report your situation to the authorities. You could be arrested, or worse, you could lose custody of your children and even lose unsupervised visitation. Your self-respect is worth more than anything this person can give you.

If You Are Abused

I've been in an abusive relationship with a man who has never hurt my children, but hurts me. He says he really wants help. Should I believe him? There are so many wonderful things about him if he could get over this.

When you are in an abusive relationship, even if he never hurts your children directly, they are still being affected. He may tell you that he was abused himself as a child and just does not know any other way. Sadly, this might be true, but it does not give him the right or excuse to abuse you. He may not be abusive to your children now, but most men who abuse their mates eventually abuse the children, too.

Abusive men can change, but they need intensive long-term psychotherapy from professionals with special training and experience. There are also support groups for men who are or have been abusers. These programs are similar to twelve-step programs for other addicts and have a very high success rate. If your boyfriend is able to make the commitment to such treatment, then you can hold out hope that you two may someday live together without violence. Don't accept his promises that he will change his behavior on his own. Experts say this is almost impossible, unless he undergoes a major transformation, such as having a deep religious experience. Remember, you cannot "love these problems away," nor are you to blame.

IF YOUR PARTNER LEAVES

My boyfriend has been living with my three sons and me for almost a year. The boys and I were really starting to feel like Jake was a member of the family. He would do things with the boys, which was great because their own dad has moved across the country and rarely sees them. Jake and I talked about marriage. I wanted a commitment, but Jake said that things would take care of themselves in time. Last Sunday the boys and I returned from a one-day trip to discover that Jake had moved out. His note said that things had gotten too complicated and he had to move on. The boys are devastated, and I simply do not know what to do.

Unfortunately, you are learning by painful experience that single mothers need to keep a clear head when it comes to allowing a dating partner to move in. It was natural for you to want to be with Jake as much as possible, and your desire to live with him is quite understandable. However, it does not sound as though Jake lied or misrepresented his feelings. No doubt he enjoyed spending time with the boys, and no doubt the boys loved every minute with Jake. The problem is that you held out hope that living together was part of a marriage plan. Things got too intense for Jake. He did not know how to handle the situation that he had helped create. Did he handle things in the most appropriate way possible? No. But rather than blame Jake entirely, perhaps there were things you, too, might have considered.

For instance, a less traumatic way to have approached this situation would have been for you and Jake to have talked out your feelings prior to his moving in and becoming such an important part of the boys' lives. Perhaps Jake alerted you that he was ambivalent about his readiness to make a long-term commitment, and you could have given more thought to his moving in. It would have been better, too, to explain to the boys that the future with Jake was precarious and that although you certainly hoped they enjoyed his company, Jake's life might take a different turn. He probably would not be living with them forever the way they live with you. In this way, the boys would have put certain limits on their feelings, which would have been appropriate given the situation. The difficulty is that the boys, picking up on your cues, trusted Jake in the same manner that they trust you. They believed that he would continue to be a part of their lives. Having lost their father, they have now lost another adult in whom they invested love and trust. But hindsight teaches us a little too late sometimes.

You can still make things better, and here is how: Have the talk with the boys now that under better circumstances would have occurred before Jake moved in. Explain to them that men and women sometimes want different things out of relationships and that this sometimes causes hurt and confusion. Tell them straight out that Jake left because you and he did not want the same things. Tell the boys that you are looking for someone to share your life with for a long time, which for adults means marriage. Jake did not want marriage for his own reasons, and this is why he left. Emphasize that Jake's departure had nothing to do with them. They were not in some way not good enough. Tell them that Jake probably misses them a great deal, which is probably very true. This will be difficult, but you will have to put your own hurt aside for now and help your boys get back on an even keel. Take the time to do things together and know that it will take time for all of you to recover from what was an unexpected and disappointing loss.

WHEN A LONG-LOST BOYFRIEND RETURNS

I broke up with my live-in boyfriend literally two days before we were to be married. I found out that he had a serious gambling problem, and I could not bring that kind of chaos into my daughters' lives. He split, and we did not hear from him for two years. Now he is back and wants to take up where we left off. I am confused and do not know what to do.

When you do not know what to do, do nothing. For you this means taking things very slowly. People do change, and it is possible that your boyfriend has completely changed and that his serious addiction no longer is a threat to the stability and peace of your home. If you want to date him again, by all means do so. See him, however, away from your home without involving the girls. Listen to what he shares with you about his life. If he is indeed in control of his addiction, you should expect to hear him say that he has been in treatment and continues to be in some type of support program like Gamblers Anonymous. Statements like "I beat this on my own" or "I still put a few bucks in the football pool every now and again but nothing like I used to" should be red flags signaling that he is still controlled by his addiction. If this is the case, run away and stay away from him. He can only bring you heartache.

Through no real fault of your own, your daughters suffered a serious loss when the wedding was canceled and he left. You cannot change what happened, but you can prevent another loss by proceeding—if you decide to pursue this relationship at all—slowly, cautiously, and with both eyes open.

HELPING THE KIDS THROUGH YOUR BREAKUP

I have been dating a man for about four years. He has become an integral part of my children's lives although their father remains attentive, supportive, and involved. My boyfriend lives with me for all intents and purposes, and the children certainly are aware that we sleep together. The problem is that I no longer love him. It is the old sad story, but I have grown and he has not. Breaking up with him will be hard enough for him, but I do not know how to handle the "breakup" of him and my children.

Relationships that are slowly dying often cause the most pain. You are right to be concerned about handling not only your feelings but those of your children as well. While you and your boyfriend work things out (or do not work things out, as the case may be), the best thing to do is to lessen his involvement and contact with them. This is not to say stop all contact immediately, but rather begin to include him less in your regular family activities. This means that you may plan your outing to the museum without him, go grocery shopping without him, and generally begin to live your lives more separately. For right now, it is okay to be vague with your children about why your boyfriend is not joining you. The old standby "He has other plans" will work nicely here. When you are absolutely definite about the status of the relationship, then tell your children and help them deal with their feelings about losing someone who has become an important part of their lives.

IF YOUR EX-BOYFRIEND WANTS CONTACT WITH YOUR CHILD

I have broken up with my boyfriend. He is just not relationship material. We want different things out of life. He has gotten so attached to my ten-year-old daughter that he wants to keep coming over to see her. He says he will miss her too much. I am not sure how I feel about this and how I should handle things.

This man may have genuinely grown to love your daughter. He may know that he lacks the commitment gene but is able to be a special adult friend to your child. On the other hand, he may want contact with your daughter solely to keep some kind of tie to you. Perhaps he cannot satisfy your need for companionship and commitment but cannot quite cut the ties with you. If this is the case, asking to keep contact with your daughter reflects a desire to use her to get what he wants. There are men, too, who are unable to make a commitment because they have serious sexual problems. This is not to say that he is a pedophile whose sexual needs are met by contact with children, but all precautions should be taken while investigating why he wants to maintain this relationship. He really may feel that she fills a special place in his life and may have a genuine "fatherly" love for her, but you need to examine his reasons.

You also need to ask yourself how your daughter feels about your boyfriend. Have you ever for even a fleeting second had a concern that his actions toward her were even slightly inappropriate? If so, the answer, of course, is that he cannot see her. If, however, you have always felt that these two got along appropriately and you can handle having him be a peripheral part of your life, then you might consider letting him take your daughter to a play or museum. Common-sense rules should always be followed. You need to know where they are going and when they will return. Overnight stays are out of the question. If your child returns from the play or museum full of exciting information about what they saw, then you can know that your instincts were correct in trusting him. If she returns with no details, or is sullen and quiet, or tells you that they did not go to the museum after all but just "hung out," then your mother radar should be on red alert. He did not keep his word, and you cannot trust him with your daughter again. You will need to tell him just that and stick to it.

BLENDING FAMILIES

If Your Boyfriend's Mother Treats You Like Excess Baggage. The most important thing to consider in this situation is not what his mother says, but how he reacts to it. If you detect a whiff of agreement or there is no effort on his part to modify his mother's remarks, then it is probably time to reassess this relationship. Nobody wants to feel second-rate. On the other hand, if your boyfriend's mother has fantasies that her son will marry a virgin with no past and begin a fairy-tale family, it is not his fault that Mom lives in romance-novel reality. Try saying to Mom, "I think Joe is lucky to be part of all the fun we have as a family." Refuse to be drawn into a discussion with his family about where this relationship might be leading, if anywhere. That is for your boyfriend and you to talk about privately. Prepare your children for remarks they may overhear, and let them know that some people require more than a little extra understanding. If his family is so nasty or abusive

that you or your children have left a family gathering or encounter in tears more than once, then it is time to take a hard look at changes that need to be made and new rules that need to be negotiated. This may mean that he socializes with his family without you and the children. Make room for compromise and accept that not all people are capable of change.

If Your Boyfriend's Family Is Not Receptive to Yours

I'm a single mother of five-year-old twin girls. I've been dating a never-married man I met through work for almost ten months. He recently invited us to his family's house for the holidays. However, when I met his mother briefly a few weeks ago, she made me feel like returned merchandise. Jeff was talking about my girls when she cut him off with a comment about when he has his own children. I know that there will be other kids at her house during Christmas—nieces, nephews, and grandchildren—but I don't want to feel rejected and especially don't want my daughters to feel left out. What should I do?

Maybe Jeff doesn't respond to his mother's obvious or even subtle pressures regarding his marrying and having children, so she dumps on you. Try not to take it to heart—Jeff is ultimately the one who has to deal with her, not you.

If Jeff talks about the twins, especially to his family, regardless of the depth of your involvement with him, it sounds as if he has a relationship with the girls, for whatever it's worth. You might want to tell Jeff that you are worried your children will feel isolated at his mother's house and you would appreciate a little extra support from him. Perhaps he could introduce them to the others.

You can also decline the invitation if you feel Jeff won't be supportive and are truly concerned that hurtful remarks from his mother will be issued your way. But you could also respond to offhand comments that make you feel unwelcome by saying, "I thought we were welcome here to share and participate in Christmas with the rest of the group. I can't help sensing that you are uncomfortable with my children and my being here." Often, people who slip you underhanded remarks suggesting their displeasure need to be asked directly what the problem is.

Most likely, your daughters won't take too much notice of Jeff's mother's feelings about "his own children" and will be happy to have other kids to play with and toys and stories to share. But children do pick up on the body language of adults quite easily. If you worry that they will feel alienated from the others because they might pick up on signals transmitted either by you or by Jeff's mother, you might want to prepare the girls first. For instance, you might tell them that you will be spending Christmas with a lot of new friends. Letting your children know that Jeff's mother sometimes has trouble with new friends will help them understand that it is not because of them that she might appear to be ignoring or rebuffing them. Let the girls know that being around Jeff's mother doesn't make you very happy sometimes, but you are excited about meeting the other "friends." You might initially want to spend a little time with the children organizing a game or activity to serve as an icebreaker. This will help everyone get off on equal footing.

Telling Your Children You Are Getting Married. If you have involved your children appropriately as this wonderful, special relationship has evolved, the fact of your actual marriage and all the planning entailed will probably not come as a big surprise. More than likely, it will seem to your children a natural turn of events. If, however, your circumstances have been such that your husband-to-be has not become an integral part of your children's lives, it is probably best to let them get better acquainted before springing the big news. Your children will have many questions no matter what. They will ask if they will be living in a different house or if their visitations, if any, with Dad will change. They may want to know if holiday routines and rituals will be different. You should be ready with answers because you and your fiancé should have settled these kinds of questions as part of your getting to know and love one another.

If your children protest loudly and seem generally devastated and upset by the news of your marriage, ask yourself

ARE YOU REMARRYING TOO SOON?

Don't jump out of the frying pan into the fire. Studies indicate that second marriages have a higher divorce rate than first-time marriages—over 60 percent. Some of the factors causing single parents to remarry too soon are lack of money, loneliness, sexual desire, lack of self-esteem (feeling you can only be defined by having a mate), requiring help around the house, and wanting a dad for your kids. None of these are good reasons for wanting a relationship. Think it out. Take the time to learn to love yourself first, especially if you have recently emerged from a long-term relationship where you functioned as the primary caretaker.

why. Do they still have hopes that you and their father will get back together again? If so, this is the time to explain gently that your life and that of their father are separate now. Your children may still be grieving and may need a greater measure of love and support to weather this big change in their lives. Your soon-to-be husband may not have formed the most affectionate of bonds with your children, and they may resent what will be his greater presence in your life. This signals the need for clear boundaries about who sets family policy and who is in charge of discipline. The children will do much better if the rules and expectations are clearly set out.

Just as you expect them to adjust, you will have to adjust to the fact that your children may never be more than lukewarm in their feelings for this man you love. The best you may be able to hope for is cordial respect. Remember

always that *The Brady Bunch* was fantasy. In real life, the adjustments in remarriage and stepparenting are among the most difficult to negotiate. Many second marriages fail over disagreements concerning the children from prior relationships. Everyone needs a chance to be heard and to have his or her feelings respected. Take things slowly and keep your expectations reasonable. Do not expect instant bonding and immediate togetherness.

Should Your Children Attend Your Wedding? It depends how they feel about your new marriage. Watching your mother pledge eternal love to a man you can barely tolerate can require more fortitude than some children can muster. Most children of divorce harbor fantasies about their parents getting back together long after there is no realistic flicker of hope left that such a reconciliation might occur. Ask your children directly if they would care to attend and participate. If they seem okay or are enthusiastic about participating, give them a simple role appropriate to their age. Very young children might carry flowers or simply stand by your side. An older child might do a brief reading. Unless your children are adults, the role of maid or matron of honor or best man or simply adult witnesses belongs appropriately to an adult friend. You and your husband might choose to include in your vows promises to care for and love the children you bring to the marriage. Including your children in this way can be very comforting and affirming to them. Remember that this is your day of joy. Your children may not be as joyful as you are, but if they choose to attend and participate, they must do it in the proper spirit of the day. Explain that if they feel they can-not be part of this joy, then it is cer-tainly their choice not to attend. This is simply part of proper social training and is not negotiable.

Spending the Night When You're Engaged. When the relationship is a committed one and marriage is planned shortly, it becomes more diffi-cult to know what to do. There are a couple of things, however, to keep in mind. First of all, the standards you set in your home will be the standards your children will follow. You may, for example, tell your ten-year-old daugh-ter that Robert is spending the night with you because you two love one another and plan to spend the rest of your lives together. Your ten-year-old will accept this, and you will see no immediate repercussions. But, later on, when those hormones hit, she will tell you how much she loves her pimple-faced but ardent suitor and how they plan in just twelve more years to get married and spend the rest of their lives together, too. Your children will not see themselves at this future time so differently than you see yourselves now. If your marriage is postponed because one of you is waiting for those final divorce papers, then the issues become even more tricky because, in essence, one of you is still married. You don't want this for yourself, and you certainly do not want to encourage your children to have relationships with married people.

If You Decide to Live Together. For right now, remember that if you decide to live together with your children's full knowledge, your children will feel fine about discussing the circumstances at home with teachers and anyone else.

Even though more and more women are sharing their lives with "partners," and not spouses, there are huge pockets in our culture where this is slow to catch on. Your little one may have lots to say at "show and tell" that you might have preferred to keep private. Older children, who might still be harboring anger and resentment, may openly refer to your husband-to-be as "the man my mother screws" and give the full report to back up the statement. If this is okay with you, then okay. It's certainly acceptable to live together—as long as you use caution. For example, some noncustodial fathers have been known to take exception to such premarital arrangements and have sometimes sued for custody and/or caused other grief. So it is usually best to avoid living together and to keep your private life separate from your children.

FROM SINGLE PARENT TO STEPPARENT

Over one million Americans become stepparents each year. There are few greater challenges than bringing together two families to create what the media calls the blended family. It is important to remember that the cre-ation of your new family order will require commitment, hard work, perse-verance, and a lot of unselfish love. It is equally important to remember that by committing yourself to the creation of this blended family, you are giving your children priceless gifts of resilience, adaptability, and tolerance. These gifts will be their reward for the many com-promises all of you will have to make to bring this new family together. There will be change, and change is always difficult and never entirely to our liking.

Your children will have mastered the ability to confront the need for change, do what needs to be done, and move ahead, but think about this: What better preparation for life can there be?

Making the Initial Adjustment. Before you can adjust to the challenges of creating a new family structure, you and particularly your children need to mourn the loss of the original family. This could mean grieving for a lost parent, whether dead or divorced, or facing the loss of the cozy little nest you created as a Mother Outside of Marriage. Additionally, kids worry that your attention to your new spouse means that you will have less affection for them. Moreover, they have to face the fact that their biological parents will never unite. Allow everyone some time to get over the past before beginning anew.

Financial Considerations. More than just deciding how you are going to divide, share, and handle routine household expenses, or who pays for vacations, the cost of rearing children needs to be itemized. Paying for food, housing, college, medical and dental bills, insurance, educational activities, and enrichment are just some of the things that are factored into the cost of raising children. You need to be clear about what your respective contributions will be. Often, a simple written contract clarifies misunderstandings and prevents serious disagreements later.

Unless you have specific arrangements, child support payments from an ex usually end when you remarry.

Feelings About Raising Someone Else's Kids. In an ideal society, it would be the lucky child indeed who not only gets to live with an extended family, but also has the support of those who were at one time a part of a previous chapter in his or her life. It seems an incredible fantasy to visualize a room filled with all the people who are connected to one child and who want what is best for that child. Unfortunately, our culture doesn't lend itself to the type of life style that is found in a commune or a kibbutz. Although we feel an extraordinary bond to our biological children, it is important, on a more spiritual level, to recognize that all children belong to the family of the human race. It is our job as adults to mother them all without prejudice, jealousy, resentment, or fear.

SETTING UP HOUSE RULES

To avoid having his kids get away with murder while your kids are constantly complaining that they have no rights, you and your new partner need to first establish rules and boundaries for the basic operations of running a house.

Make a Contract. Putting these rules in plain sight is an important first step. Print the house rules on a piece of poster paper or any large piece of paper and display them in the kitchen for all to see. Some parents find it useful to make the rules into a kind of contract and have all family members sign their names or draw pictures of themselves to demonstrate their agreement to these "Rules for Living."

Be Specific About Rules. Both you and your partner must agree to these rules. These rules must be capable of being enforced without disagreement about whether or not the rule has been broken. For example, a rule that bedtime must be at a reasonable hour only opens the door for debate and disagreement about what is a reasonable hour. It is better if the rule states that all children are to be in bed by 9:00 P.M. on school nights and 10:00 P.M. on other nights.

Picking up and keeping the house in reasonable order is another common battleground. Try making a rule that all toys should be in the toy box or on the shelves before bedtime rather than a rule that says the house has to be cleaned up before bedtime. "Cleaned up" might not mean the same thing to you that it does to your partner or to the children. In fact, a common bone of contention between men and women is basic disagreement on the definition of "clean"!

The rules need to be clear and enforceable with no room for debate. Start simply and begin with no more than four or five rules.

Choose Your Battles Wisely. It might make you nuts that the toothpaste cap is never replaced, but are you sure this is where you want to make a stand? Wouldn't dirty clothes in the hamper or a less hassled bedtime seem more appealing? Do not hesitate to make a rule forbidding foul language, hitting, or other unacceptable behaviors. Again, remember to be as specific as possible and avoid vague rules like "Be kind to everyone."

When possible, try to write the rules in a positive manner. Instead of writing "Do not turn on TV until homework is finished," try writing instead, "The TV may be turned on only after homework is finished." This small difference creates a more positive tone and adds to the general feeling of cooperation for which you and your partner are striving. Remember that if you and your partner disagree, you should work out these disagreements out of earshot of the children.

Present a United Front. When it is time to post and discuss these rules with the children, present a united front. If you and your new partner are not clearly united, the children will sense this, and then divide and conquer games will begin. Remember also that your children will fight. There will be normal sibling-type disagreements about what show to watch or whose turn it is to sit in the front seat of the car or who ate the last chocolate chip cookie. There cannot be rules to govern every possible circumstance.

Let the Children Settle Their Own Disagreements. Do not think that you have to mediate or settle every dispute. The best response is to tell them to work it out themselves. Children love the structure of rules, and you will chuckle at the complex rules they will devise if the decision is left up to them. You really do not care who sat in the front seat last, so let them work it out and save your energy for the important stuff.

Support Each Other. An important part of setting up household rules is to agree on the consequences for breaking the rules. The consequences must be clearly spelled out, and the children must know that their natural parent will support the other in enforcing these consequences. For example, if the rule is no TV until homework is finished, and your partner's child has not completed his homework, the child needs to be reminded that he cannot plop himself defiantly in front of the TV. If he responds, "You can't tell me what to do because you're not my real mother," warn him that the rule his father helped to write and will enforce is no TV until homework is complete. Emphasize that this is the rule of the household, not your rule.

It is far less likely that there will be such showdowns if each child knows that the other parent will back up the parent who is in charge for that

---

Six Tips for Helping Kids Adjust to the New Family

1. Encourage your children to share thoughts and feelings honestly and openly. Don't discount their feelings of anger, confusion, or even guilt over the former or biological parent. These feelings are to be expected and should be recognized.

2. Communicate with your children about the changing composition of the family. Let them know what is happening by reviewing the events that will take place, when and where, and how these changes will affect them. Specifically, children need to be told what their ongoing contact will be with their non-custodial parent.

3. Be sure to establish a consistent set of expectations, rules, and approaches to discipline. Children need to know what the adults of the family expect of them. Just because your family makeup is shifting, it's not a license for children to behave altogether differently than before. Bedtimes, personal hygiene habits, and dietary patterns should remain pretty much the same.

4. Don't pressure or hurry your child into accepting your or your new spouse's point of view about your new family. Your child has a different opinion. Remember, each person will have his or her own personal adjustments to make. Children need time to develop new relationships at their own pace.

5. Try to find a support group for your child. Many schools, hospitals, and mental health agencies sponsor support groups for those undergoing a change in family structure. A support group is a great way for your child to discuss and compare reactions with other children in similar circumstances.

6. If your child is reacting in a way that is out of your control, seek the advice of a mental health professional. If schoolwork is seriously affected, or if your child's emotional difficulties are resulting in inappropriate behavior at home, a good therapist can help your child make the transition more smoothly.

moment. If the children sense that one parent will soften or not support the other, then there will be defiance and chaos, and nobody, including the children, will have the privilege of living in a happy home. Be ready to back each other up.

Who Disciplines Whose Children? It is simply not realistic or practical to decide that he will discipline his children and you will discipline your own. What happens when one of you is not at home? Avoid physical punishment. Withholding privileges and using time-outs are the best consequences, but be sure you and your partner agree on them. Better yet, jointly create a system of rewards for positive behavior. The goal is to achieve cooperation, not division.

Altered Life Styles. Some of your cherished habits like uninterrupted Sunday mornings with the newspaper may need to be revised in the face of new family arrangements. Your partner may suddenly find himself listening to your daughter's endless hours of introductory violin practice, which sounds more like a chorus of dying cats. Your

new living arrangements mean that adjustments and good will are necessary. Remember, you are the adults. Your behavior will set the tone and provide the model for your children's behavior. If you and your partner are always complaining, bickering, and keeping score, chances are your kids will do so, too. But if you allow the richness that each of you brings to this relationship to flourish, a stronger family will be the result.

Maintain Connections to the Past. People who were once or still are important need to be accepted in your lives. Your new partner may have a cordial relationship with his former wife or significant other, and you should allow room for this friendship to be woven into the material of your new life. The keys here are accommodation, communication, and respect. For example, spending Christmas Eve with your former in-laws is not the best arrangement now. Can you be flexible through creative scheduling that allows you to spend time with his family, too? Maintain a positive mental attitude and a willingness to adapt to change.

24

Expanding Your World

CREATIVE APPROACHES TO COMBINING PERSONHOOD AND PARENTHOOD

One of the most remarkable discoveries that psychologists and social scientists have made about single mothers is their depth of creativity, inventiveness, and resourcefulness. It's sad that we don't read enough about the achievements of many of these women, but it's not unusual to learn that a particular successful person had spent many years as a single mom. One newly single mother who was fond of spending Sunday mornings in bed with the *New York Review of Books* wasn't a bit surprised to learn that *Midnight Lemonade*, a novel that had critics buzzing, was written by a single mother of four, who would arise at 4 A.M. every morning until her manuscript was completed. Other women, whether they are filmmakers, teachers, physical therapists, social workers, students, or those undergoing personal or career changes, have found that their experiences as single mothers prompted them to use innovative methods for balancing their personal development with their roles as mothers. Some underwent significant spiritual changes, while others discovered that their relationships with their children helped them grow and learn about the world in ways they had never perceived before becoming mothers. This chapter is about defining yourself and finding your place in the world. It's about the ways you can expand your horizons while growing as a parent and as a complete woman.

BALANCING WORK AND FAMILY

Most single mothers have to work outside the home. Those who have chosen to return to school see their education as their work. Balancing your work and your family can be difficult, but it doesn't have to be overwhelming if you have a blueprint to follow. Flexibility is a must when combining your career with children, but a blueprint or pattern that allows for this is your best bet.

Take some time to review your schedules, your child's routines, and the realistic options you have available to you. Some mothers make flow charts to order their priorities, and others simply keep lists, lists, and more lists. A calendar posted in an accessible place is a must, and so are phone numbers of "backups"—people or services that can help out in a crunch.

Keep in mind, too, not to overly schedule your child's life, and take every spare moment to reenergize yourself the way you feel is good for you, regardless of what others think. If friends urge you to get away to the beach, but you hate the sun, don't do it. If family members insist you take a nap, but you're too wired and would rather work on a report, do what your heart dictates. Learning where your center of gravity is, or where you feel the least stressed in your decisions, is the first step toward balancing these two life styles.

Returning to Work. Going back to work, whether you have been on maternity leave or you are recently divorced and reentering the work force after staying at home with the kids, can be emotionally devastating.

For the new mom, even though returning to your job is exciting and is actually a relief from the twenty-four-hours-a-day, seven-days-a-week job of beginning motherhood, it's natural to feel guilty about leaving your baby. On the other end of the spectrum is the mom who stayed home during her marriage and now has to enter the work force as a newcomer. The excitement and anticipation of this new life also brings with it feelings of insecurity. You may ask yourself, "What if I can't cut it?" or "How will I ever make enough money with my limited skills?" These are normal feelings. Rest assured that your skills will improve while you are on the job.

However, you might also want to consider getting started on a new or modified career path, or working out of your home. Another way to deal with returning to work is to become updated on what your current job demands, or to ask your new boss to let you come in a few hours for a few days to get settled in before your first big day.

Getting Your Career Back on Track. Jump-starting a career can be difficult for mothers who have taken several months of maternity leave or have been staying home to care for the kids for years. Following are tips for getting your career back on track:

◆ Network with parents you will meet at your Lamaze class, new moms' support group, day-care center, child's school, Little League, or other organizations to see what jobs are out there for you.

◆ Maintain contacts with people with whom you have worked before. Try to have lunch at least twice a month with a former coworker.

◆ Become involved in volunteer activities in your community. This sounds difficult when you're busy with a child, but one hour a week is really not too difficult to slot out.

◆ If you're returning to your regular job after maternity leave, consider job sharing if you'd rather work part-time. Like part-time work, job sharing allows you to spend more time with your baby. But there are more advantages for both employees and employers. Job-sharing positions usually include half of all benefits that full-time employees receive. Additionally, the salary is usually more than a similar part-time position. Plus, the employer benefits by getting two skilled people for the price of one. In fact, studies show that job sharers produce more than one-half of the work, thereby giving the employer more for the money. The fields of medicine, education, administration, and human resources are utilizing job sharing, and a number of major American corporations are beginning to catch on, too. However, the best way to arrange job sharing at your place of business is to find another person in your department who is interested in sharing the position, and for both of you to make a proposal to your manager.

◆ Work full-time with modified hours. This is known as flextime, a work policy that is gaining popularity with many large companies. U.S. Sprint, one of the country's top-ranking long-distance telephone services, employing a large number of single mothers, has found that allowing flexible work schedules promotes happier and more productive work-

ers while having adequate staff to handle "rush hour" work times.

◆ If you simply can't see eye-to-eye with your employer and you see no way of balancing your job with your home life, consider starting your own business. More and more women are going the entrepreneurial route as consultants, bookkeepers, copywriters, data processors, or medical transcriptionists; they are earning money through hobbies such as sewing, interior design, catering, or teaching skills like tennis, swimming, painting, or music. Network in the business forum of the National Organization of Single Mothers newsletter, *SingleMOTHER*. Subscribe to *Entrepreneurial Woman* magazine or join the National Association of Female Executives. *Income Opportunities* is another magazine that can give you great ideas for creating your own work.

◆ Work at home. With the advances in telecommunications and the new shortcuts to the information highway, working at home is a very viable option. Or if you have skills such as sewing, writing, illustration, or hair styling, working at home may be just the solution for you.

◆ Keep current in your field by reading professional journals or trade publications. They often include an employment section or job-hunting guide.

◆ Join or rejoin professional organizations. Keep your memberships current.

◆ Take classes if you need to develop new skills. Your local community college most likely will have computer courses on the latest business trends and software.

♦ Get in touch with the alumni office of your college or professional school. Call an old classmate or teacher for ideas.

♦ Look for companies that are hospitable to women: those with significant numbers of women in upper management; those with part-time or flextime work arrangements; smaller companies and start-ups. Check out *Working Mother* magazine's yearly "Guide to the Best 100 Companies."

♦ Consider part-time employment or a temporary job in your field or in a field you have wanted to work in that could lead to a full-time position.

Try Not to Feel Guilty About Working. Don't feel guilty about not spending enough time with your child because you must go to work. Studies have clocked the actual quality time stay-at-home moms spend with each child, compared with working moms. Believe it or not, the actual time difference was only eight minutes a day more for the stay-at-home parents. Possibly this is because full-time homemakers are distracted by the day-to-day task of tending to children's needs while simultaneously performing household chores. This also can result in the need to escape, whereas the working parent welcomes the change from the work place to the home front and looks forward to seeing the missed child. Also, a 1991 Gallup Poll reports that single parents are good at nurturing and spend quality time with their

---

IF YOU'RE WORKING LATE OR ON AN OVERNIGHT TRIP

Just because you can't be home to tuck your child in bed, it doesn't mean that you can't still have your usual good-night ritual. Call home and read your child her favorite bedtime story. If necessary, get extra copies of her favorite books or tapes and tuck them in your briefcase whenever you're called to put in a late night or go out of town.

---

children, most likely because they are not distracted by another adult in the household. Try to remember this rather than paying attention to the manipulated statistics slanted toward special-interest groups bent on discouraging working mothers and single parents in general.

Out-of-Town Trips. There will be times when you'll be asked to go out of town, take a business trip, work on a weekend, or put in some overtime. These can be difficult decisions, especially if you have an infant or toddler or have never been separated from your children. Always remember that the most important thing you can do for yourself and your family is to be who you are. And although it might be the most valued undertaking in your life, being a parent is not the only definition you give yourself. If you have worked hard to score points in your career and want to advance further in your job, then making that overnight sales trip might be the right decision. Do what feels right, not what you think should be the right thing. As the saying goes, "If Mom ain't happy, ain't nobody happy!"

What to Do When the Kids Have a Snow Day. When your children have an unexpected day off from school or your baby-sitter suddenly cancels and you absolutely cannot miss work, are you prepared? First, find out if you work in a kid-friendly place. Inquire about what seems to be the unwritten office rule on bringing children to the office. If you have been with the company only a short time, ask a colleague if children are ever brought to the office when there is a baby-sitting or weather emergency. Do you see other people bringing their children into the office from time to time? Obviously some work places are dangerous or inappropriate for children—clearly the case if you are an assembly line worker or a police officer or firefighter. But, in most offices, children are occasionally tolerated and sometimes even welcomed.

If your work place is able to tolerate your children in such cases, count your blessings and get prepared. Have food set aside to "nuke" for them in the office microwave and have snacks available to bring along. Juice boxes and other such high-priced convenience foods are well worth the price of keeping your children fueled up and content during your work day. You should also think ahead about what your children will bring along to keep them occupied. Even the copying machine loses its fascination after a while, and you certainly do not want your children making pests of themselves. Best suggestions are quiet activities like coloring books and board games. You should also plan to discuss ahead of any scheduling emergency the kind of behavior you expect from your children when they accompany you to the office. If your boss wears the most obvious hairpiece in America, discuss this fact with your eight-year-old well ahead of time,

BEATING THE MORNING MADNESS!

If the morning rush leaves you frenzied and frazzled—dressing, feeding, and shuffling your young child off to day care or school so you can be on time for work—try an old army tip: Dress your child at bedtime with the next morning's attire. You don't have to put outerclothes on her, but at least put on socks and underwear, and maybe a T-shirt or jogging outfit that's comfortable to sleep in. Save the cute little bunny suits and teddy bear jammies for the weekend. After all, kids really don't have much of a fashion sense at a young age, and would much prefer that you spend the few extra minutes saved in the morning cuddling them, rather than wasting time wrestling them out of their sleepwear. Naturally, this suggestion works only if your child is dry through the night.

If you're concerned that your child is too young to know the difference between night and day, and you want to have a special ritual for bedtime, you can still partially dress them for the next day and tuck them in with a special blanket or stuffed animal. Babies should be in comfortable, fire-retardant attire and not kept too warm.

rather than have him blurt out, "Your wig is really a funny color. How come it doesn't stick on your head better?" when he is introduced the morning of the big snowstorm.

When You Cannot Bring Your Children to Work. If your work place is not kid-friendly or even kid-tolerant, you will need a backup plan for bad weather or no-baby-sitter days. Look for resources close by. Is there an elderly neighbor who might welcome the extra cash and diversion for the day but who is not interested in baby-sitting full-time? Is there a high school student who might be available to sit on days when there is no school? How about a teacher or other member of the school staff who is off on days when school is closed for weather emergencies? Can you offer her a free Saturday in exchange for the help you need when schools are unexpectedly closed?

Once your plan is in place, make additional preparations at home. Set aside easily prepared, kid-favorite lunch foods for your children to take along, or simply be ready to send along their regular brown-bag lunch. If their destination house has a VCR, send along favorite tapes, which incidentally a senior citizen might actually enjoy watching with them. It is never a bad idea to send along coloring books, board games, and other quiet activities. Discuss with your children any changes in routine that might take place if your backup plan has to be put in place. For example, if your elderly neighbor is your backup sitter, discuss any special rules she might have, like staying away from her not-so-friendly cat. The peace of mind is well worth the efforts this planning involves—not to mention the stress-busting effect of knowing that you are prepared if the unexpected happens.

Should You Call in Sick to Care for Your Child? It's amazing how many parents still call up insensitive bosses claiming that they cannot come to work because their car broke down, or a power outage prevented the alarm from going off, rather than admit that they must stay home with a feverish child. Other excuses range from underground gas explosions to attending a relative's funeral for the umpteenth time rather than saying that a child needs to see a doctor or dentist or is appearing in a school play.

Before you call in sick instead of asking for time off to attend your daughter's school awards ceremony, try to think about the ways you can take time off for your child and function effectively at work.

Start by requesting a conference with your boss. Ask him or her to meet with you, preferably during your lunch hour or during a slow period. Open the talk on an upbeat note, assuring your supervisor how dedicated you are to your job and how much you want to do your very best. Let your supervisor know, too, however, that it is important for you to be honest when something comes up requiring you to attend to your son's or daughter's needs.

If this person makes critical remarks when you seek time off, make him or her aware that these comments hurt and prevent you from being truthful. But ask questions, too. Perhaps your supervisor is edgy because you are not completing your tasks or are failing to close certain sales. Does he or she feel that you are not doing your job up to par? How can your performance improve? Does your absence creates chaos?

After you've heard your boss's side, it's time to make it clear that you want to do everything possible to cooperate. For example, can you work out a buddy system with a coworker who can cover for you in the event of your absence? Can you take some work home, make calls outside of the office, send your work via computer and modem, or even come in a little earlier one day? Once your supervisor knows that you have made every effort to help the business run smoothly even when you aren't there, he or she will begin to consider your needs and will respect you more for your honesty, consideration, and commitment to work and family.

Working During the Summer.
Unless you have the budget of a movie star, filling those long summer months with safe, healthy, fun activities can seem like an impossible task. But before you succumb to the "What-am-I-going-to-do-with-the-kids-this-summer?" panic, try to realize that most working parents face the same dilemma. Know, too, that there are resources and solutions available if you know where to look.

Keep in mind that because the demand for summer child care is so great, you need to plan early. Regardless of whether you choose a pricey camp or an inexpensive swim club through your local parks and recreation service, these programs fill up fast. The best strategy is to start planning summer activities between the time you put the last of the Christmas tree decorations away and before Valentine's Day!

CONTINUING YOUR EDUCATION

Are you spending too much time wishing you could win the lottery? If you are tired of being strapped for cash or relying on public assistance or undependable child support, you should consider continuing your education. The more education you have, the more money you will make. Nothing will move your life ahead with greater certainty than improving your job skills.

Nobody said that going back to school as a single parent is going to be easy. But nothing worthwhile ever is, and the rewards of getting this valuable education are endless.

For example, you can increase your skills to advance in your job or simply to make yourself employable for the first time. Never forget that knowledge is power. People want to and need to be around people who possess a great deal of knowledge about how things work in our ever-changing world. In addition, you are setting a priceless example for your children as they watch you organize your time efficiently, study for exams, research topics for your homework assignments, and—most importantly of all—set goals and achieve them. Plus, school-age children who enjoy having a homework buddy actually relish the fact that their moms and they do homework together!

CAREER PLANNING

Here is a list of things to get you started on your new or modified career path, according to New York University's Center for Career and Life Planning:

- Self-assessment: Try to determine what you have always wanted to do, incorporating your values, interests, skills, motivation, and personality style.

- Research: Find out what kinds of jobs really exist out there by reading and talking to people in the field.

- Putting it together: Make some choices, looking at pros and cons of your job options as well as your personal, financial, and familial needs.

- Training: Read, take a course, volunteer, be an apprentice.

- Trying it out: Go after what you want. It could change your whole life!

Don't Ignore the Opportunities.
There are so many opportunities out there waiting for you. You might decide to enroll in college classes, sign up for a series of special training seminars at work, take a night course to learn to appraise antiques, get your real estate broker's license, or take correspondence courses. The list of possible educational opportunities is endless.

You're Not Too Old to Start

I have always loved interior design and have helped many friends decorate their homes. I know I have a real flair. The problem is that to get the job I want I must have at least a two-year degree. I can probably only afford to go to the local community college part-time. By the time I get my degree I'll be forty.

You are going to be forty anyway, so why not go back to college and celebrate forty with a degree? Start planning the future you want and remember that the birthdays come and go even if we have not begun to move ahead to reach our goals.

"I Don't Want to Be the Oldest Student..."

I would like to earn my bachelor's degree in nursing. I have worked as a nurse's aide for many years. I worry that I will be a lot older than my classmates in the nursing program.

First of all, it is unlikely that your age will be of great interest to your fellow nursing students. In fact, one-third of college students today are "older"— thirty-five years and up.

Your fellow students will probably envy your practical knowledge and experience and will be flocking to be your study partners, as so many mature women returning to school soon find out.

Fear of Failing

I have not opened a book in years. I always hated school and got only mediocre grades in high school. My boss wants to send me to a special company training program so that I can upgrade my skills and earn a promotion. What if I can't cut it?

Your experiences as an adult in a career training program will be a far cry from beginning algebra and world history. Probably in high school you saw little point in the subjects you were expected to learn and were distracted by normal teenage concerns like boys, dates, and parties.

Now motivation won't be a problem because education means something else to you—more money, a better life for you and your family. But since you have been out of school so long, you might want to do a little homework before school starts. Bone up on your reading, math, or computer skills. If necessary, find a high school student to tutor you.

If You Never Finished High School.
If you never obtained a high school diploma, then look into the General Educational Development (GED) Test. This test is a battery of five comprehensive examinations in social studies, science, writing, reading, and mathematics. This test was developed during World War II to help returning servicemen and servicewomen complete their

high school educations. Since then, millions of Americans have received their high school equivalency certification by passing this test.

If this opportunity interests you, your best bet is to call a local community college. Ask to speak with an admissions counselor. It is likely that the college offers classes to help prepare you for taking the GED. If there is no community college in your area, contact your high school guidance office and ask where information about this test might be obtained.

Getting a High School Diploma Through the Mail. Completing your high school education through a home correspondence program will give you the advantage of flexibility and the ability to work at your own pace. This opportunity might be just the solution if your children are still infants, dependable transportation is a problem, or you need to squeeze studying in between job and family responsibilities.

Institutions that offer high school diplomas through correspondence study are listed in the Resource Roundup at the end of this book.

Correspondence Schools. Earning a high school equivalency diploma is just one opportunity that correspondence schools provide. There are more than four hundred correspondence schools in the United States offering hundreds of courses. Some even offer accredited academic degrees.

Before enrolling, inquire about cost, the length of study, and what happens if you fail to complete the program. If your plan is to transfer correspondence credits toward a degree program, it is your responsibility to make sure beforehand

that the courses and the credit hours will be accepted by the school from which you hope to eventually graduate.

Vocational Correspondence Courses. Vocational home study courses train you in such specialized fields as locksmithing, interior design, auto mechanics, landscaping, and clerical skills. As a general rule, credits earned from such programs cannot be applied toward a college degree. Course length ranges from a few weeks to over four years of study. This might be the plan for you if your job skills are weak but you would have difficulty attending a traditional training program because of responsibilities at home.

Sound interesting? Get a free copy of the *Directory of Accredited Home Study Schools*, available from the National Home Study Council, 1601 18th Street N.W., Washington, DC 20009.

Academic Correspondence Courses. Academic correspondence courses designed specifically to earn college credits are also available. This is ideal for the mom who wants to begin earning college credits while still working and taking care of her children.

Begin by looking into programs accredited by the Independent Study Division of the National University Continuing Education Association (NUCEA). NUCEA is a professional organization of approximately seventy colleges and universities offering correspondence courses.

Obtain specific information about NUCEA correspondence courses by getting a publication entitled *The Independent Study Catalog: The NUCEA Guide to Independent Study Through Correspondence Instruction*

(Peterson's Guides, P.O. Box 2123, Princeton, New Jersey 08543. Telephone: 1-800-338-3282).

Are You a Good Tester? Several thousand colleges and universities award college and university credit based solely on examinations. These tests are called equivalency examinations, and they allow you to demonstrate college-level learning that you have acquired outside the classroom. This option could save you much time and money because it would allow you to enter a college program at the advanced level. Sometimes, successfully completing these examinations will also fulfill professional licensing and certification requirements.

How to Begin. The first step is to speak with the admissions counselor at the college or university from which you would like to receive your degree. Ask if this school will grant you credit for equivalency exams and, if so, for what courses. Will the school grant you the maximum number of credits for these exams? What will be the charge, if any, for credit transferred to your college transcript? Some colleges add credit for no charge while others charge half tuition.

Whom to Contact. The most widely accepted credit-by-exam program is the College Level Examination Program (CLEP). More than 200,000 students "CLEP out" of classes each year, because nearly three-quarters of all accredited colleges will award credit for passing scores on the CLEP exams.

If you think you might qualify to earn college credit, write for the free publications *Make Learning Pay with CLEP*, and *CLEP Colleges: Where You Can Be Tested/Where You Can Get Credit*. The address for both of these publications is CLEP, CN 6601, Princeton, New Jersey 08541-6601. Telephone: 609-951-1026.

Earn Credit for Life Experience. You can earn academic credit for skills you have acquired through your daily living, including volunteer work, noncredit courses like company in-service training, travel, independent reading, or conversations with experts. Credit can be earned toward a degree, provided you document these learning experiences and submit them to the school in the form of a life experience portfolio.

Everything you need to know is contained in an excellent guidebook entitled *Earn College Credit for What You Know* by Lois Lamdin. To get a copy, write to the Council for Adult and Experiential Learning (CAEL), 223 West Jackson, Suite 510, Chicago, Illinois 60606. Telephone: 312-922-5909.

When Correspondence School Isn't Right for You. Many single mothers discover that their progress toward a degree or certification is not rapid or steady enough. A step-by-step program of study is needed, but they don't have the time and money to commute to a campus.

Imagine a university right in your own home. This is the opportunity offered through University Without Walls (UWW), an international network of colleges and universities offering both graduate and undergraduate degrees through external study. These are not "diploma mills" but accredited institutions that specialize, among other things, in nontraditional study.

Colleges that offer short residency or nonresidency programs allow you to earn a degree while spending little or no time living on the campus. This means you could earn a degree in the field of your choice while living thousands of miles from the campus.

There are many colleges and universities that offer such opportunities. A good place to begin is to contact Mind Extension University at 1-800-727-5663. They can send you information about their program and also provide you with listings of other colleges and universities that offer short residency or nonresidency programs.

Don't Overlook Your Local Community College. Sixty percent of all jobs today do not require a four-year college degree. Your local community college may be your best bet for improving your job prospects by upgrading your skills.

Community colleges typically offer three different kinds of programs:

Certificate Programs. Certificate programs provide you with training for a specific job, like real estate appraiser, cosmetologist, dental laboratory technician, or legal secretary. For these kinds of jobs you do not need or probably want extra courses in subjects like sociology or political science. Students who enter these types of programs are looking to prepare for new careers, make themselves eligible for promo-

tion, or just stay current with new knowledge in their field.

The course of study can range anywhere from a couple of weeks to two years, depending upon what coursework is required. The opportunities that such certificate programs provide are very often not available at two- or four-year university-sponsored degree programs.

Associate Degree in Applied Science. An associate in applied sciences (SAAS) degree is awarded to students who complete sixty hours of credit—about four semesters—in a specific sequence of courses. These courses are not meant to be the freshman and sophomore years of a traditional four-year degree program. These two-year programs are designed to prepare students for entry into the work force immediately in fields such as dental hygiene, interior design, office administration, police science, and finance and credit management.

Transfer or Associate in Arts Degree. Students who think they might wish to obtain a four-year degree eventually often begin by enrolling in a community college to obtain an Associate in Arts degree, which generally takes four semesters full-time to complete. Such a degree will transfer to a four-year institution so that a bachelor's degree can be earned. Some students find such a plan a big money-saver—certainly of interest to the strapped-for-cash single mother—and others find they need this first step to gain the confidence and experience to continue their education.

My high school grades were a nightmare. I would really love to begin attending classes at the university part-time, but I know they will not accept me into a degree program with my terrible high school record.

Enrollment in a community college would be a good idea. The good grades you will earn will be considered better evidence of your abilities than your high school grades. In other words, time spent doing well in a community college can prepare you to enroll in a more selective four-year program when your high school record is less than fabulous.

Should I Think About Enrolling in a Private Career School?

I see ads on television all the time for schools that promise high-paying jobs as a professional after you complete their state-of-the-art education program in whatever. What is the story with these schools?

The schools you see advertised on television are called private career schools or proprietary schools. They are private businesses and their purpose is to make a profit. Some of these schools do grant associate degrees, although the faculty is less permanent than in a community college. On a more positive side, these schools are more sensitive and quicker to change in response to economic forces and changes in the job market than more traditional schools.

These schools will ask you to sign a contract, and their programs will typically be more expensive than community colleges. The courses offered will be very practical and will be oriented toward getting a job upon completion of the program. Some typical courses of study at such schools include auto mechanics, truck driving, and computer

technology, but other courses are also available. Hands-on experience is offered, and a new training program usually begins every three or four weeks.

A Word of Caution About Private Career Schools. Before you sign the contract, ask: What will happen if I don't complete the course work? Does the school offer career counseling and placement? What percentage of graduates receive jobs in their field? How long does it take for a graduate to find a job? What are the names of some employers who hire the school's graduates? If the responses are not satisfactory, don't enroll.

Make sure you also take a tour of the school and speak to the current students. They will tell you the real story. Ask for the names of some recent graduates and contact them directly to see how they rate the training they received.

How Will I Pay for This? Lack of money is the biggest obstacle for a single parent thinking of returning to school, followed by worries over time management. Let's face it, education after high school is not cheap. Not only do you have tuition costs but there are books and transportation costs, and child care to consider. But don't view the money you'll need or the income you'll lose by not working while attending school as a waste. Think of it as an investment. Studies have shown that those with post-high school training will earn a minimum $750,000 during their lifetime, much more than a person with only a high school diploma. Additionally, there are various part-time jobs that are ideal for moms attending classes, including tutoring, cleaning houses and offices, and working as a courier. Many single moms take in sewing, custom alterations, and even ironing because these can be done at home after their children are asleep.

Where Are the Big Bucks? The biggest sources of financial aid are the colleges, universities, and other types of schools themselves. In fact, ninety percent of financial aid is campus-based money. This means that when you apply for admission to the school of your choice, you must also apply for financial aid. Schools may have different forms and requirements, but all require promptness and legibility. Type, if possible, rather than handwrite. Seek help from the school's financial aid director.

Federal Aid. There are five major student financial aid programs through which most students requiring financial aid receive help. These programs are administered by the federal government though the Department of Education. Two are grant programs, which means this is money you will not have to pay back. These grant programs are the Pell Grant and the Supplemental Educational Opportunity Grant (SEOG). Two other programs are loan programs, which means, of course, that you will have to pay this money back with interest, although usually at a rate lower than current rates. These are the Perkins Loan and the Stafford Student Loan. The fifth program is the College Work Study (CWS), which helps colleges provide jobs for students receiving financial aid.

What You Should Know About Financial Aid

All state, federal, and campus-funded programs of financial aid are accessible through the Free Application for Federal Student Aid (FAFSA). This form is absolutely free and can be obtained in any high school guidance office. You must submit a completed FAFSA as soon after January 1 as you can, but not sooner or it will be returned to you. Most financial aid awards are given on the basis of need, and need is determined by the information you provide on the FAFSA. Complete this form properly and in a timely way, to avoid losing your eligibility to receive aid from federally sponsored programs.

If you need help filling out the form or have questions, call the Federal Student Aid Information Center during regular business hours at 1-800-4-FED-AID.

After you apply for federal student aid, you will receive a Student Aid Report in about a month. This report will contain the information you provided, but it will also give you information about your eligibility for certain federal aid programs and will be used to determine your further eligibility for campus-based aid.

Other Sources of Financial Aid. Although most financial aid money comes from the schools themselves and from the federal government, you should thoroughly investigate other sources of possible aid. Millions of dollars of aid money goes unclaimed every year because the students who were eligible were not aware that such money was literally theirs for the asking. Many scholarships, for example, are for people who come from specific towns or belong to certain organizations. This is one of those situations where a little legwork and time in the library can really pay off.

Who Is Eligible to Participate in These Federally Sponsored Programs?

For most programs you must be enrolled at least half-time at an approved college or program of study. You must be a United States citizen or permanent resident. You must use the aid for educational expenses, and you cannot be in default on another student loan or owe a refund on a federal grant. You must qualify on the basis of need.

What to Expect After You Apply for Financial Aid.

Your college or university will put together a financial aid package for you. This package will give a breakdown of the campus-based aid you will receive as well as the federally sponsored loans and other grants for which you are eligible. Your college financial office can help you apply for any federally sponsored aid to which you are entitled. This financial aid package, given to you in the form of a one-page statement, will also tell you at a glance how much money you will have to provide in order to meet the expected costs of books and tuition.

What About Time Management?

Treat going to school as you would going to a job. The same rules that you would apply to showing up at work apply to receiving your education. The pay is different, but the credit you'll earn from school is more rewarding in the long run.

I am scared that I will not be able to handle all the responsibilities of going to school and raising my children. I feel selfish, like I will be shortchanging them, but I really want to go to school.

You're not selfish for wanting to improve conditions for yourself and your children. You may actually become a better role model by showing them how you set goals and deal with conflicting demands. They may wind up more self-reliant, too.

My teenage children are thrilled that I am going to be a student at the local community college. I should be preparing them for the changes my school attendance will bring. What should we discuss?

Talk to them about making compromises. Although they may lose the on-call chauffeur, the always available cook, and the always open ear, they are getting a happier, more successful mother. Prepare your children for what changes in routine and expectations may occur. Reassign chores ahead of time, and go through a rehearsal to see if you can work some of the kinks out of the system before the first day of school arrives.

The key to a successful educational career is time management. You will have to be organized every single day in order to fit everything in. At the same time, you will have to be adaptive enough to accommodate unexpected changes in routine, like when a child gets sick or the weather is uncooperative.

Ten Tips for Doing Your Best in School

1. Keep the vision of your goals in front of you. How will you know when you have achieved your goal? Will it be the moment you are handed your diploma? Will it be the moment you see your name

and title on the door? Keep a vision in your mind of that moment and use it to keep you motivated and focused on the task at hand. If your goal is symbolized by a picture, keep that picture handy and look at it often.

2. Share your vision with others. Other people cannot help you if they have no idea what your dreams or goals might be. Some people might resent your ability to go after what you want, but most people will support you and help you in ways you never would have asked for.

3. Write down your goals. Make your goals specific. For example, I will have taken all my required courses by the spring of next year. I will do this by taking two courses each semester and one course during the summer. Or, I will attend every optional career seminar offered, even if it is scheduled on Friday afternoon. Make a contract with yourself and sign your name. Promise yourself to move ahead with a well-thought-out plan.

4. Plan on paper. Once something is written down, it is a plan. If you keep it only in your mind, then it is just an idea without form or substance.

5. Get organized. Do not think you are going to plop your stuff down on the kitchen table every night. Find a shelf, a box, or a secondhand file cabinet in which to store all your school materials. The kitchen table can certainly turn into your "school desk" at night, but you need a definite and well-organized place to put everything. Otherwise, you will waste valuable study time looking for things you have misplaced or for things the children have somehow managed to "borrow."

6. Single mothers do not have the option to procrastinate. Students without the responsibilities you have may be able to put off studying or writing a paper until the last minute. Guaranteed, the first time you put off an important school paper, your kids will get the flu and the paper will not be done on time. The best way to manage the inevitable stresses of juggling multiple responsibilities is to do things as they need to be done. Then, when your assignments are completed, you can enjoy without guilt the time away from the pressures of school.

7. Rethink your standards. Does your house have to be spotless? Is watching that TV show really that important? Can you set aside certain hobbies or interests while you are in school? At work, you may volunteer for fewer extra projects or work less overtime. This is a time to concentrate on the task at hand—to finish school so your goals can be realized.

8. Learn to delegate. Think about what you absolutely do not have to do yourself and then don't do it. Your children will be infinitely better off as independent creatures capable of packing their own lunches and picking up after themselves.

9. Learn to say no. While you are in school, you must learn to say no to demands that do not help you to move along with your studies or personally benefit you and your children. If this is difficult for you, get a friend to help you role play.

10. Treat yourself once in a while. Pat yourself on the back, buy yourself a candy bar, and savor every unhealthy but nonetheless scrumptious mouthful. Take a walk in the sunshine while reciting in your head recent accomplishments. Enjoy hearing, if only in your head, "Congratulations. Dr. Jones loved your presentation, and you got a B on a quiz that you were sure you failed." If you are not going to say good things about you, who is?

CREATING AN EXTENDED FAMILY

Emotions are contagious. Moods are like social viruses—some people have a natural ability to transmit them, while others are more likely to catch them. Women were reported to be in negative moods almost twice as much as men, although studies indicate that women were generally happier than men.

One way to catch positive feelings is to be around upbeat people. Avoid toxic people—they just pull you into their mood. Another way is to join a support group.

Seeking Self-help Through a Support Group. Support and self-help groups are a great way to balance positive and negative feelings. According to a Gallup Poll, one American in three belongs to some kind of support or self-help group. George Gallup, Jr., says, "In our fragmented society, where loneliness and isolation are so prevalent, it is encouraging to see so many people reaching out to each other. It's a very hopeful sign for the future."

Many scientists also agree that participating in self-help groups can lead to longer and healthier lives.

How to Organize a Support Group. Don't waste your time reinventing the wheel. Visit some support groups to observe how they operate. You can even borrow tips from their material, their flyers, and their meeting formats. Even if there is no other group in your area for single parents, visiting a new moms' group, sitting in on a regular gathering of divorced parents, or attending a meeting for parents of children who have Attention Deficit Hyperactivity Disorder can prove invaluable in the ideas that you can come away with. Although twelve-step programs such as AA, Al-Anon, and Parents Anonymous have been the sanest thing for those suffering from addictions or other spiritual diseases, the National Organization of Single Mothers (NOSM) does not believe that single mothering is something from which one requires recovery. However, NOSM does believe that many of the negative beliefs single mothers carry around can benefit from a group structure that looks to a force or power that is higher or stronger than the individual.

Don't Overlook the Word "Mutual." You need to find a few others who want to help you start the support group. If you try to manage everything yourself, you will find yourself burning out somewhere down the road. Besides, it is to the other members' benefit to be part of planning activities and tending to the initial tasks required in starting a self-help group. If a few women feel as though they are there to be rescued, their feelings of helplessness and powerlessness cannot be overcome, and they will remain dependent on others to provide their well-being. With everyone pulling her own weight, the collective power in such a group can be increased to the point where everyone becomes empowered.

Select a Steering Committee. A steering committee or core group is necessary to assign chores to other members, particularly if you are planning for fairly large gatherings. For example, one person can handle refreshments, another can be responsible for greeting visitors and handing out name tags, and still others can manage the child care and publicity for the group.

Find a Suitable Place for Your Meetings. Until you can find a home for your group, such as a library, community center, church or synagogue, school, hospital, or human service agency, try meeting at members' homes. You can also arrange to have a monthly bring-your-own picnic meeting at a local park or recreation center. Start out by rotating members' houses and apartments until you find that you have outgrown these facilities. One of the advantages of small groups in your home is that you can all take turns watching the children. Also consider the best times

for these meetings and try to stick to them. Would day, weekends, or evenings be better for most members? It's easier for people to remember the meeting time if it is always the same day of the week or month. Keep in mind, too, that you can start with very informal gatherings that spend only a few minutes on the business aspects of your support group. For example, one California chapter of NOSM simply holds a potluck supper twice a month at a large recreation facility. The adults can enjoy good conversation, music, and food while the little ones run around in the nearby playground or play on the provided equipment.

Publicize Your First Meeting. In general, when starting a support group, reaching potential members is not easy, but with all the single mothers out there looking for others with whom to network, it may not be that difficult, either. Remember that your local media are always looking for community events to announce to their viewers or readers. For instance, most news shows on local channels, local newspapers, and area magazines have a community calendar that permits free listings. Be sure to print up a flyer or a press release that you can mail or fax to every radio and TV station, and even to corporate newsletters and house organs. Not only might businesses and companies in your community have employees who would be interested in joining a support group, but these corporations might want to participate to show the community their concern for families. Keep in mind, too, that you can place flyers or notices in places where single mothers congregate. Doctors' offices, dental clinics, post offices, schools, day-care centers, community centers, hospitals, libraries, pharmacies, and grocery stores are excellent places to publicize your group. If you receive any resistance—say, a building custodian tells you that solicitation is forbidden in the office complex where you are about to post notices—reply that this is for a nonprofit support group and you are certain that this facility would want to do its share in promoting a resource to help families. By being clear and focused on what you want to see come out of such a support group, you will be able to sell this idea more easily to those members of your community from whom you seek assistance.

Plan Your Meeting Agenda. Here are the five most important considerations when planning future meetings:

1. Purpose of the group. Although you should have this pretty much figured out at your initial meeting, you may learn from members what areas of concern are strongest, and what areas do not require much attention. For instance, if most of your members are MOMs and not divorced women, then addressing issues such as finding male role models may be more welcome than discussing methods of coparenting or which lawyers are best for a custody battle. Conversely, if your group is primarily composed of divorced women who are having trouble collecting child support, then this would be a stronger area of focus than, say, talking about donor insemination.

2. Membership. Recruit members through publicity (see previous section).

3. Meeting format. You can arrange to have a monthly bring-your-own picnic meeting at a local park or recreation center, or your meetings can be as formal as, say, having a guest speaker or lecturer.

4. Telephone tree. Give each member approximately three names of people to whom they are responsible for relaying information about group activities or updates. Also, each member should be able to call people on their list for mutual support, venting, and even small talk.

5. Raising money. Groups charge a small membership fee and at some meetings pass around a basket for funds to help with the cost of hiring baby-sitters and to pay for paper, printing/copying, and postage and mailing.

Other Activities. You may want to have professionals in your community speak to your group, or you may be even more industrious and plan large projects such as building a day-care center for single-parent families. Go slowly, and work with a parent agency as your needs and group size grow. Be sure to keep abreast of all legal and federal regulations pertaining to nonprofit groups raising money for major projects.

FINDING A SPIRITUAL HOME

One single mother in her mid-thirties who has been building a quality life for herself and her boys looks back to a time when she relied strongly on others to make the simplest decisions. "I don't know why I stayed in bad relationships, or why I let my second husband, the father of one of my children, dictate what I felt, thought, and did. I just didn't have any other sources of strength, I guess. He was like a god to me."

At that time, she belonged to a church, yet had much difficulty getting him to attend. So she, like many others who couldn't drag their partners to a particular house of worship, gave up on her spiritual search. She felt that if her significant other didn't accompany her, then it was meaningless. But nothing could be further from the truth. Attending a house of worship often has as much to do with spiritual fulfillment as with serving as a social outlet.

Why It's Important to Find a Spiritual Center. Religious scholars have noticed that even though various religious dogmas and beliefs dictate different practices and rituals, most were developed for one basic reason: to give families living under patriarchy (which accounted for most religions founded on Judeo-Christian principles) rules for living morally and with conformity under a set of standards designed to help males and females cohabit. But many are finding that these religious standards don't celebrate the home headed by a single female, whether or not she is a mother. Because of this, there has been a great advancement in what is known as the women's spiritual movement, geared toward more "female affirming" spirituality.

Now, this doesn't mean that you should immediately join a cult of goddess worshippers or study Wicca to cultivate powers against which men have no defense. Nor should you run out and purchase crystals or herbs in search of a New Age religious experience because you feel rebellious against a

"Father God." What it does mean is that God is important but He does not necessarily take the form of a male entity or father figure. Remember, many of those who need God as a father figure may have had fathers at home but missed the experience of being "fathered." It also means that along with the democratization of society, in which women are gaining more power over their lives, there is a democratizing of religion, too.

For households headed by single mothers, particularly where Mom often feels overwhelmed and lacks a full-time supportive adult with whom to share tasks, the belief that there is something bigger than themselves is very comforting. But you don't need traditional beliefs to be spiritual. God can be anything, look like anything, and be called by any name or not be called by a name at all. Just know that you are not alone. No matter how big some crises you face appear to be, the world will continue regardless, so why not let go of some of the stress and find a little peace by focusing on something bigger than yourself?

I'm a twenty-nine-year-old single woman who recently gave birth to the sweetest, most wanted baby. His father left the day before he was born. When I showed up last week at a neighborhood church, the members suggested that I need to be "saved." They stress that a deeper relationship with the Lord will provide my son with a "loving, all-knowing father," but frankly their concern upsets me. Does God have to be a "father" in order for my family to thrive? I have found an inner strength since the birth of my son, but now I'm confused. I do want a spiritual life for myself and my son, but we don't need to be saved from the choices about parenting I have made.

Religion is a deeply personal subject and no one should suggest or urge anyone to move from one place of worship to another or to convert to another religious faith. Any way you choose to believe in God is all right for you and your family. It might be helpful, however, for you to be aware that many churches today are actively seeking to meet the needs of their single-parent members. Some women report that less traditional synagogues and churches meet their needs best, while others have worshipped at the Unitarian Universalist Association, a church that embraces single mothers and the right to believe your own way. Based on Judeo-Christian ideals, it is not as New Age as some might think. (Thomas Jefferson and Benjamin Franklin both attended Unitarian churches.)

You're right—you don't need more "saving" as a single mother than does anyone else. Your own path of spiritual growth might eventually lead you to choose to worship with a congregation that is more embracing of single parents.

Casting Stones

I am in my late twenties, and my fiancé died while I was in my fourth month of pregnancy. Most resources for widows seem to be for elderly women. Also, I feel that because I wasn't married before I became pregnant I am being unfairly judged. The women at my church where I've tried to establish a support group

can't relate to me. And married mothers who attend my church and are the same age make me feel self-conscious and out of place. Even though my religious community claims they are recognizing single motherhood, I sometimes feel like they are "casting stones" because of my unwed mother status. What can I do?

Former first lady Eleanor Roosevelt said a lot when she remarked: "Nobody can make you feel inferior without your consent."

Sometimes we allow others' opinions of us to dictate how we feel about ourselves. And, all too often, we misread their inability or uneasiness to relate to issues that are rarely part of their daily scope as being inconsiderate or judgmental.

It's up to you to convey the message that you want to be a part of their activities, or at least be accepted in your religious community for who you are, whether widowed, unmarried, divorced, or even single by choice. But don't expect people, especially those limited or unexposed to nontraditional life-style situations, to initiate a close or intimate relationship with you. It's a sad fact of life, but there are and will always be some people who are immovable and whom you will never be able to please. But it's *always* worth a try.

Since your attempts at organizing a support group are meeting a brick wall, why not consider joining another church, one a little more embracing of single parents? Just be careful not to join a group that feels that being a single parent is a shortcoming. Make sure they accept it as a viable family life style.

GROWING WITH YOUR CHILDREN

Being a parent doesn't mean always being in the position of teacher. We learn about the world around us through the eyes of children if we are just willing to look at what they see. Parent development, like child development, is not a one-way street. It's a growth process that lasts as long as you are willing to let it.

Inasmuch as we are the ones to show children how to hold a paintbrush, how to tie their shoes, and how not to hurt themselves, our children can teach us to create and to heal. They help us establish new routines and ways of thinking and doing things, such as creating new family traditions—sources of joy that can emerge from something that once was painful. As long as you focus on your parental development, your children will continue to grow, too.

Seasonal Celebrations and Holidays. Establishing new traditions is the secret to getting through holidays and celebrations such as birthdays, Fourth of July picnics, and other events. Trying to make things fit a certain scheme or reliving what you did before you became a single mother is only an invitation to disappointment and failure. The flexible person who doesn't try to halt change experiences the most joy in whatever comes her way. For example, if you and your child's father celebrated Mother's Day in bed (after he served breakfast), don't ruin your day by pining for what can't be. Instead, think up new ways to celebrate, such as going out to breakfast or brunch.

If Memorial Day was a time when you cooked out with your ex, why not celebrate his birthday that day instead, and you and your kids can get to indulge in gooey birthday cake, candles and all. If Passover is important to you, learn the Haggadah (available from any synagogue) and conduct a seder with your friends and family with you heading the Passover table!

Beating the Holiday Blues. It's just before Christmas and here it comes— the final assault of television ads flashing their rapid succession of "perfect-family" holiday images—you know, where the teary wife finds a diamond in her yogurt placed by her hunky husband. Or where eternal happiness is found, if not in a bottle of good scotch, then certainly in a bottle of cologne. And of course, the kids will never again misbehave because they got megacrates of brain-sizzling electronic gizmos and dolls that laugh, cry, teach sex education, and painfully mature so they won't have to.

It's enough to make anyone feel depressed, especially single parents. But a real Thanksgiving, Christmas, Hanukkah, New Year's, or Kwanzaa celebration is what you make it. Here's help for driving away the holiday blues and assuring you and yours a really fabulous time.

◆ Feeling like less of a family because there is no man around to carve the bird? Arm yourself with *Why Do I Think That I Am Nothing Without A Man* by Penelope Russianoff (Bantam Books) and *Necessary Losses* by Judith Viorst (Ballantine Books). Read anything by Erica Jong and load up on Marge Piercy's works. Get your hands on every book for, by, and about successful, independent women, such as the biography of remarkable author and single mother George Sands. Or witness her notorious seduction (under the piano) of legendary composer Chopin by renting *Impromptu* from your local video store.

◆ Round up the kids and head down to a shelter or soup kitchen and volunteer to help with a sumptuous holiday meal. You'll be setting a great example for your children by showing them that your family has ample warmth and love to share on the holidays with other families who are currently undergoing some kind of burden. Invite a single mother and her children to dinner. There are also many battered women's shelters with long files containing names of families who would love to spend a holiday in your very gracious household.

◆ If you're still feeling alienated in the face of the media's blaring version of a traditional holiday, have your family enjoy a totally backwards, fabulously silly, nontraditional celebration. Laugh at all the frenetic people rushing around in overdrive, while you maintain a very relaxed, low-key attitude. Be carefree—roll in the leaves or snow with your kids. On Christmas Eve, stay up all night, play-

ing with the stuff you opened the day before. Participate in a Hanukkah festival at a local synagogue or attend midnight mass at a Catholic church, regardless of your religious preference. Serve your kids' favorites: hotdogs, popcorn, peanut butter and jelly on crackers, instead of turkey. Eat in front of the TV (hopefully this is something that you rarely do) and make sure you start the meal with dessert. Your kids will always remember such holidays with much fondness, unless they really do like yams.

◆ Buy gifts that require no batteries. You'll save money down the road and do more for the environment. Give your kids simple things that they'll use often, such as a kite or musical instrument. Furnish gifts that require children to use their imagination, including paper, fabric, and other artists' materials to encourage them to create their own picture books. Make items with your children for relatives and friends. Let your kids color large sheets of newsprint to use for wrapping paper, bearing in mind that "classy" is really the outcome of remarkable creativity. Encourage older children to share a special talent or skill. If your fifteen-year-old son is a whiz in the kitchen, team up and make jars of chilled soups, dips, or salsa to give as gifts. See how innovative you can be.

◆ Be frugal: Make ornaments. String popcorn and cranberries. Find a cheap photo-reprint service and make photo-postcards of your family (pets included, or course) to function as greeting cards. The postage will also be less. If your children are away during the holidays visiting relatives or the other parent, wait until after the holidays to buy their gifts. They won't even know the difference and you'll save considerably. Plan next year to celebrate the holidays on a tight budget. Shop the week after Christmas to ensure the best cost, usually half price on most items.

◆ Adopt a grandparent. Celebrate the holidays with a senior citizen at a local center or retirement home.

◆ Round up all the single and married people you know who are not attending or preparing a holiday dinner this year. Ask everyone to bring a dish, and have a wonderful potluck celebration at your place.

◆ Handprint homemade gift certificates offering such services as a manicure or hairstyle for your neighbor, or give your child's teacher a coupon announcing a special visit to the class where you'll share your favorite book, record, or story. Teachers love it when parents volunteer. Surely, you can muster up one lunch hour in a year.

◆ If you can't altogether cut it out, limit television viewing. At this time of the year, most ads are targeted toward consumers who faithfully buy into the mass commercialization of Christmas. Don't be suckered by toy, cosmetic, and jewelry ads or seductive alcohol spots that suggest you need to be part of a couple in order to have a satisfying holiday. Remember, the goal of the sellers of these products is one thing—to make lots of money. And the most efficient way for advertisers to rake in the bucks is to convince viewers that their lives will be complete if

only they have an abundance of toys for the kids, a cold beer, a partner who always smells good, or a sexy car. What nonsense. Just say no!

◆ Invite all the members of your support group to feast. Recruit some teenagers to assist with child care and pay them with the two or three dollars that each parent chipped in. If you don't belong to a support group, then make it your New Year's resolution either to join or start one.

Father's Day. It's Father's Day again, you're a single mother, and your five-year-old comes home from kindergarten with stories about the Father's Day gifts he had to make at school. Here are some things to remember to ensure that this Father's Day won't have you hiding under the bed avoiding "daddy questions."

It's unlikely that your child is the only one in his class without a father living at home. Half of all children today are raised during some time of their lives in single-parent families.

There is no reason for your child not to participate in creative class projects that recognize Father's Day. Just as it is okay not to have a father heading the household, remember that just because "Dad" lives in the home does not mean a child is being fathered. However, there are a number of fatherly types who can be recognized for overall contributions to children, particularly those serving as healthy role models.

◆ Send Mr. Rogers a Father's Day card because he makes so many kids feel that they are part of his special family. Any male friend, family member, associate, or acquaintance who has shown significant fathering qualities, including patience, empathy, and mentoring, can be acknowledged on this day.

◆ Other men can be the recipients of homemade cards, drawings, or other objets d'art: the softball coach who first showed your little boy the correct way to bat lefty; the repairman who fixes things with his power tools; the neighborhood policeman who kids can rely on when they are lost or alone; or the local pharmacist whom paid a little extra attention to your child's needs.

◆ Some families honor their big, lovable German shepherd—the pet who played daddy by protecting their bodies and their home—with a bag of doggie bones.

Since all children are connected at least biologically to a "father," even those by adoption and donor insemination, tell your child whatever you know about his or her father and let it be the child's decision whether or not to recognize him on this day. Or take it a step further, and rename Father's Day. "Parent's Day" is a creative way to encourage participation by your child and coax out of him another work of art for you!

Traveling with Kids. If you think you can't afford to take a vacation during the summer or any other time you and the kids have off, think again. It takes a lot of preparation and planning, but if you do your homework, you can have a memorable vacation that you and the kids will talk about for many years. Following are seven great ideas:

1. Start out by including your kids in the plans. Your older one can help

TRAVELING SOLO WITH BABY AND YOUNG CHILDREN

While on the road remember to adhere to safety rules and be prepared for the unexpected with these tips:

Bring a car phone.

Have your car checked out thoroughly before departing.

Never drive even a few feet if kids are not buckled up correctly.

Bring healthy snacks and drinks to avoid spending at fast-food joints.

Provide distractions for the kids: books, crayons, drawing paper, music, and even story tapes you can all listen to.

Prepare your children ahead of time. Let them know specifically how you expect them to behave in the car. Simple rules like "keep hands, feet, and objects to yourself" will help prevent squabbles.

Be sure kids are dressed for the temperature inside the car so they'll be comfortable.

Avoid stopping at unfamiliar, isolated places. Visitors' centers can direct you to kid-friendly restaurants, hotels, and activities.

Be adventurous, but cautious. Some well-meaning travelers may offer assistance if you appear overwhelmed. Seek help only from police or local area merchants if you

TRAVELING SOLO WITH BABY AND YOUNG CHILDREN

A solo trip to visit Grandma or taking a little time off to soak up some sun may seem unwieldy when you have a baby. Here are some Dos and Don'ts to make your vacation rewarding for you both:

+ Don't romanticize your vacation. Lower your expectations, and raise your flexibility quotient, advise many experienced travelers. It's probably a mistake to think you'll be lying on the beach, nodding yes or no to what flavor tropical drink you want is the perfect vacation with children.

+ Do see traveling with children as a chance to bond with them by getting away from day-to-day pressures and routines. Share activities you wouldn't normally fit in at home. Lying in the grass, having a picnic, or taking pictures are a simpler alternative to visiting every landmark, carrying a bored or sleepy child.

+ Do lighten up on the packing. Essentials only: you'll already be lugging suitcases, baby, and baby gear. Ditch the stroller for a backpack (for older babies) or a papoose-style carrier or sling for infants so your hands are free. The Federal Aviation Administration strongly recommends children under 40 pounds ride in a car seat while flying, so be sure to ask if the airline loans or rents car seats.

+ Don't keep others in the dark. If visiting friends or family, alert them early on of your needs. This doesn't mean they need to redo their homes, but childproofing areas where baby may explore, or keeping the cat in their bedroom if your child has allergies, will make the visit easier on everyone. Your hosts also know their location best, so recruit them to find some inexpensive family-friendly activities. Larger cities and towns often have more public recreational services such as parks, zoos, and cultural centers. Don't expect "free" babysitting, but welcome the respite if friends or family offer you some baby-free time!

you address postcards requesting pamphlets and brochures from information services in the areas you'd like to visit, such as chambers of commerce, state tourist bureaus, and automobile clubs. Little ones can help you stamp the postcards and tear ads out of magazines and newspapers.

2. You can also find ways to supplement the funding of your trip with a little ingenuity. Consider bartering your talents. If you are a writer, ask hotels, airlines, resorts, or theme parks about the possibility of creating favorable publicity in the form of a news or magazine article in exchange for reduced rates or complimentary services. Or maybe you are an expert in a field such as real estate, cooking, money management, or decorating. Offer the entertainment director at a resort or on a cruise ship your services in speaking on a topic like "How to start a mail order business," and see if that can earn you a free vacation.

3. Consider traveling with one or more other adults to share some of the expenses. It's cheaper to rent a whole beach house and split the cost than to pay for daily motel rates. If you can't find a traveling companion, resist or challenge those places that have rates "based on double occupancy," as they are discriminating against single parents.

4. If you're a city dweller, ask travel agents, county chambers of commerce, or farm cooperatives about spending your vacation on a farm in exchange for picking vegetables and milking the cows. At least the kids would love this idea. But if you don't, check out colleges with unused dorms during the summers. Many will rent out rooms cheap. Your local parks and recreation department may offer getaways for the whole family at great deals, too.

5. Hosteling International/American Youth Hostels have bargain basement prices on dorm-like arrangements and private rooms, but offer surprisingly comfortable accommodations all over the United States and abroad. NOSM support groups and their families can expect even better deals. Plus, hosteling is a great way to meet interesting people from all over the world.

6. Be sure to investigate deals through your church, school, or any organization to which you belong. Remember to check out the features of any hotel or motel. You want a fridge and a microwave in your room to defray the costs of restaurants every time your kids are hungry. Better yet, see if the rates

---

THE DOS AND DON'TS OF COMBINING PERSONHOOD WITH PARENTHOOD

- Don't expect to do the impossible. Managing your work and social life and family shouldn't be a juggling act.

- Do remember that more than half of the work force consists of women with children under six. You aren't alone when you feel you're being pulled from both ends.

- Don't leave everything for the eleventh hour. Be prepared in case of emergencies.

- Do give yourself frequent pats on the back.

- Don't let negative assumptions about your life style affect you. Think instead of how your being a single mother is helping others by bringing back the extended family—one of the things our country really needs. Communal caring for our children and each other is the way a society thrives best. Be proud of your pioneering spirit.

---

include a pool or access to workout facilities, and ask if they offer babysitting services of any kind.

7. Do you have a daughter in scouting? Offer to be a group leader for an excursion to the beach, mountains, or camping at the state park. More and more single parents are finding that although this may not be the quickest way to rest and relaxation, you're still getting away from it all, and what's a few more

girls when you're already taking your own kids? Plus, you'll enjoy chatting with other adults.

Above all, lower your expectations and raise your enjoyment threshold. And start preparing now because it's never too early to plan for a good time.

SO YOU WANT ANOTHER CHILD...

I have a a five-year-old son by a man I've known most of my life. We're no longer together, but his family is very involved in my son's life. In fact they are the greatest grandparents, aunts, and uncles ever, even more than my own family. I have always wanted two children and would like another child before I turn 40. The catch is I'd like this person to be the donor but I'm catching flack from my own family for wanting another child outside of marriage. Is this really so bad? My son and I are doing great and I know I'm a good mom.

If adoption is not a choice for you and you're currently not in a relationship with a man who wants children, there's nothing wrong with expanding your family as you had originally planned. Plenty of moms space their children out, allowing them to nurture a new baby while the firstborn is ready to begin preschool or kindergarten. And because your age is a factor, you're wise to begin planning your second child now. Another plus in your situation is the involvement of your children's paternal relatives offering them grandparents and other extended family, beyond your own.

You're not alone. Lots of single women want more children. If the father consents on this agreement, go for it. Let your family know that this is something to which you've given lots of thought, and you would appreciate their support. Just be sure you're comfortable with this scenario and able to explain to your children why (Dad's) grandma and grandpa are more involved in their lives than their natural father.

AFTERWORD

In the time since the research on this book began, I have received thousands of letters from readers of *Single-MOTHER* and my nationally syndicated newspaper column, "Single ... With Children," and from members of the National Organization of Single Mothers. The voices in these letters inspired me to ask questions about the joys and concerns of heading a single-parent family, to seek solutions, and above all to challenge the prevailing assumption by "traditionalists" that single mothering is not normal.

From your words, and from the combined experience of co-author Leah Klungness and myself, I found that single mothering is indeed not only normal, but can provide a healthy environment in which to raise children, particularly compared to the stresses of families suffering from gender inequities.

So that I may remain current and responsive to the needs of single-mother families, I encourage you to write to me or contact me via the Internet. I will include your questions and suggestions in my library of information for new editions of this book. Send your questions or comments to:

National Organization of
    Single Mothers, Inc.
P.O. Box 68
Midland, NC
            28107-0068

E-mail:
singlemothers@aol.com
or visit our Web site at:
www.singlemothers.org

— A. E.

RESOURCE ROUNDUP

Following is a comprehensive listing of addresses and phone numbers of organizations that have services of interest to single-parent families. Be sure to inquire about pamphlets, packets, and information when contacting these groups. Additionally, many of these national networks can refer you to local members or to local referral agencies.

For the most complete, up-to-date listing of resources in your area, look to United Way's "First Call For Help," a directory of available support services in your community. Check your local phone directory for the number of your local United Way agency. You can purchase your own copy of "First Call For Help," or head to your nearest United Way agency or library to use theirs. This directory is updated every year or two. You may be able to purchase an older edition "at cost" by inquiring at any United Way agency.

Adoption

Adoption Horizons, Inc.
899 Petersburg Road
Carlisle, PA 17013
717-249-8850

Adoptive Families of America Inc.
*This organization has nearly four
hundred books and tapes available.
Call to request a catalog.*
2309 Como Ave.
St. Paul, MN 55108
www.adoptivefam.org

American Academy of Adoption
    Attorneys
Box 33053
Washington, D.C. 20033-0053
202-832-2222

International Families
*Information and support for those
wishing to pursue foreign adoption.*
Contact: Becky Panagos
International Families
PO Box 1352
St. Charles, MO 63302

The National Adoption Center
1500 Walnut St., Suite 701
Philadelphia, PA 19102
800-862-3678
800-TO-ADOPT
www.adopt.org

North American Council on
    Adoptable Children
970 Raymond Ave., Suite 106
St. Paul, MN 55114
members.aol.com/nacac

*Note: The National Center on Women
and Family Law and special divisions
of the American Bar Association
(ABA) also have information on
adoption. Contact the bar association
in your area to obtain further information. (See Legal Information)*

Women of Color Resource Center
2288 Fulton Street, Suite 103
Berkeley, CA 94704
510-848-9272
colorogirls@igc.org

Child Abuse/Sexual Abuse

National Clearinghouse on Child
  Abuse and Neglect Information
www.calib/nccanch
National Committee to Prevent Child
  Abuse
www.childabuse.org
National Council on Child Abuse and
  Family Violence
www.nccafv.org

Child Care

American Academy of Pediatrics
www.aap.org
Childhelp USA
*A 24-hour hotline to help with parenting
  problems and questions.*
800-4-A-CHILD

Information Kit on Employer-Assisted
  Child Care (2nd printing, 1990).
  For more information on the kit,
  call NAEYC at 800-424-2460.

National Association for the
  Education of Young Children
  (NAEYC)
1509 16th Street NW
Washington, D.C. 20036-1426
800-424-2460
www.naeyc.org

National Association of Child Care
  Resource and Referral Agencies
  (NACCRRA)
1319 F Street NW
Suite 810
Washington, DC 20004
202-393-5501
www.naccrra.net

Parents Anonymous
909-621-6184
www.parentsanonymous~natl.org

Ten to Eighteen
Northwest Parenting Publishing
1530 Westlake Ave., Suite 600
Seattle, WA 98109
800-794-1018

Child Support

American Child Support Collection
  Association
  *National association of private profes-
  sional collection agencies. Call for the
  number of the agency nearest you.*
P.O. Box 691067
San Antonio, TX 78269
1-800-729-2445

Association for Children for
  Enforcement of Support (ACES)
  *National. Founded 1984. Information
  for parents who have custody of their
  children and have difficulty collecting
  support payments.*
2260 Upton Ave.
Toledo, OH 43612
www.childsupport-ACES.org
Child Support Enforcement (CSE)
800-801-KIDS
www.supportkids.com
E-mail: info@supportkids.com

EX-POSE
  *An organization created to help ex-
  spouses get information about military
  benefits. A small membership fee is
  charged for this service.*

National Child Support Network
800-PAY-KIDS
http://www.childsupport.org

Office of Child Support Enforcement
  Administration for Children and
  Families
U.S. Department of Health and
  Human Services
370 L'Enfant Promenade SW, Fourth
  Floor

Washington, D.C. 20447
(In most states, CSE offices are listed under Department of Social Services or the human resource services agency in the government section of your phone book. For a listing of all state offices, contact the CSE office listed above.)

Custody

Joint Custody Association
International. Founded 1979. Helps divorcing parents to achieve joint custody and provides information concerning family law research.
Contact: James A. Cook, President
10606 Wilkins Ave.
Los Angeles, CA 90024
310-475-5352
www.jointcustody.org

National Center for Missing and Exploited Children
2101 Wilson Boulevard, Suite 550
Arlington, VA 22201-3052
800-THE LOST (843-5678)
www.missingkids.com

United Fathers of America
595 City Drive, Suite 202
Orange, CA
714-385-1002

Disabilities

The Arc
Publishes handbooks for families and can help find local resources.
800-433-5255

Exceptional Parent
This magazine is for parents with disabled children. A one-year subscription is $28.
800-247-8080

Feingold Associations of the U.S.
National. Founded 1976. Help for families of children with behavioral or learning problems through a program of awareness regarding diet, food, and synthetic additives.
Box 6550
Alexandria, VA 22306
703-768-3287

Learning Disability Association of America
Organization formed by concerned parents, devoted to defining and finding solutions for the broad spectrum of learning problems.
Contact: Jean Peterson, Executive Director
4156 Library Road
Pittsburgh, PA 15234
412-341-1515
www.ldanatl.org

National Information Center for Children and Youth with Disabilities
Federal clearinghouse; vast resource materials, free by mail.
P.O. Box 1492
Washington, D.C. 20013-1492
800-695-0285
http:\\www.nichcy.org

National Parent Network on Disabilities
This federal funded organization provides information, training, and support for parents.
703-684-6763

Parent Network
Links families with similar challenges.
500 Balltown Road
Schenectady, NY 12304
800-305-8817
www.parenttoparentnys.org
E-mail: parents2par@aol.com

Shriners Hospital for Crippled
  Children
  Network of hospitals and rehab cen-
  ters offering free orthopedic care for
  kids, infants though age eighteen, whose
  parents cannot otherwise afford it.
800-237-5055.
2900 Rocky Point Dr.
Tampa, FL 33067-1435
813-281-0300

Education
College Board Web Site
This site contains a database of scholar-
  ships sources.
http://www.collegeboard.org

National Association of Financial Aid
  Administrators
http://www.finaid.org
http://www.nasfaa.org

Planning for College; Nontraditional
  Education: Alternative Ways to
  Earn Your Credentials; and GED
  Diploma. Get all three government
  publications for just $1.75 by call-
  ing 1-888-878-3256 and ask for
  "Nontraditional Educational
  Package."

S.R.N. Express
This site provides a free Web version of
  the database of the Scholarship
  Resource Network.
http://www.rams.com/srn/search.htm
Student Loan Marketing Association
http://www.salliemae.com

**Employment Information and
Counseling**
American Businesswoman's
  Association
9100 Ward Parkway
P.O. Box 8728
Kansas City, MO 64114
816-361-6621
www.abwahq.org

Displaced Homemakers Network
1625 K Street NW, Suite 300
Washington, D.C. 20006
202-467-6346
www.womenwork.org

National Association for Female
  Executives (NAFE)
127 West 24th St.
New York, NY 10011
800-927-6233

Women Employed
  Founded 1973. Promotes economic
  equity for women through education
  and advocacy.
22 W. Monroe St., Suite 1400
Chicago, IL 60603-2505
312-782-3902

Financial
Better Business Bureau of
  Metropolitan New York
Request a free copy of "A Beginner's
  Guide to Secured Credit Cards."
257 Park Ave. S.
New York, NY 10010

MoneyMinded
A great source for personal-finance infor-
  mation with a lifestyle-forced twist.
www.moneyminded.com

National Consumer Law Center
"Surviving Debt" can be ordered for
  $15.
18 Tremont St.
Boston, MA 02108
617-523-8089

Social Security Information Office
800-722-1213

Girls

An Income of Her Own
Program that provides teenage women with the experience and inspiration to achieve.
P.O. Box 987
Santa Barbara, CA 93120
800-350-2978

Girls Incorporated
Serving girls and women between the ages of six and eighteen.
30 E. 33rd Street
New York, NY 10016
212-689-3700

Girls State/Girls Nation
Opportunity for teenage girls to learn how our system of government works.
777 North Meridian Street
Indianapolis, IN 46204
317-635-6291

Grandparents Raising Children

AARP
601 E Street NW
Washington, D.C. 20049
202-434-2296
AARP.org

Health/Medical

National Immunization Information Hotline
800-232-2522
800-232-0233 (Spanish)

National Library of Medicine: Office of Public Information
Provides a list of over 300 health hotlines.
8600 Rockville Pike
Bethesda, MD 20894
(301) 496-6308

Homesharing/Housing

The Cohousing Company
1250 Addison, Suite 113
Berkeley, CA 94702
510-549-9980
www.cohousingco.com

Cooperative Resources and Service Project
3551 Whitehouse Place
Los Angeles, CA 90004
213-738-1254
Shared Living Resource Center
2337 Parker St. #9
Berkeley, CA 94704-2841
www.sharedliving.org
E-mail: slrcnorword.igc.org

Legal Information

Nolo's Pocket Guide to Family Law
A great quick legal reference. Also available in book form.
http://www.nolo.com/ChunkDIV/DIV.index.html

NOW Legal Defense Fund (National Organization of Women)
99 Hudson Street
New York, NY 10013
212-925-6635

Office of Public Affairs
Legal Services Corporation
400 Virginia Ave. SW
Washington, D.C. 20024
(202) 336-8800
(To request information about local legal services for low-income clients.)

Women's Legal Defense
1875 Connecticut Ave. NW, Suite 710
Washington, D.C. 20009
www.nationalpartnership.org

Lesbians and Gays

Momazons
P.O. Box 02069
Columbus, OH 43202
614-267-0193

National Center for Lesbian Rights
870 Market Street, Suite 570
San Francisco, CA 94102
415-392-6257
www.nclrights.org

Parents and Friends of Lesbians and
    Gays (PFLAG)
202-638-4200
Straight Spouse Support Network
http://www.glpci.org/~sssn/

Mental Health/Counseling

Alliance for Children and Families
    (was Family Service America)
www.alliance1.org

American Association of Marriage
    and Family Therapists
    *Send stamped self-addressed envelope
    for listing of recommended therapists
    in your area.*
1133 15th Street NW, Suite 300
Washington, D.C. 20005
800-374-2638

American Psychological Association
750 First Street NE
Washington, D.C. 20002-42422
202-336-5500

Covenant House Nineline
*Crisis intervention referral and informa-
    tion for troubled teens and families*
800-999-9999

Depression After Delivery

Emotions Anonymous
    *National. Founded 1971. Fellowship
    that shares strengths, experiences, and
    hope with each other, utilizing the
    Twelve Steps in order to gain better
    emotional health.*
P.O. Box 4245
St. Paul, MN 55104
615-647-9712
Fax: 651-647-1593
www.emotionsanonymous.org
E-mail: eaisc@mtn.org

Family Service America
11700 W. Lake Park Drive
Milwaukee, WI 53224
414-359-1040

Mental Health Net
*A general guide to on-line mental health
    topics.*
www.cmhc.com

National Alliance for the Mentally Ill
*This group provides information and
    assistance to families.*
800-950-6264

National Association of Social
    Workers
750 First Street NE, Suite 700
Washington, D.C. 20002
202-408-8600

National Depressive and Manic
    Depressive Associations
    *Founded 1986. Mutual support and
    education by providing information on
    the biochemical nature of depressive
    illnesses.*
Contact: Merchandise Mart
Box 3395
Chicago, IL 60654
312-939-2442

Overeaters Anonymous
International. Founded 1960.
Fellowship to help overcome eating
disorders. Based on the Twelve Steps.
P.O. Box 92870
Los Angeles, CA 90009
213-936-6252

Recovery, Inc.
National. Founded 1937. A communi-
ty mental health organization that
offers a self-help method of will train-
ing; techniques to control attitudes
toward nervous symptoms and fears.
802 N. Dearborn Street
Chicago, IL 60610
312-337-5661
www.recovery-inc.com

Sex and Love Addicts Anonymous
International. Founded 1976. Based
on the Twelve Steps for those who
want to change their behavior.
P.O. Box 1964
Boston, MA 02105
617-625-7961

Youth Crisis Hotline
Counseling and referrals for teens in
crisis.
800-448-4663

Mentors

Big Brothers/Big Sisters
230 N. 13th St.
Philadelphia, PA 19107
215-567-7000

One-to-One
2801 M Street NW
Washington, D.C. 20007
202-338-3844

On-line Education

Distance Education Clearinghouse
www.uwex.edu/disted/home.html

Distance Education Resources
www.ola.bc.ca/ola/library/interesources

The Internet University
http://www.caso.com/iu.html

Peterson's Education Center
http://www.petersons.com

Sexual Harrassment/Job Discrimination

9 to 5, The National Organization of
    Working Women
800-522-0925

"Pregnancy and Parental Leave
    Resource Kit"
    A booklet that explains the Family
    and Medical Leave Act in greater
    detail. The cost is $5.00.
Write to: The NOW Legal Defense
    and Education Fund
99 Hudson Street
New York, NY 10013

Single Parenting

National Organization of Single
    Mothers, Inc. (NOSM)
    Clearinghouse of information and net-
    work of support to single mothers.
    Helps establish support groups and
    publishes a bimonthly newsletter,
    SingleMOTHER.
P.O. Box 68
Midland, NC 28107-0068
704-888-KIDS

Parents Without Partners
National. Founded 1957.
Membership organization of divorced
parents, regardless of the age of the
children, and widowed persons.
401 North Michigan Ave.
Chicago, IL 60611
www.parentswithoutpartners.org

Single Mothers By Choice (SMC)
National. Founded 1981. A support
network for women having children
while not in a permanent relationship
with a man.
Contact: Jane Mattes
P.O. Box 1642
Gracie Square Station
New York, NY 10028
212-988-0993
E-mail: mattes@pipeline.com

Single Parent Resource Center
International. Founded 1975.
Network of single-parent self-help
groups, information, and referrals.
1165 Broadway
New York, NY 10001
212-947-0221

Sperm Banks and Fertility Clinics
* Accredited by the American Association of
Tissue Banks

American Association of Tissue Banks
Contact for listings of sperm banks or
clinics in your area.
1350 Beverly Road, Suite 220A
McLean, VA 22101
703-827-9582
www.aatb.org

American Society for Reproductive
Medicine (ASRM)
Formerly the American Fertility
Society. This national association will
provide listings of local sperm banks or
clinics that work with single women.
1209 Montgomery Highway
Birmingham, AL 35216-2809
205-978-5000

Biogenetics*
PO Box 1290
Mountainside, NJ 07092
800-637-7776
www.sperm.com

California Cryobank*
Also has branches in Cambridge,
MA, and Palo Alto, CA.
1019 Gayley Avenue
Los Angeles, CA 90024
800-231-3373

Xytex Corporation
1100 Emmett St.
Augusta, GA 30904
800-277-3210
www.xytex.com

Stepfamilies
Stepfamily Association of America, Inc.
Founded 1979. Self-help programs
that offer information and educational
resources for stepfamilies.
215 Centennial Mall South, Suite 212
Lincoln, NE 68508
402-477-7837
650 J Street, Suite 205
www.stepfam.org

The Stepfamily Foundation
333 West End Ave.
New York, NY 10023
212-877-3244

Substance Dependency

Alcoholics Anonymous
  International. Founded 1935.
  Fellowship sharing experiences,
  strengths, and hopes to help each other
  recover from alcoholism. The original
  Twelve Step, Twelve-Tradition
  Program.
Box 459
Grand Central Station
New York, NY 10163
212-686-1100

Al-Anon Family Groups
  International. Founded 1935.
  Fellowship of men, women, and chil-
  dren whose lives have been affected by
  the compulsive drinking of a family
  member or friend.
P.O. Box 862 Midtown Station
New York, NY 10018-6106
212-302-7240
800-344-2666
(Also contact Alateen at this location.)

Families Anonymous
Support for family members and friends
  concerned about a loved one's drug or
  alcohol abuse
800-400-0900

National Clearinghouse for Alcohol
  and Drug Information
800-729-6686
www.health.org

Women for Sobriety
  National. Founded 1976. Program
  designed to help the woman alcoholic
  achieve sobriety and overcome depres-
  sion and guilt.
Box 618
Quakertown, PA 18951
215-536-8026

Travel

Family Hostel, University of New
  Hampshire
6 Garrison Ave.
Durham, NH 03824
800-733-9753

Special Information to Send for

"Debt Zapper Kit." Can help you get
out from under excessive credit card
debt. Contact the Bankcard Holders
of America, 524 Branch Drive, Salem,
VA 24153. The cost is $15. You sup-
ply the number of credit cards and the
total amount of money owed. Debt
Zapper will help you lay out a repay-
ment plan.

"Extending Your Family: The Guide
for Single Parents" by Shoshana
Alexander. Ninety-minute audio cassette from Sound Tree Catalog, 800-
333-9185. Explains how single parents
are creating a new kind of family with
help from friends, mentors, and other
loving adults.

The Social Security Book: What Every
Woman Absolutely Needs to Know
(14117). For a free copy, send a post-
card to the title and stock number, followed by: AARP Fulfillment
(EE0114), 1909 K St. NW,
Washington, D.C. 20049. 202-434-
2277

"Where to Write for Vital Records."
Government publication that explains
where to get copies of birth, death,
marriage, or divorce certificates. Send
a check for $6.95 payable to Federal
Reprints, Box 70268, Washinton, D.C.
20024.

Your Pension Rights at Divorce: What Women Need to Know. Write to: Pension Rights Center, Department MM, 918 16th Street NW, Washington, D.C. 20006. 202-296-3776

Moms With Modems...

One of the best ways to get support when you can't leave the house is through the Internet. To simplify your search for sites catering to single mothers or which archive articles and resources you can use, here are some picks to click:

Singlespot.com—Unique product and gift ideas for single parents, as well as online information, support, and resources.

http://www.divorcemag.com
http://www.women.msn.com
http://www.familyeducation.com
http://www.laze.net/stacey
http://www.ysp.ourfamily.com
http://www.makinglemonade.com
http://www.momsonline.com
http://www.singlemothers.org
http://www.parentsplace.com
http://www.parentsoup.com
http://www.parentswithoutpartners.org

(Note: Depending on your Internet access and service provider's capabilities, you may not be required to type in http://www. You may only need to key in the site address or simply preface your entry with www.)

RECOMMENDED READING

Adoption

Adoption: A Handbook of Hope, Suzanne Arms (Celestial Arts).

The Adoption Resource Book, Lois Gilman (HarperCollins).

Geborener Deutscher. A newsletter for German-born adoptees and their birth/adoptive families c/o William L. Gage, 805 Alvarado Dr. NE, Albuquerque, NM 87108.

The Handbook for Single Adoptive Parents, Hope Marindin (Committee for Single Adoptive Parents).

Raising Adopted Children: A Manual for Adoptive Parents, Lois Rusaki Melina (HarperCollins).

Waiting to Forget, Margaret Moorman (W.W. Norton & Company).

Child Care

The Child Care Sourcebook: The Complete Guide to Finding & Managing Nannies, Au Pairs, Baby-Sitters, Day Care & After School Programs, Ellen O. Tauscher (Macmillan).

The Complete Guide to Choosing Child Care, Judith Berezin (Random House).

Disabilities

Nobody's Perfect, Nancy B. Millier, MSW, Ph.D. (Paul Brookes Publishing Company).

Pride Against Prejudice: Transforming Attitudes to Disability, Jenny Morris (New Society Publishers).

Divorce

Creative Divorce: A New Opportunity for Personal Growth, Mel Krantzler (New American Library).

Divorce Casualties: Protecting Your Children From Parental Alienation, Douglas Darnall, Ph.D. (Taylor).

Divorce and Money: How to Make the Best Financial Decisions During Divorce, Voilet Woodhouse and Victorial Felton Collins with M.C. Blakeman (Nolo Press).

Divorce Help Sourcebook, Margorie L. Engel (Visible Ink).

The Divorced Parent, Stephanie Marston (Morrow).

The Fresh Start Divorce Recovery Workbook by Bob Burns and Tom Whiteman (Fresh Start).

How to Forgive Your Ex-Husband and Get On with Your Life, Marcia Hootman and Patt Perkins (Warner).

Life After Divorce: Create A New Beginning, Sharon Wegscheider-Cruse (Health Communications).

Second Chances, Judith S. Wallerstein and Sandra Blakeslee (Ticknor and Fields).

Surviving the Breakup: How Children and Parents Cope with Divorce, Judith S. Wallerstein and Joan Berlin Kelly (Basic).

What Every Woman Should Know About Divorce and Custody, Gayle Rosenwald Smith, J.D. and Sally Abrahms (Perigee)

Donor Insemination

Having Your Baby by Donor Insemination: A Complete Resouce Guide (Houghton Mifflin).

Lethal Secrets: The Shocking Consequences and Unsolved Problems of Artificial Insemination, Annette Baran and Reuben Pananor (Warner Books).

Fathering

Father Love: What We Need, What We Seek, What We Must Create, Richard Louv (Pocket).

Fathers and Babies: How Babies Grow and What They Need from You from Birth to Eighteen Months, Gene Marzollo (HarperCollins).

Fathers, Sons and Daughters: Exploring Fatherhood, Renewing the Bond, ed. Charles Scull (J.P. Tarcher).

How to Father a Successful Daughter, Nicky Marone (McGraw-Hill).

The Nurturing Father: Journey Toward the Complete Man, Kyle Pruett (Warner).

Questions from Dad: A Very Cool Way to Communicate with Kids, Dwight Twilley (Charles Tuttle).

Single Fathers, Geoffrey L. Greif (Lexington Books).

The Single Father's Cookbook, Nick Silva (Writeworks).

The Single Fathers' Handbook: A Guide for Separated and Divorced Fathers, Richard Gatley and David Koiulack (Anchor/Doubleday).

Finance/Saving Money

Financial Self-Confidence for the Suddenly Single: A Woman's Guide, Alan Ungar, C.F.P. (Lowell House).

Free Money for Children's Medical and Dental Care, Laurie Blum (Fireside).

Great Buys for Your Kids, Sue Goldstein (Penguin).

How to Turn Your Money Life Around: The Money Book for Women, Ruth Hayden (Health Communications).

The Single Person's Guide to Buying a Home, Elaine J. Anderson (Betterway Books).

Wake Up and Smell the Money, Ginger AppleGarth

Women and Money: The Independent Woman's Guide to Financial Security for Life, Frances Leonard (Addison-Wesley).

Girls/Women Without Mothers

Letters from Motherless Daughters, Hope Edelman (Addison-Wesley).

Motherless Daughters, Hope Edelman (Addison-Wesley).

Grief/Widowhood

Being a Widow, Lyn Caine (Arbor House).

The Courage to Grieve, Judy Tatelbaum (Harper and Row).

On Death and Dying, Elisabeth Kubler-Ross (Macmillan).

When My Dad Died, Janice Hammond (Cranbrook Publishing).

When My Mommy Died: A Child's View of Death, Janice Hammond (Cranbrook Publishing).

Job/Career

Working from Home: Everything You Need to Know About Living and Working Under the Same Roof, 4th Ed., Paul and Sarah Edwards (Jeremy P. Tarcher/Putnam).

Kids (and for parents to read with kids)

Adoption Is for Always (Adoptive Families of America).

At Daddy's on Saturdays, Linda Walvoord Girard (Albert Whitman & Company).

Beginnings: How Families Come to Be (Adoptive Families of America).

A Chair for My Mother, Vera Williams (Morrow).

Changing Families: A Guide for Kids and Grownups, David Fassler, M.D., Michele Lash, M. Ed., A.T.R., and Sally B. Ives, Ph.D. (Waterfront Books).

Did My First Mother Love Me? (Adoptive Families of America).

Dinosaurs Divorce: A Guide for Changing Families, Laurene Krasny Brown and Marc Brown.

The Divorce Workbook: A Guide for Kids and Families, Sally B. Ives, Ph.D., David Fassler, M.D., and Michele Lash, M. Ed., A.T.R. (Waterfront Books).

Do I Have a Daddy?, Jeanne Warren Lindsay (Morning Glory Press).

Families Are Different, Nina Pellegrini (Holiday House).

Helping Children Cope with Separation and Loss, Claudia Jewett Jarratt (Positive Books for 21st Century Kids).

How to Live with a Single Parent, Sara Gilbert (Lothrop, Lee & Shepard).

How to Survive Your Parents' Divorce: Kids' Advice to Kids, Gayle Kimball, Ph.D. (Equality Press).

Kids Are NON-Divorceable, Sara Bonkowski (Assisting Christians to Act Publishing).

The Kids' Book About Single-Parent Families, Paul Dolmetsch and Alexa Shik (Doubleday).

Mom's House, Dad's House, Isolina Ricci, Ph.D. (Simon & Schuster)

My Kind of Family: A Book for Kids in Single-Parent Homes, Michele Lash, M. Ed., A.T.R., Sally Ives Loughridge, Ph.D., and David Fassler, M.D. (Waterfront Books).

My Mother's Getting Married, Joan Drescher (Dial/Pied Piper Books).

My Mother's House, My Father's House, C.B. Christiansen (Viking).

My Real Family: A Child's Book About Living in a Stepfamily, Doris Sanford (Questar Publishers).

Tell Me A Real Adoption Story (Adoptive Families of America).

When My Dad Died, Janice Hammond (Cranbrook Publishing).

When My Mommy Died: A Child's View of Death, Janice Hammond (Cranbrook Publishing).

Why Was I Adopted, Carole Livingston (Adoptive Families of America).

Parenting

Beyond Discipline: Parenting That Lasts a Lifetime, Edward R. Christophersen (Westport Publishers).

The Challenging Child: Understanding, Raising and Enjoying the Five "Difficult" Types of Children, Stanley I. Greenspan, M.D. (Addison-Wesley).

The Complete Guide to Choosing Child Care, Judith Berezin (Random House).

Controlling the Difficult Adolescent: The REST Program (The Real Economy System for Teens), David B. Stein (University Press of America).

The Courage to Raise Good Men, Olga Silverstein and Beth Rashbaum (Viking).

Families Apart: Ten Keys to Successful Co-Parenting, Melinda Blau (G.P. Putnam's Sons).

The Family Bed, Tine Thevenin (Avery Publishing Group).

For the Sake of the Children: How to Share Your Children with your Ex-Spouse in Spite of Your Anger, Kris Kline and Stephen Pew, Ph.D. (Prima Publishing).

The Handbook for Latchkey Children and Their Parents, Thomas and Lynette Long (Berkeley Books).

Healthy Parenting: How Your Upbringing Influences the Way You Raise Your Children and What You Can Do to Make it Better for Them, Janet G. Woititz (Simon and Schuster).

Healthy Sleep Habits, Happy Child, Marc Weissbluth (Ballantine).

How to Talk So Kids Will Listen and Listen So Kids Will Talk, Adele Faber and Elaine Mazlish (Avon).

In Praise of Single Parents, Shoshana Alexander (Houghton Mifflin).

Keys to Single Parenting, Carl E. Pickhardt, Ph.D. (Barrons)

One on the Seesaw: The Ups and Downs of a Single Parent Family, Carol Lynn Pearson (Random House).

Positive Discipline for Single Parents, Jane Nelson, Cheryl Erin, and Carol Delzer (Prima Publishing).

Raising Boys, Steve Biddulph (Celestial Arts).

Safe at School: Awareness and Action for Parents of Kids Grades K-12 (Free Spirit Publishing).

The Single Parent Family: Living Happily in a Changing World, Marge Kennedy and Janet Spencer King (Crown).

Solve Your Child's Sleep Problems, Richard Ferber, M.D. (Fireside).

Successful Single Parenting: A Practical Guide, Anne Wayman (Meadowbrook).

A Tribe Apart: A Journey into the Heart of the American Adolescence, Patricia Hersch.

When Your Child Drives You Crazy, Eda LeShan (St. Martin's).

Whole Child/Whole Parent, Polly Berrien Berrends (Perenial).

Pregnancy and Childbirth

What to Expect When You're Expecting, Arlene Eisenberg, Heidi Murkoff, and Sandee Hathaway, BSN (Workman).

Relationships

Bad Guys, Brook Hersey (Bishop Books).

Cupid, Couples, and Contract, Lester Wallman with Sharon McDowell, (Master Media Ltd.).

Encouragements for the Emotionally Abused Woman: Wisdom and Hope for Women at Any Stage of Emotional Abuse Recovery, Beverly Engel, MFCC (Fawcett Columbine).

Getting Married After 40 - Advice & Inspiration From 100 Women who Found Good Men & Happy Marriages, Carmen Anthony (Adams Media Corp.).

Get Your Tongue Out of My Mouth, I'm Kissing You Goodbye, Cynthia Heimel (Ballantine).

Infidelity: A Survival Guide, Don-David Lusterman, Ph.D. (New Harbinger).

Keeping the Love You Find: A Guide for Singles, Harville Hendrix (Simon and Schuster).

Why Do I Think I Am Nothing Without A Man, Penelope Russianoff (Bantom).

Resource Books

Child Custody Made Simple, Webster Watnik (Single Parent Press).

The Intentional Family: How to Build Family Ties in Our Modern World, William J. Doherty, Ph.D. (Addison-Wesley).

The Mommy Guide: Real Life Advice and Tips from over 250 Moms and other Experts, Susan Bernard (Contemporary Books).

Nolo's Pocket Guide to Family Law, Robin Leonard and Stephen Elias (Nolo Communications).

The Self-Help Sourcebook: Finding and Forming Mutual Aid Self-Help Groups, Barbara White and Edward J. Madara (American Self-Help Clearing House).

The Women's Information Exchange National Directory, compiled by Deborah Breecher and Jill Lippitt (Avon).

Single Mothers

The Complete Idiot's Guide to Single Parenting, Sara Dulaney (Alpha Books).

Lives on the Edge: Single Mothers and Their Children in the Other America, Valerie Polakow (University of Chicago Press).

Mother Journeys: Feminists Write About Mothering (Spinsters Ink).

Operating Instructions: A Journal of My Son's First Year, Anne Lamott (Pantheon).

Pitied But Not Entitled: Single Mothers and the History of Welfare, Linda Gordon (Free Press).

The Single Mother Book: A Practical Guide to Managing Your Children, Career, Home, Finances and Everything Else, Joan Anderson (Peachtree).

The Single Mother's Companion, edited by Marsha Leslie (Seal Press).

Single Mothers by Choice, Jane Mattes (Times Books).

Solo Parenting: Raising Strong and Happy Families, Diane Chambers (Fairview Press).

Two of Us Make a World: The Single Woman's Guide to Pregnancy, Childbirth and Beyond, Sherill Tippins (Henry Holt).

When Baby Makes Two: Single Mothers by Chance or Choice, Jane Stonesifer (Lowell House).

Where's Daddy?, Claudette Wassil-Grimm, M.Ed. (The Overlook Press).

Stepparenting

The Courage to Be a Stepmom: Finding Your Place Without Losing Yourself, Sue Patton Thoele (Wildcat Canyon).

The Enlightened Stepmother: Revolutionizing the Role, Perdita Kirkness Norwood with Teri Wingender (Avon).

How to Win as a Stepfamily, Emily B. Visher, Ph.D. & John S. Visher, M.D. (Brunner/Mazel).

Keys to Successful Stepmothering, Philippa Greene Mulford (Barron's).

Making It as Stepparents: New Roles/New Rules, Claire Berman (Harper and Row).

My Mother's Getting Married, Joan Drescher (Dial/Pied Piper Books).

My Real Family: A Child's Book About Living in a Stepfamily, Doris Sanford (Questar Publishers).

Stepfamilies: A Guide for Working with Stepparents and Stepchildren, John and Emily Visher (Brunner/Mazel).

Stepmotherhood: How to Survive Without Feeling Frustrated, Left Out or Wicked, Cherie Burns (HarperCollins).

The Stepparenting Challenge: Making It Work, Stephen J. Williams, Sc.D. (Mastermedia Limited).

Travel/Moving

Great Vacations with Your Kids, Majorie Adoff Cohen and Dorothy Jordan (Dutton).

How to Take Great Trips with Your Kids, Sanford and Joan Portnoy (The Harvard Common Press).

Moving with Children: A Parent's Guide to Moving with Children, Thomas T. Olkowski, Ph.D., and Lynn Parker, LCSW (Gylantic Publishing).

Videos

Single Parenting, Jean Rosenbaum, M.D. and Veryl Rosenbaum, PSA (JVM Productions). Distributed by Video 11, P.O. Box 1429, Durango, CO 81302.

Magazines, Newsletters, and Other Periodicals

Adoptive Familes
AFA
3333 Highway 100N
Minneapolis, MN 55422
612-535-4829

Chain of Life
(Issues in adoption and child welfare)
P.O. Box 8081
Berkely, CA 94707

Essence magazine
1500 Broadway
New York, NY 10109

Full-Time Dads
P.O. Box 577
Cumberland, ME 04096
207-829-5260

HipMAMA
P.O. Box 9097
Oakland, CA 94613

Mothering magazine
515 Don Gaspar
Santa Fe, NM 87501

Parenting
301 Howard Street, 17th Floor
San Francisco, CA 94105

SingleMOTHER
(News journal of the National Organization for Single Mothers)
P.O. Box 68
Midland, NC 28107
704-888-KIDS

Single Mothers by Choice Newsletter
P.O. Box 1642
Gracie Square Station
New York, NY 10028
212-988-0993

The Single Parent
(Journal of Parents Without Partners)
401 N. Michigan Ave
Chicago, IL 60611
312-644-6610

Working Mother
230 Park Avenue
New York, NY 10169

BIBLIOGRAPHY

"ABA Reports Impact of Domestic Violence on Children." *Youth Law News*, July–August 1994.

Abarbanel, Karin. "The Four Money Stages of Entrepreneurs." *Executive Female*, May/June 1994.

Bachu, Amara. "Fertility of American Women: June 1992." *Current Population Reports*, Series P-20, No. 470.

Besharov, Douglas J. *Combating Child Abuse: Guidelines for Cooperation between Law Enforcement and Child Protective Agencies* (Lanham, MD: University Press of America).

"The Best of Single Parenting." *The Single Parent*, May/June 1988.

Boo, Katherine. "The Return of the Extended Family." *Washington Monthly*, April 1992.

Boorstein, Michelle. "Married With Children? For an Institution, an Uncertain Time." Associated Press, Aug. 30, 1999.

Borders, L. DiAnne, Ph.D. "Where's Daddy?" *Adoptive Families*, January/February 1995.

Branden, Dr. Nathaniel. "Drawing Boundaries." *New Woman*, March 1994.

Brenes, Margarita Elena; Eisenberg, Nancy; and Helmstadter, Gerald C. "Sex Role Development of Preschoolers from Two-Parent and One-Parent Families," *Merrill Palmer Quarterly* 31, No. 1, January 1985.

Burnham, Sophie. "Confronting Loneliness." *New Woman*, August, 1992.

Buxbaum, Martin. "Success" (poem), from "Dear Abby." *Newsday*, January 7, 1994.

Child Support Report, Vol. XXI, No. 1-No. 9, January-September 1999.

Children and Divorce, The Future of Children, Volume 4, Number 1, Spring 1994.

Chollar, Susan. "Happy Families: Who Says They All Have to be Alike?" *American Health*, July/August 1993.

Connell, Christopher. "Birth Rate for Unmarried Women Up More Than 50%." *Associated Press*, May 1995, from a report by Stephanie Ventura, National Center for Health Statistics.

Coontz, Stephanie. *The Way We Never Were: American Families and the Nostalgia Trap* (New York: Basic Books/Harper Collins, 1992).

DeParle, Jason. "Census Reports a Sharp Increase Among Never-Married Mothers: Puncturing Stereotypes of Out-of-Wedlock Births." *New York Times*, July 14, 1993.

Eckel, Sara. "Single Mothers; Many Faces." *American Demographics*, May, 1999.

Engber, Andrea. "And Baby Makes Two." *American Baby*, July 1999.

Engber, Andrea. "Family Matters." *Working Mother*, December 1994.

Engber, Andrea. "How Single Moms Can Handle Father's Day." *Working Mother*, December 1994.

Engber, Andrea. "Just the Two of Us." *American Baby*, August 1998.

Engber, Andrea. "How to Talk About 'Dad'." *Universal Press Syndicate*, March, 1998.

Engber, Andrea. "Real-Life Custody Battles That Outdo Woody and Mia." *Woman's Own*.

Engber, Andrea. "Single Motherhood in the Workplace." *Working Mother*, September 1994.

Engber, Andrea. "Why You Shouldn't Tell Him He's a Dad." *Universal Press Syndicate*, June 1997.

Erickson, Nancy S., Esq. *Child Support Manual for Attorneys and Advocates.* National Center on Women and Family Law, Inc. 1992.

Family and Conciliation Courts Review, Volume 32, Number 4, October 1994.

Family and Conciliation Courts Review, Volume 33, Number 1, January 1995.

Figes, Kate. "Sex, Lies and the British Backlash." *Everywoman*, July 1994.

Fine, Suzanne. "The Stay-at-Home Fantasy." *Working Mother*, September 1994.

Gilbert, Eliza. "Pregnancy Discrimination Alert." *Working Mother*, June 1994.

Greif, Geoffrey L.; and Pabst, Mary S. *Mothers Without Custody* (Lexington, MA: Lexington Books/D.C. Heath, 1988).

Hansen, Karen; and Garey, Anita Ilta. *Families in the US: Kinship and Domestic Politics* (Temple University Press, Philadelphia, 1998).

Hicks, Tyler G. "10 Easy to Start Home Businesses." *Income Opportunities*, October, 1993.

Hite, Shere, *The Hite Report on the Family: Growing Up Under Patriarchy* (New York: Grove/Atlantic 1995).

Holcomb, Betty. "Working Mothers on Trial." *Working Mother*, January 1995.

Kleesattel, Gina. "The Kindness of Strangers." *SingleMOTHER* No. 23, March/April 1995.

Kuriansky, Dr. Judy; and Brockway, Laurie Sue. "Would You Have a Baby on Your Own?" *New Woman*, July 1988.

Lamott, Anne. "Life Without Father Need Not be Lonely." *New York Times*, August 5, 1993.

"Left Alone at Home: O.K., or a Danger?" *New York Times*, October 6, 1994.

Lewin, Tamar, "The Good Mother: Rise in Single Parenthood Is Reshaping U.S." *New York Times*, October 5, 1992.

Millar, Heather. "How to Act Like a Grown-up When Picking Up Your Stepchild." *Parenting*, September 1992.

"Money Report." *New Woman*, November 1994.

National Child Support Enforcement Association. *NCSEA News*, Vol XXIII, Fall 1994, Vol. XXVIII, Fall 1999.

"On the Importance of Being Tribal and the Prospects for Creating Multicultural Community." *Utne Reader*, July/August 1992.

"The 100 Best Companies for Working Mothers." *Working Mother*, October 1994-1999.

"The Path to Joy." *New Woman*, August 1994.

Peay, Pythia S. "Walking Your Own Spiritual Path." *New Woman*, September, 1992.

Pollitt, Katha. "Fair Is Fair: What About Unwed Fathers?" *The Nation*, January 30, 1995.

Pollitt, Katha. "Viewpoint: Motherhood Without Marriage." *Glamour*, December, 1993.

Quindlen, Anna. "Done in by Day Care." *New York Times*, July 30, 1994.

Raspberry, William. "Success and the Single Mother." *Washington Post*, January 12, 1994.

Rhodenbaugh, Suzanne. "Better Dead Than Unwed?" *Utne Reader*, May-June 1995.

Risman, Barbara J. "Intimate Relationships from a Microstructural Perspective."

Rosen, Margery D. "Getting Your Baby to Sleep." *Child*, May 1999.

Rubenstein, Carin. "New Advice on How to Raise Little Boys to Be Good Men." *New York Times*, August 11, 1994.

Search Institute Source Volume X, Number 2, June 1994.

Short, Oona. "And Baby Makes … Two." *First*, October 19, 1992.

Statistical Abstracts of the U.S. 1994.

SingleMOTHER, Issues 18–22, May 1994–February 1995.

SingleMOTHER, Issues 40-50, January 1998-September 1999.

Single Parents: A Reference Handbook, (ABC-CLIO, 1999).

Stein, David B. *Controlling the Difficult Adolescent: The REST Program (The Real Economy System for Teens)*. (Lanham, MD: University Press of America).

Stephenson, June, Ph.D. *The Two-Parent Family Is Not the Best*. (Diemer, Smith, 1991).

Webber, Mary S. "Wrong Analysis of Single Parent Births." *St. Louis Post-Dispatch*, December 21, 1993.

"Where Are All the Fathers?" *Los Angeles Times*, November 18, 1992.

Whitehead, Barbara Dafoe. "Dan Quayle Was Right." *Atlantic Monthly*, April, 1993.

Wolfelt, Alan D. Ph.D. "What Bereaved Childen Want Adults to Know about Grief." *Bereavement Magazine*, October, 1989.

The Women's Advocate, (National Center on Women and Family Law, March 1995, Volume 16, No.2, May 1995, Volume 16, No. 3).

Wong, Yin-Ling Irene; Garfinkel, Irwin; and McLanahan, Sara. "Single-Mother Families in Eight Countries: Economic Status and Social Policy." *The Social Service Review*, June 1993.

INDEX

The Everythng® Bedtime Story Book

The *Everything® Bedtime Story Book* is a wonderfully original collection of 100 stories that will entertain the entire family. You can change bedtime from a dreaded task to a wonderful family experience, as you share some of literature's great children's classics. Perfect for any age—from babies to toddlers, and beyond—*The Everything® Bedtime Story Book* will inspire young readers, and take parents back on a trip to their own childhood.

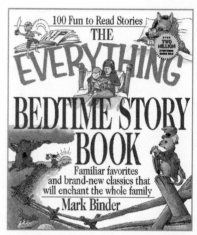

Trade paperback, $14.95 ($22.95 CAN)
ISBN: 1-58062-147-3

ABOUT THE AUTHORS

Andrea Engber is founder and director of the National Organization of Single Mothers, and editor-in-chief of *SingleMOTHER*, the voice of the organization that has been awarded a "Parent's Choice" Award and hailed by the media as the best source of available information for single mothers. She has written for and advised major magazines on single-parenting issues, including *Redbook, New Woman, Working Mother, Woman's Own, Parenting, American Baby, American Woman,* and *Parents* magazine, and is often cited as one of the country's leading sources of single-mothering statistics and information.

A former contributing editor for *Working Mother* magazine, Engber wrote a single-parenting column for their two million–plus readership. She currently pens a nationally syndicated weekly column, "Single … With Children" and serves as America Online's Single Parent Pro at Moms Online. In 1995 she was honored with the No-nonsense American Woman Award for her combined efforts toward helping single mothers and their families. Engber lives in North Carolina with her fourteen-year-old son, Spencer, her partner Bob, along with four cats, five dogs, occasional horses, and several other animals.

Leah Klungness, Ph.D., is a recognized authority on single parenting. She has been quoted in *Redbook, Working Mother, Parents, Parenting,* the *Boston Globe,* the *New York Times,* and *Newsday,* and has appeared on television and radio talk shows. She is a member of the editorial board and a featured columnist for *SingleParents* magazine, as well as a member of the professional advisory board and a regular contributor to *Singlespot.com.* Dr. Klungness's expertise comes from a blend of direct experiences as single parent, school psychologist, psychologist in private practice, and elementary school teacher. Dr. Klungness earned her doctoral degree while single parenting her two children. Her son, Andrew, is an attorney and her daughter, Sarah, a college student. Counseling many single women and their families, Dr. Klungness has come face-to-face with real issues facing single parents. She resides in Locust Valley, New York.